HOW DID CHRISTIANITY REALLY BEGIN?

A Historical-Archaeological Approach

HOWARD M. TEEPLE

Revised Edition

RELIGION AND ETHICS INSTITUTE
EVANSTON, ILLINOIS

Series: Truth in Religion, 4

BR
129
,T44
1994

Published by
Religion and Ethics Institute
Evanston, IL 60204

Revised Edition
Copyright © 1994 by
Religion and Ethics Institute, Inc.
P.O. Box 5510
Evanston, Il 60204
U.S.A.

First Edition © 1992

Library of Congress Catalog Card Number
94-066911

ISBN 0-914384-05-8

Printed in the United States of America by
BookCrafters, Chelsea, MI

HOW DID CHRISTIANITY REALLY BEGIN?

A Historical-Archaeological Approach

Books by same author

The Mosaic Eschatological Prophet (1957; monograph based on
author's Ph.D. dissertation, University of Chicago)

The Literary Origin of the Gospel of John (1974; sources and
revision of the text in antiquity)

The Noah' s Ark Nonsense (1978; expose of the claims that the
Flood occurred and that Noah's ark exists) Series: Truth
in Religion, 1.

The Historical Approach to the Bible (1982; survey of the
history and nature of the main historical methods of
understanding the Bible; award from National
Conference of Christians and Jews) Series: Truth in
Religion, 2.

I Started to Be a Minister : *From Fundamentalism to a Religion
of Ethics* (1990; the author's autobigraphy) Series:
Truth in Religion, 3.

The Religion and Ethics Institue, Inc. (REI) is an educational
nonprofit organization devoted to research in religion and ethics.
Unlike many religious institutions, it is not tied to the traditions
of the past, but searches for new knowledge and new directions,
provided they are consistent with science and reason. Its
purpose according to its charter is "to promote the discovery and
distribution of sound historical and scientific knowledge in the
fields of religion and ethics." It seeks an accurate understanding
of the past and present, but its primary concern is the
development of the future.

Membership in the institute is open to all at moderate
cost.

TO

GLADYS

my loving wife,
my helpmate,
my inspiration

CONTENTS

PREFACE

How did Christianity really begin? How much church tradition is reliable? How much is fact and how much fiction in Acts and the gospels in the New Testament? What did Jesus actually say and do?

These and similar questions have puzzled historians and biblical scholars, especially in the last two centuries. The conclusions drawn have varied tremendously, even conflicting with each other. A wide range of reconstructions of Christian origins and of lives of Jesus have been written. Why is there so much disagreement among them? What is the truth?

Many factors have interfered with the human efforts to discover the past:

1. The evidence is conflicting and ambiguous, even in the New Testament.

2. Much important literary and archaeological evidence was unknown or misunderstood until the twentieth century.

3. Many ancient church traditions are faulty and through the centuries have given Christians erroneous views of the origins of their religion. (Other world religions have a similar problem.)

4. Some vital historical and literary methods of interpreting the ancient literary sources were unknown until recent decades.

5. The ancient sources are so numerous, yet generally unavailable except in a few research libraries, that few investigations of the subject are sufficiently comprehensive.

6. Knowledge of the situation in the early Christian communities—especially their intellectual problems—has not been sufficiently applied.

7. Information about the Jewish environment of the early Christians was deficient until the Dead Sea scrolls and the Charlesworth edition of the Jewish Pseudepigrapha were published.

8. The influence of the gentile environment upon the early Christians has not been adequately recognized.

9. Bias, that old enemy of truth, is still a hindrance.

This book is the culmination of five decades of the author's quest to learn what Jesus actually taught and how the Christian movement really began. An account of the quest is given in the author's autobiography, *I Started to Be a Minister: From Fundamentalism to a Religion of Ethics* (REI, 1990). His interest in the subject was aroused by his undergraduate studies at Willamette University, a Methodist school in Salem, Oregon. That led to a Ph.D. in Bible at the University of Chicago. Two years as a research assistant in the International Greek New Testament Project (then at Emory University) provided excellent training in textual criticism of the New Testament.

The author's research has been both intensive and comprehensive, using especially The University of Chicago Library, The United Library at Garrett-Evangelical and Seabury-Western Theological Seminaries, and his own library. He and his wife Gladys visited many museums, libraries, and archaeological sites in Europe to obtain significant but little-known information about the gentile environment of early Christianity—especially the Hellenistic mystery religions.

We are fortunate to live at a time when so much historical information is coming to light. The Dead Sea scrolls are rightly hailed as important sources for the understanding of Christian beginnings, but some other sources, which have not received publicity, are equally significant. Examples are the Jewish *Testament of the Twelve Patriarchs* and the pagan mystery cult of Mithras. A virtue of the present book is that it includes the evidence from a multitude of sources. The author strove earnestly to be objective, not seeking to attack or defend Christianity.

All too frequently writers in the field are biased—often unconsciously—in favor of defending the Bible, Jesus, or the Christian faith in general. This book investigates controversial issues such as the divinity of Jesus and the persecution of Jewish Christians by Jews.

This work is based on a comprehensive survey of sources, quoted extensively. It incorporates new research on the following subjects: the role of John the Baptist, the life of Jesus, comparison of the ethical teaching in the synoptic gospels with that in contemporary Judaism, the problems of the early Christians and the effect on Christian doctrine, and the literary strata in the Gospel of John.

The symbols used to represent strata in John are those used in the author's *The Literary Origin of the Gospel of John* (REI, 1974): S designates the Signs Source, or Gospel of Signs; G designates the semi-Gnostic sources(s); E stands for the author or editor of the gospel; R represents the Redactor. Recognition of the Signs Source is increasing among scholars, and acceptance, with much modification, of Rudolf Bultmann's "Revelation Speeches" sources (cf. the present writer's "G") will probably occur eventually.

Only Mark is cited when a pericope (see Glossary) is also in Matthew and/or Luke, indicated by "Mark par." Q passages may be indicated by "Matt. par" or "Luke par," or by "Matt. . . . = Luke . . ." Some of the English translations of the Bible are from the Revised Standard Version and some are the author's. Passages in the Jewish Pseudepigrapha are quoted by permission from James H. Charlesworth's edition, *Old Testament Pseudepigrapha*, but do not necessarily follow the same format. The quotations from other sources are a mixture of my translations and those of others. Laity should know that capitalization of letters is a decision of the translator; in ancient Greek and Hebrew texts no distinction is made between what we call capital and lower case letters.

Paul Gehl, William Murphy, and Rolf Erickson—all members of the board of directors of the Religion and Ethics Institute—were very helpful with their criticism of the manuscript and with the additional information they supplied. Rita Djuricich labored industriously with great perseverance to typeset the manuscript of the original edition. Throughout, the author's wife Gladys contributed proofreading and library research. They all deserve our hearty gratitude.

The author has made minor revisions of the first edition. Kristin Stoneking has corrected its typographical errors and reset the type to reduce the number of pages. She majored in English at Rice University and currently is a graduate student at Garrett-Evangelical Theological Seminary. We acknowledge with deep gratitude her meticulous work and congenial cooperation.

We are deeply indebted to the professors at The University of Chicago for the thorough historical training they provided, and to the late Merrill Parvis in the "Project" for transmitting his expertise in textual criticism. Thanks, too, to the libraries which provided vital resources, and to the three professional librarians at The United Library: Alvin Caldwell, David Himrod, and especially Newland Smith. Finally, this book would have been impossible without the work of the pioneering historians and biblical scholars, past and present.

Evanston, 1994

ABBREVIATIONS

Apocrypha
   Sir.—Ecclesiasticus, or Wisdom of Jesus, Son of Sirach
   Tob.—Tobit
   Wis.—Wisdom of Solomon
Apostolic Fathers
   Barn.—Epistle of Barnabas
   1, 2 Clem.— 1 Clement, 2 Clement
   Did.—Didache, or *The Teaching of the Twelve Apostles*

Herm., Mand.	*Shepherd of Hermas,*	Mandates
Sim.		Similitudes
Vis.		Visions

Ignatius, *Eph.*	*Letter to the Ephesians*
Mag.	*Letter to the Magnesians*
Phil.	*Letter to the Philadelphians*
Rom.	*Letter to the Romans*
Smyr.	*Letter to the Smyrnaeans*
Trall.	*Letter to the Trallians*

Martyr. Poly.—Martyrdom of Polycarp
Polycarp, *Philip.—Letter to the Philippians*
Church Fathers
ANF—Ante-Nicene Fathers
Eusebius, *H.E.—Historia Ecclesiastica* (Church History)
Irenaeus, *Adv. Haer.—Adversus omnes Haereses* (Against All
     Heresies)
Jerome, *Adv. Pelag.—Dialogi adversus Pelagianos* (Dialogues
     against Pelagius)
Origen, *Celsum—Contra Celsum* (Against Celsus)

Justin,	*1 Apol.*	*1 Apology*
	2 Apol.	*2 Apology*
	Dial.	*Dialogue with Trypho the Jew*

Origin, *Celsum—Contra Celsum* (Against Celsus)
Dead Sea Scrolls
CD—*Damascus Document*
IQM—*War of the Sons of Light with the Sons of Darkness*
1QpHab—*Habukkuk Commentary*
IQS—*Manual of Discipline*
Misc., Ancient

John,	E—author, or editor, of Gospel of John
	G—semi-Gnostic sources
	R—redactor

Abbreviations

S—Gospel of Signs source
Josephus, *Ant.*   *Antiquities of the Jews*
        Apion *Contra Apion* (Against Apion)
        Vita   *Life of Josephus*
        War.   *The Jewish War*
Mishnah, *Abot*—*Pirqe* (or *Pirke*) *Abot* (Sayings of the
      Fathers)
Philo, *Cher.*   *De Cherubim* (On the Cherubim)
      Decal.   *De Decalogo* (On the Decalogue)
      Immut. *Quod Deus sit Immutabilis* (That God
                Is Unchangeable)
      Legat. *Legatio ad Gaium* (Legation to Gaius)
      Mos.   *De Vita Mosis* (On the Life of Moses)
      Opif.   *De Opificio Mundi* (On the Creation of
                the World)
      Som.   *De Somniis* (On Dreams)
      Spec.   *De Specialibus Legibus* (On the Special
                Laws)

Modern

ANRW *Aufstieg und Niedergang der Römischen Welt*
BAR   *Biblical Archaeology Review*
HBD   *Harper's Bible Dictionary* (1985)
IDB   *Interpreter's Dictionary of the Bible*
JBL   *Journal of Biblical Literature*
NTS   *New Testament Studies*
OTP   *Old Testament Pseudepigrapha* (Charlesworth, ed.)
par   parallel(s) in one or two of the other synoptic
        gospels
RGG   *Religion in Geschichte und Gegenwart*

Pseudepigrapha

Jub.—*Jubilees*
Pss. Sol.—*Psalms of Solomon*
Sib. Or.—*Sibylline Oracles*
T. Abraham—*Testament of Abraham*
T. Moses—*Testament* (or *Assumption*) of Moses
T. 12 Patr.—*Testaments of the Twelve Patriarchs*
      T. Ben.   *Testament of Benjamin*
      T. Judah *Testament of Judah*
      T. Levi   *Testament of Levi*

GLOSSARY

apocalypse: A writing purporting to contain a divine revelation of God's plan for the world.

apology; apologetics: Writing intended to persuade the reader; it may be a defense of one's religion or an effort to promote it or both. Contrary to the modern usage in which a person says, "Sorry, I was wrong," in this usage he says, in effect, "Hey, I am right."

apostles vs. disciples: As used in this book, "apostles" refers to early Christian missionaries who had not been followers of Jesus during his lifetime. "Disciples" designates those who had been his followers before his death; some of them were founders of the Christian community at Jerusalem.

catholic: Refers to the "universal" Church, the churches in general, except the Gnostic churches. It does not refer to the Roman Catholic Church, which was established later when the bishop of Rome succeeded in asserting his authority over other churches in the West.

eschatology: Beliefs about "the last things," i.e., the end of the present world or age, and the future coming of the kingdom of God and the new age. A Jewish and Christian idea with roots in ancient Iranian religion.

genre: The type of literature, such as gospel, letter, or tract, defined by its structure.

gentiles: Refers either to gentile Christians or to pagans who were neither Christians nor Jews.

God-fearers: The "men who feared God" were gentiles who worshipped the Jewish God, Yahweh, and attended synagogue services, but did not join Judaism (e.g., Cornelius in Acts 10).

Hellenistic: A mixture of Greek and Near Eastern elements, it was the predominant culture of the Mediterranean world before the Roman culture became prevalent.

kerygma: The early Christian "procla-mation," the message preached by apostles.

logos: Greek word meaning "reason" or "word." In Platonic philosophy it referred to divine Reason. In Judaism it became a term for God's speech or words at the Creation. In the Prologue of the Gospel of John it becomes a title for Jesus.

"man of God": A man to whom a deity has given supernatural power to perform miracles.

magic: A technique by which a human accomplishes, or

appears to accomplish, something very unusual.

miracle: A divine act, or an act man accomplishes by divine aid.

paganism: The culture of the Near East, Greek, and Roman worlds, apart from that of Judaism and Christianity. Jews and Christians denounced it, but, like Judaism and Christianity, it included both "good" and "bad" features, when judged from a modern point of view.

parousia: The second "coming" or "presence" of Jesus.

Pentateuch: The Torah, or Law (lit. "instruction"), the first five books of the Hebrew Bible, or Old Testament.

pericope: A saying or narrative unit, self-contained, in a biblical text, especially in the gospels.

Q: The source, or more probable, sources, besides the Gospel of Mark, used by the authors of the Gospels of Matthew and Luke.

testimonia: They were quotations from the Old Testament that circulated independently and were used as proof-texts to support one's preaching or writing. The Essenes at Qumran used them, and the early Christians did too.

We-section in Acts: Selections in the Book of Acts from a diary of someone who accompanied Paul on (only part of?) his second missionary journey. It refers to those missionaries as "we" instead of "they."

1

LOST AND FOUND:
CHRISTIAN BEGINNINGS

The historical origin of Christianity has been misunderstood through the centuries because much of the knowledge of it was soon lost. Only a small portion of the events in the first century were ever recorded. The little evidence that we do have is often confusing; historical facts are mixed with promotional apologetics, legends, and miracle stories.

Jesus' life is difficult to discover because he wrote no records and—contrary to tradition—neither did his disciples. Jesus was crucified around A.D. 30, but the four gospels in the New Testament were not written until A.D. 75-100; none of the authors had ever known Jesus. The Jerusalem church, founded by Jesus' disciples, fled to Pella in the year 70 during the First Jewish War, and left us no writings.

As for the history of the churches in the first century, our earliest accounts are in Paul's letters (A.D. 50-58) and the Book of Acts (ca. 85). Paul had direct knowledge of a few events, but he mentions them only briefly. After all, he was writing letters, not a church history. The author of Luke-Acts wrote a history of Christianity's first few decades, but like the other gospel authors, his desire to promote the Christian faith affected his account, and his material must be used with care. In the second century the church historian Hegesippus wrote five books against the Gnostic Christians. Only a few fragments of them have survived, incorporated in Eusebius' *Ecclesiastical History*. The fragments deal mainly with the history of the Jerusalem church.

The canonical gospels have been a handicap as well as a help, for they have given us unreliable portraits of Jesus. In them beliefs and arguments of the early churches have been ascribed to him. Separating the authentic (actual words and deeds of Jesus) in the gospels from the unauthentic has been a major concern in biblical scholarship in the last two centuries.

The suggestion that some words and deeds of Jesus in the gospels may not be historical is an idea that may dismay some laity, but the evidence is decisive. The differences between the Gospel of John and the other three canonical gospels provide one type of evidence. In John the portrait of Jesus disagrees strongly with that in the synoptic gospels. Was Jesus a humble man who said, "Why do you call me good? No one is good except God" (Mark 10:18)? Or was he a boastful god who claimed divinity and said, "No one comes to the Father [God] except through me" (John 14:6)? Did Jesus regard repentance as the basis of salvation, as in the synoptic gospels (Mark 1:15), or is being "born again" the basis, as in John 3:3? Those two ideas are very different, as their occurrence elsewhere in the ancient world clearly shows. Both the theology (doctrines about God) and the christology (doctrines about Jesus as the Christ, or Messiah) in John cannot be reconciled with the theology and christology in the synoptic gospels. The radical differences between these gospels tell us that Jesus could not possibly have said all that the gospels ascribe to him.

The miracle stories in the gospels and Acts also warn us that some of the material is not reporting actual history. Nineteenth-century Christian liberalism tried unsuccessfully to rationalize them as exaggerated accounts of actual events, but parallels in contemporary Jewish and pagan literature reveal that they originated as miracle stories, which were abundant and readily believed in antiquity. In the modern world we cannot reasonably believe that the dead were revived by a spoken word or that demons that could be seen and heard were exorcised from the sick. A further warning consists of the gospel sayings on the lips of Jesus that deal with church problems which did not arise until after his death. Did he foresee all those problems? If so, why are the solutions presented often inconsistent, and why did Jesus not foresee problems that arose *after the gospels were written?* The only sensible answer is that these statements originated in the churches and that the gospel authors were looking back at what had happened between Jesus' crucifixion and the time when they wrote. The gospels' extensive mixture of the life of the churches with the life of Jesus makes the gospels both complex and unique in ancient literature.

Eusebius of Caesarea wrote his church history early in the fourth century. He, too, was more concerned with promoting the faith than with reporting its beginnings. Writing

2

three centuries after Jesus, his sources for the first century A.D. were the canonical gospels, the Jewish histories written by Josephus, and some late church legends. Eusebius used Josephus in a vain effort to defend the stories of Jesus' birth, and he followed the argument of the church father Africanus when he denied (wrongly) that the genealogies of Matthew and Luke disagree with each other. Eusebius also refused to admit that there had been any changes in church doctrine, except by heretics. Kirsopp Lake expressed it thus:

> It cannot be too strongly emphasized that Eusebius, like all early church historians, can be understood only if it be recognized that whereas modern writers try to trace the development, growth, and change of doctrines and institutions, their predecessors were trying to prove that nothing of the kind ever happened. According to them the Church had had one and only one teaching from the beginning; it had been preserved by the "Succession," and heresy was the attempt of the Devil to change it.[1]

The church fathers in general misunderstood Christian beginnings for several reasons: (1) they lacked sufficient information; (2) they were involved in numerous disputes, so they interpreted the Bible and early Christian history to support their own beliefs; (3) they used unreliable methods of interpreting the Bible; they even misquoted the Bible to make it fit their views.

UNRELIABLE METHODS OF INTERPRETATION

Exegesis is the effort to "lead out" of a text what it really says. Eisegesis is the subjective "leading into" a text what one wants to find there. Needless to say, eisegesis results in misunderstanding the Bible, and it has been used many, many times through many centuries.

Misinterpretation of the Jewish Bible, which Christians call the Old Testament, began in Judaism. First, late biblical authors reinterpreted early biblical books, mainly the Psalms and those in the Law, or Pentateuch, and the Prophets. Later, various Jewish sects misinterpreted the Hebrew text of the Jewish Bible: for example, in commentaries (Hebrew: *pesherim*) on the Prophets and Psalms that are among the Dead Sea scrolls. Next, the rabbis too reinterpreted the Hebrew Scriptures in oral teaching which later was codified in the Mishnah and Talmud.

In the third and second centuries B.C. Jews in Alexandria translated the Hebrew Scriptures into Greek; this version is called the Septuagint. The translators added to their Bible the books known today as the Apocrypha, which are now in the Anglican and Roman Catholic Bibles, but not the Jewish Bible. The Bible of Jesus and the Jerusalem church was the Hebrew Scriptures, but the Bible of most other churches and the New Testament writers was the Septuagint.

The early Christian communities had numerous intellectual problems, including the difficulty of convincing the world that Jesus was the Messiah, or Christ, expected by many Jews. A major way of trying to solve the problem was to claim that Jesus' life and Christian faith were all according to God's plan. They used Jewish literature--especially the Septuagint--as evidence that Jesus and the Christian movement fulfill Scripture. This apologetic use of the Old Testament is reported in Acts 18:28, where it is said that a Jewish Christian, Apollos, "powerfully refuted the Jews in public, showing by the Scriptures that Jesus was the Christ." The gospels portray Jesus as saying that he and events fulfill Scripture. According to Luke, Jesus even trained his disciples in such matters after his resurrection.[2] The early Christians had several methods of making their religion fulfill Scripture: by explicitly quoting or referring to the Old Testament; incorporating an Old Testament idea in their own writing, without quoting the passage; by interpreting actual events as fulfillment of Scripture; and by creating stories to serve as "events" to fulfill prophecy.

The author of the Gospel of Matthew often quoted Scripture as prophecy fulfilled in Christianity. For example, in 1:23 he cited Isaiah 7:14 as prophecy fulfilled: "All this took place to fulfill what the Lord had spoken by the prophet: 'Behold, a virgin shall conceive and bear a son, . . . '" (but Isaiah is not referring to Jesus' mother, and the correct translation is "young woman," not virgin). Actually, Isaiah was writing about a Jewish king whose "name shall be called Immanuel" (which was not Jesus' name) when "all the land will be briars and thorns" (Isa. 7:24), which did not happen in Jesus' day.

When material from the Old Testament was used without referring to the source, a later writer might either mention or quote the source. An instance of this is in Mark 4:12, wherein

Jesus teaches in parables so that outsiders "may indeed hear but not understand, lest they should turn again and be forgiven." Mark derives this idea from Isaiah 6:9-10, but does not say so. When the author of Matthew copied Mark, he added that this fulfills a prophecy of Isaiah which he proceeds to quote (Matt. 13:14-15); thus Matthew made plain what Mark was doing. In Isaiah it is not a prophecy of the future; the Lord is commanding Isaiah to tell the people (in his own day) to hear and not understand so that they will not repent and be saved. Justin realized that Christians applied to the future various biblical statements in the past tense, so he explained it thus: "The things which he (the Spirit of prophecy) knows absolutely will take place, he predicts as if already they had taken place" (*1 Apol.* 42).

To make Old Testament passages fit--more or less--, writers often ignored the setting, changed past or present tense to future tense, and reinterpreted a word or phrase to serve as the basis. A similar procedure is followed in the Dead Sea scrolls and the writings of the church fathers.

The vain effort to make the Old Testament prophesy Christianity persisted in patristic literature, the Reformation, and today in Protestant fundamentalism. This error had to be discovered and corrected. Pioneers in this were Theodore of Mopsuestia (5th c.), Anthony Collins (1724), and C.H. Toy at Harvard (1884).

The dishonest tactic of quoting and misinterpreting biblical passages by ignoring the evidence of the surrounding verses also occurs today as often as in the past. The tactic is called "proof-texting" and "lifting passages out of context." It was denounced by Theodore of Mopsuestia. Another form of the sin of omission is to say "the Bible says" and then quote a verse one likes, conveniently ignoring the parts of the Bible that "says" the opposite. Instead of that procedure, the whole Bible should be considered. The study of the Bible should be comprehensive, not piecemeal.

The worst of the church fathers' methods was allegorical interpretation of the Bible, which was employed extensively in the second and third centuries, especially by Clement of Alexandria and Origen. In this method the interpreter seeks for hidden meanings in the text and arbitrarily states that A is B (or anything else) and that C means D (or anything else). Obviously this method enables one to make the Bible say

5

anything he wants it to say (but some people still achieve that goal without the use of allegory!). Paul uses it in Galatians 4:22-26 in his interpretation of Genesis. Before Christians used allegorical interpretation, the Greek Stoics applied it to Homer's poetry, and Philo applied it to the Jewish Scriptures.

In the first half of the Middle Ages both Jewish and Christian interpretation of Scripture was traditional. Jews repeated the rabbis' comments preserved in the Talmud; Christians repeated the exegesis of the church fathers. Christian scribes wrote in the margins of biblical manuscripts excerpts and summaries of the church fathers' comments; these medieval notes are called *catenae*. This method prepared the way for scholasticism's mixture of patristic, allegorical, and mystic interpretation. Thomas Aquinas, influenced by Aristotle's writings, modified it in the direction of reason. The biblical text itself was no longer studied, and interest in the conditions in which the Bible was written was completely lacking.

Other errors have appeared in modern times. One is the assumption that the Bible is self-explanatory. Actually, many passages cannot be adequately understood without additional information. Even worse is the illusion that the Holy Spirit guides one's interpretation when one reads the Bible. The "Spirit" has a record of giving very different interpretations of the same passage to different people!

The belief arose that the whole Bible is the literal Word of God, and therefore it must be a unity, with no inconsistencies, no errors. This view has often caused believers to misinterpret the book by trying to force disparate passages to agree with each other. The evidence that the Bible is not the Word of God includes inconsistencies, errors, miracle stories, and the misinterpretation of the Old Testament in the New Testament.

A common mistake is to assume that the expression "the Scriptures" in the New Testament refers to the whole Bible. Actually, it refers only to the Old Testament; the only Christian books that the New Testament refers to as Scripture are Paul's letters, and that occurs only once, in 2 Peter 3:15-16, written in the second century. Needless to say, in Jesus' day none of the New Testament books had yet been written.

In spite of its weaknesses, the Bible is still our primary-- though not our only--source of information about Christian beginnings. But we can never discover and understand the past

6

by employing unreliable methods of interpreting ancient literature, including the Bible.

DISCOVERY OF HISTORICAL METHODS[3]

Fortunately, a few Christian scholars did try to understand the Bible better. Remarkable in their day were the scholars at Antioch in the third, fourth, and fifth centuries. Influenced by Greek rhetoric and philosophy, they rejected the allegorical method and insisted on literal interpretation of the Bible. They established a monastery school at Antioch that is referred to as the "School of Antioch." It paid attention to the context of passages, to the philology of the text, and to what little was known of the historical setting. One of the school's teachers, Theodore of Mopsuestia, insisted that the Old Testament does not predict Jesus. Involved in the theological controversies of the fifth century, the school was condemned for heresy and ceased to exist.

Pope Damasus, dismayed at the disagreement in the readings in the Old Latin manuscripts of the canonical gospels that were circulating in the churches, commissioned Jerome (late in the fourth century) to establish the correct reading of the Latin text of those gospels. Jerome expanded the project to include the whole Bible. He soon saw that he must go back to sources, so he translated the New Testament from its original language, Greek. He began to translate the Old Testament from the Greek version, the Septuagint, but Jewish scholars convinced him that he should translate it from its original language, Hebrew. Thus Jerome arrived at two essential principles of biblical scholarship; *establish* the text in its original language, and *translate* the text from its original language.

In the following centuries both Jews and Christians neglected philological interpretation in favor of traditional interpretation of the Bible. But Jews later learned from Arabs the methodology of systematizing grammar. Contact with Jewish biblical scholars in the twelfth century introduced some Christian scholars to the Hebrew text of the Old Testament and to Hebrew grammar, and then they too interpreted directly from the Hebrew text. The monastic school of St. Victor in Paris led the way.

In the thirteenth century Christians in the West first began to study the Greek text of the New Testament. At that time Robert Grosseteste at Oxford University learned Greek and applied his new knowledge to biblical study. When the Turks conquered Constantinople in 1453, Byzantine Christians fled to Italy, bringing with them the Greek language, the Greek text of the New Testament, and the Greek classics. That event resulted in the West in increased grammatical study of the Greek text of the New Testament.

Grammatical study of the text naturally led to literal interpretation, which exposed the fallacy of allegorical and spiritual interpretations. Study of the text in its original language instead of in a translation is very important because the meaning of the words and grammar in the second language may be different from that in the original. Thus some of an author's thought may be lost or misunderstood when a translation is used as a source.

The late medieval period saw the emergence of many types of tools essential for biblical study. In addition to grammars, Hebrew and Greek lexicons (dictionaries) were produced, and linguistic commentaries on the Bible were written. In the thirteenth century Christians first produced geographies of Palestine and concordances to the Bible and patristic literature. The first Jewish concordance to the text of the Hebrew Scriptures was compiled by Isaac Mordecai ben Nathan in the fifteenth century. Johannes Reuchlin wrote a combined Hebrew lexicon and grammar that was very influential among German scholars (1506).

Accurate understanding of the Bible and Christian beginnings could not be achieved until conditions arose that permitted a change in attitude and the discovery of new knowledge. The establishment of monastic and cathedral schools began with Charlemagne in the eighth century. Many universities were founded in Europe in the twelfth to fifteenth centuries. Then, as now, schools led the way. Philosophy tended to open minds to new concepts about the past. Influenced by Aristotle, some medieval philosophers and theologians exalted reason, which at times clearly contrasted with traditional religious faith. Martin Luther and the Protestant Reformation opened the way for some new biblical interpretation in the first half of the sixteenth century, but the intense Catholic-Protestant controversy that followed produced dogmatism on both sides that closed the door. In the seventeenth and eighteenth centuries some philosophers advocated the questioning and the investigation of religion. The rise of science in the same period fostered freedom of thought and the use of scientific methodology.

Now let us shift from a chronological account to a topical, or subject, approach to the development of historical methods of understanding the Bible. These methods eventually led to interest in and recovery of the historical beginnings of Christianity.

Textual Criticism

Textual criticism consists of establishing the original text as nearly as possible, using rules derived from the history of the transmission of the text.

Study of the Greek text of the New Testament was handicapped until that text was restored to its original form, or at least close to the original. The Greek text, new in the West, was an improvement over the Latin text, but the Greek manuscripts varied so much from each other that they created the same kind of problem that Jerome had faced with Old Latin manuscripts, namely, the uncertainty of the reading in the original text. The Dutch scholar Erasmus was a pioneer in establishing textual criticism. Early in the sixteenth century, with the aid of John Colet's collations of the variant readings in manuscripts, he tried to determine the original text of the Greek New Testament. But he failed to find it because the text had already been changed before those manuscripts were written in the tenth to thirteenth centuries. When monks in the Greek monasteries had transmitted the text by copying manuscripts, they made alterations in the text, sometimes accidentally, sometimes intentionally.

The best and earliest manuscript of the Greek text of the New Testament as a whole (though a few leaves are missing) is Codex Vaticanus, or Codex B, written in the middle of the fourth century. It was acquired for the Vatican Library by Pope Nicholas V (1447-1455). It remained unknown to biblical scholars until after Napoleon stole it when he conquered Italy (the French returned it after Napoleon's defeat). In the nineteenth century Constantin Tischendorf searched for similar manuscripts in libraries all over Europe and the Near East. At the Greek Orthodox monastery of St. Catherine on Mount Sinai he found another important New Testament manuscript written in Greek in the latter half of the fourth century. Now in the British Museum, it is known as Codex Sinaiticus.

Three very important Greek papyri of New Testament books are still earlier, written around A.D. 200. All were purchased in this century from dealers in Egypt. P[46], in the Chester Beatty collection, is a nearly complete manuscript of the Pauline Epistles. In the Bodmer Library near Geneva are P[66], consisting of most of the Gospel of John, and P[75], consisting of Luke and John.

Even these earlier manuscripts contain alterations of the original text, but they lack the changes and insertions scribes made later. For example, they contain neither John 5:4, with its legend that an angel "troubled" the water in a pool, nor John 7:53-8:11, the story of the woman taken in adultery. Where alterations occur in even our earliest documents, determining the original text can be difficult. To deal with that situation, scholars have created rules of textual criticism to use as guides in selecting the probable original reading from the variant readings. Johann Bengel was the first to set forth a set of such rules, in 1734.

Before textual scholars could analyze the variants, however, they had to find them by collating many manuscripts, verse by verse, word by word. A leader was John Mills at Oxford University in the eighteenth century. He spent 30 years collating nearly 100 Greek New Testament manuscripts and found 30,000 variant readings.

Literary Criticism

Biblical literary criticism is the study of the literary aspects of the writings. It has numerous subdivisions.

1. *Linguistics.* After the text has been established, the next most basic step is to understand the language of the text. Historically and logically this begins with study of the grammar and syntax. The first biblical grammars were Hebrew grammars. After learning scientific linguistic methodology by attending Muslim schools in Spain, Jewish scholars—especially some in southern France—produced Hebrew grammars. Saadia ben Joseph in the tenth century was the scholar who established Hebrew philology as a systematic way of studying the Hebrew Bible. In the thirteenth century Roger Bacon wrote Greek and Hebrew grammars and insisted that knowledge of the Greek and Hebrew languages is necessary for understanding the Bible.

Equally vital for linguistic study is lexicology, knowledge of the meaning of words. Hebrew lexicology began in the tenth century with Jewish grammarians. Eventually Christians compiled both Greek and Hebrew lexicons, or dictionaries. Modern lexicons of Hellenistic Greek (in which the New Testament is written) and classical Hebrew are the result of exhaustive examination of the meaning of the words in other contemporary literature as well as in the Bible.

Beginning in the thirteenth century Christians compiled concordances to the Bible and patristic literature, a tedious task. The first Jewish concordance to the Hebrew Scriptures was produced in the fifteenth century. Concordances are very useful tools, now as then.

Ideally everyone who studies the Bible should know the languages of the original text, namely, classical Hebrew and Hellenistic Greek. Both languages are difficult to learn, however, and few laity or clergy have the time or opportunity to learn them. This is regrettable, for even a cursory knowledge is helpful in understanding the more advanced commentaries.

2. *Style*, the arrangement of words, can help us to recognize an author's mood and to decide whether the words are to be taken literally or figuratively. Also, style can be a criterion of whether a book was written by its traditional author, whether written by one author or several, and whether or not a passage is a later insertion.

3. *Recognizing reinterpretation of the text.* One of the problems in understanding the Bible is caused by ancient reinterpretation of the text. We saw above that scribes altered the text when they copied manuscripts. Here we are concerned with alterations in the meaning of the text that are made outside the text itself.

a. The text at times was deliberately misquoted to promote a person's or a group's argument or point of view. This trait is characteristic in the Dead Sea scrolls and the writings of the church fathers, and therefore those quotations are useless for establishing the original text.

b. Another method was to reinterpret passages, not only by lifting them out of context, but also by changing the meaning of some of their details. An example is in Daniel. Jeremiah wrote that seventy years will elapse before God restores the nation (29:10). When Daniel was written centuries later, that event had not occurred, so the author of Daniel 9

11

reinterpreted—by using an angelic vision as a device—the seventy years to mean "seventy weeks of years," that is, 7 x 70, or 490 years (9:2, 24).

c. The third method of reinterpreting text is to retell its story to make it promote a particular idea or point of view that differs from that of the original narrative. In writing 1 and 2 Chronicles the Chronicler retold some of the accounts in the books of Samuel and Kings in order to idealize David and bolster the position of the Levites and singers in the Temple. The author of *Jubilees* (2nd c. B. C.) retold the story in Genesis and Exodus to enhance the authority of the Jewish Law, particularly concerning certain rites and the Sabbath.

4. *Literary types.* The Bible consists of narratives, drama, poetry, proverbs, and apocalypse (divine revelation of God's plan for the world). Recognizing these types of literature is relatively easy, but learning the characteristics of each requires study.

The Israelites learned the style of writing proverbs from the Egyptians and even included some Egyptian proverbs in their own Book of Proverbs. From the Canaanites they borrowed poetic parallelism and incorporated it in their own poetry and songs. In one form, synonymous parallelism, the same thought is expressed in different words in each of the two lines of a couplet:

The desire of his heart you did grant him,
And the request of his lips you did not deny him
(Ps. 21:2).

In antithetical parallelism the thought in the second line contrasts with that in the first line:

Weeping may tarry for the night,
But joy comes with the morning (Ps. 30:5).

Knowledge of literary parallelism is necessary to understand Matthew's story of Jesus' entry into Jerusalem. In the similar accounts in Mark 11 and Luke 19 only a colt is involved, but in Matthew 21 Jesus simultaneously rides on both a colt and an ass! The cause of this remarkable feature is that the author of Matthew treats the story as a fulfillment of Zechariah 9:9:

Lo, your king comes to you;
triumphant and victorious is he,
humble and riding on a ass,
on a colt, the foal of an ass.

Matthew's author failed to recognize the synonymous

parallelism in that verse; he did not realize that the colt is the same animal as the ass in the preceding line.

Robert Lowth, professor of poetry at Oxford, was the first Christian to understand the parallelism in Hebrew poetry (1753).

5. *Authorship.* Both Jews and Christians ascribed some of their writings to their prominent religious leaders in the past to give the books more authority. In some cases the author wrote pseudonymously. An example is 2 Peter, whose author says he is Peter, but its content reveals that it was written too late to have been composed by Peter. Often the false authorship was assigned by others years later—for example, the Epistle to the Hebrews, which tradition erroneously ascribed to Paul. Jews had a special reason for ascribing a book to an ancient prophet. Pharisees taught that God had withdrawn his Holy Spirit until the last days of the present age and therefore no more prophets will arise in the meantime. If a current book was believed to have been written by an ancient prophet, however, it could be accepted as divinely inspired. Christians, too, had a special reason. Gnostic heretics claimed that some of their books were written by early apostles, so less radical, or catholic, Christians made a similar claim for some of their own writings.

Suspicions arose early concerning the authorship of some biblical books. In the second century the Nazarenes, a Jewish-Christian sect, rejected the tradition that Moses wrote the Pentateuch (the Torah), the first five books of the Bible. In the third century a gentile Christian, Origen, doubted that Paul wrote the Epistle to the Hebrews because it lacks Paul's diction and roughness of style. His pupil Dionysius concluded from the linguistic evidence that the Book of Revelation and the Gospel of John must not have been written by the same "John." In the medieval period some Jewish scholars concluded that Moses did not write the Pentateuch; Ibn Ezra in the twelfth century concluded that Isaiah was written in two parts by two different authors. In the same century the Christian Hugh of St. Victor remarked that the Wisdom of Solomon (in the Apocrypha) was not written by Solomon. Luther and Calvin questioned the traditional authorship of some biblical books.

The basis for rejecting traditional authorship is often a different literary style in each of two books alleged to have been written by the same writer. Sometimes the content was plainly

13

written later than the date of the alleged author. The old erroneous assumptions about authorship have caused readers to place a book in the wrong environment at the wrong date and then try to force it to harmonize with the writing of the traditional author whose ideas may have been quite different. The authors of the New Testament books are unknown to us, with the exception of Paul. Church tradition assigned fourteen epistles to Paul, but today the maximum number that can be reasonably ascribed to him is nine.[4] Some scholars accept only seven or less. With the exception of Philemon, all of the nine contain redactors' insertions. If we do not recognize those passages as insertions made by a later writer, we are liable to conclude either that Paul did not write the book, or else that Paul was not consistent in his style and thought. Much of the inconsistency in Paul's letters is the result of insertions by redactors or scribes. The gospels could not have been written by disciples who accompanied Jesus, for the gospels' contents reveal that the authors had slight knowledge of his life.

      6. *Comparative literature.* Basic to understanding the Bible is the recognition that its writings are similar to other ancient literature and that it must be studied by the same methods. In the eighteenth century Johann Semler rejected the doctrine of the divine inspiration of the Bible, and Johann Wettstein recognized that the Bible is a product of its times and environment. Therefore other ancient literature from a similar environment must be studied to learn how their authors wrote; this provides insight into what the biblical authors were saying.

Source Criticism

      Source criticism is the detection of a written source or sources incorporated in a book by the author. In the absence of copyright laws in antiquity, authors freely used sentences and even blocks of material from another man's writing without giving credit. Many ancient Jewish, Christian, and pagan documents are composite.

      Source criticism of the Old Testament began with H. B. Witter in 1711 when he observed that there are two Creation stories in Genesis (1:1-2:4a; 2:4b-25). From this small beginning evolved the famous Graf-Wellhausen hypothesis of the origin of the Hexateuch (first six books of the Bible), according to which editors combined and revised sources (documents J, E, D, and P) over a period of centuries. The authors of Matthew and Luke used the Gospel of Mark as a source, and they used another source (or sources) which biblical scholars have called "Q," from the German word *Quelle*, "source." Q generally (with a few exceptions) is in both Matthew and Luke, but not in Mark. Karl Lachmann, professor of classical philology at Berlin, in 1835 was the first to recognize on a sound basis these two main written sources in Matthew and Luke ("the Two Document Hypothesis").

Biblical writers' use of sources can be misleading. The author of Mark begins by combining a quotation from Malachi 3:1 with one from Isaiah 40:3 and erroneously ascribes both to Isaiah. Later he combines two unrelated sayings which he attributes to Jesus (9:49-50). The first saying refers to eternal punishment as identical with being "salted with fire." In the second saying "salt is good." The sayings do not belong together either in thought or in their concepts of salt. The author of Mark placed them together because he treated "salt" as a catchword connecting them; this literary device occurs frequently in John. Mark's arrangement makes Jesus appear illogical.

When an ancient writer used source materials, he usually did not revise them to make them harmonize or agree with each other or with all of his own ideas. The resulting document was a mixture of his ideas and the ideas in the sources, which could make the author appear to be unreasonable. In a narrative this type of writing can make a character appear senseless or inconsistent.

Redaction Criticism

Redaction criticism consists of the detection and analysis of either an author's revision of his source material or a later redactor's revision of the book. Redaction was accomplished by changing the text and/or inserting new material. Sometimes both source criticism and redaction criticism apply to a document. Often a redactor composed the material he inserted. Various motives could prompt a redactor to make changes; he might wish to polish the style, add a story, or insert his own ideas. When he inserted his own point of view, a redactor did not necessarily remove from the earlier text the features that conflicted with his own views.

A redactor inserted 1 Corinthians 12:31-13:13, the inspiring ode to love, to counteract Paul's exhortation to the

Corinthians to "desire the spiritual gifts, especially that you may prophesy" (1 Cor. 14:1).[5] Paul advocated prophesying and speaking in tongues, but the redactor believed that love is far more important. Another redactor added chapter 21 to John and made some insertions in the body of the gospel.

Redaction is easy to detect and analyze when both the original text and the revised text have been transmitted to us. Though rare, that situation occurs in the synoptic gospels. The authors of Matthew and Luke revised Marcan material when they used it as a source, and by comparing the three gospels arranged in parallel, we see plainly the changes those two authors made in the Marcan account, and often we can detect why.

As early as 1823 Gustav Seyffarth demonstrated that the last chapter of John must have been added later by a different writer, for its style is so unlike that of the rest of the gospel (which plainly closes at the end of chapter 20). In 1850 Bruno Bauer concluded that the author of Mark imposed on his source material his own notion that Jesus forbade spirits and people to make his healings known. In the twentieth century redaction criticism of the Bible has advanced by leaps and bounds.

Criticism of the Synoptic Gospels

An important field is synoptic criticism, which is the analysis of the synoptic gospels and comparison of them with each other in the light of the various historical methods of New Testament study. This method is usually based on the theories that the authors of both Matthew and Luke used Mark and the material we call "Q" as sources. In this method the scholar tries to detect the earliest form of the text and to analyze the causes of the changes in Matthew and/or Luke.

Historical Criticism

This field includes knowledge of the time, place, and circumstances in which a book or passage was written, the author's purpose, his own background, and the environmental background of the book and its ideas. In short, it is concerned with the whole historical situation.

The famous pioneer in this field of New Testament study was Hermann Reimarus, who tried to place Jesus in his Jewish setting and the gospels in their Christian setting (1778). Prior to the eighteenth century, Christians lacked historical sense; they imagined that conditions in ancient times were the same as in their own day. Jean Terretini, professor of church history at Geneva, urged biblical interpreters to "put ourselves into those times and surroundings" (1728). Johann Gabler apparently was the first to note the importance for biblical study of recognizing the differences among various periods of time (1787). In the nineteenth and twentieth centuries archaeology has assisted historians tremendously in recovering conditions in the past.

Form Criticism

Form criticism rests on the premise that the literary forms in parts of the Bible originated in oral tradition and should be studied in the light of their *Sitz im Leben* ("situation in life"), that is, the situation in the community that led to their origin. The literary form is believed to be a guide in determining the historicity of a narrative and authenticity of a saying. At the beginning of the twentieth century Hermann Gunkel applied form criticism to Genesis and the Psalms. Paul Wendland applied the form-critical method to the synoptic gospels in 1912; in the next two decades this work was continued in depth by three other German scholars: Karl Schmidt, Martin Dibelius, and Rudolf Bultmann. These form critics observed the characteristics of folk lore in the contemporary Mediterranean world and saw parallels in the gospels. Brief healing stories tended to have three parts: the illness, the healing, and the proof of healing (the lame walk; the blind see). Form critics called attention to the "pronouncement stories," concise narratives ending with a pronouncement by Jesus.

Form criticism should be used with care. It can demonstrate that a narrative is not reporting history and that a saying has been altered from its original form. It cannot, however, prove by means of the literary form that they are genuine, for unhistorical accounts and unauthentic sayings can take any form. Bultmann used form criticism to detect the original form and the later altered form of a pericope (saying or story unit). He erred, however, in tending to think that the original form must be a genuine saying of Jesus. Actually, an unauthentic saying could be altered later as readily as an authentic one. Also, the form critics have contended that an oral tradition of Jesus' authentic teaching circulated generally in the early Christian communities and is preserved in the synoptic gospels, but that hypothesis does not stand up under examination.[6]   Some of the gospel pericopes, or units, originated in the writing of the authors, not oral tradition. An oral tradition of the apostles' preaching, however, may have circulated among the churches. Recognition of the situation in the life of the churches is indeed very important, but in general it belongs in the category of historical criticism, not form criticism.

THE HISTORICAL APPROACH

The types of criticism should be used together; each contributes only a part of the total picture. When all the types, or methods, are combined in the task of understanding Scripture, the resulting system is called the historical approach to the Bible. The pioneers in establishing it appeared in the eighteenth century in Germany: Johann Ernesti, Johann Semler, Johann Michaelis, J. G. Eichhorn, and Hermann Reimarus.

Structural criticism is too subjective to be included in the historical approach. It seeks to find the meaning of a text for modern culture, but the alleged meaning varies tremendously according to the beliefs and interests of the individual interpreters, who tend to see what they want to see.

Canonical criticism deals with the question, Which books belong in the Bible? That question was a lively issue for centuries, but today it is regarded as minor because there is not a clear distinction between the nature of the books in the Bible and some of those outside it. Whether a book is or is not in the canon has no bearing on the value of its evidence for discovering the beginning of Christianity. Besides, for centuries Christians disagreed on which books belong in the Bible.

NATURE OF THE BIBLE

Mistaken ideas of the nature of the Bible have also led people astray in regard to the beginning of Christianity. The belief that the Bible is literally the word of God and therefore every sentence is true, with no errors or inconsistencies, has obscured the Bible's variety of thought and historical setting, and caused laity and clergy alike to try to force disparate passages to agree with each other. The inevitable result is misinterpretation of the book.

Lost and Found

The Bible was written by authors in ancient times, for readers in those days; if the authors had written for the modern world, their contemporary readers would not have understood what they were talking about. And we will not understand what they were talking about if we fail to learn all we can about the ancient settings in which the book was written. We should learn also each author's motives for writing; often an author was trying to promote certain beliefs or viewpoints. Such writings have been labeled "apologetics." Because the ancient world was so different from ours, we must beware of translations and interpretations of the Bible which ignore its antiquity and try to make it fit the modern world. The excessive authority given to the Bible is responsible for the error of modernizing it, which prevents the Bible from speaking for itself.

The primary purpose behind the writing of the four canonical gospels is not biographical but apologetic: to persuade readers that "Jesus is the Christ," as John 20:31 frankly states. A related purpose is to help solve both the internal and external problems of the churches.

Also erroneous is the hypothesis that the gospels were originally written in Aramaic, and later were translated into Greek. The main argument for it is the presence in the gospels of Aramaisms, or Semitisms; that is, words and syntax characteristic of the Aramaic language. The hypothesis goes back to Johann Eichhorn in his *Introduction to the New Testament* (1804-1812), and was energetically advanced by Gustav Dalman in 1898. But a contemporary of Dalman, William Moulton at Cambridge University, recognized that Semitisms had been incorporated into the Greek language as a result of the widespread use of Greek in the Near East—an example of inter-cultural influence. In 1931 Ernest C. Colwell demonstrated through the examination of Greek papyri in Egypt that Aramaic words and expressions had become a part of the Hellenistic Greek language in which the New Testament is written.[7] No one claims that Paul's letters were originally written in Aramaic, even though they contain the Aramaic expressions *abba,* "father" (Rom. 8:15; Gal. 4:6) and *marana tha,* "our Lord, come" (1 Cor. 16:22). Further evidence is the fact that the gospel authors quote the Old Testament from the Greek version, the Septuagint, instead of from an Aramaic version; if the authors had written in Aramaic, they surely would have quoted Scripture in Aramaic, not Greek! Nevertheless,

19

this theory had a large following in Britain and America in the first half of the twentieth century. The root of the popularity of the oral-tradition and Aramaic-gospels hypotheses was that both would provide sources that were earlier than the text that has been transmitted to us. This appealed to conservatives eager to maintain the authenticity of gospel traditions.

If we are to use the Bible successfully as a source, we must be fair to it and recognize it for what it is and study the whole book and the total environment in which it was written. And we must avoid the quagmires of erroneous theories, ancient and modern, about the nature of the gospels.

When used carefully, however, the Bible can tell us much about the beginning of Christianity.

SOURCES OUTSIDE THE BIBLE

Other ancient sources besides the Bible shed light on Christian beginnings, either directly or indirectly. Study of the sources should be preceded by learning ancient history—at least Near Eastern and Greco-Roman history from the time of Alexander the Great (336 B.C.) to the middle of the second century A.D.

ARCHAEOLOGY

Ancient sites, artifacts, and manuscripts found by archaeologists and others have furnished evidence important for our task. Archaeology has contributed to our knowledge of all three environments of the New Testament: Jewish, Christian, and pagan, or gentile. Archaeology's contributions to the understanding of the Old Testament have been much publicized. New light on the Near Eastern environment of the Old Testament and the Hellenistic and Roman background of the New Testament is particularly significant. Some writers, however, eager to support the Bible, have misused archaeology. They report cases where archaeological discoveries agree with the Bible, but they conveniently omit the cases where archaeology disagrees with it. The late Millar Burrows at Yale reported both, accurately and fairly.[1]

JEWISH SOURCES

Christianity began as a movement within Judaism, and neither Jesus nor his disciples had any intention of starting a new religion. The earliest Christians were Jews and thought as Jews. To understand what happened we must know what Jews thought. Jewish culture was an important factor in shaping early Christianity. Also, controversy developed between Christians (both Jewish and gentile) and non-Christian Jews, and the issues between them concerned religion.

Dead Sea Scrolls

In 1947 a Palestinian shepherd boy, Muhammad adh-Dhib, accidentally discovered ancient leather scrolls written in Hebrew, wrapped in linen, and stored in earthen jars in a cave near the northwestern shore of the Dead Sea. Bedouins and archaeologists later found more manuscripts in other caves nearby. A copper scroll was also found. The leather scrolls were difficult to unroll and the copper scroll had to be cut into narrow pieces because it was impossible to unroll. Many tiny fragments of scrolls were in the caves too, and trying to piece them together has been a tedious task. Remains—ranging from fragments to the whole book—of virtually all the Old Testament books were found, along with writings—its own and others—that the sect had stored in the caves. Those writings include the *Manual of Discipline* (or *Rule of the Community*), *Damascus Document*, *The War of the Sons of Light with the Sons of Darkness*, and *Thanksgiving Hymns*.

The scrolls soon precipitated many disputes among scholars. Parallels with some New Testament ideas, such as repentance, new covenant, and belief that the world would soon end, along with the practice of sharing all things in common (like the Jerusalem church in Acts) raised the question of whether the sect was Jewish or Christian. Its founder was called "the Teacher of Righteousness," and a few scholars thought that he must have been Jesus. The date of the scrolls was another issue. A Jewish sect in the Middle Ages, the Karaites, held some similar ideas, and Solomon Zeitlin, editor of the *Jewish Quarterly Review*, insisted that the scrolls were written by that sect. The date was settled in 1951-1956 when archaeologists excavated the sect's communal building and cemetery at Qumran near the caves. The pottery and coins found there showed that the site was occupied in the first century B.C. and first century A.D. No coins were later than A.D. 68. The excavation and manuscripts together convinced most biblical scholars that the group was the Essenes, a sect described by Josephus.[2] Other issues in the first two decades after the scrolls were discovered arose also. Was John the Baptist an Essene? Are the scrolls part of the background of the Gospel of John?

Edmund Wilson's lengthy article in *The New Yorker* in 1955 suddenly brought the scrolls to the attention of the

American public. Many wild speculations about them appeared. Professor Millar Burrows at Yale University wrote two books which, together with Wilson's article, brought much common sense to bear on the subject.[3]

From the standpoint of providing new insight into Christian beginnings, the discovery and publication of the Dead Sea scrolls has been the most significant archaeological event of the twentieth century. The scrolls have enlarged our knowledge of the Jewish environment of early Christianity.

Jewish Pseudepigrapha

Although the Old Testament with its Apocrypha provides some necessary knowledge, the Jewish Pseudepigrapha give us more insight into Jewish thought contemporary with Christian beginnings, for they were generally written from 200 B..C. to A. D. 200. Some of the ideas written a century or two before the Christian era were still very much alive in New Testament times. These books have been called "Old Testament Pseudepigrapha" because they were generally written pseudonymously in the name of a personage in the Old Testament; they were never in the Old Testament however.

Early in the eighteenth century Johannes Fabricius was the first person to collect a few of these books. R. H. Charles of Oxford University edited an English translation of seventeen documents in 1913. Today Charles' work has been superseded by the excellent comprehensive collection edited by James H. Charlesworth. In the Charlesworth edition fifty-two Pseudepigrapha, plus fragments of lost Judeo-Hellenistic works, have been translated into English with critical introductions by an international team of scholars that Professor Charlesworth organized. The project was greatly assisted by the work of the Pseudepigrapha Seminar which met at the annual meetings of the Society of Biblical Literature. Some Pseudepigrapha influenced books in the New Testament.

The synoptic gospels manifest knowledge of the Son of Man concept of the Messiah, or Christ, found in the Parables section of *1 Enoch*, a book in the Pseudepigrapha. The description of the fallen angels in Jude 6 incorporates quotations from *1 Enoch* 10 and 12. The Pseudepigrapha and the Jewish sects which produced them had a strong impact on the ethics of the synoptic gospels.

The Pseudepigrapha demonstrate that there was great

variety of thought in early Judaism and that Jews both inside and outside of Palestine were influenced by Egyptian, Persian, and Greek thought. Some of the books are apocalypses, purported revelations from God or his angels to a famous person in the past about the coming end of this age. This information, previously hidden, is revealed to Old Testament figures such as Adam, Abraham, Enoch, and various prophets. Some of the Pseudepigrapha are in the form of "testaments" in which the Old Testament personage passes on to his descendants before his death knowledge that Israel should know and preserve. Other forms of these writings are psalms, prayers, wisdom literature, and legends that present a variety of religious ideas.

The Mishnah

The Torah, or Pentateuch, in the Bible was called the Written Law. Questions arose on the meaning and application of the Written Law, and Pharisaic rabbis made decisions which served as guidelines for the future. These interpretations of the Torah, originally transmitted orally, were called collectively the Oral Law. Sometimes the Sanhedrin, the court in Jerusalem, rendered decisions between conflicting rabbinic opinions. Similarly, in the modern world a new situation may arise that is not clearly covered by existing laws; when the case is taken to civil court, a judge may give a new interpretation of the law, setting a precedent which other courts may follow. One of the many problems arising from the Written Law in Judaism was that the law prohibits work on the Sabbath (Exod. 20:10), but the question often arose, Is a particular act work or not? Consequently rabbis rendered opinions on such questions. Later this Oral Law was written down, and late in the second century of the Christian era Rabbi Judah Ha-Nasi ("Judah the Prince") in Galilee edited them in his compilation now known as the Mishnah. The Talmud is mainly a collection of later rabbinic commentary on the Mishnah. Parts of the Mishnah report rabbinic teaching in New Testament times, including that of the two prominent schools, those of the rabbis Hillel and Shammai. Unlike the Pharisees, two other Jewish sects, the Sadducees and the Essenes, did not adopt the Oral Law.

Josephus (ca. A.D. 38-100)

In A.D. 66 Josephus assumed the supreme military

command of Jewish forces in the Jewish revolt against Rome. When the Romans defeated his army the next year, he went over to the Roman side and urged Jews to surrender. The Roman armies besieged and conquered Jerusalem, thoroughly destroying the city and its Temple, the center of Jewish nationalism and religion, in A.D. 70. Thenceforth unpopular with the other Jews, Josephus settled in Rome and wrote a detailed account of the war. Next he wrote *The Antiquities of the Jews* in which he purported to narrate the history of the Jews from the Creation to the beginning of the First Jewish War against Rome. Writing at a time of high tension between Jews and gentiles, Josephus retold Jewish history with a bias as a means of defending his people. Pagan writers had charged that Jews were a people of recent origin and had made no contributions to human culture. Josephus argued that the Jewish nation was as old as any other and that the law of Moses (the Torah) is older than any other law. He also wrote *Against Apion* as an apologia, or apology, for Judaism. Near the close of his life Josephus wrote a brief *Life* defending his role in the Jewish War.

Josephus' works are valuable to us for his firsthand account of the Jewish War and for the demonstration of some of the literary devices used also in early Christian and other ancient writings. We need his brief description of John the Baptist (*Ant.* 18.5.2) to correct and supplement the gospels' accounts.

Philo (ca. 20 B.C.-ca. A.D. 50)

Philo lived in Alexandria, a city with a large Jewish quarter. Born of a wealthy Jewish family, he received a Hellenistic education. Familiar with Greek philosophy, especially that of Plato and the Stoics, he wrote many allegorical commentaries on the Septuagint version of the Jewish Bible and combined Jewish and Greek ideas into theological philosophy. He wrote a full account of the mission of his delegation sent to Rome by Alexandrian Jews in A.D. 40 to persuade the emperor Gaius Caligula to nullify the order that Alexandrian Jews must worship the emperor's image. This account provides insight into the worship of Rome and its emperors, a practice which became an important factor in church history.

After Alexander the Great conquered the Near East in the fourth century B.C., Greek language became the international language and Greek culture became popular throughout the region. During this Hellenistic period (330-64 B.C.) Near Eastern elements were fused with the Greek, producing a syncretism, a blending, of the two types of culture. Tension developed between Jews who adopted Greek culture and Jews who opposed it as inimical to their traditional faith. Philo was one of the Jews who tried to combine the two worlds. The motivation for such efforts was twofold: to ease tensions within the Jewish community between traditional and Hellenistic Jews, and to persuade gentiles that Judaism was in harmony with Greek culture.

Philo sought to harmonize Jewish religion and Greek philosophy by finding in the Torah the good doctrines which are in Greek philosophy and by asserting [falsely] that the philosophers had learned them from Moses. He interpreted Scripture allegorically to try to prove his points. Another Alexandrian Jew, Aristobulus, who probably lived in the second century B.C., had made the same claims, using the allegorical method in his commentary on the Torah. Philo maintained that there are two senses, literal and allegorical, in Scripture and that the latter is more important.

Philo's task was a difficult one. Jewish religion and Greek philosophy were so very different from each other that they did not fit well together. Other Jews, too, struggled to solve the problem. Later, church fathers had a similar problem when they tried to harmonize Christian theology with Greek and Roman philosophy.

One of Philo's problems was the utterly different concepts of the nature of God. In the Jewish Scriptures God is the personal god Yahweh. In Plato God is an abstraction; it is Mind, the supreme Idea, the Good; it is without attributes and is recognizable only by reason (Greek: *logos*). In pantheistic Greek Stoicism, too, God is not an individual, but is Universal Reason (*logos*), or Universal Law, a force which pervades and controls the whole universe. Philo offered a compromise between an abstract God and a personal God who created the Universe. He maintained that the Universe was made not directly by God, but by his agent, the Logos, Reason, which thus is the intermediary between God and the world. Philo calls the Logos "Son of God," "Paraclete," "Mediator," and "Archangel."

Stoics taught that man should obey the laws of nature.

Philo connected this with Judaism by stating that the Jewish law is in harmony with the laws of nature.

Philo's concept of the human soul is based on the dualism derived from Plato: the spiritual versus the physical (see Plato's *Phaedo*). The ultimate goal for man is to realize that his soul is from God and should return to him. The soul originally descended from outer space and became imprisoned in a human body. The body and the physical world in general are imperfect; man can free himself temporarily from them through a vision of God obtained in ecstasy. Through mysticism (and Torah, added Philo) man can understand the nature of God and thereby attain moral and philosophical perfection. If man frees himself from attachment to the physical world, at death his soul will return to God.

Philo's adaptation to Greek philosophy helps us to visualize what was happening in Hellenistic Judaism in Alexandria as Christianity began.

CHRISTIAN SOURCES

Apostolic Fathers

After the New Testament, the most important Christian source for our purpose consists of the group of writings known as the Apostolic Fathers. They were given that name because of the erroneous assumption that all were written by persons who had known the original apostles. Most were written in the first half of the second century. The collection and publication of these documents began in the seventeenth century. They include:

1. *1 Clement*. This letter was written by the church at Rome to the church at Corinth. Tradition assigns authorship to Clement, bishop of Rome near the close of the first century, but actually the authorship is uncertain. Many Christian works were attributed to a "Clement" and this could be one of them. The writer cites Paul's letters, the Gospels of Matthew and Luke, and the Epistle to the Hebrews. Both Matthew and Hebrews were probably written around A.D. 90, so *1 Clement* must be later. A date in the late 90s is generally accepted.

This letter was written to solve the problem of strife in the Corinthian church; some members had rebelled against its leaders. In the first century many—especially Jewish-Christian—churches adopted the type of organization of the synagogues, that of governance by "the elders," the oldest men in the congregation. In the second century some churches were beginning to use the system of one man, "a bishop," as head of the local church; this practice was borrowed from some Roman organizations. In *1 Clement* the church's leaders are elders against whom a few persons have rebelled, and the writer urges the guilty to submit to the elders (chaps. 47, 54, 57). In chapter 44, however, the crisis in Corinth is "strife for the title [or office] of bishop." Did the rebels want to change the system of leadership from elders to a bishop, with one of their own as the bishop? Or did the church have both a council of elders and a bishop? In chapter 42 the claim is made that the apostles in the past went from city to city and appointed their first converts to be "bishops and deacons." We suspect later redaction here because that sentence is inconsistent with the author's support of the elders as the leaders and because assigning apostolic authority to later church practices and beliefs became a standard propaganda device in early Christianity. If the author was bishop of Rome, why would he support the elders and not those who wanted a bishop?

Beliefs as well as personal ambition may have been involved in Corinth. The author tries in three chapters (24-26) to prove that there will be a resurrection of the dead. One suspects that the rebels had rejected the belief and that the author felt compelled to defend it. It is clear that his main concern was to restore harmony in the church, for as he states, the dissension had caused slander of the church's name and loss of members.

2. *The Two Ways.* A short Jewish writing which contrasts the two ways of living, "the way of light" and "the way of darkness," was attached to the end of the *Epistle of Barnabas* (chaps. 18-21), which is in the Apostolic Fathers. The evidence that it is Jewish is that it contains nothing specifically Christian and does contain expressions especially characteristic of early Judaism. Its contrast between two "ways," good and evil, has its roots in the Old Testament, where "the way of the righteous" is opposed to "the way of the wicked" (Ps. 1:6). *The Two Ways* uses the Jewish expression "walk" to refer to one's conduct ("walk in the way," *Barn.* 19:1).

In 1899 a Latin translation was found of a Jewish-Christian document originally written in Greek, perhaps around A.D. 100. It has been labeled the *Doctrina.* It is a variant form of *The Two Ways,* adding "life" and "death" as synonyms for "light" and "darkness"; this was probably suggested by

Jeremiah 21:8, "Behold, I set before you the way of life and the way of death." Only its liturgical ending, which may have been added by Jewish Christians, is definitely Christian. It contains the commandments to love God and your neighbor and gives the Golden Rule, but does not ascribe them to Jesus. Some scholars have thought that the author derived them from the synoptic gospels, but that is improbable because these teachings were in Judaism too and the form of the Golden Rule here is the Jewish negative form ("Do not do"), not the Christian positive form ("Do"). The evidence indicates that we have here early Jewish-Christian use of a Jewish literary source. The themes in *The Two Ways* are ethical, not doctrinal.

3. *Didache*, or *The Teaching of the Twelve Apostles*. This church manual was written around the middle of the second century, perhaps in Syria. *Didache* (pronounced did-a-KAY) is a Greek word meaning "teaching." The contents of the manual are definitely not the teaching of Jesus' disciples. Its Greek text was discovered by P. Bryennios in 1873 in a monastery in Constantinople. The first half is based on the *Doctrina*, but the second half gives instructions for performing Christian rituals, particularly baptism, fasting on Wednesdays and Fridays, the Lord's Prayer (quoted from the Gospel of Matthew), and the Eucharist. The *Didache* also warns against false teachers and false prophets, and gives advice for Sunday church service and the appointment of bishops and deacons (no mention of elders). It closes with a warning that the Lord is coming soon.

4. *Epistle of Barnabas*. This is a Christian treatise, not a letter, by an unknown gentile author. It probably was written in Alexandria. Its entire Greek text was discovered in the biblical manuscript Codex Sinaiticus, where it was accepted as a book of the Bible. At the time that it was written, hostility between Jews and Christians was intense, and Christianity was separating from Judaism. Consequently some Christians discarded the Jewish Scriptures. An alternate course of Christian action was to keep the Old Testament as Scripture, but reinterpret it to remove offensive Jewish features, that is, to dejudaize it. The gentile author of *Barnabas* attempted to do so by means of allegorical interpretation of it. Whereas Philo had recognized that Scripture has a literal meaning also, the author of *Barnabas* rejected literal interpretation as the device of a wicked angel who deceived the Jews! Using proof texts and allegory, he forces the Old Testament to support Christianity instead of

Judaism. He rejects Jewish sacrifices, fasting, food laws, observance of the Sabbath, and the Jewish Law in general ("we should not be shipwrecked by conversion to their Law," 3:6). The author freely applies the term "Lord" to both God and to Jesus (2:5-6). He is also very concerned with defending Christianity by explaining why Jesus had to die.

5. *Shepherd of Hermas.* The literary form of this book, written in Rome, is that of an apocalypse, or revelation. Its three sections are the Visions, the Mandates or Commands, and the Similitudes or Parables. The author, Hermas, had been a Christian slave, but his owner, a woman named Rhoda, had set him free. As a merchant he became wealthy by unlawful means, but lost all his property in a persecution. Finally he and his family repented. Writing in the first person, Hermas records revelations he receives from a lady who is the Church and from the angel of repentance, who is dressed as a shepherd. The book derives its title from this angel who is Hermas's "shepherd" who will instruct him with commandments and parables. "'For I was sent,' said he, 'to be with you who repent with your whole heart, and to strengthen you in the faith'" (Mand. 12.6.1).

The author was deeply concerned with repentance as basic in Christianity and particularly with the problem of sin after baptism. Hermas was also deeply concerned with morals and ethics; his book was so esteemed for its moral value that some early churches used it as a textbook for catechumens, as the church father Athanasius reported.

6. *Ignatius,* bishop of Antioch, was condemned to be killed by lions in the Coliseum at Rome during Emperor Trajan's persecutions of Christians in Anatolia and Syria. En route to Rome soldiers conducted Ignatius through coastal cities of Anatolia. While he was in Smyrna he wrote letters to the churches of the cities of Ephesus, Magnesia, Tralles, and Rome, and later, while he was in Troas, he wrote to the churches in Phila-delphia and Smyrna and to Polycarp, the bishop of Smyrna.

Ignatius was eager for martyrdom as the sure way to gain eternal salvation. He is not humble as he boasts of his willingness to die for the faith. He also strove to counteract the danger of the churches' replacing their faith with docetism, the Christian heresy that maintained that Jesus only seemed to die on the cross and to be resurrected. As a safeguard against the docetics, he urged the laymen and the elders to be in harmony with the bishop (*Eph.* 4).

Ignatius, too, warns against following the practices of Judaism, particularly the observance of the Sabbath instead of the Lord's day (Sunday). He briefly supports ethics: be meek, humble, pure, and do not retaliate. He, too, expected the end of the world soon.

Several other writings—some only fragments—are also in the Apostolic Fathers. Of special interest to us is the eyewitness account, *Martyrdom of Polycarp*. In the year 156 Polycarp was condemned and killed in Smyrna. When arrested, he refused to call Caesar "Lord" and offer sacrifice, so he was burned alive before a crowd in the arena.

Justin Martyr

Justin was a gentile born in Samaria around A.D. 100, and when he was about thirty years old he converted to Christianity. Next he taught at Ephesus, where he engaged in a lengthy debate with a Jew, Trypho. He wrote an account of the dispute entitled *Dialogue with Trypho the Jew* around A.D. 135. Later he moved to Rome, where he opened a Christian school and wrote *1 Apology* (ca. 155) and *2 Apology* (ca. 161). He refused to make Roman sacrifices, and was beheaded ca. 165. His *Dialogue* gives us valuable insight into the issues between Jews and Christians; many of the issues arose even before the gospels were written. His *1 Apology* gives us valuable information about baptism and the Lord's Supper in the churches. His information about the life of Jesus is drawn from the gospels.

Christian Apocrypha

These early Christian writings have been called New Testament Apocrypha. Although they have some of the same literary forms, such as gospels, acts of various apostles, and apocalypses, they are generally quite different from the New Testament in content and were never in our Bible. Therefore I prefer to call them "Christian Apocrypha."

Are there any early Christian sources outside the Bible that provide reliable information about the life of Jesus? A few isolated sayings are attributed to him, as well as sayings in apocryphal gospels. Today Christians and non-Christians alike

31

are eager to learn more about Jesus, and the discovery of another gospel is hailed in the media with much fanfare. Nevertheless, these sayings and gospels do not deserve the hype they receive. A few consist of a canonical gospel expanded by a writer who added his own words. Some combine elements of several or all canonical gospels with later features dealing with church problems. Some gospels, such as the infancy gospels, consist of legends about Jesus; some were written to promote a particular theology such as Gnosticism. As a result of the break between Judaism and Christianity some are critical of Jews and Judaism; for example, the *Gospel of Peter.* On the other hand, three Jewish-Christian gospels written in the first half of the second century support the Jewish law and practices: *Gospel of the Nazaraeans, Gospel of the Ebionites,* and *Gospel of the Hebrews.* Unfortunately, these three are lost except for a few quotations in the church fathers. The various acts of apostles in the Christian Apocrypha are very unreliable historically, but they display additional variety in early Christian thought.

Nag Hammadi Codices

In 1945 a bedouin discovered thirteen leather codices buried near the modern town of Nag Hammadi along the Nile river. The codices contain 46 tractates, six of which were already known. These manuscripts are written in Coptic, but linguistic features indicate that they are translations of texts originally written in Greek in the second and third centuries. Many are Gnostic, some of which are Christian. Publication of most of the documents was delayed for 25 years because of military and political conditions in the Middle East and because of misunderstandings and rivalry among scholars. Professor James M. Robinson, director of the Institute for Antiquity and Christianity (founded by E. C. Colwell) at Claremont, played an active role in securing publication of the manuscripts.

In the first half of the fourth century the monk Pachomius founded a flourishing monastic movement along the Nile. He built his own monastery and church near Nag Hammadi, and the monastery became the administrative center of other monasteries which sprang up in the area. The production of the codices was contemporary with its existence. Papyrus letters and business documents dated from A.D. 333-348 were reused to thicken the leather cover of Codex VII. Sometime in the latter half of the fourth century the codices were buried beside a grave near caves in a cliff.

The relation of the codices to Pachomius' monastery is not clear. In 367 A.D. Archbishop Athanasius wrote an Easter letter in Greek condemning heretics, and Theodore, the contemporary head of the Pachomian monastery, deposited a Coptic translation of it in the monastery. Did the letter cause Gnostic monks to be expelled from the Pachomian monastery along with their heretical library? And did they then make the nearby caves their dwelling place, eventually being buried with the manuscripts at the foot of the cliffs? The fact that the codices were buried in a jar indicates a desire to preserve, not destroy them, so they must have been buried by Gnostics.

The Nag Hammadi library supplies much information about Christian heresy, but nothing new about the historical Jesus. The *Gospel of Thomas* in this collection, however, has attracted much attention as a possible source of some actual sayings of Jesus. Some of Jesus' sayings in it are not in the Bible, while other sayings are modifications of canonical sayings. Close inspection of the sayings reveals two predominant traits. Often a saying consists of one from the synoptic gospels with another idea added, and the sayings, whether expansions of the synoptics or independent of them, tend to express Gnostic ideas. Here are two samples: "Jesus said, 'Blessed are they who have been persecuted within themselves. It is they who have truly come to know the Father.'" (*Gos. Thom.* 69). The first clause is based on Matthew 5; the rest is a Gnostic addition.

(Jesus said,) "When you come to dwell in the Light, what will you do?" (*Gos. Thom.* 11). This is Gnostic thought. The human soul has come from above, the abode of Light, and if you are a Gnostic, your soul will return and dwell in it.

A characteristic of Gnostic literature is the A-B, B-C, C-D literary pattern of chain linkage, as in this case: "Jesus said, 'Let him who SEEKS continue seeking until he FINDS. When he FINDS, he will become TROUBLED. When he becomes TROUBLED, he will MARVEL, and he will rule over the All'" (*Gos. Thom.* 2). Neither the literary form nor the thought is characteristic of Jesus in the canonical gospels.

Comparison of the *Gospel of Thomas* with the canonical gospels is facilitated by two recent workbooks.[4] The non-canonical materials in *Thomas* demonstrate efforts to foster Gnosticism by reinterpreting and expanding canonical material.

Reinterpretation of sayings ascribed to Jesus was a prevalent device of the Gnostics of the second century. To explain why other Christians had not heard of such teaching, they placed the sayings in a setting which infuriated the early church fathers. The setting was that of the resurrected Jesus giving secret revelations to a particular disciple or to "the Twelve"; the revelations, of course, were Gnostic teaching! The church father, Irenaeus (A.D. 180), denounced their tactics (*Adv. Haer.* 2.27.1).

GENTILE SOURCES

Professor Frederick C. Grant, among others, recognized the importance of knowing the gentile environment of early Christianity: "the New Testament student ought to know Greek literature—all of it—. . . There are certain religious ideas found in Greek literature which are simply indispensable for the interpretation of the New Testament . . . Of course they really are there, in the Bible—but the ordinary reader is not likely to see them when he reads only the Bible without the parallel literature of Greece."[5]

Until late in the nineteenth century nearly all Christians strongly resisted any suggestion that their religion might have been influenced by paganism. That is still true of conservative biblical scholars. Nevertheless, the influence did occur, mainly through gentile converts who retained some of their former ideas and practices, adapting them to their new religion. Another source of such influence consisted of Hellenistic-Jewish converts who had already adapted some Greek elements to their form of Judaism.

Edwin Hatch was a pioneer in recognizing some Greek influence on early Christianity. His lectures delivered at Oxford in 1880 and 1888 were published and stimulated further research, especially in Great Britain. In the United States Shirley Jackson Case of the University of Chicago (particularly with his book published in 1929, *Experience with the Supernatural in Early Christian Times*) was an important factor in leading American scholars into this field. Other important books on the subject have followed.[6]

Some of the pagan source materials have been collected and published mainly for the benefit of New Testament scholars. Some collections contain both Jewish and gentile sources.

Gentile Philosophy

Ethics were well developed in Greek and Roman philosophy. Not all pagan thought and conduct was wicked and depraved, though some propagandists have wanted us to think so. Ethical standards were generally high among philosophers. Socrates led the way.

"The Good" is a term Plato applied to the eternal reality, God. Numenius (A.D. 150-200), a Neopythagorean, said that the First God (among three) is "the Good." Development of Plato's use of the word may have led indirectly to the Jesus saying in Mark 10:18, "Why do you call me good? No one is good, except one, God." Plato declared that mankind's primary duty is to seek knowledge of the Good. He taught in the *Timaeus* (90) that we have a "divine principle within us." This reminds us of Paul's teaching: "Do you not know that your body is a temple of the Holy Spirit within you, which you have from God?" (1 Cor. 6:19). Plato's *Crito* reports Socrates' ethical teaching, and in chapter 10 Socrates says: "Then we ought neither to requite wrong with wrong nor to do evil to anyone, no matter what he may have done to us." This is a forerunner of the famous rejection of revenge in Matthew 5:38-39.

Stoic philosophy, too, contributed noble ideals to the ancient world, and the writings of Epictetus and Marcus Aurelius are important sources. Stoics taught that virtue is based on knowledge and that mankind should live in harmony with nature and reason. Stoics developed the concept of "conscience," an idea accepted by Paul and a few other New Testament writers.[7] They also produced sets of rules to guide households (German scholars call them *Haustafeln);* this literary type occurs in Colossians 3:18-4:1, which is expanded in Ephesians 5:22-6:9.

Some Cynic philosophers were wandering preachers who were much concerned with ethics. Many philosophers combined Cynic and Stoic ideas. Cynics produced lists of vices and virtues; Paul uses the same literary form in Galatians 5:19-23.

In the sixth century B.C. Pythagoras taught the transmigration of souls. This superstition was not new; it was known in primitive societies and ancient Hinduism, and was taught by the Buddha, a contemporary of Pythagoras. Pythagoras believed that souls are divine, have fallen to earth from heaven, and are confined as in a tomb in the bodies of men, animals, and even plants. The only escape from the cycle is by a "way of life" in which the soul is purified through study. Other religions devised various methods of escape. Pythagoras founded a religious society in which women were equal with men, meat was not eaten because of the blood brotherhood between humans and animals, and ethics and purification of the soul were stressed.

Organized Pythagoreanism was persecuted and in the fourth century it disappeared, but the philosophy revived in the form of Neopythagoreanism at the same time that Christianity began. Apollonius of Tyana in Asia Minor was a Neopythagorean philosopher who was contemporary with Jesus. He was an ascetic wandering teacher and a miracle worker who healed the sick. He was a "man of God," to use the modern term for a human to whom some deity had given supernatural power to perform miracles. After his death a hero cult in his honor was founded, with a temple dedicated to him at Tyana. Flavius Philostratus wrote *The Life of Apollonius of Tyana*. Its details are unreliable, but it does present some interesting parallels to our canonical gospel accounts of Jesus as a wandering teacher and miracle worker.

Mystery religions[8]

Some of these popular religions originated in Greece (cults of Demeter, Dionysos, the Great Gods of Samothrace, and Orpheus); others were Near Eastern religions (Cybele and Attis, Isis and Sarapis, Mithra, and the Syrian Goddess), that became mystery cults as the result of contact with the Greek mysteries. In the Hellenistic and Roman periods these cults spread rapidly all around the Mediterranean and as far north as Germany and Britain. Their popularity resulted from the fact that they were personal religions; the deities cared for each individual personally. Membership in one cult did not prohibit membership in another; unlike Judaism, Christianity, and Islam, they were not exclusive religions.

Although they differed greatly from each other, all of these cults held a basic doctrine: the rituals of initiation into membership conferred salvation, consisting of divine protection in this life and an eternal happy life after death. In some of them the *mystai*, or members, were baptized, partook of a ritual meal, and observed a drama of the life and death of the deity. Through initiation and other ceremonies the devotees obtained mystical union with the god; having become one with the deity, they were partly divine and hence assured of blessed immortality. Thus all members were equal, regardless of sex, race, or social status. Stoics taught that *all* persons are equal, but in the mysteries it was only members who are equal. Paul in Galatians 3:28 has an attitude similar to that in the mysteries: "There is neither Jew nor Greek; there is neither slave nor free; there is neither male nor female; for you are all one in Christ Jesus." The last clause puts equality on the basis of religious membership, as in the mystery religions.

Some Hellenistic Jews, like Paul, had some knowledge of the mystery religions, but those gentile Christians who formerly were members of the cults were best equipped to bring in and adapt cultic ideas and practices to the new religion.

Source material on the mysteries is relatively scarce because members were pledged to secrecy—which is why they were called "mysteries"—, especially about the initiation ceremonies.

Isaac Casaubon (1559-1614), a classical scholar at Geneva, Paris, and London, was the first to make a serious study of the possible influence of the mystery religions on Christianity.[9] He concluded that they were the source of the Christian sacraments.

Hero Cults[10]

The hero cult was another type of pagan religion with significance for Christian beginnings. The cult was created by deifying and worshiping a human being; some were legendary beings, some were historical; with some we are not certain whether they existed or not. Usually these personages were so honored because of their outstanding accomplishments. Hercules was worshiped because of his feats of miraculous strength. Asklepios (Latinized as Aesculapius) in Homer's *Iliad* is a mortal physician, but later he was deified and a cult established with its center at Epidauros in Greece. The cult spread, and at the sanctuaries of Asklepios remarkable cures were claimed, some apparently real. The cult combined actual medical procedures with the patients' faith that the god, in the form of a snake, would heal (hence two snakes became a part of the symbol of the medical profession today). Healing the sick and the crippled was a major concern in antiquity.

Roman Imperial cult

In ancient times there were two ways in which a human ruler could be regarded as divine. He could be viewed as divine from birth, as in the case of the kings of Egypt. Or he could become divine by apotheosis, deification by the gods, either during his reign or after his death, as a result of his great deeds, as in the hero cults.

When Alexander conquered Egypt, he allowed priests there to hail him as a god, for he realized that thus the Egyptians were more likely to submit to his rule. Two years after Julius Caesar's death, the Roman Senate bestowed on him the title "Divine Julius." Augustus, the first Roman emperor, sought no divine titles, but the citizens of two cities in Asia Minor honored him with temples dedicated "to Roma and Augustus." In the first century A.D. the Roman people were willing to worship some emperors after death, but they rejected the claims of the emperors Caligula, Nero, and Domitian that they themselves were divine during their lifetime. At the end of the second century Emperor Septimius Severus was the first to firmly establish the belief in the divinity of the living emperor.

Gnosticism

The roots of the heresy, Christian Gnosticism, are in the Greek world in the teachings of Pythagoras and Plato. The dualism between the earthly and the heavenly, the physical and the spiritual, and the importance of knowing its significance, developed in Hellenistic mysticism. Christian Gnosticism contains both Jewish and pagan ideas, but its basic ideas are pagan. The roots are not in Judaism, for no pre-Christian Jewish Gnostic thought has ever been found, and hostility to Judaism is characteristic of Gnostic writings, both pagan and Christian. Pagan Gnostic documents written in the second and third centuries A.D. are the Hermetic writings and some of the books found at Nag Hammadi.

Knowledge of the sources, both biblical and non-biblical, helps us to transport our minds into the ancient past and get "the feel" of the environment in which the early churches emerged. The knowledge can also give us insight into the situation in the early Christian communities, the problems they faced, and the variety of their efforts to solve them.

3

THE JEWISH ENVIRONMENT

Because Christianity began in a Jewish environment and the earliest Christians were Jews, we must understand that complex environment in order to understand another complex subject, Christian beginnings. This chapter is limited to the most basic features; later we will observe other Jewish aspects in direct relation to early Christianity.

PALESTINIAN POLITICAL HISTORY

Hebrews originally filtered into Palestine in the patriarchal age (ca. 2000-1500 B.C.) and settled among the Semites already there. These Hebrews generally came from Hurran, or Haran, at the northern end of the Fertile Crescent, but their ancestors had migrated to Hurran from Mesopotamia. These migrations are epitomized in the story of Abraham's migrations (Gen. 11:31; 12:4-5). Between 1500 and 1300 B.C. some Hebrews entered Egypt. Around 1470 Egypt defeated Syria in the Battle of Megiddo and thereafter controlled Palestine—more or less—until ca. 1250. Egyptian cultural influence is demonstrated by Egyptian artifacts that archaeologists have found in Palestine. As a result of frequent wars, control of the land seesawed among Egyptians, Mitanni (Hurrians), and Syrians, but at times the ruling nation was too weak to exert much control.

In the Exodus (ca. 1250?) Moses led the Israelites, the Hebrews in Egypt, to Canaan.[1] The Israelites gained control of the land partly by military conquest—assisted by Hebrews already living in Canaan—and partly by gradual assimilation. They divided the land among their twelve tribes and formed a loose confederacy. As a defence against the Philistines, they formed a monarchy under Saul (ca. 1020 B.C.), who was succeeded by kings David and Solomon. In 922 the monarchy split into the northern kingdom, Israel, and the southern kingdom, Judah. Israel continued until 721, when its capital city, Samaria, fell to the Assyrian king, Sargon II. Judah endured until Nebuchadnezzar II, king of Babylonia, conquered Jerusalem in 587. He took priests and other Jewish leaders as captives to Babylon; the period of their captivity is known as the Exile. When Cyrus II, king of Persia, conquered Babylonia in 539, he released the captives; some of those Jews returned to Jerusalem, but others stayed in Babylon because they were prospering there. (It is customary to refer to the people as "Israelites" between the Exodus and the Exile, and as "Jews" thereafter.)

Persia controlled Palestine until Alexander the Great defeated the Persian king, Darius III, at Issus and marched through Palestine on his way to Egypt in 332 B.C. After Alexander's death three of his Macedonian generals vied for as large a piece of the empire as they could get and hold. One, Ptolemy I, seized control of Egypt and Palestine, and his descendants held nominal control over Palestine 312-198 B.C. Thus while the Ptolemies ruled Palestine, its rulers were Greeks, not Egyptians. They lost control of Palestine when defeated by the Seleucid, Antiochus the Great, at Panium in 198 B.C.; the Seleucid dynasty was descended from one of the three Macedonian generals. The Jewish Hasmoneans revolted against the Seleucid king, Antiochus IV Epiphanes, in 166 and ruled most of Palestine until Pompey made Judea a vassal state of Rome in 63 B.C. In 40 B.C. the Roman Senate appointed a non-Jew, Herod the Great, as king over Palestine except portions of the coast. When he died in 4 B.C., Rome divided his kingdom among his three sons: Herod Archelaus became ethnarch of Judea, Samaria, and Idumea; Herod Antipas became tetrarch of Galilee and Perea; Herod Philip became tetrarch of a region northeast of the Sea of Galilee. In A.D. 6 Augustus banished Archelaus and made his territory the Roman province of Judea. Pontius Pilate became its procurator, or governor, in A.D. 26, but was removed from office in 36 because of his tactless treatment of Jews and Samaritans. In 41 the Roman emperor Claudius bestowed on Herod Agrippa I, grandson of Herod the Great, the kingship of all Palestine. After his death in 44, Judea was again governed by Roman procurators. When the Jews revolted against Rome in 66-70, the Romans destroyed Jerusalem and its Temple. A second Jewish revolt against Rome (132-135, led by Simeon bar Kosiba) also failed.

NATIONALISM

Nationalism was intimately connected with Jewish religion, begining with the Exodus. Moses brought along the worship of the tribal god, Yahweh (translated as "the Lord" in many English versions of the Bible),[2] which he acquired while working for his father-in-law, a Midian priest (Exod. 3). Although later tradition claimed that Yahweh had been the god of Abraham, Isaac, and Jacob too, historians are certain that the claim originated later to support Yahweh-worship after Moses introduced the Israelites to it. Archaeologists have found Yahweh's name on Palestinian inscriptions, but all are later than the Exodus, which suggests that Yahweh worship in Palestine began after the Exodus. The belief that Yahweh had led the Israelites to Canaan had a powerful impact upon Judaism, and later tradition expanded and interpreted it to support the worship of Yahweh. Also, a feeling of separateness from other peoples was generated by the doctrine of election, the belief that Yahweh had chosen the Israelites to be his own people. "Yahweh your God has chosen you to be a people for his own possession, out of all the peoples that are on the face of the earth" (Deut. 7:6). (In Jesus' day a Jewish sect, the Essenes, believed in the divine election of their sect only, not all Jews.) Because Yahweh had chosen them and led them out of Egypt, they should worship only him. "I am Yahweh, your God, who brought you out of the land of Egypt, out of the house of bondage. You shall have no other gods before me" (Exod. 20:2-3). At first this was henotheism, the worship of only one god while believing that other gods exist. Many tribes, cities, and nations in the ancient Near East had their own special god, though they usually worshiped other gods too. But Israel's prophets insisted on the worship of only Yahweh, for he had selected, or elected, only the Israelites. This belief is understood in Jeremiah 30:22, where the Lord says to Israel, "You shall be my people, and I will be your God."

Nationalism was also stimulated by the belief that Yahweh helped their ancestors conquer Canaan. This faith is demonstrated by the Israelites' practice of taking their god in "the ark of God" [a box in which Yahweh, probably in the form of a stone, dwelt] with them into battle to help them defeat enemies, and their consternation when the Philistines captured it (1 Sam. 4:17-22). Thus the Conquest was a holy war of which

Yahweh approved. Centuries later Israelite writers used it to bolster Yahwism and eradicate foreign religions (Num. 33:51-53). The Deuteronomist even went so far as to represent Yahweh as commanding a holocaust of non-Jews during the Conquest: "But in the cities of these peoples that Yahweh your God gives you for an inheritance, you shall save alive nothing that breathes, but you shall utterly destroy them, the Hittites and the Amorites, the Canaanites and the Perizzites, the Hivites and the Jebusites, as Yahweh your God has commanded; that they may not teach you to do according to all their abominable practices which they have done in the service of their gods, and so to sin against Yahweh your God" (Deut. 20:16-18). What a terrible model for future generations, and it is in the Torah! Centuries after the Exodus the tradition arose that Yahweh had promised the land of Canaan to the Israelites in perpetuity (Gen. 17:8; Deut. 34:4).

The belief that Yahweh had made covenants with his people also encouraged nationalism. Other peoples in the Near East had similar beliefs, but the effect was more enduring in Israel because of the tradition of the Sinaitic covenant and because the covenants were incorporated in Scripture. Prophets denounced those who broke the Sinaitic covenant (Jer. 11:3-5). Even though the people have broken their covenant with Yahweh by worshiping foreign gods, he says, "I will establish with you an everlasting covenant" (Ezek. 16:60).

Jews were often subjected to foreign rule. They were successively ruled by the Assyrians, Babylonians, Persians, Macedonians, and Romans. The taxation that accompanied foreign dominance augmented the desire for national freedom. Subjection to foreign powers was especially difficult to accept when Jews recalled their independence and power under David, Solomon, and the Hasmonean rulers. Also, the reality did not fit the theory that Yahweh, who ruled the whole earth, was protecting them, his chosen. The prophets offered two main solutions: (1) The foreign invasions were divine punishment for Israel's unfaithfulness to Yahweh (Jer. 30:14), and (2) Yahweh will punish the other nations on "the day of the Lord" (Ezek. 30:3-5). The Exile especially was a very severe blow to national pride. Some prophets held out the hope that the remnant of the Jews scattered abroad will be saved and will return to their homeland and to "the mighty God" (Isa. 10:21; 11:11-12) and the nation will be restored (Jer. 30). After the Exile the Jews gathered in Judea regarded themselves as the "remnant that has escaped" (Ezra 9:15), and centuries later the Essenes viewed *themselves* as the remnant (CD 1:4-5).

During the Exile the Jewish priests in Babylon became very nationalistic and codified Israelite laws and composed additional ones. Nationalism inspired the rebuilding of Jerusalem and its Temple, which the Babylonians had destroyed. The priest Ezra came from Babylon with authority to enforce "the law of Moses." National pride was restored.

Nationalism burst into flames under the persecution by the Seleucid king, Antiochus IV Epiphanes in 166 B.C. Encouraged by the Hellenizing party among the Jews, he tried to unify his kingdom by forcing the orthodox Jews to stop practicing their religion and to adopt Greek culture, which had become the international culture of the Mediterranean world. The Maccabees led a successful revolt, establishing the Hasmonean dynasty which ruled most of Palestine until Rome gained control in 63 B.C. The revolt is recorded in 1 Maccabees in the Apocrypha.

Nationalism waned somewhat in the first century B.C., but revived with the rule over Palestine by the Herod family and by the Roman procurators. Their rule brought heavy taxation, which aroused hostility to foreigners in general and the rulers in particular. Jews often attempted in vain to revolt, culminating in the Second War against Rome, led by Simeon bar Kosiba. The numerous revolts are described in chapter 7 below.[3]

Not all Jews were so nationalistic, however. Efforts of some Jews to turn toward gentiles and their culture are reported below in chapter 6, "Ethical Teaching."

When Jews were under foreign rule, they longed for the restoration of the nation, with peace and prosperity (Jer. 33). Yahweh himself will be the king of the new kingdom, reigning from Jerusalem in some prophecies (Zech. 14; Micah 4:7). In Zechariah, Yahweh will stand on the Mount of Olives as king of all the world and smite with a plague all the peoples who waged war against Jerusalem. All who survive will go annually to that city "to worship the king, the Lord of hosts [lit.: Yahweh of armies], and to keep the feast of booths."

THE MESSIAH

Some writers expected that the king of the ideal Jewish

kingdom would be a Messiah, God's agent. The English word Messiah is an approximate transliteration of the Hebrew word *Meshiach,* "Anointed One." The basis for the term was the ancient Israelite practice of anointing a new king by pouring oil on his head. At Yahweh's command Samuel thus anointed David to be king, "and the Spirit of Yahweh came mightily upon David from that day forward" (1 Sam. 16:13). The anointing was regarded as performed by Yahweh himself, and the king was called "Yahweh's anointed" (2 Sam. 19:21).

In retrospect David's kingdom seemed to be the ideal kingdom and David the ideal king. Therefore a prevalent expectation was that the messianic king would be the "Son of David," that is, a descendant of David. Descendants of David were on the throne of Judah from its beginning to its end, inspiring the anachronistic pledge of Yahweh to David: "I will raise up your offspring after you, . . . and I will establish the throne of his kingdom forever" (2 Sam. 7:12-13). Isaiah 9:6-7 may refer to Hezekiah, a contemporary reforming king of Judah, but Isaiah 11:1-5 definitely refers to a future, ideal Davidic king: he is a shoot from Jesse (David's father); "the Spirit of the Lord shall rest upon him, the spirit of wisdom and understanding"; "with righteousness he shall judge the poor, and decide with equity for the meek of the earth"; "he shall smite the earth with the rod of his mouth, and with the breath of his lips he shall slay the wicked." Other prophecies of the future coming of a Davidic king are in Jeremiah 23 and in a book in the Jewish Pseudepigrapha, *Psalms of Solomon* (17-18).

Psalms of Solomon was written in the first century B.C., close enough to the time of Jesus to demonstrate messianic ideas that were in the air in his day. Here is a selection of aspects of the Son of David in its description: "See, Lord, and raise up for them their king, the son of David, to rule over your servant Israel in the time known to you, O God. Undergird him with the strength to destroy the unrighteous rulers, to purge Jerusalem from gentiles who trample her to destruction; in wisdom and in righteousness to drive out the sinners from the inheritance; . . . to destroy the unlawful nations with the word of his mouth; . . . he will condemn sinners by the thoughts of their hearts. He will gather a holy people whom he will lead in righteousness; . . . And he will have gentile nations serving him under his yoke, . . . And he will be a righteous king over them, taught by God. There will be no unrighteousness among them in his days, for all shall be holy, and their king shall be the Lord Messiah. . . . He will strike the earth with the word of his mouth forever; he will bless the Lord's people with wisdom and happiness. And he himself (will be) free from sin, (in order) to rule a great people. He will expose officials and drive out sinners by the strength of his word. . . . God made him powerful in the holy spirit and wise in the counsel of understanding, with strength and righteousness. . . . His words will be purer than the finest gold, the best. . . . His words will be as the words of the holy ones [angels], among sanctified peoples." He is "the king of Israel."

The Son of David Messiah was clearly a human being, but in Isaiah 11 and the *Psalms of Solomon* he has acquired a supernatural attribute, the power to kill people and destroy nations by the words of his mouth. He is not divine himself, but God has given him this supernatural power. Some pagans, too, believed that the gods bestowed supernatural powers, such as the power to perform miracles, upon certain chosen humans.

Another type of Messiah that appeared in Jewish thought shortly before the beginning of the Christian era was the Son of Man. He is briefly described in scattered portions of the Parables, or Similitudes, section of *1 Enoch* (chaps. 37-71). The original Parables section ended with chapter 69, and chapters 70-71 were added when *1 Enoch* was compiled to connect the Parables to the man Enoch, who is not in the Parables proper.

In the Parables the Son of Man has existed with God from before the universe was created. All righteous, faithful Jews are "elect ones" (chosen by God), but the Son of Man is especially "the Elect One" because God chose him to be the Messiah. God has hidden him, but at the proper time God will reveal him. The Son of Man will come to earth, sit on his throne of glory, and judge the risen dead. Immortality will be on earth; the righteous will "wear garments of glory," and "they shall eat and rest and rise with that Son of Man forever and ever." "He is the light of the gentiles." The title, Son of Man, sounds like he was human, but the fact of the matter is quite the opposite (see chapter 12).

A prevalent belief was that the Messiah will be a prophet. The Son of David will have the Spirit of the Lord resting upon him, according to Isaiah 11:2, and thus he will be the Prophet-King. By New Testament times various other concepts of the Prophet-Messiah had appeared. He would not necessarily be a descendant of David, although that view was still prevalent. He might also be a Prophet like Moses, based on a reinterpretation of Deuteronomy 18:18. The types of Messiah are discussed further in chapters 12 and 13.

ESCHATOLOGY

During the Persian period Jews were in contact with Zoroastrianism, the Persian religion, and they adopted and adapted some of its beliefs. The Zoroastrians believed in angels, demons, and the dualism of two spirits, the Good Spirit and the Bad Spirit, to which was attached the dualism of Truth vs. Falsehood, Light vs. Darkness, Life vs. Death. This dualism is behind the Essenes' belief in two spirits: the spirit of Truth and Light and the spirit of Error and Darkness.

A major feature of Zoroastrianism was its eschatology. The word "eschatology" is derived from the Greek term meaning "last things" and signifies beliefs about the resurrection of the dead and the last judgment at the end of the present world, or present age. Zoroastrians believed that at death souls receive a preliminary judgment and reside temporarily in heaven or hell until the resurrection of the dead bodies and the final judgment. Then the souls return to the bodies, with the wicked going to eternal punishment and the righteous remaining in the new incorruptible world on earth.

The Sadducees did not believe in immortality. The Pharisees believed that after death souls are stored in chambers in the heavens until the day of judgment, at which time they will be reunited with their bodies, which God will raise from their graves (he will restore the body from the tailbone, which the Pharisees thought would never decay). The righteous, now transformed into imperishable bodies, will live forever on a new, imperishable, perfect earth. The wicked will be punished forever in the fires of Gehenna. The Essenes, however, believed in the immortality of souls in heaven, never on earth, and therefore did not believe in the resurrection of the body.

The eschatological new world will be similar to the national, or political, new kingdom in that it will be perfect with an ideal ruler, with Jews still God's chosen people in it. Unlike the natural kingdom, however, in the eschatological kingdom people will live forever, and they will consist of the righteous dead whom God has raised as well as the righteous who are living at the time that the end occurs. In Isaiah 65-66 Yahweh will make a new heaven and earth.

Belief in the resurrection of the dead appears in Isaiah, Daniel, and *Psalms of Solomon*.

Your dead shall live; their bodies shall rise (Isa. 26:19).

And there shall be a time of trouble, such as never has been since there was a nation till that time; but at that time your people shall be delivered, every one whose name shall be found written in the book. And many of those who sleep in the dust of the earth shall awake, some to everlasting life, and some to shame and everlasting contempt (Dan. 12:1-2).

"Those who fear the Lord shall rise up to eternal life" (*Pss. Sol.* 3:12).

The judgment is described concisely in *1 Enoch*:

And there shall be a judgment upon all, . . . And to all the righteous he [God] will grant peace. . . . They shall all belong to God and they shall prosper and be blessed; and the light of God shall shine unto them. Behold, he will arrive with ten million of the holy ones [angels] in order to execute judgment upon all. He will destroy the wicked ones (1:8-9).

Humans are not necessarily the only ones to be punished. Isaiah 24:21 mentions the punishment of heavenly powers.

When Jews adopted the eschatology of a final and endless Age to Come with God reigning directly from Jerusalem, a compromise arose between it and the old national Jewish kingdom with a human Messiah. The compromise was the belief that the rule of the Messiah would be temporary, and God's direct rule was postponed until after it. In *4 Ezra* the temporary Messianic Age will last only 400 years, while in the Jewish source in the Book of Revelation it lasts 1,000 years. With the rabbis it varied from 40 to 1,000 years.[4]

Eschatology is widely accepted in the Pseudepigrapha, especially by the apocalyptic writers. In some writings all the dead will be raised for judgment, but in others only righteous Jews will be raised, not gentiles or wicked Jews. In some writings the Messiah will overthrow the foreign rule and then turn over the kingdom to God; in others God will accomplish all without the aid of a Messiah. God will be the judge at the judgment, except that in the Parables of *1 Enoch* the Son of Man will be the judge. Some Hellenistic Jews did not believe in eschatology and instead accepted belief in the final immortality of the soul in heaven. Philo and the Wisdom of Solomon set forth that view; its basis is the doctrine that souls originated in heaven and therefore the souls of the good will return there.

THE TEMPLE

During the Exodus, when the Israelites were desert nomads, they carried with them a tent-shrine, the "Tent of Meeting," or "Tabernacle." When Moses entered it, Yahweh as a pillar of cloud descended and stood at the door. There Moses and Yahweh met. "Thus Yahweh used to speak to Moses face to face, as a man speaks to his friend" (Exod. 33:11). Any other Israelite who wanted to meet with Yahweh could go to the tent too (Exod. 33:7). Other tribes had a similar practice with their gods; traces of a Midianite tent-shrine have been found at Timna.

After the Israelites settled in Canaan, they constructed the "Ark of the Covenant," a box in which Yahweh's presence was believed to dwell continuously. A housing was built for this ark, and it became the official shrine of the Israelite tribal league. The location of this central shrine has been debated, but at least it was at Shiloh when the league came to an end. When David became king, he had the ark (now called "the ark of Yahweh" and "the ark of God") transferred to Jerusalem and installed "inside the tent which David had pitched for it" (2 Sam. 6:17). Many Israelites had objected to the political change from tribal organization to a monarchy under Saul. David strengthened the monarchy by moving the ark, thus making Jerusalem the religious center as well as the political center. Solomon went even farther in this direction. He built the magnificent Temple in Jerusalem and placed the ark in the Holy of Holies, the inner sanctum at the rear of the Temple. Then Solomon said to Yahweh, "I have built you an exalted house, a place for you to dwell in forever" (1 Kings 8:13). As the only temple in the kingdom, the house of Yahweh became the heart of the holy city and the nation. The description in Exodus 25-31 and 35-40 of the elaborate Tabernacle in an elegant setting is not really a description of the Tent of Meeting in Moses' day, but rather a description of the Ark of Yahweh in the Temple. This is an anachronism by the writers of the P source, ascribing later conditions to an earlier period.

The First Temple, Solomon's, was built by a Phoenician architect from Tyre and was patterned after Phoenician and Syrian temples. After seven years of construction it was completed around 952 B.C. Many Greek and Roman temples had an impressive large statue of the deity standing on the floor or seated on a throne at the rear of the main room, clearly visible as worshipers entered. Near Eastern temples usually had either a small statue in a niche at the rear or else statue(s) in an inner room at the rear into which only priests were allowed to enter. In ancient Egypt, in the case of some pharaohs, a statue of the deified king stood in an inner room at the rear of the pharaoh's tomb; only priests could enter it. The Holy of Holies was a modification of the inner chamber; Yahweh dwelt in it, but had no statue. He may have been represented there by a small ungraven stone. Since the government in Judah was a theocracy, the Temple priesthood had great influence. The Temple was destroyed by the Babylonians in 587 B.C.

After the Exile Cyrus II, the Persian king, authorized the Jews who had been captives in Babylon to return to Jerusalem and rebuild the city and its Temple. He returned to them the gold and silver vessels which the Assyrian king, Nebuchadnezzar, had taken from the Temple. Under the leadership of the high priest Jeshua and the governor Zerubbabel, the Second Temple was built on the site of the First in 520-515 B.C. Because there was no longer an Israelite king on the throne, the Temple priesthood exercised much civil authority in addition to their religious authority. But in the next few centuries the Temple was plundered and allowed to deteriorate.

Herod the Great embellished the Second Temple so extensively that this final form is often called "Herod's Temple." Construction began in 20 B.C. and continued for decades. The Temple was covered with gold and was the same size as its predecessors. Its setting, however, was vastly enlarged, with wide courtyards surrounded by elaborate colonnades with monumental gates. The architectural style of the whole complex was no longer Phoenician, but Greco-Roman. Herod's goal was twofold: to impress the Romans with the elegant structure and, as a non-Jew himself, to please the Jews, his subjects. The Temple faced east, toward the sunrise, like many Near

Eastern temples; the worship of sun gods was the ultimate source of this practice. The outer courtyard was called the "Court of the Gentiles" because gentiles were allowed to enter it. Inscriptions on the wall surrounding the inner courtyard and Temple warned gentiles not to enter those areas, under penalty of death. From the front to the back of the Temple complex proper, the arrangement and accompanying restrictions were in this order: The Women's Court, into which Jewish women could enter; next, the Court of Israel, into which only Jewish men could enter; the Priests' Court, into which only priests could enter; finally, the Holy of Holies, into which only the high priest could enter.

Worshipers in various Near Eastern religions made pilgrimages to cultic centers, or shrines, to bring offerings, offer sacrifices, and celebrate religious feasts. Before Solomon built the Temple, Israelites made pilgrimages to cultic centers such as Shiloh, where the "yearly feast of Yahweh" was held (Judg. 21:19), and Solomon himself made pilgrimages to "the great high place" at Gibeon (1 Kings 3:4). The Temple replaced the local shrines in these functions, especially after the reforms of King Josiah (7th c.). Deuteronomic law required three journeys per year for males: "Three times a year all your males shall appear before Yahweh your God at the place which he will choose: at the feast of unleavened bread, at the feast of weeks, and at the feast of booths. . . . every man shall give as he is able" (Deut. 16:16-17). In Jesus' day enormous crowds came to Jerusalem for the feasts.

The loss of its religious center, the Temple, in the First Jewish War against Rome was a tremendous shock to Jews. Judaism survived, however, because the role of the Temple was transferred to the homes and synagogues. Within a few decades Rabbi Johanan ben Zakkai established an academy and a new Sanhedrin court at Jabneh (Greek name: Jamnia), on the coast; his academy established Pharisaism as dominant in Judaism.

PRIESTS

According to tradition Aaron (Moses' co-leader in the Exodus) and all his descendants were to be priests, and they were accordingly anointed with oil and entitled to wear priestly garments. Only this family line could be priests. At first they served in the various cult centers, but in Josiah's reform the other centers were abolished and all priests had to serve in the Temple. In addition to the priests of Aaronic descent, a large group called the Levites were ordained as priests to serve in the Temple. With so many priests confined to one center, there were more priests than work. So more ritual was devised for them to perform, and they were separated into divisions in order to rotate the work (cf. Luke 1:8-9). Many had to find other work such as farming. The Levites were relegated to the role of Temple servants (Ezek. 44:10-11). In 1 and 2 Chronicles the author tries to elevate the status of the Levites.

The high priest was at the head of all the priests, the Temple, and the Sanhedrin, the council or legal court in Jerusalem. He was so powerful that he also controlled many functions of the political government of Judea. Herod the Great, however, deprived him of all but ceremonial functions, but under Roman rule he and the Sanhedrin regained considerable power.

The Essenes rejected the Jerusalem Temple and its priests because the Essenes believed that those priests were corrupt, did not follow the correct calendar, and had profaned the Temple. They wrote a scroll which describes the new Temple which would replace the contemporary one in the new kingdom. In the *War* scroll (2:1-6) they describe the number, organization, and functions of priests and Levites in the future new order. In the new kingdom a messianic Aaronic priest, the priestly Messiah, will come to supervise properly all religious matters.

ORIGIN OF PARTIES AND SECTS

Zadok (a descendant of Aaron) and his descendants controlled the high priesthood in Jerusalem from the time of Solomon until 171 B.C. Then their dynasty ended partly because of rivalry for the office and partly because Jews in Jerusalem were sharply divided between the Hellenizers, who adopted Greek culture, and the orthodox, who continued to observe the Jewish Law. Hellenizers usurped the office of high priest by bribing the king, Antiochus IV Epiphanes. The transfer of the high priesthood, with all its power, from the Zadok priests to the Hellenizers infuriated the Zadok priests and the party of the Hasidim ("the pious ones"). When Antiochus and the Hellenizers tried to force Greek culture on the Jewish population, the Maccabees revolted, resulting in the establishment of the Hasmonean line of Jewish kings, who were neither descendants of Zadok nor even Levitic priests. The Hasmoneans, at first quite orthodox, drifted toward concern for personal power and indifference to strict Judaism, and thus lost the support of the Hasidim.

Out of this turmoil, sometime in the middle of the second century B.C., new sects and parties emerged. One group, claiming (perhaps rightly) to be descendants of Zadok, migrated from Jerusalem to Qumran and formed the sect of the Essenes.[5] The party of the Sadducees gained control of the Temple and for political reasons were friendly with the Hasmoneans and later with the Roman rulers. The sect of the Pharisees grew out of the Hasidic movement. They carried their teachings to the towns outside Jerusalem and eventually established synagogues with rabbis as teachers. The Mishnah and Talmud contain their teachings from the beginning of the Christian era to the fourth century. The Sadducees rejected the Pharisees' belief in immortality and angels. Judging from the Pseudepigrapha, other Jewish religious groups, or sects, arose outside of Palestine.

THE LAW, OR TORAH

The first five books of the Bible are called the Torah, a Hebrew word that means "instruction," but is generally translated into English as "law," Contrary to the tradition which refers to them as "the law of Moses," they were not given by Moses in the thirteenth century but are composite works with layers of material composed and edited from the ninth to sixth centuries B.C. The contents of the books reveal their later origin.

The earliest code in the Torah is the Covenant Code (Exod. 21:1-23:19), which contains an Israelite adaptation and revision of Babylonian laws, particularly the laws of Hammurabi (17th c. B.C.), which archaeologists have discovered. The Israelite version of those laws is more humane. The Decalogue, or Ten Commandments (Exod. 20:2-17), is ancient too; to give it authority, it is erroneously represented as received by Moses at Mount Sinai.

Using some of these earlier laws, some person or group wrote down a collection of laws which Hilkiah the high priest found in the Temple in 621 B.C. King Josiah read the words of this "Book of the Law" to all the elders of Judah and "made a covenant before Yahweh, to walk after Yahweh and to keep his commandments and his testimonies and his statutes, with all his heart and all his soul, to perform the words of this covenant that were written in this book" (2 Kings 23:3). Thus Josiah adopted the book as the law of his kingdom.

The event was very significant in Israel's history. First, it set a strong precedent for Jewish rejection of foreign religions. Judah had become a vassal state of Assyria in 721 B.C. Then Ahaz, the king of Judah, added worship of Assyrian gods to the worship of Yahweh in the Temple. This act was deeply resented by the Yahwists (devout worshipers of Yahweh), and when Ahaz's son Hezekiah became king, he cast out the Assyrian religion and rebelled unsuccessfully against Assyria. His son, King Manasseh, made peace with Assyria and reintroduced worship of Assyrian and Canaanite deities. While Josiah was the king of Judah, the Israelites regained their political freedom, and Josiah instituted a reform based on this Book of the Law.

Second, the event was significant as the beginning of Judaism as a religion of the Law. The adoption of the Book of the Law by means of making a sacred covenant with Yahweh made observance of it especially binding. The principle was accepted by future generations when the Law was expanded.

Third, the Book of the Law was the earliest form of the Jewish Bible. It probably consisted of an earlier version of chapters 5-28 in Deuteronomy. Other laws were added later. The Priestly Code in Exodus, Leviticus, and Numbers was compiled before, during, and after the Exile. Eventually the Pentateuch became the Law. Leviticus 17-26 is called the Holiness Code because of its theme that Israel should be holy even as Yahweh is holy.

The need for deciding just how the Law should be applied in various situations—especially in changed conditions centuries later—led to interpretations of the Law. An example is the law forbidding work on the Sabbath; the question often arose, Should a particular activity be classified as work or not? In Jesus' time all three main Jewish sects were interpreting the Torah. The Sadducees interpreted it strictly according to the written text. The Pharisees interpreted it more loosely, which enabled them to reinterpret it to fit current conditions and attitudes. They transmitted their interpretations of the Law

53

orally by teaching them in the synagogues and by training disciples. Therefore their interpretations became known as "the Oral Law" in distinction from "the Written Law," the Pentateuch. To give the Oral Law equal standing with the Written Law, the Pharisees erroneously claimed in the Mishnah that Moses received it at Sinai (*Abot* 1:1). Torah, or Law, in its narrow sense consists of only the Written Law; in its broad sense it includes the Oral also.

Guided by divine revelation—they believed—, the Essenes interpreted the Law to support the beliefs of their sect. When the Holy Spirit revealed a new interpretation of the Torah to an Essene, it was his duty to pass the revelation on to the brethren. Some members wrote commentaries on Old Testament books by copying the Hebrew text and inserting their interpretations of it.

The necessity of observance of the Torah was one of the most basic beliefs of the three major Jewish sects. The belief was reinforced by the conviction that the Law is identical with God's wisdom and will last forever. The Book of Baruch in the Apocrypha states this concisely: "She (wisdom) is the book of the commandments of God, and the Law that endures forever" (4:1). Nevertheless, there was a school of thought in early Judaism that held that the present Law would last only until the new age or kingdom came; then God would give a new law.[6]

THE ESSENES

When the Hasmonean kings took over the high priesthood, a "Teacher of Righteousness" led his followers out from Jerusalem into the desert and established the priestly sect of Essenes with headquarters at Qumran near the Dead Sea. They maintained that they were "the sons [i.e., the descendants] of Zadok" of Ezekiel 44:15-31 and therefore were the priests entitled to the high priesthood and control of the Temple. They believed that the usurping priesthood followed the wrong calendar and did not conduct the Temple services properly. These Essenes asserted that they were the righteous remnant and that Yahweh had made the New Covenant (Jer. 31:31-34) with them. They were the true Jews, "the sons of light." They believed that the end of the present age was near when, with God's help, they would win a holy war against "the sons of darkness." They thought that they fulfilled prophecies in the

Scriptures. In the art of misinterpreting Scripture by lifting passages out of context, they could match anyone, past, present, or future! During the first Jewish war against Rome the Essenes hid their library in the caves of Qumran; the Romans soon occupied their community building, as archaeological excavation has proved. The Essenes at Qumran did not survive the war, for they never retrieved the library. Other Essenes lived in Palestinian towns and survived, for the sect was known to Hegesippus in the second century A.D.[7]

ETHICS

Ethics, the question of right and wrong, arose in primitive society largely as a self-defence mechanism. Conduct that was harmful to the individual, family, or tribe was regarded as wrong. When nations were formed later, they had a similar attitude: anything harmful to the nation was wrong.

The Old Testament reflects the development from nomadic life to settled life in Canaan and eventually life in a kingdom. Standards of conduct practiced among nomadic tribes were strict, but tended to be modified when the tribes settled down to agricultural and urban life. In Israel the new settled conditions caused some confusion at first in religion and ethics. "In those days there was no king in Israel; every man did what was right in his own eyes" (Judg. 17:6).

Some of the old tribal ways persisted, however, including sexual morality and the dominance of the male as the father and husband, which gave women an inferior social status. Women were the property of the father or husband; he could sell his daughters into slavery (Exod. 21:7-11), and he could divorce his wife (Deut. 24:1-4), but she could not divorce him.

A continuing issue in Judaism was the question of particularism, or exclusiveness, versus universalism. Should fair treatment be extended to all peoples, or only to the members of one's own group? Are outsiders inferior to insiders? Tribal existence had fostered higher ethical standards of treatment of persons within the tribe than of those outside it. Prostitution, witchcraft, and idolatry in Canaanite, Philistine, and Assyrian religions, and human sacrifices in Canaanite and Phoenician religions caused a low opinion of the peoples who engaged in such practices. Intermarriage with foreigners was forbidden because it was liable to lead Israelites into immorality and cause them to turn away from worshiping Yahweh (Deut. 7:3-4). Another cause of prejudice against outsiders was that sometimes their group was a tribal or national enemy of one's own group. The belief that the god Yahweh had chosen the Israelites as his own people was not so detrimental at first while the Israelites were henotheists, that is, while they believed that other gods exist. In the Near East many nations, including Israel, had their own god or gods. But when the Israelites became monotheists and believed that only one God exists, and he has chosen them above others, the foundation was laid for an attitude of separateness, exclusiveness, and superiority.

During the Exile many of the Jews in Palestine became lax in observing Israelite religion; some married foreign wives and adopted their religion. Ezra revived Jewish exclusiveness by forcing Jerusalem Jews to separate from the gentiles and to divorce their gentile wives:

And Ezra the priest stood up and said to them, "You have trespassed and married foreign women, and so increased the guilt of Israel. Now then make confession to Yahweh, the God of your fathers, and do his will; separate yourselves from the peoples of the land and from the foreign wives" (Ezra 10:10-11).

Unfortunately, this event had a lasting effect, for it was recorded in the Book of Ezra, which later was canonized as Scripture. Gentiles were regarded with disdain simply because they were gentiles.

Yet in the early Hellenistic period many Jews looked favorably upon the Greeks and their culture, but after Antiochus IV suppressed Jewish religion, antipathy toward foreigners prevailed again. In Jesus' day the Roman rulers with their heavy tax levies were especially hated.

Nevertheless, some nobler individuals rose above the narrow attitude. "You shall not wrong a foreigner or oppress him, for you were foreigners in the land of Egypt" (Exod. 22:21). "And I charged your judges at that time, 'Hear the cases between your brethren, and judge righteously between a man and his brother or the foreigner who is with him'" (Deut. 1:16). The authors of Second Isaiah, Jonah, and Ruth were willing to accept gentiles into the Jewish faith. The Pharisees are reported in the Gospel of Matthew to have compassed sea and land to win a convert (23:15). Yet these efforts applied only to gentiles who converted to Judaism, thereby placing a limitation on the movement toward universalism. The non-Jew was not really accepted as equal. Particularism, or exclusiveness, naturally tended to accompany nationalism. But congenial contact with other peoples and their culture served to moderate the narrow view. The Wisdom literature of the Old Testament (Job, Proverbs, Ecclesiastes) tends to speak in terms of the problems of humanity in general, not just those of Jews. Contact with Egyptian culture and ethics was a constructive influence. Harry Elmer Barnes remarked: ". . . it seems that the Egyptians were the first to evolve a moral code based on the concepts of justice, truth, individual worth, and personal equality. . . . The Egyptians were probably the first to develop a consciousness of individual worth, as set off against the family, clan, and nation."[8] Centuries before the Israelite prophets, there were Egyptian reformers who cried out for justice, who protested the exploitation of the poor by the rich. An example is the story of "The Eloquent Peasant," written around 2000 B.C. In it the sun-god Ra urges mankind to "speak the truth, do the truth." A pioneering work in recognizing the Egyptian contribution to the ideal of an ethical society was James Henry Breasted's *The Dawn of Conscience* (1933). The Israelites were influenced by Egyptian culture, including its ethics and practical wisdom. A clear example is the fact that Proverbs 22:17-23:11 is based on the earlier Egyptian document, the *Wisdom of Amenemope*. The first scholar to recognize the source of those verses in Proverbs was the German Egyptologist, Adolf Erman in 1924.[9]

Alexander the Great treated as equals the peoples he conquered and tried to unite them with Greek language and culture, which became very popular. Some Jews discarded Judaism in favor of Hellenism. Other Jews sought to accommodate the two worlds by reinterpreting Judaism along the lines of Greek philosophy. In Wisdom of Solomon 6, wisdom is identified with God's words and is available to gentiles; "she goes about seeking those worthy of her," including the kings of the world. In the Jewish Pseudepigrapha the *Testaments of the Twelve Patriarchs* was strongly influenced by Stoic universalism. The world should obey God's Law, which includes Stoic principles of virtue. Jewish sins against it will prevent it from enlightening the nations: "You [Jewish sinners] will bring down a curse upon our nation, because you want to destroy the light of the Law which was granted to you for the enlightenment of every man" (*T. Levi* 14:4). Hellenism pulled Jews in the direction of universalism, but Jewish tradition pulled them toward particularism.

Various noble ideals were in the Jewish background of early Christianity, and were honored as essential: justice, love, truth, and charitable concern for the poor, widows, orphans, and the sick. Specific ethical principles are described in chapter 6 below; here we note statements upholding righteousness and goodness in general, beginning in the Old Testament. "Let justice roll down like waters, and righteousness like an ever-flowing stream," wrote Amos (5:24). "What does Yahweh require of you but to do justice, and to love kindness, and to walk humbly with your God," wrote Micah (6:8). Yahweh is "the God of truth" (Isa. 65:16)

Ethical concern in Judaism developed further under Greek influence, especially in the last two centuries B.C. and the first century A.D. In the Apocrypha the trend is manifest in Tobit and Sirach. "Live uprightly all the days of your life, and do not walk in the ways of wrongdoing. For if you do what is true, your ways will prosper through your deeds" (Tobit 4:5-6). Observe that living uprightly is equated with doing what is true; truth and righteousness are one, as with the Essenes. The Jewish Pseudepigrapha, especially the *Testaments of the Twelve Patriarchs*, uphold righteousness and goodness in general. "Run from evil, . . . cling to goodness and love" (*T. Ben.* 8:1-2). The *Testament of Benjamin* 4-6 describes at length the virtues of the good man, whom others should imitate. The *Sibylline Oracles* (3:630) admonish readers to "honor righteousness and oppress no one."

The Christian and pagan environments of the early churches were very important too. Along with additional aspects of Judaism, they will be discussed as we search to learn how Christianity began. Our search begins with two Jewish prophets who appeared in Palestine around A.D. 30, John the Baptist and Jesus of Nazareth.

4

JOHN THE BAPTIST

JEWISH BAPTIST MOVEMENTS

In ancient Israel religious significance had long been attached to the bathing of the human body. The Israelites believed that bathing was necessary to cleanse themselves after defilement from physical contact with dead bodies, lepers, and unclean animals, and after childbirth. In the period of the Second Temple the idea developed that the body should be bathed in order to have a proper relationship with Yahweh. The deity is holy, and should not be insulted by approaching him when one is unclean. Leviticus 16:2-4 portrays Aaron the priest as ordered to bathe his body before putting on holy garments and approaching the holy place, the mercy seat of the ark of Yahweh. It became the custom for the high priest to bathe on Yom Kippur before appearing before the Lord. Jews performed ablutions before entering the Temple, and the Pharisees required Jews to wash themselves before prayer. The emphasis on physical cleanliness was related to the Jewish belief that body and soul belong together and should be clean together.

When Christianity began, numerous Jewish bathing, or baptizing, movements were appearing. Perhaps they drew inspiration from a literal interpretation of the metaphor in Ezekiel 36:25: "I will sprinkle clean water upon you, and you shall be clean from all your uncleannesses, and from all your idols I will cleanse you." In my doctoral studies I encountered a very thorough French study of the subject, *Le Mouvement baptiste en Palestine et Syrie*, by Joseph Thomas (1935). Although his discussion of the Essenes needs to be updated, the book remains an excellent survey of Jewish and Christian baptism movements from 150 B.C. to A.D. 300. I am now using it as a partial guide in sketching, in chronological order, the Jewish groups that practiced ritual bathing.

The Essene sect, pre-Christian in origin, had its monastery headquarters at Qumran, not far from the Jordan

River where John baptized. According to Josephus, there were many other Essenes in Palestinian towns. He reports (*Wars* 2.8.5) that the Essenes bathed before their noon and evening communal meals, to which only members in good standing were admitted. He states that they enter their communal dining room as into "a holy temple." A priest said grace both before and after the meals. Thus the bathing was a physical cleansing which prepared members for participation in their meals, which apparently were given some religious significance. Although the Essenes regarded themselves as "those in Israel who had repented" and had separated themselves from other Jews (CD 4:2-3), neither Josephus nor the Dead Sea Scrolls associate repentance with their bathing.

Josephus has left us the best description of the nature of John the Baptist's baptism. John preached to Jews that the baptism would be acceptable to God, "not for the purpose of the forgiveness of sins, but for the purification of the body, supposing that the soul was thoroughly purified beforehand by righteousness" (*Ant.* 18.5.2). Thus John's baptism was consistent with the Jewish belief that bathing does not cause forgiveness of sins, but cleanses the body while repentance and righteousness cleanse the soul. This belief was definitely held by the Essenes. Men who walk in the way of wickedness cannot be cleansed from sin by bathing: "For men cannot be purified unless they repent their evil" (1QS 5:13-14). John's baptism differed from that of the Essenes in that his was not repeated daily and was offered to all Jews who desired it.

Although our primary interest is in John, let us continue to sketch the development of bathing in early Judaism, and then return to John. About twenty-five years after John's death Josephus, at the age of sixteen, became a disciple of Banus for three years (*Vita* 2). Banus was an ascetic hermit who lived in the desert, made his garments of leaves and bark, and ate only food that grew in the wild. John too had lived in the wilderness like a hermit; his food consisted of locusts and wild honey (Matt. 3:4). Banus, says Josephus, "bathed himself in cold water frequently, both by night and by day, in order to preserve his purity." Apparently he did not baptize other people, and there is no evidence that he connected his bathing with repentance. He had disciples, however—at least Josephus was one temporarily.

A few church fathers mention a Jewish bathing sect

which they called the Hemerobaptists, that is, "Daily Baptists."
According to Epiphanius it was one of the seven Jewish sects
which fled from Jerusalem when the Romans attacked the city in
A.D. 70. He remarks that the Daily Baptists have the trait of
bathing in water daily, in spring as in autumn, in summer as in
winter. He associated their bathing with purification from sins.
The author of the *Apostolic Constitutions* states that they bathe
each day before their meals and strictly cleanse their rooms and
table utensils (6.6.5). Although bathing before meals is like the
Essenes, Hegesippus lists them and the Essenes as separate
Jewish sects.[1]

The fourth book of the Jewish *Sibylline Oracles*
contains a poem written around A.D. 80-90 that pertains to
baptism. The author probably lived in Syria or Asia Minor. He
exhorts "wretched mortals" to:

... wash your whole bodies in perennial rivers. Stretch
out your hands to heaven [i.e., pray] and ask forgiveness for your previous deeds and make propitiation for
bitter impiety with words of praise; God will grant
repentance and will not destroy. He will stop his wrath
again if you all practice honorable piety in your hearts.[2]

Like John the Baptist, the author associates bathing with
repentance and warns against imminent divine judgment. Both
men regard repentance, not baptism, as the factor that causes
God to forgive. Unlike John, this author is addressing gentiles,
and clearly the baptism of converts to Judaism is involved here.
John, however, baptized Jews, not new proselytes. As for the
association of prayer with baptism, this probably became a
standard feature of the initiation of proselytes into Judaism. The
connection may have been suggested by interpreting literally the
metaphorical use of "wash" in Isaiah 1:15-16. An early stage of
the connection between prayer and baptism may be reflected in
the third book of the *Sibylline Oracles* written in mid-second
century B.C. The passage is not dealing with proselytes, but
rather describes pious Jews as "at dawn they lift up holy arms
toward heaven, from their beds, always sanctifying their flesh
with water."[3]

The Palestinian Targum on Exodus, dated in the third or
fourth century A.D., demonstrates that baptism in some Jewish
communities, at least, was used in initiating proselytes. Exodus
12:43-44 states that no foreigner may eat the Passover, but that a
(foreign) slave may do so "after you have circumcised him." In

its translation of these verses the Targum adds "and given him a ritual bath."

JOHN'S LIFE AND DISCIPLES

When we try to recover the actual life of John the Baptist, we meet two problems which we will encounter on a larger scale in retrieving the actual life of Jesus. First, the material that reports or at least reflects authentic history must be separated from the unreliable material which in many cases was produced for propaganda purposes. Second, the authentic tradition that has been transmitted to us is meager. The bulk of the traditions about John that we have are Christian; therefore we will have to take early church history into account in order to separate the wheat from the chaff about John.

The earliest Christian documents that report John's activities, Mark and Q, know of no stories about his birth. Our reliable information begins with John appearing in the wilderness, baptizing in the Jordan River, and preaching. He may have been located only at the southern end of the Jordan, as implied by Mark's statement that all Judea and Jerusalem went out to him, or perhaps he ranged all along the Jordan, as Matthew and Luke imply. Josephus and the synoptic gospels agree that John was very popular with the crowds. Many Jews in Palestine believed he was a prophet (Matt. 14:5).

As for John's message, Josephus is probably correct in describing him as "a good man, who commanded Jews to practice virtue, both as to righteousness toward one another and piety toward God" (*Ant.* 18.5.2). But Josephus omits the eschatological element, which was basic and which Q, Matthew, and Luke rightly include. The reason that John's preaching and baptism were so popular is that he emphasized that the anticipated kingdom of God was coming very soon, so if Jews would repent at once, they would pass the Judgment and enter the kingdom. Matthew 3:2 makes the point explicit: "Repent, for the kingdom of heaven is at hand." (In Matthew "kingdom of heaven" is substituted for "kingdom of God" because the word God was regarded as holy.) Clearly the early Christians believed that John's message was eschatological. The necessity of Jews repenting before the Judgment was a Jewish belief stated clearly in *1 Enoch* 50: The Elect One (the Messiah) will cause people to "repent and forsake the deeds of their hands"; at the Judgment "the unrepentant in his presence shall perish." Q's metaphor of trees cut down and "thrown into the fire" (Luke 3:9 par) plainly refers to the Judgment and fiery punishment of the wicked.

The preaching ascribed to John in Q (Luke 3:7-9 par) and in Luke 3:10-14 has been regarded by some scholars as authentic material transmitted by John's disciples. I find features in it that point to a Jewish-Christian origin. "You brood of vipers" sounds like a Christian epithet for non-believing Jews during the sharp controversy between Jews and Christians that was raging when the Q traditions were formed. Also, the injunction to the crowd not to rely on descent from Abraham to save them is similar to the Christian argument against Jews in John 8. The statement here, "every tree therefore that does not bear good fruit is cut down and thrown into the fire," is ascribed to Jesus verbatim (except "therefore") in Matthew 7:19. Finally, "soldiers," presumably Roman, are in the crowd in Luke, and that does not fit John's situation. He preached to and baptized Jews; only they were already conditioned by training to be concerned about repentance and the Judgment. Soldiers responding to preaching does fit the situation of the Christian apostles, however, for some Roman soldiers joined the early churches; those soldiers may have been "God-fearers" attending synagogue services.

John's preaching that the kingdom of God was coming soon naturally made some Jews wonder if he were the Christ (Luke 3:15). At this time the word "Christ," or "Messiah," referred to the "Anointed One," whoever he might be, who with God's help would free Jews from foreign rule. It did not necessarily refer to Jesus. Christian laymen today are so accustomed to using "Christ" as a name for Jesus that it is difficult for them to realize that originally the term could apply to any "anointed" leader. Whether John believed that he was the Christ is unknown; statements of his denial of that claim are unhistorical, as we will see. His disciples may have believed in his messiahship during his lifetime; certainly after his death they and converts to his sect honored him as the Christ, as the intense rivalry between the Christians and the Baptist's sect indicates. The *Clementine Recognitions* (in the Christian Apocrypha) states: "Some of the disciples of John, who seemed to be great ones, have separated themselves from the people and proclaimed their own master as the Christ" (1:54). The belief that John was a prophet did not at all prevent followers from believing that he was the Messiah.

The Jews who believed that John was the Christ would naturally expect him to lead a revolt to overthrow the current rulers and prepare for the coming rule, or kingdom, of God which he preached was near at hand. According to Josephus, John's popularity caused Herod Antipas to imprison him in Machaerus in Perea, east of the Dead Sea, and there put him to death, lest he induce the crowds to revolt. The synoptic gospels have substituted a different motive for his execution by Antipas: John had criticized him for divorcing his wife and marrying Herodias, his sister-in-law. This, too, may have been a cause of his death, although the story of Salome's dance is surely legendary (Mark 6:17-29). Although Mark states that all the people of Judea went out to John, and none of the gospels mention the people of Perea, across the Jordan, John must have operated in Perea at least part of the time, for Herod had jurisdiction over Perea but not Judea. Herod could not have had John arrested in Judea.

After the death of both John and Jesus, their followers became bitter rivals. The intense polemic against John in all four Gospels demonstrates that fact. Why the hostility? Because both sects claimed that their master was *the* Christ, and the Baptists could say that Jesus, baptized by John and preaching the same basic message, was only a disciple of John. John's sect continued well into the second century and probably the third. The two sects began with the same basic message, yet the Baptists disappeared while Christianity grew and survived. Why? Because the former remained one of many Jewish sects, but Christianity became interracial and international, opening the door to many more converts.

JOHN AND CHRISTIANITY

The early Christians were indebted to John, for his message inspired Jesus to continue the work after John's death. According to Mark 1:15, Jesus preached the same basic theme as John (Matt. 3:2). The friendly connection between the two men, however, caused some problems later between the followers of John and the followers of Jesus. Both groups believed that their master was the Christ.

The fact that Jesus derived his basic message from John

may have suggested to non-Christian Jews that John, not Jesus, was the Messiah. A solution to the question of which man is the Christ is offered in the Q source of Matthew and Luke. John is portrayed as sending some of his disciples to ask Jesus if he is the Messiah. "Are you he who is to come, or shall we look for another?" Jesus tells them to report to John that the blind, lame, lepers, and deaf are healed, the dead are raised up, and the poor have the good news, or gospel, preached to them (Luke 7:18-23 par). This answer, in effect, is that Jesus is the Christ, for he is doing the work of the Christ. The answer rests on a messianic interpretation of passages in Isaiah.[4] This story contrasts sharply with the gospel stories and sayings in which John already knows that Jesus is the Christ. There is one other gospel tradition, however, in which John has to be told—in this case, by a sign—that Jesus is the Messiah. God has told John that upon whomever he sees the Holy Spirit descend and rest, that one is the Son of God who baptizes in the Holy Spirit (John 1:32-34).

In defence of their belief that Jesus was the Christ, early Christians downgraded John. The synoptic gospels portray John as preaching, before he baptized Jesus: "After me comes he who is mightier that I, the thong of whose sandals I am not worthy to stoop down and untie. I have baptized you with water, but he will baptize you with the Holy Spirit" (Mark 1:7-8). Thus John and his baptism are inferior to Jesus and his baptism. John's inferiority to Jesus is the theme in the Christian saying ascribed to the Baptist in the Gospel of John: "He must increase, but I must decrease" (3:30).

A problem was that John came first and that Jesus apparently learned his basic message from him. It may have been said that Jesus was only a disciple of John. In those days the earlier was generally assumed to be better than the later. The Gospel of John portrays John as proclaiming of Jesus, "He who is coming after me was ahead of me [in rank] because he was first of me" [in time] (1:15). The reasoning is based on the doctrine of incarnation: Jesus existed in the heavens before he came to earth, and therefore he is earlier than John and outranks him.

Another problem was that John had baptized Jesus. John's baptizing the crowds of Jews was in connection with his call for repentance, and the baptism of Jesus was not an exception. It indicated that Jesus thought that he had sinned and was now repentant. This idea was especially troublesome because in Jewish prophecies of the future Christ he was expected to be sinless, completely righteous. The author of Matthew tried to solve the problem by depicting John as protesting, "I need to be baptized by you, and do you come to me?" (3:14). Thus John is again belittled in comparison with Jesus.

Nevertheless, many early Christians realized that John had played an important role in paving the way for their movement. This led them at times to praise and upgrade him. In a pericope in Q we find Jesus giving limited praise to John: "I tell you, among those born of women none is greater than John; yet he who is least in the kingdom of God is greater than he" (Luke 7:28 par). In other words, no non-Christian is greater than John, but even the least of Christians is; John is outside the kingdom! This attitude tells us that the saying originated in the churches; it is incredible that Jesus would regard the martyr John as outside the kingdom of God.

One method of explaining John's role was to interpret him as the divinely-sent prophet who would be the forerunner of the coming of the Judgment and the new kingdom. Isaiah 40:3 states: "A voice [God's] cries: 'In the wilderness prepare the way of the Lord [Yahweh, or God], make straight in the desert a highway for our God.'" Mark 1:3 par quotes that verse, but changes it to read, "the voice of one crying in the wilderness," so that the voice is not God's, but John's. The author of Mark did this to try to make John fulfill prophecy.

When we turn to the Q material, we find in Luke 7:27 par a quotation from Malachi 3:1, which reads, "Behold, I send my messenger [of the covenant] to prepare the way before me." Q changes it to read, "Behold, I send my messenger before your face, who shall prepare your way before you." Observe the change in thought: The anonymous messenger has become John, and the Lord's way has become Jesus' way.[5]

These Christian traditions—whether they originated in apostolic preaching, written gospel sources, or the composition of the gospel authors—supported the claim that Jesus, not John, was the Christ. But they did not explain why John was involved with Jesus and the birth of Christianity. The early Christians believed that all that happened to Jesus was according to divine plan. If that was the case, what was John's role in that plan? Why was John necessary? The apostles produced two answers: (1) John was the forerunner who came to prepare the way for Jesus, and (2) his function was to identify Jesus as the Christ, to make him known to Israel.

Some Jews expected that the prophet Elijah would appear on earth again just before the kingdom of God arrived. But why Elijah? Although eventually some Jews thought that Isaiah and Jeremiah might return, they had died and could not appear on earth again until their bodies were resurrected. Elijah, however, was different. According to 2 Kings 2:11 God had taken Elijah alive to heaven in a whirlwind. Thus God could readily send him back to earth *before* the general resurrection of the dead.

Belief in Elijah's return first appears at the end of Malachi in the Old Testament. In 3:1 Yahweh will send "the messenger of the covenant" before he himself comes to his Temple to establish his kingdom. The messenger will "prepare the way before me," says Yahweh. Later someone attached two verses at the end of Malachi, interpreting the messenger as Elijah:

> Behold, I will send you Elijah the prophet before the great and terrible day of the Lord comes. And he will turn the hearts of fathers to their children and the hearts of children to their fathers, lest I come and smite the land with a curse. (4:5-6).

Here Elijah is the eschatological prophet whom Yahweh will send at the end of this age. His function will be to reconcile fathers and children. Written in the second century B.C., Sirach 48:10 expands his role to fit the nationalist hope: he will "restore the tribes of Jacob." The scribes said that Elijah must come first, and Jesus is reported as agreeing (Mark 9:11-12).

In the middle of the second century A.D., Justin reported Trypho as saying that "we [Jews] all expect that Christ will be a man [born] of men, and that Elijah when he comes will anoint him" (*Dial.* 49).[6] Here Elijah has a different function: he will anoint the Messiah. If that belief was current in Judaism in the first century A.D. as well, it is very significant. Trypho adds, "yet as Elijah has not come, I declare that he [Jesus] is not Christ."

This Jewish background tells us why many Jewish Christians felt compelled to regard John as Elijah. Other Jews besides Trypho have said that Jesus could not have been the Christ, for Elijah had not yet returned to prepare the way for the coming of the Lord.

The Baptist is specifically identified with Elijah in Matthew and Mark.[7] In Matthew 3:4 this claim is given support by describing John as dressed the same way as Elijah (2 Kings 1:8). The belief that John was sent by God to prepare the way for Jesus caused some Christians to criticize those who did not believe John (Matt. 21:32) or who charged that he had a demon (Luke 7:33). The desire to honor John even resulted in the claim in a birth legend that he and Jesus were related; when speaking to Mary, the angel Gabriel refers to John's mother, Elizabeth, as "your kinswoman." The author of Matthew admits that John was not regarded as Elijah during his lifetime ("for they did not know him," Matt. 17:12).

The birth stories about the Baptist are very Jewish in tone, a fact which has led some biblical scholars to theorize that the stories are drawn from traditions transmitted by the Baptist's sect. The theory is very questionable. Although the stories contain typical Jewish views, we must remember that in the first century many Christians, too, were Jews with typical Jewish beliefs. The birth stories about Jesus in Matthew and Luke, which certainly are not derived from John's disciples, are of the same nature as those about John, which are only in Luke. All these stories are Christian legends which use Old Testament materials copiously. The birth stories about John are only part of the Christian effort to upgrade John as the forerunner.

The second Christian explanation of the role of John is that God sent him to identify Jesus as the Christ. The Gospel of Signs source in the Gospel of John depicts the Baptist as explicitly rejecting the idea that he is Elijah (1:21). Instead, the Baptist's function is to identify Jesus as the Christ and point him out to Jews: "I came baptizing with water in order that he might be revealed to Israel" (1:31). In the Gospel of John the Baptist himself does not know who Jesus is until he sees the Holy Spirit descend on Jesus (1:32-34). In contrast, in Luke 1:41 John as a fetus recognizes Mary's voice and leaps in the womb.

It is not surprising that the Gospel of John rejects the belief that the Baptist was Elijah, for he did not accomplish what Elijah was expected to do. He had not reconciled fathers and children (as far as we know) nor had he restored Israel as a nation. Even some pericopes in the synoptic gospels reflect the belief that Elijah is still in heaven. He an Moses appear in visionary form at the Transfiguration (Mark 9:4), and at Jesus' crucifixion bystanders think that Jesus is calling to Elijah (Mark 15:35). Two church fathers, Tertullian and Hippolytus, rejected the claim that John was Elijah.[8]

A compromise view was that John was not Elijah, but he had his spirit. In the birth stories an angel tells John's father that John will go forth "in the spirit and power of Elijah" (Luke 1:17). Justin told Trypho that the same Spirit of God that was in Elijah was in John, and that Elijah himself will come with Jesus when he returns to earth (*Dial.* 49).

5

JESUS OF NAZARETH

Did Jesus ever live, or is he just a mythological figure? Several scholars, having observed that much in the gospels is unhistorical, have concluded that the whole story about Jesus is a myth. In the ancient world stories about mythological persons were abundant, so it would not be unusual if Jesus were mythological too. The miracle stories in the gospels and the mystical Jesus from heaven in the Gospel of John are certainly mythological. In 1850 Bruno Bauer decided that Jesus was not a historical person, and recently G. A. Wells reached the same conclusion. The most famous work of this kind written in English is Arthur Drews' *The Christ Myth* (1924).

Nevertheless, there really was a man known as Jesus of Nazareth. He was not the first historical person to have legends written about him after his death. Alexander the Great, Julius Caesar, and many others also received that honor. Hero cults arose which deified a hero after his death, as we have observed.

The gospels contain much more than miracle stories. They contain other material which originated in the early Christian communities and tell us a lot about Christian origins. They also contain a few historical facts about Jesus in the gospels give us a glimpse of an actual life; there was no reason for the authors to mention them if they were pure fiction. If the Christians had created the person of Jesus out of thin air, their story of his life would not have included features that were contrary to Jewish expectations of the coming Messiah, features which early Christians tried desperately to explain in their efforts to persuade others, especially Jews, that Jesus was the Christ and fulfilled prophecy. A fictional Jesus would have conformed much better to the messianic hope and not have generated so many difficult problems for the early Christian communities. (A fuller discussion of this topic is in chapter 25.)

THE SEARCH FOR JESUS

"Who Was Jesus?" is the title of a *Time* magazine survey of recent scholarship on the subject.[1] This significant question has often been raised both within and outside of Christianity, from the first to the twentieth centuries. The canonical gospels do not present a consistent picture of Jesus, and the enormous differences between John and the other three canonical gospels have always been confusing. The earliest attempt (ca. A.D. 170) to reconcile the confusing diversity was Tatian's *Diatessaron*, an interweaving of the four gospels in an effort to construct one continuous account. It was so popular in the Syrian churches that it replaced the four "separated" gospels there until bishops put an end to it in the fifth century. The earliest attempts to write a life of Jesus were made in England in the middle of the eighteenth century when three men each wrote a biography of him: Thomas Chubb, Thomas Morgan, and Matthew Tindal. In the nineteenth and twentieth centuries many more lives of Jesus were written, which vary from each other so much that it is impossible that all—if any—are accurate. Causes of the variety include the authors' selection of biblical passages to use as sources, their interpretation of the passages, and their own theology. Christian liberals portrayed Jesus as human, an act which aroused the ire of Christian conservatives and led them to write biographies of a divine Jesus. The result was bitter controversy, which stimulated more detailed and more comprehensive biblical study by both groups.

The canonical gospels are virtually our only sources for the life of Jesus. Apocryphal gospels and fragments have been found, but none contain any new information about Jesus that is reliable. But the gospels in the Bible are not very reliable either. Reporting the real life of Jesus was not the purpose of the biblical authors and besides, they did not know many details anyway. They wrote to aid the Christian communities in their efforts to win converts and to solve a wide variety of problems in the churches. Consequently, many unauthentic sayings and incidents are ascribed to Jesus, and the task of discovering what Jesus actually said and did is very difficult.

CRITERIA OF AUTHENTICITY

In order to judge whether gospel material is authentic or

71

not, we need to establish objective, historical criteria to use as guidelines. The criteria which the present writer judges to be valid are listed in the Appendix.[2]

Separating the authentic from the unauthentic is more difficult in regard to Jesus than John the Baptist. In the case of Jesus the unhistorical traditions are more numerous, and the issues and the motives which caused their creation are more abundant and complex.

JESUS' BIRTH

His name was "Jesus," not "Christ." In earliest, or primitive, Christianity, Jesus was sometimes called "Jesus, the Christ," that is, Jesus, the Messiah, in Jewish fashion. Christ was a title, not a personal name. But when gentiles were converted to Christianity, many were unfamiliar with Jewish-Christian usage and thought that the expression was a proper name. Thus "Jesus, the Christ" became "Jesus Christ."

His parents were Mary and Joseph. Joseph is his father in two pericopes in Matthew. In 13:55, when Jesus teaches in a synagogue in his own country of Galilee, the people exclaim over his wisdom and mighty works and ask, "Is not this the carpenter's son?" The carpenter is surely Joseph; the carpenter certainly is not the Holy Spirit of the virgin birth tradition! Also, the genealogy at the beginning of this same gospel attempts to trace Jesus' ancestry back to Abraham, the traditional father of the Jewish race. This genealogy traces Jesus' ancestry through Joseph, not Mary; obviously whoever composed it regarded Joseph as Jesus' father, for otherwise the genealogy has no bearing on Jesus' ancestry. The genealogy in Luke expressly states that Jesus was "the son of Joseph" (3:23). "As was supposed" is clearly an insertion by a later scribe to try to eliminate conflict with the virgin birth story. Luke's genealogy, like Matthew's, is pointless if Joseph was not the father of Jesus.

In Luke 4:22 the Galileans say of Jesus, "Is not this Joseph's son?" In the Lucan story of Jesus teaching in the Temple at the age of twelve, Joseph and Mary are his "parents" in 2:41 and 2:43, and in verse 48 Mary herself says to Jesus, "Behold, your father and I have been looking for you." In the Gospel of Signs source in the Gospel of John (1:45) Jesus is "the son of Joseph." 1 Clement 32:2 regards Jesus as a

72

descendant of Jacob (ancestor of Joseph): "From him [Jacob] physically the Lord Jesus came."

Conservative biblical scholars have tried in vain to discount this evidence. Some early Christians tried too. The "as was supposed" insertion into the Lucan genealogy is a case in point. The same purpose is behind a change in the fifth-century Codex A and Codex C; they change "his parents" in Luke 2:43 to "Joseph and his mother" to avoid referring to Joseph as Jesus' parent. The scribes who wrote these two codices were not systematic, however, for they neglected to eliminate the word "parents" in verse 41 and Mary's reference to Joseph as Jesus' father in verse 48. We are surprised when we first encounter such scribal inconsistency, but after we become familiar with ancient manuscripts we find that such inconsistency was frequent when authors incorporated source material or changed it or scribes copied and altered the text.

Jesus' parents were Jews, and Jesus and his four brothers had Jewish names (Mark 6:3); the name Jesus is the equivalent of the Hebrew name Joshua. Jesus was very probably born in Nazareth. He definitely was not born in Bethlehem, for if he had been, it would not have been necessary to create the two contradictory and implausible stories in Matthew and Luke which locate his birth in Bethlehem in an effort to make his life fulfill prophecy. (See chapter 12 below.)

The birth stories about Jesus in Matthew and Luke are just as legendary as those about John the Baptist.[3] The purpose of the stories about Jesus is not historical, but christological; that is, they were written not to report history but to promote beliefs about Jesus as the Christ.

The fantastic stories of the virgin birth of Jesus, with God's Holy Spirit as his father instead of Joseph, are not in the Gospels of Mark and John, and with good reason. In Mark the natural birth of Jesus, with Mary and Joseph as parents, is clearly assumed. In John a virgin birth would not be incompatible with the Incarnation doctrine. In that gospel Jesus, a spirit, was already the Word and the Son of the Father (not son of the Holy Spirit) in heaven before he came to earth and was incarnated in a human body. Mary, the mother of Jesus, is not even mentioned in John.

As Raymond Brown has recognized, the virgin birth idea may be earlier than Matthew and Luke, and probably originated in Hellenistic Jewish Christianity.[4] The stories contain several Jewish aspects, including an annunciation by an angel (Matt. 1:20; Luke 1:26). The Hellenistic Jew Philo wrote allegorically of Hebrew patriarchs who were begotten by God; for example, Jacob's mother "Rebekah . . . became pregnant from God."[5] The ultimate source of Hellenistic Jewish ideas about supernatural birth was paganism. Greek and Roman stories related that the heroes Hercules, Asklepios, Plato, Alexander the Great, Julius Caesar, and Augustus were the sons of a god and a woman. Although in the myths those heroes were the result of sexual intercourse, Plutarch agreed with the Egyptians that such was not really the case, for the act was accomplished through the "spirit of a god."[6] This is essentially the same idea as that in Matthew and Luke.

The Christian birth stories, as far as we know, were not copied directly from Hellenistic stories, but the similarity of some themes shows that stories of miraculous birth were "in the air" in the superstitious ancient world and must have suggested to Christians the desirability of having their own stories. Compare this legend about the birth of Apollonius of Tyana, who was born around A.D. 20, reported by his disciple Damis. Before he was born the god Proteus appeared to his mother in the form of an Egyptian deity and told her that the child she was about to bear would really be the god Proteus himself. Later, just as the hour of his birth was approaching, his mother was instructed in a dream to walk out into a meadow. She fell asleep lying on the grass, swans danced around her and cried out all at once. She leaped up, which cause her to bear the child.

> But the people of the country say that just at the moment of the birth, a thunderbolt seemed about to fall to earth and then rose up into the air and disappeared aloft; and the gods thereby indicated, I think, the great distinction to which the sage was to attain, and hinted in advance how he should transcend all things upon earth and approach the gods, and signified all the things he would achieve (*Life of Apollonius* 1. 5).

Diogenes Laertius reported that three philosophers agreed on this story of Plato's birth:

> [They] all say that there was at Athens a story that when Periktione was ripe (for bearing children) Ariston was trying desperately but did not succeed (in producing any children). Then when he had stopped his efforts, he saw a vision of [the god] Apollo. Therefore he abstained

from any further marital relations until she brought forth a child.[7]

Why were the Christian virgin birth stories created? Primarily to enhance Jesus as the Christ for missionary purposes in the Greco-Roman world. The early apostles were in competition with other religions which offered deities and demi-gods who performed miracles, healed the sick, raised the dead, protected their followers, and bestowed eternal salvation on their devotees. A Christ who was half-divine, half human, seemed more likely to be able to accomplish such things than one who was entirely human.

How could the Holy Spirit impregnate Mary? What was the rationale behind the notion? The explanation is in the origin of the word "spirit." Both the Hebrew and Greek words for spirit originally meant wind and breath. Ancient man observed that when men and animals died, they ceased to breathe. Gods are alive, so they must breathe too, and they can breathe the breath of life into humans and animals. This idea is expressed in Psalm 104:30: "When you [the Lord] send forth your Spirit [or breath], they [the creatures of the earth] are created." (In the preceding verse the Lord can take away the breath of life too.)

But why a virgin for a mother? In the ancient world the virginity of the bride insured the paternity of the offspring. Another reason for virginity was to make the birth pure. A belief in antiquity was that sexual intercourse defiles, and only a virgin is a clean, pure woman. "For blessed is the barren woman who is undefiled, who has not entered into a sinful union," states Wisdom of Solomon 3:13. Romulus, a mythical founder of Rome, was believed to be the son of the god Mars and the virgin priestess Rhea Silvia. Pythagoras was said to be the son of a virgin. Justin reports Trypho as saying: "... it is said that Perseus has been born from Danae, still a virgin, by him they call Zeus flowing down upon her in the form of gold" (*Dial.* 67:2).

Before the canonical gospels were widely circulated in the churches and used as sources of Christian faith, the majority of Christians did not believe in the virgin birth. Paul never mentions it because the notion had not yet entered Christianity. It does not appear in the New Testament outside of Matthew and Luke. In the Jewish-Christian *Didache* both David and Jesus are described in the same human terms; both are God's child or servant (Greek: *paidos*; *Did.* 9:2).

The virgin birth stories created many problems for the early Christians. First, they contradicted the known fact that Joseph was Jesus' father. Second, they conflicted with the genealogies which traced Jesus' Davidic descent through Joseph. Nevertheless, even within the birth stories the authors of Matthew and Luke retained the claim that Joseph was a descendant of David (Matt. 1:20; Luke 1:27). To reconcile the virgin birth with the claim that Jesus was a descendant of David, both Ignatius and Justin in the second century asserted that it was Mary who was a descendant of David.[8] The virgin birth also conflicted with the Incarnation doctrine. If Jesus originated with Mary, he did not pre-exist in heaven. Therefore the Gospel of John, with its Incarnation theory, does not mention the virgin birth. Ignatius was the earliest writer known to expressly accept both doctrines.[9]

Another resultant problem was the false Jewish charge that Jesus was an illegitimate child, born out of wedlock. The charge is alluded to in the Gospel of John. The Jews said to Jesus, "We were not born of fornication" (8:41) and "they answered him, 'You were born in utter sin, and would you teach us?'" (9:34). The same charge is alluded to in the *Gospel of Thomas*: "Jesus said, 'He who will know the Father and the Mother will be called "the son of a harlot"'" (105).

JESUS' BAPTISM

The earliest actual incident in Jesus' life that is known to us is his baptism by John the Baptist, but we do not know any of the details, and apparently the gospel authors did not either. The account in the synoptic gospels is interesting for what it reveals of early Christian efforts to portray Jesus as the Messiah. Two main features are involved here:

1. The Holy Spirit of God descends from the heavens in the form of a dove and comes "on" (Q; a traditional Jewish idea) or "into" (Mark; a Hellenistic idea) Jesus. A belief in the Old Testament is that God anointed prophets with the Holy Spirit: "The Spirit of the Lord God is upon me, because the Lord has anointed me . . ." (Isa. 61:1-2a). In Luke 4:17-21 most of that passage is applied to Jesus. In Isaiah 11:2 the future king, a descendant of Jesse and David, is predicted to have the Spirit of Yahweh: "And the Spirit of the Lord shall rest upon him." In *Psalms of Solomon* 17:37 in the Jewish Pseudepigrapha this

76

idea is applied to the Son of David Messiah, who will not weaken because "God made him powerful in the holy spirit and wise in the counsel of understanding, with strength and righteousness,"[10] "In him [the Elect One, the Messiah] dwells the spirit of wisdom" (*1 Enoch* 49:3). In the *Testament of Judah* we find this prophecy of the coming Messiah: "And the heavens will be opened upon him to pour out the spirit as a blessing of the Holy Father. And he will pour the spirit of grace on you" (24:2-3). This belief that the Messiah will give the Spirit to others after he receives it from God is probably behind the idea that Jesus will baptize with the Holy Spirit (Mark 1:8 par), that he poured out the Holy Spirit at Pentecost (Acts 2:33), and that he bestowed the Spirit on his disciples soon after his resurrection (John 20:22). The most developed Jewish expression of this messianic idea is in the *Testament of Levi:*

> The heavens will be opened,
> and from the temple of glory sanctification will come upon him,
> with a fatherly voice, as from Abraham to Isaac.
> And the glory of the Most High [God] shall burst forth upon him.
> And the spirit of understanding and sanctification
> shall rest upon him (18:6-7).

This passage is clearly a primary source of the synoptic account of Jesus' baptism, used to support the claim that Jesus was the Christ.

2. "A voice came from heaven, 'You are my beloved Son; with you I am well pleased'" (Mark 1:11 par). This passage does not imply the deity of Jesus, but only that he is the Messiah, the Christ. The words of the voice from heaven are a combination of extracts from two verses in the Old Testament that early Christians interpreted as prophecies of the Messiah. (1) "You are my Son" is from Psalm 2:7, where the words are presented as those of Yahweh to the current—not future—king of Israel. (2) "With you I am well pleased" is derived from Isaiah 42:1, "Behold my servant, whom I uphold, my chosen [or: elect], in whom my soul delights; I have put my Spirit upon him." Two aspects of the Isaiah passage suggested to the author of Mark that it would fit into his account of the baptism, namely, "my chosen," or "my elect,"[11] which had become a term for the Messiah in the Jewish Pseudepigrapha, and the idea that God put his Spirit on "his servant" (elsewhere in Mark Jesus is also

regarded as the "servant" mentioned in Second Isaiah).

The typical fundamentalist interpretation of such agreement between the Old and New Testaments is that this shows that Jesus is the Christ foretold in the Bible and that it also proves that the Bible is true. The truth of the matter, however, is that the early Christian writers, striving to represent Jesus as fulfilling Old Testament prophecy, used the Old Testament as a *source* in apostolic preaching and in writing the gospels. So of course there is some agreement between the Old and New Testaments! But it is at the cost of misinterpreting the Old Testament; the passages in the Psalm and in Isaiah refer to kings in the past, not to Jesus!

Why are virtually all biblical scholars certain that John baptized Jesus? Because it is not an incident that early Christians, eager to convince others that Jesus was the Christ, would invent. On the contrary, it was a problem for them to explain, for the Messiah was not expected to be baptized and, above all, he was expected to be sinless, whereas Jesus' going to John to be baptized implied that he thought he had sinned. The Marcan account of the baptism, incorporated in Matthew and Luke, deals with the problem indirectly by transforming it into the occasion whereby the Messiah received the Holy Spirit. In addition, Matthew (3:14-15) deals with it directly by having John protest that Jesus should baptize him instead. The *Gospel of the Nazaraeans* (early 2d c.) also deals with the problem explicitly: When his mother and brothers suggest that they all go and be baptized by John, Jesus replies, "Wherein have I sinned that I should go and be baptized by him?"[12] When gentile Christians concluded that Jesus was divine, the apologetic problem was compounded.

Many biblical scholars have misinterpreted the baptism story by declaring that it depicts what Jesus "experienced" when he was baptized. Actually, the story tells us nothing about his experience. What it does tell us is that the author of Mark, or possibly a source, has produced it to solve two problems with one master stroke: the problem of explaining Jesus' baptism by John and the problem of supporting the claim that Jesus was the Messiah.

JESUS AND THE KINGDOM OF GOD

Jesus went from his home in Nazareth in Galilee to the

place where John was baptizing in the Jordan River. After John was arrested and beheaded, Jesus returned to Galilee and began to preach. According to Matthew 3:2 and 4:17, both men preached the same basic message: "Repent, for the kingdom of heaven [God] is at hand." Mark 1:4 and 1:15 also indicate that both men preached the same gospel. Further evidence is that, according to Mark 6:16, the activities of the two men were so similar that Herod thought that Jesus was John the Baptist risen from the dead. John had disciples (John 1:35), and possibly Jesus was one of them before John's death. Mark 1:15 adds "believe in the gospel" to Jesus' message. The Greek word translated as "gospel" means "good news"; that is, it was good news that the ideal kingdom was about to be established very soon. This was the original meaning of the Christian use of the word; later the churches interpreted the term as either a type of book or Christian doctrine as a whole.

The call to repent was directly related to the proclamation of the imminent coming of the kingdom. Jews and proselytes to Judaism could enter the kingdom only if they were righteous at the time of the last judgment. Therefore a personal cleansing from all sin must be accomplished immediately before it was too late. (Rabbi Eliezer said, "Repent one day before your death" [*Abot* 2:10], so that you will not have time to sin again.)

There is no doubt that Jesus preached the urgency of repentance. That was the main theme in his basic message and in the preaching of the apostles (Mark 6:12;; Acts 3:19). Jesus' preaching must have been the apostles' source. Jesus regarded preaching, not healing and performing miracles, as his main task: "Let us go on to the next towns, that I may preach there also; for that is why I came out" (Mark 1:38). The importance of repentance in contemporary Jewish thought is well attested. Examples will be given in the next chapter, "Ethical Teaching."

Some biblical interpreters have claimed that Jesus' preaching was new because the expression "kingdom of God" is not in the Old Testament. The absence of the exact expression is insignificant, however, for the idea abounds there. The idea is quite explicit in Micah and Zechariah. "And Yahweh will reign over them in Mount Zion, from this time [the latter days, 4:1] forth for evermore" (Micah 4:7). "And Yahweh will become king over all the earth" (Zech. 14:9).

As historical study developed in the nineteenth century, biblical scholars began to recognize that belief in eschatology (the end of this world, the Judgment, and the coming of the kingdom of God) was a Jewish idea. Many Christians disliked that fact, for they wanted Christianity to be unique. They also disliked the superstitious nature of such beliefs. Therefore conservative Christians often ignored them and concentrated on ecclesiastical doctrines instead, while liberal Christians portrayed Jesus as reinterpreting "kingdom of God," viewing it as an ideal society, independent of Jewish nationalism.

The liberals' interpretation was based mainly on two passages. The statement, the kingdom of God is "in the midst of you," or is "among you" (Luke 17:21), was mistranslated as "in you," which suggested that the kingdom is spiritual. In John 18:36 Jesus says, "My kingdom is not of this world"; this, too, suggested that the kingdom is spiritual. Actually, neither saying is authentic. "Nineteenth-century Christian liberalism," as it has been called, was advocated by the German theologians Friedrich Schleiermacher, Heinrich Holtzmann, and Adolf Harnack, who tried to de-judaize Jesus by eliminating the eschatology. Early in the twentieth century some Americans followed this reinterpretation of Jesus by advocating the "social gospel" kind of Christianity, namely, that Jesus did not preach eschatology, but the gradual building of a just society in the world, an ideal which churches should energetically promote. Advocates of this "Christian social gospel" included Washington Gladden, Walter Rauschenbusch, and Shailer Matthews. But two German scholars, Johannes Weiss and Albert Schweitzer, carefully compared Jesus' message with contemporary Judaism and found that they were of the same nature. This is the firm conclusion of historians today.

Recently a few scholars have tried to revive the de-judaizing movement by claiming that Jesus' message was non-eschatological. Many of us would like to think that Jesus was modern enough to discard all the erroneous beliefs of his day, but the evidence, alas, is against it. If we have any reliable evidence at all of what Jesus taught, it is Mark 1:15, in which he says, "The time is fulfilled, and the kingdom of God is at hand. Repent." Matthew and Mark agree that this was Jesus' basic message. If his disciples remembered and transmitted any of his teaching, it would naturally be his basic message which was repeated to different people in different places rather than a saying uttered only once on a particular occasion. The saying in Mark 9:1 also portrays Jesus as declaring that the kingdom of

God is coming soon: "Truly I say to you, there are some standing here who will not taste death before they see that the kingdom of God has come with power." This saying may not be historical, but at least it has as good a claim to authenticity as any sayings used by the "non-eschatological Jesus" school of thought. Those scholars have relied heavily on the fact that some of the kingdom sayings of Jesus do not regard the kingdom as imminent; they have failed to recognize that these sayings originated in the church—not with Jesus. Many of the sayings are later explanations of the delay in the coming of the kingdom, so these sayings naturally emphasize slowness of growth rather than the imminent coming of the kingdom.

The earliest churches clearly expected the end of the world soon, and why would they preach that if the idea had not already been implanted by Jesus? Faith in Jesus' resurrection would not create the belief, for the death and resurrection of the Messiah were not features of Jewish beliefs about the coming of the end. Admittedly, in the first few weeks after Jesus' death, his resurrection was believed to be the beginning of the Resurrection Day, but that was a temporary factor, for the non-appearance of the general resurrection of the dead disproved that belief. The early Christians must have derived from Jesus their hope in the imminent coming of the kingdom. Jesus had received the idea from John the Baptist.

A related question, much debated, is whether Jesus thought that the kingdom was coming in the future or was already present. The kingdom is future in his basic message and in Mark 9:1, as we have seen. It is also future in the Lord's Prayer in the Sermon on the Mount: "Thy kingdom come." In the early church, however, opinion was divided. Apparently one view was that the initial phase of the kingdom had begun with the coming of the Christ; this apparently is the thought in Luke 17:21, "the kingdom of God is in the midst of you."

DID JESUS BAPTIZE?

Since Jesus preached the same basic message as John, did he also baptize others, as John had done? Here is the evidence:

Against

1. The synoptic gospels give no indication that he

81

baptized (but they are not biographies; perhaps the authors chose to omit his baptizing).

2. If Jesus returned to Galilee, he departed from the Jordan River, which was John's water supply for baptizing, and probably would be Jesus' too.

3. John was called the Baptist; Jesus was not (but was John given that title to distinguish him from other Johns?).

4. Perhaps the ritual of baptism was introduced into the primitive church by former disciples of John.

5. The tradition in Matthew and Luke that John forecast that Jesus would baptize with the Holy Spirit and fire is not authentic, and is not evidence either for or against Jesus' baptizing with water.

For

1. Since Jesus continued John's mission after John was arrested, he would probably continue the baptism as well as the message, for the two features were closely related.

2. A passage in the Gospel of Signs, incorporated in John 3:22, states that Jesus baptized in Judea.

3. John 4:1 states that Jesus baptized more disciples than John. (The next verse states that Jesus himself did not baptize, but his disciples did. This verse, however, is an insertion by a later scribe [as linguistic evidence shows], who was probably influenced by the synoptic gospels.)

4. According to Acts 2:38 Peter preached, "Repent, and be baptized . . ." The apostles baptized, and the most plausible explanation is that they were continuing Jesus' practice. If they were not, why did they introduce the ritual? Apparently Jesus continued John's practice after John's death, and the disciples continued Jesus' practice after his death. Strong evidence is the fact that John, Jesus, and the disciples all combined repentance and baptism, a distinctive feature.

5. The absence in the synoptic gospels of any tradition that Jesus baptized others does not prove that he did not do so. The gospels are unreliable in many respects and this may be one of them. The authors may have omitted it in an effort to separate the careers of the two men. The Gospel of John deals with the problem by saying that Jesus baptized *more* disciples than John. The synoptics' solutions are to omit any mention of Jesus' baptizing and to claim that he—unlike John—baptized with the Holy Spirit. Evidence of the synoptics' unreliability is

that their sayings of Jesus omit his basic theme, the call to repentance.

In the light of the total evidence, it is probable that Jesus did baptize.

DID JESUS THINK HE WAS THE CHRIST?

This question was much debated at the beginning of the twentieth century and was known as the question of "Jesus' messianic consciousness."

Against

1. One belief in early Christianity was that God made Jesus the Christ when he raised him from the dead. Paul wrote that Jesus "was designated [by God] Son of God [i.e., the Christ] in power according to the Spirit of holiness [i.e., the Holy Spirit] by his resurrection from the dead" (Rom. 1:4). And in a speech ascribed to Peter in Acts, we read: "God raised up this Jesus, and . . . being therefore exalted at the right hand of God [i.e., Jesus' ascension], and having received from the Father what was promised, namely the Holy Spirit,[13] he has poured out this which you see and hear. . . . Let all the house of Israel therefore know that God has made him both Lord and Christ, this Jesus whom you crucified" (2:32-36). Since some early Christians believed that God made Jesus the Christ by his resurrection and ascension, they must not have believed that Jesus thought that he was the Christ before his crucifixion.

On the other hand, the idea that Jesus became the Christ when God raised him from the grave is an idea that apparently began as an explanation of why Jesus did not overthrow the Roman rule, namely, that he could not do it until he returns as the Son of God "in power." They who created this doctrine were not interested in the question of Jesus' messianic consciousness. To them, the important thing was to solve the problem of Jesus' messianic failure, that is, his failure to accomplish the main task of the Messiah. Thus, their explanation was that Jesus did not perform the messianic task because he was not yet the Messiah.

2. In Mark Jesus is portrayed as telling his disciples not to tell others that he is the Christ (8:29-30). If the story is authentic, Jesus is suppressing the idea that he is the Christ. But if unauthentic, it may be a later effort to explain that though

the disciples thought he was the Christ, he did not say so. (But in the same gospel he does say so publicly in his reply to the high priest [14:61-62], and biblical scholars have concluded that Jesus' commands of secrecy to disciples and demons in Mark is a literary device to explain why most Jews did not believe that Jesus was the Christ.)

3. Another argument has been that Jesus referred to the Son of Man, a name for the Messiah, in the third person, so he did not regard himself as the Christ. (But Jesus' teaching in Mark 8:31 plainly identifies the Son of Man with himself, and besides, none of the Son of Man sayings is authentic anyway, so none tell us what Jesus thought.)

For

1. In some gospel pericopes Jesus is represented as thinking that he was the Christ. These include his confession to the high priest, his acceptance of the idea when Peter confesses him to be the Christ (Mark 8:29), and other passages. (But these too are unauthentic, so all they demonstrate is that some early Christians thought that Jesus thought that he was the Christ.)

2. After the disciples were convinced that Jesus was raised from the dead, they definitely believed that he was the Christ, for that theme became central in their preaching. The resurrection faith alone could hardly create the belief in his messiahship, for a dying and rising Christ was contrary to all messianic expectations. Therefore the disciples must have believed before his death that he was the Messiah; that belief, badly shaken by his death, was restored by faith in his resurrection. And where did they get the belief that he was the Messiah? The most probable source is Jesus himself.

3. All four gospels agree that the Romans put a sign on Jesus' cross labeling him as "the king of the Jews," an appropriate label for someone believed to be the Jewish Messiah. Thus the Romans, at least, thought that Jesus and his followers believed that he was the Christ before his crucifixion.

I find the last two arguments above very convincing.

Although Jesus believed that he was the Christ, that belief was not a major theme of his preaching. Contrary to the Gospel of John, the synoptic gospels portray Jesus' major theme as the proclamation of the kingdom, not the proclamation of himself. The repentance of Jesus' listeners was not dependent upon Jesus' identity; repentance was a matter between man and God, a matter in which the Messiah was not essential.

CONTEMPORARY ATTITUDES TOWARD JESUS

Many people who heard Jesus were very favorably impressed. Mark in particular reports that crowds came to him. He attracted disciples, or followers, who traveled with him, including women.[14] The attitude toward Jesus was very different in his hometown of Nazareth. The villagers there did not believe that he was the Christ. They knew his parents and they knew his brothers and sisters, and "they took offense at him" (Mark 6:3 par). *Skandalizo*, the Greek word here translated as "took offense," occurs frequently in early Christian writings in reference to lack of faith in Jesus, which is consistent with the people's "unbelief" at the end of this story. In this pericope Jesus quotes a proverb: "A prophet is not without honor, except in his own fatherland." As applied here, the proverb is intended to refer not to the whole country of Galilee, but only to Nazareth, as Luke's version of the story (4:16-24) makes clear.

Even Jesus' own family did not believe in him. Mark adds to the proverb the words "among his own kin and in his own house." Luke's version of the proverb (4:24) omits these two embarrassing additions and Matthew omits the mention of kin. These additions indicate that neither Jesus' immediate family nor his other relatives were convinced that he was the Christ. The gospels contain other evidence that supports this conclusion. A tradition in Mark, copied with modification in Matthew and Luke, is that as Jesus was sitting with a crowd around him, his mother and brothers came and called to him. Instead of going to them, he looked around at those sitting with him and said, "Here are my mother and my brothers!" (Mark 3:34). Jesus' mother is also downgraded in Luke 11:27-28, where a woman says to Jesus, "Blessed is the womb that bore you." Jesus responds, "Blessed rather are those who hear the word of God and keep it." The author of John inserted in his source material his own remark, "For even his brothers did not believe in him" (7:5). In the story of the wedding at Cana (drawn from the Gospel of Signs) Jesus' abrupt reply to his mother suggests that the Christian community in which the gospel was written thought that Jesus' attitude toward his mother was not very cordial or for some reason it did not feel very friendly toward her. The story represents her as supporting Jesus, however, for she tells the servants to do whatever he tells them to do (John 2:4-5). The Johannine miracle story of the wedding is not historical, but some actual history must be reflected in these references to the family. Considering that Jesus' oldest brother, James, eventually became head of the Jerusalem church, and that Mary, the mother of Jesus, was later exalted by the churches, the invention after the crucifixion of the idea of tension between Jesus and his family is quite unlikely. We can only conclude that during Jesus' lifetime his family did not think that he was the Christ.

There is even a tradition that Jesus' friends thought that he was out of his mind. "Then he went home; and the crowd came together again, so that they could not even eat. And when his friends heard it, they went out to seize him, for they said, 'He is beside himself'" (Mark 3:19-21). We are not surprised that the authors of Matthew and Luke chose to omit this one! Mark fails to provide a reason for the friends' opinion; attracting a large crowd certainly does not indicate that one is insane. If Jesus traveled around trying to cast out demons, did that cause friends to think that he had lost his mind? Or was his preaching the cause? This tradition probably reflects history, for it, too, is not the type that churches would want to create.

That story is immediately followed in Mark by a pericope in which scribes from Jerusalem accuse him of being possessed by Beelzebul and of casting out demons by means of that demon. I am suspicious of this pericope, however, because so often in the synoptic gospels conflicts between the apostles and the scribes are placed back in a setting in Jesus' life. Was it Jesus' exorcisms or the apostles' exorcisms that were denounced as the work of the demon Beelzebul? According to John 10:20 Jews charged that Jesus had a demon and was mad; this passage may be based on nothing more than the Marcan pericope.

Admittedly, Jesus was mistaken in thinking that the present world was about to end, but in his environment that need not indicate insanity. The Essenes thought essentially the same thing, and the Pharisees believed that it would happen eventually. (Why, even in the twentieth century people have thought that the world was about to end, and they were not insane. Wacky, but not necessarily insane!)

DID JESUS CHOOSE TWELVE DISCIPLES?

This question has been much debated. Biblical scholars generally agree however, that whether historical or fictional, the Twelve symbolize a new twelve tribes of Israel.

The case for a historical Twelve: (1) They are mentioned in the gospels and in Acts 6:2 they are the leaders of the Jerusalem church. (2) Judas, the traitor, is one of the Twelve. Would he have been, if the Twelve are only fictional? (3) In Acts 1 the eleven disciples cast lots and thus chose Matthias to replace Judas as one of the Twelve.

The case for a fictional Twelve: (1) In the synoptic gospels and Acts (except 6:2) the inner circle usually consists of Peter, James, and John, not the Twelve. (But these three were early martyrs, and therefore were given this special honor.) (2) When Paul visited the Jerusalem church a few years after Jesus' crucifixion, he stayed fifteen days with Peter and saw no other apostles except James, Jesus' brother (Gal. 1:18-19). He never mentions the Twelve, perhaps because such a group did not exist. (3) The lists of the names of the Twelve in the synoptic gospels do not agree with each other entirely. (4) As the controversy between Judaism and Christianity grew, Christians contended that they were the New Judaism that replaces the Old Judaism. That point of view could easily lead to the claim that twelve disciples were chosen by Jesus to be founders of the Church, even as Yahweh had chosen twelve patriarchs to be the founders of Israel. The New Twelve replaces the Old Twelve. It is improbable that Jesus would think that way, for he was not separating himself and his disciples from Judaism.

6

ETHICAL TEACHING

The word "teacher" (Gk: *didaskalos*) is applied to Jesus more than forty times in the four gospels. The fact that he had disciples may be evidence that he was a teacher, though it could indicate only that they assisted him in preaching that the kingdom of God was coming. The word was applied to others too; tax collectors called John the Baptist by that name (Luke 3:12), which was applied to other Jews too (Luke 2:46; John 3:10).

In Mark Jesus is called "Rabbi" by Peter, a blind man, and Judas,[1] but New Testament scholars are generally convinced that Jesus was not a rabbi. Unlike the rabbis, Jesus was not primarily interested in interpreting the Law, he did not require his disciples to study the Law, and he did not claim for himself the authority of the Jewish fathers. Unlike them, he had women followers, he associated with "sinners," and (John 7:15) had never studied.

In the synoptic gospels—but not in John—Jesus frequently uses parables in his teaching. A parable is a concise story that presents by analogy, either implicitly or explicitly, an idea an author wished to explain or teach. Rabbis used them frequently to explain scriptural passages and to emphasize their own teaching (e.g., *Abot* 3:18). In the synoptics, however, they are not used to explain Scripture. Although the purpose of parables is to make ideas clear, we find in Mark 4:11-12 this surprising statement on the lips of Jesus: ". . . for those outside everything is in parables, so that they may indeed see but not perceive, and may indeed hear but not understand!" The use of parables to keep one's message hidden instead of clarifying it is utterly implausible. Later we will see that this strange notion emanated from the author of Mark.

Albert Schweitzer thought that Jesus taught ethics that would apply only for the "interim" before the new kingdom came. The interim ethics theory is rightly rejected today, for the gospels and the Jewish background alike indicate that the same ethics are needed both before and after the coming of the kingdom of God. The ethics are in accordance with the will of God in this world, or age, and there is no reason for God to change his will in this matter in the new age.

Much of the teaching in the gospels will be discussed later. Here we will examine the ethical teaching in the synoptics, which is quite unlike the teaching in John.

NEW ETHICAL TEACHING?

According to Mark 1:27, when Jesus was teaching in the synagogue at Capernaum, "they were all amazed, so that they questioned among themselves, 'What is this? A new teaching?'"[2] Let us focus on the ethical statements in the synoptic gospels and ask, How new was the ethical teaching of Jesus, or at least that attributed to him? Are the ideas new?

Since Jesus was a Jew raised in the Jewish setting, the logical procedure is to compare the teachings with those in contemporary Judaism. Jewish traditions from nearly the whole first century A.D. should be included because of the possibility that the gospel authors and their sources may have assigned to Jesus teaching that was current in their day. Only the earliest of the rabbinic parallels will be employed, for the rabbinic literature was written much later than the gospels, but the Mishnah especially does contain some traditions from the first century A.D. Scholars in the past have relied too heavily on rabbinic traditions.[3] We will look at the Old Testament, the Jewish Apocrypha and Pseudepigrapha, the Dead Sea scrolls, and a few early teachings in the Mishnah.

I investigated this subject in depth, using the following procedure: From a synopsis of the synoptic gospels, select the ethical teachings and classify them according to subject in two broad categories, general ethics and specific ethics. Next, search in the Jewish literature for the same or very similar ethical principles or ideas. Very helpful is the pioneering study by H. Maldwyn Hughes,[4] long neglected. Use of the recent Charlesworth edition of the Jewish Pseudepigrapha is absolutely essential.

GENERAL ETHICS

The general nature of ethics in the synoptic gospels provides the framework in which the specific ethics are to be applied. General ethics and wisdom are closely related to each other in Wisdom of Solomon (1:4; 8:7) and in Plato (*Phaedo* 69B).

Righteousness
This virtue is a basic ideal in the Sermon on the Mount. "Blessed are those who hunger and thirst for righteousness" (Matt. 5:6). "But seek first his [God's] kingdom and his righteousness, and all these things shall be yours as well" (Matt. 6:33).

The Old Testament abounds with praise of righteousness. In it too God himself sets the example: "For the Lord is righteous; he loves righteous deeds; the upright shall behold his face" (Ps. 11:7). "Righteousness delivers from death" (Prov. 10:2). Teaching righteousness was an ideal as well; the Essenes honored highly their former "Teacher of Righteousness."

Doing the Will of God
Although this could involve acts of piety such as prayer and rituals, it often consisted of ethical conduct. In the gospels, ethics are not explicitly connected with doing the will of God, but probably are understood in three passages: In the Lord's Prayer, "Thy will be done, on earth as it is in heaven." In Matthew 7:21, "Not everyone who says to me, 'Lord, Lord,' shall enter the kingdom of heaven, but he who does the will of my Father who is in heaven." In Mark 3:35 doing the will of God replaces family ties as the basis for true relationship to Jesus: "Whoever does the will of God is my brother, and sister, and mother."

As for the Jewish parallels, the expression "will of God" does not occur in the Old Testament in an ethical sense. The idea, however, is present in the belief that God's people should obey his commandments, for surely in the Old Testament God's commands are expressions of his will. But in the second century B.C. doing God's will was stated explicitly in ethical terms. In the *Testament of Naphtali* 3:1 we find: "Do not strive to corrupt your actions through avarice or to beguile your souls by empty phrases, because those who are silent in purity of heart will be able to hold fast God's will and to shunt aside the will of Beliar" (i.e., Satan). In the next verse God's will is identical with "the Law of God." In *Jubilees* 21:2 Abraham in his old age says, "Throughout all the days of my life I have been remembering the Lord and sought with all my heart to do his will and walk uprightly in all his ways."

Reward and Punishment

Another general ethical feature is the teaching that God will reward individuals for goodness and punish them for wickedness. This idea abounds in the synoptic gospels, early Judaism, and ancient pagan literature. It also occurs in the Old Testament: "Righteousness delivers from death" (Prov. 10:2). "Cancel your sins by practicing righteousness, and your iniquities by showing mercy to the oppressed" (Dan. 4:27).

In the gospels and in early Judaism we find the idea that God's reward or punishment will be in direct proportion to the way man treats his neighbor. It is expressed verbatim in both as "measure for measure." The measure for measure principle was probably a popular proverb. It was enunciated in ancient Egypt long before Judaism existed. "The measure you give will be the measure you get, and still more will be given to you," states Mark 4:24 par. In *Sotah* 1:7 in the Mishnah we find: "With what measure a man measures out, it will be measured to him again." I did not find in the Jewish sources a specific statement that even more will be given beyond the individual's measure, however. The idea of tit for tat between God and man is also expressed without using the word "measure." *Testament of Zebulon* 5:3 states: "Whatever one does to his neighbor, the Lord will do to him." Compare Paul's "Whatever a man sows, that he will also reap" (Gal. 6:7). Sometimes both the Jewish and Christian sources connect the idea with a specific ethic, though not necessarily the same one. Rather similar is the connection with forgiveness in the synoptics and with mercy in one of the *Testaments of the Twelve Patriarchs*. "Forgive, and you will be forgiven," states Luke 6:37; a similar saying is in Matthew 6:14. "Have compassion toward every person with mercy, in order that the Lord may be compassionate and merciful to you" (*T. Zeb.* 8:1).

"Good Works" as a Term for Good Deeds

In Matthew 5:16: "Let your light so shine before men, that they may see your good works and give glory to your Father who is in heaven." *Testament of Naphtali* 8:5 teaches that God will remember "your good work." *Abot* 4:11 states: "Repentance and good works are as a shield against [divine] retribution."

Two Ways

The righteous life and the wicked life are contrasted as two "ways" of living. In the Sermon on the Mount we read: "The gate is wide and the way is easy that leads to destruction, . . . the gate is narrow and the way is hard that leads to life" (Matt. 7:13-14). In the *Testament of Asher* 1:3, 5, we find: "God has granted two ways to the sons of men; . . . The two ways are good and evil." The Essenes, too, believed in the two ways, as in *Manual of Discipline* 3:20-21: "In the hand of the Prince of Lights is dominion over the sons of righteousness; in the ways of light they walk. And in hand of the Angel of Darkness is all dominion over the sons of error; and in the ways of darkness they walk."

Repentance

Repentance for one's sins was regarded as necessary in order to obtain a blessed immortality. "Unless you repent, you will all likewise perish" (Luke 13:5). As we know, a call to repentance was Jesus' basic message. In Luke 15 the parables of the Lost Sheep, Lost Coin, and Prodigal Son teach that God rejoices over sinners who repent.

Repentance was certainly a Jewish idea and practice. The Hebrew word *shub*, "repent," literally means "turn back," "return." When used in this religious sense, it means to turn back from one's evil way and return to the Lord and the good way. Isaiah 55:7 states the doctrine concisely:

Let the wicked forsake his way,
    and the unrighteous man his thoughts;
Let him return to the Lord, so that he may
    have mercy on him,
and to our God, for he will abundantly pardon.

Pharisees, Essenes, and unknown sects in Syria all emphasized repentance. Here are some examples. "Yet to those who repent he [the Lord] grants a return, . . . Turn to the Lord and forsake your sins" (Sirach 17:24-25). "You, O Lord, according to your great goodness, have promised repentance and forgiveness to those who have sinned against you; . . . that they may be saved" (Prayer of Manasseh 7). "Repentance destroys disobedience, . . . and guides the deliberative powers to salvation" (*T. Gad* 5:7). "I [God] will not hold out in anger against those who repent of transgression; yet I will have no compassion on all those who turn aside from the way" (1QS 10:20-21).[5]

SPECIFIC ETHICS

A few of these are so closely related to each other that perhaps they should be combined. This is the case with charity and helping the poor, with humility versus vanity, mental morality in general and mental sexual morality, love of enemies and non-retaliation, particularism versus universalism, and the poor versus the wealthy. They can be compared more precisely with the Jewish background, however, if we keep them separate. We will list only the close parallels.

Anger

In the Sermon on the Mount: "But I say to you that everyone angry with his brother is liable to judgment" (Matt. 5:22). "Brother," like "neighbor," refers to another member of one's own religious group, as in contemporary Jewish sectarian writings. In Judaism the first four chapters of the *Testament of Dan* are devoted to denouncing anger and falsehood; they contain the same theme as Matthew. An Essene rule was that "one should not speak to his brother in anger" (1QS 5:25).

Charity

Giving alms will provide you with "treasure in heaven" (Luke 12:33 and Mark 10:21 par). In Judaism a father tells his son that by giving alms "you will be laying up a good treasure for yourself against the day of necessity. For charity delivers from death" (Tobit 4:9-10).

Divorce

In Mark 10:2-12 divorce is forbidden and Genesis 1:27 is quoted. The Essenes at Qumran forbad a man to marry two women in his lifetime, and cited the same passage from Genesis in their *Damascus Document* (4:20-21). This prohibits bigamy; does it prohibit divorce?

Forgiveness

In the Lord's Prayer (Matt. 6:12) we find: "Forgive us our sins, as we also have forgiven those who sin against us."[6] A Jewish parallel is in Sirach 28:2, "Forgive your neighbor the wrong he has done, and then your sins will be pardoned when you pray." All three—Matthew, Luke, and Sirach—have the "measure for measure" theme, and all associate it with prayer. Also, Luke 17:3 and *Testament of Gad* 6:3-7 teach that if a "brother" sins against you and repents, forgive him.

Golden Rule

The positive form from Q (Matt. 7:12=Luke 6:31) is in the Sermon on the Mount: "As you wish that men would do to you, do so to them." A negative form is in Tobit 4:15: "What you hate, do not do to anyone." Hillel is quoted similarly in the Talmud (*Shabbat* 31a). Although the Christian form is positive and the Jewish form negative, the idea is the same. The negative literary form of rules was common in ancient Judaism; for example, the Ten Commandments. Matthew 7:12 adds "for this is the Law and the prophets," which is similar to Hillel's "this is the whole Law; the rest is commentary." (Some form of the Golden Rule is in all the major world religions. The earliest instance in the West is in the writing of the Greek historian, Herodotus, 5th c. B.C.)

Humility

In the parable of the Praying Pharisee and the Publican (Luke 18:9-14) the lesson is: "For everyone who exalts himself will be humbled, but he who humbles himself will be exalted." I did not find a close verbal parallel earlier than *Erubin* 13b in the Talmud, which reads: "Everyone who humbles himself, the Holy One, blessed be He, exalts him; and everyone who exalts himself, the Holy One, blessed be He, humbles him." The two sayings are almost identical and both must have arisen in Judaism. Humility was regarded as a virtue in Judaism long before Jesus' day. "Humility goes before honor" (Prov. 18:12). "Toward the scorners he [the Lord] is scornful, but to the humble he shows favor" (Prov. 3:34). In Isaiah 57:15 God dwells "with him who is of a contrite and humble spirit"; a similar idea is in *Testament of Joseph* 10:2. "The greater you are, the more you must humble yourself; so you will find favor in the sight of the Lord" (Sirach 3:18).

Hypocrisy

In Q we read: "You hypocrite, first take the beam out of your own eye, and then you will see clearly to take out the chip that is in your brother's eye" (Matt. 7:5=Luke 6:42). *Karphos*, here translated as "chip," is the Greek word for a small piece of wood or straw. Here it is used metaphorically and is connected with the command not to judge. In Sirach 1:29 the reader is commanded: "Be not a hypocrite in men's sight, and keep watch over your lips." Of Rabbi Tarphon (ca. A.D. 100) it was reported: "If someone would say to him, 'Take the splinter out of your eyes,' he would say to him, 'Take the beam out of your eyes.'"7 A similar parallel is in the Talmud in *Arachin* 16b. Travers Herford suggested that this saying, like some of the other parallels, may have been based on a popular proverb.8

Judging Others

"Judge not, that you be not judged," is in Q (Matt. 7:1=Luke 6:37). I did not find in early Judaism this complete prohibition of passing judgment on others, but Hillel came close: "Judge not your fellow until you are in his place" (*Abot* 2:5). In contrast, the Essenes regarded as a duty the passing of judgment on other Essenes who had committed various offences (1QS 6 and 7).

Love of Personal Enemies

This idea is in Q in the Sermon on the Mount: "Love your enemies; do good to those who hate you" (Luke 6:27), and "Love your enemies, and pray for those who persecute you" (Matt. 5:44). *Testament of Joseph* 18:2 combines praying for and doing good to your enemy: "If anyone wishes to do you harm, you should pray for him, along with doing [him] good." In *Testament of Benjamin* 4:3 the good man "loves those who wrong him as he loves his own life." Compare Proverbs 25:21-22.

Love Your Neighbor

This Second Commandment is in Leviticus 19:18, where, as in Mark 12:28-31 and parallels, a "neighbor" is a member of one's own religion. *Jubilees* 36:4 teaches that "brothers" (i.e., Jews) should love "each other as themselves." The Essenes taught love of only the members of their own sect, "the sons of light" (1QS 1:9-11). The Two Commandments, love God and love your neighbor, are combined in the synoptic gospels, in *Testament of Dan* 5:3, and in *Testament of Issachar* 5:2.

Meekness

"Blessed are the meek, for they shall inherit the earth" (Matt. 5:5) has a parallel in Psalm 37:11, "the meek shall possess the land." *2 Enoch* advises, "Walk . . . in meekness" (66:6).

Mental Morality—General

The ancient world was moving in the direction of ethical concern for thoughts and motives, not just actions. "Blessed are the pure in heart, for they shall see God" (Matt. 5:8). In the Jewish background we find in Psalm 24: "Who shall stand in his [the Lord's] holy place [Mount Zion]? He who has clean hands and a pure heart." The Psalmist is talking about the Day of the Lord when the Lord will come to Mount Zion and the righteous standing on Mount Zion will see him; in verse 6 the Psalmist classifies the pure in heart as "of those who seek him, who seek the face of the God of Jacob." "Create in me a clean heart, O God," states Psalm 51:10, and "cleanse your heart from all sin," advises Sirach 38:10. Returning to the synoptics: "What comes out of a man is what defiles him. For from within, out of the heart of man, come evil thoughts" (Mark 7). *Testament of Gad* 5:5 states that the man who is just and humble "is completely unwilling to wrong anyone, even in his thoughts."

Mental Morality—Sexual

In both the synoptics and Judaism sexual morality included absence of lustful thoughts. In the Sermon on the Mount: "But I say to you that everyone who looks at a woman lustfully has already committed adultery with her in his heart" (Matt. 5:28). The same idea is in the *Testament of Benjamin*, *Testament of Issachar*, and the *Damascus Document*.

Mercy

Mercy is upheld as a virtue in both the Sermon on the Mount and in Judaism, particularly Micah 6:8 and *Testament of Judah* 18:3. The thought in Luke 6:36, "Be merciful, even as your Father [God] is merciful," is also in *Sifre* 93b: "As long as you have mercy on men, they [i.e., God] will show mercy to you from heaven."

Particularism, or Jewish Exclusiveness

In Mark 7 Jesus at first refuses to exorcise a demon from the daughter of a Syrophoenician woman. In Matthew's version (chap. 15) the prejudice against gentiles is increased, and Jesus says, "I was sent only to the lost sheep of the house of Israel," and he refers to gentiles as "dogs" (15:24-26). Jewish bias against gentiles is very explicit in Jubilees 22:16:

Separate yourself from the gentiles,
and do not eat with them,
and do not perform deeds like theirs.
Because their deeds are defiled
and all their ways are contaminated, and
despicable, and abominable.

Jubilees 30:7 adopts a very harsh position:

And if there is any man in Israel who wishes to give his daughter or his sister to any man who is from the seed of the gentiles, let him surely die, and let him be stoned because he has caused shame in Israel. And also the woman will be burned with fire because she has defiled the name of her father's house and so she shall be uprooted from Israel.

Jubilees represents an intense reaction against Hellenist Jews who were adopting Greek culture. The prohibition of mixed marriages, however, was prevalent in Judaism and has its roots in the Old Testament.[9]

Peace

"Whatever house you enter, first say, 'Peace be to this house,'" says Jesus to the disciples in Luke 10:5. "Peace to you" occurs in Judaism as early as Judges 19:20. "Peace" as a greeting and as a blessing when parting was an old Near Eastern custom.

Christians are commanded to be at peace with one another in Mark 9:50, and peaceful relations among Israelites are called for in Genesis 13:8 and Psalm 125:5.

I did not find a verbal parallel to "Blessed are the peacemakers" (Matt. 5:9), though Hillel may have implied it when he said, "Be of the disciples of Aaron, loving peace, and pursuing peace" (*Abot* 1:12). The Jesus saying that he came not to bring peace, but "division" (Luke 12:51) or "a sword" (Matt. 10:34), does not harmonize well with "Blessed are the peacemakers."[10]

Perfection

"You must be perfect, as your heavenly Father is perfect" (Sermon on the Mount). Deuteronomy 18:13 states, "You shall be perfect before the Lord, your God"; in the Septuagint version the same Greek word, *teleios*, is used for "perfection" that is used in the Sermon. But in Deuteronomy, the application is not to ethics, but to rejecting "abominable" gentile religious practices. The Essenes, however, included ethics when they described themselves as "the holy men who walk in perfection of way" (1QS 9:9).

The Poor

Deep concern for the poor is characteristic of both the synoptics and early Judaism, except that Matthew 5:3, 6 spiritualizes "the poor" and "hunger" in the Beatitudes (Luke 6:20-21 is the earlier form). In Luke 14 Jesus instructs a Pharisee to invite only the poor and crippled when he gives a feast, because they cannot repay him. Feeding the hungry is an ethical ideal in Sirach 4. *Abot* 1:5 in the Mishnah goes farther than merely inviting the poor to a meal: "Let your house be opened wide and let the needy be members of your household."

Retaliation

Non-retaliation is the principle in Q's famous "turn the other cheek" saying, and the "law of retaliation" in the Torah (in Exod., Lev., and Deut.) is rejected in the Sermon on the Mount. But retaliation is rejected in some Jewish writings too, including Leviticus 19:18, *Testament of Gad* 6:7, Sirach 28:1, and *2 Enoch* 50:4. Proverbs 24:29 rejects tit for tat: "Do not say, 'I will do to him as he has done to me; I will pay the man back for what he has done.'" The turn-the-other-cheek metaphor is explicit in Lamentations 3:30, where a man should "give his cheek to the smiter," and thus bear the yoke of the Lord.

Ten Commandments

Observing these commandments is essential in all three synoptic gospels (Mark 10 par) as well as in Judaism.

Universalism

The only pericope in the synoptics that indicates a universalistic attitude is the parable of the Good Samaritan in Luke 10. A limited form of universalism is in Deutero-Isaiah, *1 Enoch*, and *2 Enoch*; namely, all gentiles will be saved provided they become Jews and worship Yahweh, the Lord. Paul's attitude is analogous: all persons will be saved provided they believe in Jesus the Christ (Gal. 3:26-28). In the synoptic parable, however, the Samaritan apparently is accepted as a "neighbor"—and thus an equal—without having to become either a Jew or a Christian. Two Jewish writings go all the way in accepting all humans as equal: In the *Testament of Issachar* 7:6-7 the patriarch declares, "I loved every human being as I love my children," and he instructs his children to "walk with all mankind in sincerity of heart." The *Testament of Abraham* (1st or 2d c. A.D.) makes no distinction between Jews and gentiles.

Vanity

Vanity is a sin in Matthew 6, where one should give alms quietly, offer prayers secretly, and fast inconspicuously, instead of doing these things in ways to attract public attention. The same idea is in Proverbs 21:14, "A gift in secret averts [divine] anger." The rationale of giving secretly was that giving publicly embarrasses and shames the recipient, who should be spared the humiliation. Vanity in general is deplored in *Testament of Benjamin* 6:4, where the good man does not receive glory from men.

Wealth

In contrast to Matthew, Luke is hostile to the rich, and very sympathetic with the poor. The parable of the Rich Man and Lazarus in Luke 16 teaches that the rich who are indifferent to the plight of the poor will spend eternity in Hades. Amos 6 and 8 denounce the rich who trample on the poor. Job 27 and *Testament of Judah* 17:1 denounce wealth.

The theme of the parable of the Rich Fool in Luke 12 is that you cannot take it with you when you die. The same theme is in Proverbs 11:4, "riches do not profit on the day of wrath," and in the Pseudepigrapha in *Pseudo-Phocylides* 110, "It is impossible to take riches and money (with you) into Hades."

The five general ethics and the 23 specific ones we have observed were all in Judaism in the time of Jesus. The only possible exceptions are the honor accorded to peacemakers and the strict prohibition of passing judgment on anyone, but Hillel, who preceded Jesus, had already come close to those views. We cannot honestly say that Jesus taught new ethical ideals, for they were all somewhere in the Jewish environment. To exalt Jesus as a teacher, churches claimed that "no man ever spoke like this man" (John 7:46) and that he gave "new teaching." The apologetic motive for such statements is discussed below in the chapter "The Great Controversy." In our final chapter we will examine the question of whether Jesus actually taught the ethics in the synoptic gospels.

JESUS' DEATH

Why was Jesus crucified? Was he a revolutionist? Were the Jews or the Romans mainly responsible for his death? These and related questions have been investigated chiefly in the twentieth century,[1] although an introductory examination was made in the eighteenth century by Hermann Reimarus.

The questions arose because of conflicting evidence in the canonical gospels and various improbabilities in the Passion story. The conduct of both the Jewish trial and the Roman trial of Jesus is inconsistent with the legal procedures of those courts. The gospel portrait of Pilate as kind-hearted and reluctant to sentence Jesus, accused of being a rebel, "the king of the Jews," is contrary to Josephus' report of Pilate's cruelty.[2]

THE PALESTINIAN BACKGROUND

Bandits and rebels! Rebels and would-be kings! Bandits who were rebels who wanted to be kings! They arose all too frequently from the time of Herod the Great in 4 B.C. to the Bar Kosiba revolt in A.D. 132-135. Jewish armed bandits robbed individuals in the countryside and/or looted and burned cities for the sake of plunder or because they hated the inhabitants. Many started insurrections because they hated Roman rule and wanted to establish an independent Jewish kingdom with their leader as king. The uprisings occurred especially at a time of change in government leadership. Josephus' description of the situation following Herod's death gives us a glimpse of the turmoil then:

At Sepphoris, a city of Galilee, Judas, son of Hezekiah, . . . got a multitude together and broke into the royal armory and armed his men and attacked the others who were eager to rule. In Perea also Simon, one of the servants of the king, relying on his handsome appearance and great stature, put a crown on his own head. He went about with a band of robbers he had collected and burned down the palace at Jericho and many other costly buildings, procuring spoils for himself by snatching them from the fire. . . . At this time a shepherd called Athrongeus also set himself up as king. He based his hopes on his physical strength, courage, and his four brothers like himself. He put a troop of armed men under each of his brothers, while he himself as king attended to more important affairs. He put a crown on his head, and with his brothers continued to overrun the country, . . . killing both Romans and those [Jews] of the king's party, nor did any Jew escape him if he could gain [by robbing him].[3]

When Augustus in A.D. 6 replaced Herod Archelaus' kingship over Judea and Galilee with direct Roman rule, he sent Quirinius to levy taxes there. Judas the Galilean (not the Judas who betrayed Jesus) stirred the Galileans to armed revolt, saying that they would be cowards if they paid taxes to the Romans.[4] He exhorted the people to assert the freedom of the Jewish nation, saying that God would help them. His appeal induced a large number of men to follow him eagerly, and they robbed and murdered other Jews who refused to join them. They even demolished cities and burned the Temple in Jerusalem. Thus they too were robbers as well as patriots. Josephus does not say that Judas wanted to be king; instead, he says that Judas was the founder and teacher of a sect which was quite unlike the other Jewish sects.[5] Scholars disagree on whether it was the sect later known as the Zealots; Josephus first applies that name to a sect at the outbreak of the Jewish War against Rome in A.D. 66.

There was yet another type of Jewish rebel: the messianic Prophet. Rebels of this type were self-proclaimed "prophets" who expected to usher in the eschatological kingdom of God, or New Age. Some believed that new Mosaic times would precede the coming of the kingdom, and each thought of himself as a prophet like Moses who would lead his followers in a new Exodus. This notion was derived partly from Deuteronomy 18:15-18, which was interpreted erroneously as a prophecy of the coming of a prophet like Moses in the last days before the judgment day. Josephus reports two of these persons specifically: Theudas (ca. A.D. 45) and a Jewish prophet from Egypt (a decade later).[6] Claiming to be a prophet, Theudas persuaded many Jews to join him in the wilderness east of the

Jordan River and then to march to that river, which at his command would divide and allow them to cross it. Fadus, the Roman procurator of Judea at that time, stopped the enterprise with his horsemen, who killed many and captured the rest. The troops took Theudas alive, cut off his head, and carried it to Jerusalem. The Jew from Egypt came to Jerusalem, and he too said he was a prophet (Josephus calls him a "false prophet"). He led 30,000 men (Josephus may have exaggerated the number) from the wilderness to the Mount of Olives, promising that he would make the walls of Jerusalem fall down so that they could take the city from the Romans and he could rule over it. The procurator, Felix, prevented the attack on the city by killing and capturing the prophet's followers.

Other false prophets, or false Messiahs, also appeared in the days of Felix. Josephus describes them as impostors and deceivers who, after inducing the mobs into a state of spiritual frenzy, led them into the wilderness, pretending that there God would show them signs and wonders that would indicate that freedom from Roman rule was near at hand. Felix's soldiers killed many of them too.[7] Mark 13:22 warns: "False Christs and false prophets will arise and show signs and wonders to lead astray, if possible, the elect." Although represented as a prediction by Jesus, the specific information indicates its origin in the churches; the passage evidently refers to the same false prophets that Josephus condemned.

Some features of these various uprisings are important for understanding Christian origins:

1. The frequent Jewish uprisings in Palestine explain why the Romans were wary, quick to suppress any uprising or potential uprising.

2. The Greek word *lestes*, "bandit," "robber," in Josephus' writings often refers to rebels, including some who aspired to become king. The label was appropriate, for many rebels robbed individuals, palaces, and cities.

3. A Jewish claimant to the throne need not think that he was an eschatological type of messianic king. That is, he might not think that the judgment day and the end of the present age would come soon. On the other hand, the majority of the rebels did believe that, as their conduct demonstrates, and many Jews hoped that one or another of the rebels would usher in an eschatological kingdom.

4. The prophet-type leaders evidently thought of

themselves as prophets like Moses, for their plan was to gather their followers in the wilderness of Transjordan and then, like Moses, perform miracles there and lead their group to the Jordan River. They would also lead the way across the river. In the Old Testament it is Joshua, not Moses, who accomplished the crossing, but such a minor discrepancy seldom bothered ancient peoples. The fact that Theudas expected the Jordan River to divide at his command (as Moses had divided the Red Sea, according to Exodus 14) shows that Theudas thought of himself as the new Moses.

5. The prophet-type leaders often aspired to be king of the Jews, and therefore we should not be surprised that they wanted to capture Jerusalem, the capital of the future kingdom. A man could be both a prophet and a king; a millennium earlier Israel's first king, Saul, was also a prophet (1 Sam. 10:10-13).

What does all this have to do with the actual life of Jesus? And what does it have to do with the gospel traditions about Jesus?

WAS JESUS AN INSURRECTIONIST?

The mood of the masses in Palestine was one of hatred of the Roman rulers, partly because of traditional Jewish nationalism and partly because of the heavy Roman taxation. Considering that mood and the frequency of incipient insurrections, it would not be surprising if Jesus, too, was an insurrectionist. There is evidence both for and against that conclusion.

Pro: Jesus Was a Rebel
1. Jesus and his disciples believed that he was the Christ, and in their environment the belief was prevalent that the Christ would be the king of the Jewish nation. The belief would naturally cause Jesus to plan to lead a revolt against Rome and establish the kingdom of God, which would also be the Jewish kingdom.

2. All four gospels report that the Romans put on Jesus' cross the title, "King of the Jews"; Mark 15:26 states that this was their "charge" against him. The Roman Senate had granted that same title to Herod the Great. This shows that the Romans thought that he was a rebel or at least a potential rebel, for Jewish kingship was incompatible with Roman rule (except

when the Romans selected a vassal king who would be subservient to them).

3. The Romans crucified Jesus, and crucifixion was a typical Roman method of punishment for political insurrection, either actual or planned. It was used for some other crimes too, however.

4. Mark 15:7 reads: "And among the rebels in prison, who had committed murder in the insurrection, was a man called Barabbas." Matthew omits the word "insurrection," but Luke 23:19 describes Barabbas "a man who had been thrown into prison for an insurrection started in the city, and for murder." What was that insurrection? Since Jesus was crucified along with two "robbers" who probably were rebels, and the crucifixion occurred soon after an insurrection, is it not probable that Barabbas and the three men crucified were all involved in that insurrection and that Jesus, as "King of the Jews," was its leader? The gospel authors had good promotional reasons for suppressing that embarrassing fact.

5. In Mark 15:27 and in the parallel passage in Matthew the two men crucified with Jesus are *lestai*, "robbers," the same Greek word that Josephus applied to political rebels. In Luke the political implication has been removed by calling the two men "criminals" instead of robbers.

6. Although all four gospels portray Jesus as a peaceful man (except in the passage which portrays him as saying he came to cause strife), that is an apologetic portrait. The gospel authors wished to assure the Romans that Christians were loyal members of the empire, and therefore they masked the nature of the charge against Jesus. The Gospel of John illustrates this. In S, the Gospel of Signs source, "the high priest asked Jesus about his disciples and his teaching" (John 18:19). The author of John omitted Jesus' answer in S and substituted an evasive statement he himself composed, ascribing it to Jesus: "I have spoken openly to the world. . . . Why do you ask me? Ask those who heard what I spoke to them." In S Pilate asks the Jews, "What accusation do you bring against this man?" (18:29). The author of John censored the Jews' charge and substitutes another evasive answer he composed: "Unless he was doing wrong, we would not have delivered him to you." A few verses later, from S, Pilate asks Jesus, "What did you do?" Again John omits Jesus' answer in S and substitutes a quotation from his semi-Gnostic source, G, in which Jesus says, "My

kingdom is not of this world." In this G passage Jesus admits he is a king, but he is the Gnostic, not earthly, type. Plainly the author of John and his G source went to great lengths to counteract the idea that Jesus was a rebel; this makes us suspect that they may have been covering up something. And if Jesus was so innocent, why did the Romans crucify him?

7. According to the synoptic gospels the crowds hailed Jesus as king and Messiah when he entered Jerusalem (Mark 11:9-10 par). This is not evidence that Jesus started a rebellion, but, if historical, it indicates that there was a popular view that he was the Messiah and would become king of "the kingdom of our father David that is coming" (Mark). If this event is not historical, the story at least shows that the author of Mark associated Jesus with the coming of the Jewish kingdom.

8. In Acts 1:6 the disciples ask the risen Jesus, "Lord, will you at this time restore the kingdom to Israel?" The saying is not authentic, but it reflects the historical fact that the disciples had expected Jesus to establish the Jewish kingdom.

9. The author of Luke reinterpreted the parable of the Pounds (Luke 19:12-27) by inserting verses 14 and 27 (cf. the parallel parable of the Talents in Matt. 25:14-30 to which they have not been added). The insertions clearly make the point of the parable to be that Jesus' enemies did not want him to reign over them. This is a reference to the general Jewish disbelief that Jesus was the Christ. Does it also refer to Jewish refusal to join him in a revolt?

10. According to Luke 23:2 the Jewish council in Jerusalem made this charge against Jesus when they delivered him to Pilate: "We found this man perverting our nation, and forbidding us to give tribute to Caesar, and saying that he himself is Christ a king." Considering the total situation, it is very plausible that this was indeed the real cause of Jesus' arrest.[8] A few verses later the accusation is expanded: "He stirs up the people, teaching throughout all Judea, from Galilee to this place." It may be significant that this passage is identifying "teaching" with the rebellious words in verse 2. Biblical scholars and laymen alike usually assume that Jesus' teaching could not contain rebellious statements, but should we arbitrarily rule out the possibility? The fact that it was a Jewish charge does not prove that it was false, especially when we consider allusions made by the Christian writers themselves.

11. According to Luke 22:36-38 Jesus wants his

disciples to have swords. When they say they have two, he says, "It is enough." Does this pericope reflect an armed conflict that occurred when Jesus was arrested?

12. The theory that Jesus' teaching about the Temple or his casting out the money-changers would cause his crucifixion is implausible. The Jewish authorities would have taken care of that problem themselves, as they did with Stephen, and Pilate would not have involved himself with Jewish internal affairs.

Con: Jesus Was Not a Rebel

1. Josephus reports various Jewish insurrections, but says nothing of one started by Jesus, which suggests that Jesus did not start one. (But Mark and Luke mention an insurrection that immediately preceded Jesus' crucifixion, and Josephus does not mention it either. The insurrection in which Barabbas was involved must have occurred, for no Christian purpose would be served by creating the reference to one.)

2. Perhaps there was no connection between Jesus and the insurrection which preceded the crucifixion, as the gospels depict.

3. If Jesus believed that the kingdom of God was near at hand, he may have believed that God himself would set the time—as the Essenes at Qumran believed—, and therefore Jesus need not start a rebellion. (Other rebel prophets, however, started rebellions.)

4. The main mission of both the Baptist and Jesus was to preach the urgency of repentance because the kingdom of God was coming soon. This is quite different from the activities of the aspirants to the throne that Josephus reports, including those of prophets-like-Moses. Although belief that oneself is the Messiah would theoretically lead to insurrection, preaching repentance would not be a method of "taking the kingdom by force."

5. Josephus' description of John the Baptist does not say that he was a political rebel. Instead, Josephus states that Herod Antipas killed John, a good man, because "he feared lest the great influence John had over the people might put it into his power and inclination to raise a rebellion." Jesus preached the same message as John, so he probably did not start a rebellion either.

6. And in the morning, a great while before day, he [Jesus] rose and went out to a lonely place, and there he

prayed. And Simon [Peter] and those who were with him followed him, and they found him and said to him, "Everyone is searching for you." And he said to them, "Let us go on to the next towns, that I may preach there also; for that is why I came forth" (Mark 1:35-38).

This pericope has the ring of authenticity. Nothing miraculous or mythological is in it, and neither does it serve any apologetic or promotional purpose. If Jesus regarded his mission as one of preaching repentance, it seems improbable that he would lead an armed revolt. (But teaching the people not to pay taxes to Rome [Luke 23:2] would be consistent with revolt.)

A Third Possibility

Another possibility is that at first Jesus did not intend to start a revolt, but the crowds and his disciples pressured him into doing so, and that caused his arrest.

1. That is what Herod Antipas feared would happen with the Baptist, and perhaps it really happened with Jesus.

2. One of the incidental pericopes that may reflect actual history comes from the Gospel of Signs in John 6:15: "Perceiving then that they [the people] were about to come and to seize him in order that they might make him king, Jesus withdrew again into the mountain alone." This indicates that the crowd wanted to make him king, but Jesus was reluctant to assume the role.

3. In order to arrest Jesus, the priests had to bribe Judas to lead the arresting officers to him (Mark 14:43). If Jesus led an insurrection, he may have escaped and gone into hiding, and consequently Judas' betrayal was necessary for the Jewish authorities to find him. Josephus reports that the Egyptian prophet who led a revolt escaped.

4. The early Christians, like Josephus, wished to please the Romans, so they minimized the evidence of revolt against them. That the early Christians would tone down Jesus' connection with an insurrection is quite understandable, but that they would invent evidence that he was involved in one is quite implausible. It is also improbable that Jews could create it from nothing and convince Pilate of the false charge. And the incidental references, written by Christians, that point to Jesus' involvement need to be explained.

What conclusion should we draw? The third possibility

best fits the total evidence. It explains how Jesus could preach repentance, later decide that he was the Messiah, the Christ, and finally become the leader of an incipient revolt. It also explains the origin of the belief that Jesus was the Christ.

PROBLEMS IN THE PASSION STORY

Jesus' trial before the Sanhedrin, the Jewish council or court, presents problems when examined historically. Three facts tell us that the high priest could not have charged Jesus with blasphemy (Mark 14:61-64): (a) In Judaism blasphemy was disrespect for God and his name, Yahweh; the worst blasphemy was the worship of idols (Ezek. 20:27-31). Jesus' admission that he was the Christ was not blasphemy—it was not an affront to God. (b) If the charge had been blasphemy, the high priest would not have sent Jesus on to Pilate. Pilate was concerned only with maintaining law and order and Roman control of the country; as for Jewish theology, he could not have cared less. (c) If the Sanhedrin had convicted Jesus of blasphemy, the punishment would have been death by stoning, not crucifixion, and the sentence would have been carried out by Jewish authorities, not the Romans.

In the Gospel of John two high priests, Annas and Caiaphas, are involved; that cannot be historical, for there was only one high priest at a time. This literary contribution to historical confusion is the result of lack of knowledge of who was high priest in Jesus' day. The author of the Signs source in John and the author of Matthew state correctly that he was Caiaphas (John 18:13; Matt. 26:57). Mark does not name the high priest. But the author of Luke-Acts, who evidently did not know, thought that he was Annas, who had preceded Caiaphas; in Luke 3:2 and Acts 4:6 he erroneously states that Annas was high priest. Afterwards a scribe tried to correct those texts; he added "and Caiaphas" in both verses. The author of John tried to harmonize his Signs source with Luke-Acts by inserting into John 18:13 "first" and "Annas, for he was the father-in-law of." In S, the Gospel of Signs, the verse read: "They led him to Caiaphas, who was high priest that year." But after the author of John revised it to agree with the Annas tradition, it read: "First they led him to Annas, for he was the father-in-law of Caiaphas, who was high priest that year." In John 18:24 either the author of John or the later redactor continued the effort to harmonize the whole by having Annas send Jesus back to Caiaphas. The effect of all this has been to create a literary puzzle for biblical scholars to argue about!

Jesus' trial before Pilate also presents problems. In all four gospels Pilate asks Jesus if he is "king of the Jews." That—not blasphemy—was evidently the charge against him when they brought him to Pilate in Luke 23:2, a charge of sedition. In the synoptics Jesus does not deny the charge, but replies, "You have said so," which in effect is an affirmative answer, as in Jesus' reply to Judas at the Last Supper (Matt. 26:25). In John Jesus gives an evasive response and then the author adds from the semi-Gnostic source, "My kingdom is not of this world" (18:36). Christian Gnosticism, which viewed the world as inherently evil, rejected the notion of a kingdom of God or a kingdom of Jesus on earth; the author of John used this Gnostic idea to refute the charge that Jesus wanted to set up a political kingdom. In John the kingdom is spiritualized and it no longer is God's—it is Jesus'.

JESUS AND THE TEMPLE

Jesus' "Cleansing" of the Temple

The traditional explanation of Jesus' arrest is that it was the result of his "Cleansing of the Temple." This name has been given to the story of Jesus' driving the merchants out of the Temple and overturning the tables of the money changers (Mark 11:15-18). Mark does indeed connect the cleansing with the desire of the Temple priesthood to kill him: "the chief priests and scribes heard it and sought a way to destroy him." Luke 19:47, however, breaks the connection by inserting a reference to Jesus' teaching in the Temple, thus implying that the teaching was the cause of the hostility. Matthew's version of the story omits any connection between the Cleansing and the arrest. In it (21:14-16) the cause of the indignation of the chief priests and scribes is Jesus' healing in the Temple and children's hailing him as "the Son of David." At Jesus' trials before the authorities, disruptive conduct in the Temple is not a charge against Jesus.

In the Gospel of Signs incorporated in John, the Cleansing is transferred from near the end of Jesus' career to its beginning (2:14-16). Neither the Signs source nor the author of John connect the Cleansing with Jesus' death.

Did the Cleansing of the Temple actually occur? If Jesus had actually created such a disturbance in the Temple, the Temple police would have immediately arrested him, as several scholars have remarked. The trade and money changing were too profitable to allow a violent protest against it go unpunished, regardless of Jesus' popularity. Also, the trade and money changing took place outside the Temple, not inside as the Cleansing story depicts it. Additional evidence that the incident is not historical is that it evidently is one of the stories composed to "fulfill" the Scriptures. The inspiration for the story is evidently Zechariah's description of the ideal conditions that shall prevail when "the day of the Lord comes": "And there shall no longer be a trader in the house of the Lord of hosts on that day" (14:21). The story is fleshed out by ascribing to Jesus quotations from two Old Testament passages: "My house shall be called a house of prayer for all nations" from Isaiah 56:7, and "you have made it a den of robbers," adapted from Jeremiah 7:11.

Jesus' Teaching in the Temple
Did Jesus' teaching in the Temple cause his arrest by the Temple authorities? According to Mark 11:18 the chief priests and scribes wanted to kill Jesus because they feared his teaching. The account in Luke 19:47, derived from Mark, implies it. The account of Jesus' arrest in Mark 14:49, reproduced in Matthew and Luke, also implies a connection between his teaching and the desire to kill him: "Day after day I was with you in the Temple teaching, and you did not seize me." The point of the saying is that the logical time to arrest Jesus would have been while he was teaching (assuming Mark's theory that it was the teaching that caused the arrest). Mark has an explanation, however: "they tried to arrest him, but feared the multitude" (Mark 12:12 par). Scholars have debated whether or not fear of the multitude would have stopped the chief priests. A problem is that the gospels are not consistent as to what aspect of Jesus' teaching caused the priests' hostility, and we have observed that in some verses teaching is not the cause. On the other hand, if Jesus taught, either inside or outside the Temple, that he was the Christ, the king of the Jews, that surely would arouse the fear of the Temple authorities, who wanted no Jewish rebellions.

Did Jesus teach in the Temple at all? At first glance this

appears to be a foolish question, for many statements in the gospels say that he did. Nevertheless, several features in the gospels raise doubts. The gospels portray Jesus as preaching in the Temple over a period of time, not just at Passover. "Day after day" indicates that Jesus taught there for many days. If Jesus had taught in the Temple, surely he would have been arrested sooner.

A second cause of doubt is the Temple as the locus of Jesus' teaching. Why would Jesus choose the worst possible place to teach? Jesus taught the coming of the kingdom of God, the resurrection, and the judgment, and hence the need for repentance, but these were Pharisaic beliefs that the Sadducees rejected, according to Josephus. And the Temple cult was closely associated with the Sadducees, as Acts 4:1-3 indicates. Jesus could have found crowds to teach on the streets without teaching in the headquarters of the enemy, where his teaching activity would probably have lasted only a day, not "day after day."

Jesus' teaching in the Temple does not fit his situation, but attributing it to him does fit the situation of the early Christians. The passage in Acts 4 reports that "the priests and the captain of the Temple and the Sadducees" had the apostles arrested "because they were teaching the people and proclaiming in Jesus the resurrection from the dead." The author of Matthew plainly regarded the Sadducees as enemies, for he added "and Sadducees" (16:6) to Mark's warning against the Pharisees (8:15). We have seen that the gospel authors strove to exalt Jesus as a teacher. In subsequent chapters we will see how they depicted Jesus in his teaching as superior to the Pharisees and their scribes, a reflection of the controversy between them and the apostles after Jesus' death. The gospel authors naturally thought that Jesus' teaching was also superior to that of the chief priests and their scribes, for Christian teaching directly contradicted some Saducean beliefs. This early Christian viewpoint is most developed in Luke, beginning with the story of Jesus teaching in the Temple at the age of twelve. The theory, or apologetic, begins in Mark, however, with Jesus teaching there at the close of his career. The fact that the Saducean priests were responsible for Jesus' arrest must have furnished an incentive for asserting the superiority of Jesus' teaching in the Temple.

WHO KILLED JESUS?

Two early Christian apologetic goals—in addition to explaining Jesus' death—are combined in the Passion story. The hostility between Jews and Christians that developed in the first century caused Christians increasingly to shift the responsibility for Jesus' death on to the Jews. Also, the necessity of accommodation with the Roman authorities as Christianity expanded caused Christians to strive to assure them that the relations between them had always been friendly. One means of promoting that goal was to portray Pilate as innocent of Jesus' death.

The shift of all blame on to the Jews begins in Mark 14:55-56: "Now the chief priests and the whole council sought testimony against Jesus to put him to death; but they found none. For many bore false witness against him, and their witness did not agree." It is highly improbable that the council found no valid evidence against Jesus, yet found him guilty anyway! This picture of the council as determined to convict Jesus regardless of real evidence, depicts the Jewish authorities as very unscrupulous and acting contrary to their own laws, even in their own court. Matthew makes the descendants of Jews guilty also by having the Jewish crowd say, "His blood be on us and on our children!" (27:25).

The gospels exonerate Pilate, portraying him as reluctant to crucify Jesus. But no Roman procurator would let the crowd make the decisions for him, especially when the charge was sedition. In addition to his desire to release Jesus instead of Barabbas, Pilate concludes that Jesus is innocent and asks, "Why, what evil has he done?" (Mark 15:14 par). In Luke 23:4 Pilate declares, "I find no crime in this man." In Matthew Pilate's wife sends this word to him: "Have nothing to do with that righteous man [Jesus], for I have suffered much over him today in a dream." The idea in this is that she has had a divine revelation attesting to Jesus' innocence. The author of Matthew expands further the whitewashing of Pilate by depicting him as washing his hands publicly and saying, "I am innocent of this man's blood; see to it yourselves." In John, too, Pilate finds no guilt in Jesus, and Jesus' enemies have become "the Jews" (18:38).

Who was responsible for Jesus' death, Jews or Romans? Neither Jews as a whole nor Romans as a whole, but the Sadducean priests, the Sanhedrin, Judas, and Pilate.

WHAT REALLY HAPPENED?

After we learn the historical setting and the promotional, or apologetic, motives of the gospel authors, we can recover some actual history.

The Sadducees and the Roman government had a mutual interest in maintaining the political status quo. The Romans naturally wanted to keep political control, and the wealthy Sadducees had a policy of collaborating with the Romans; they rightly feared the consequences of sedition, for when Jews revolted a few decades later, the Romans killed many and destroyed the Temple. The Sadducees' attitude must have been the same as that expressed later by Josephus. When many Jews in Jerusalem wanted to revolt from the Romans, he told them that they were inferior to the Romans "not only in martial skill, but also in good fortune." He urged them not to act so rashly and bring terrible consequences "upon their country, their families, and themselves. And this I said with vehement exhortation, because I foresaw that the end of such a war would be most unfortunate for us."[9]

The Sadducees wanted to arrest Jesus, either because they feared he might start a revolt, or because he had started one. The latter is more probable, for a rebellion occurred about the time of Jesus' arrest, Pilate acted as if Jesus had publicly proclaimed himself "King of the Jews," and Jesus apparently was in hiding, for the Temple authorities did not know where to find him until Judas led their police to him.

Judas Iscariot, one of Jesus' disciples, went to the chief priests and agreed to betray Jesus in return for money. How much money, we do not know; the "thirty pieces of silver" in Matthew 26:15 is drawn from Zechariah 11:12 to try to connect Christian beginnings with Scripture—a technique often used by the gospel authors. The chief priests wanted to arrest Jesus secretly, for he was popular with the crowds and they rightly feared that his arrest in the presence of the multitude might cause a tumult (Mark 14:1-2). The chief priests had special reason for fearing the crowds then, for the Passover was near, a time when crowds of Jews came to Jerusalem to celebrate that feast. The crowds offered sacrifices in and outside the Temple courtyard. The priests knew that a slaughter of Jews offering sacrifices at

Passover in Jerusalem had occurred when the crowds rioted when Herod Archelaus came to power in 4 B.C. [10] Therefore at night Judas led "a crowd with swords and clubs, from the chief priests and the scribes and the elders" to Jesus and his disciples in the Garden of Gethsemane, probably on the Mount of Olives near Bethany where Jesus was hiding. Judas identified Jesus by kissing him, and the armed band promptly arrested him.

Mark reports two details that serve no Christian promotional purpose and thus are probably historical. A man who was with Jesus drew his sword and cut off an ear of a slave of the high priest; this feature suggests that there may have been a fight. Luke adds the mythological feature that Jesus touched his ear and healed him. Another detail is Mark's statement that a young man with Jesus was dressed in only a linen cloth; when they seized him, "he left the cloth and ran away naked." This indicates that the Jewish authorities arrested more than Jesus. Then the disciples forsook Jesus and fled. [11]

The arresting officers took Jesus to the high priest, and Peter followed from afar. The next morning the Sanhedrin tried Jesus. During the trial Peter was afraid and when asked, denied that he was a disciple of Jesus. This tradition must be historical, for it is not the type of story that early Christians would want to invent and tell about a disciple who became a hero in the early church. Whether he denied Jesus three times is questionable, for 3, 7, 12, and 40 were popular numbers in antiquity, partly as the result of Pythagorean influence.

After the trial by the council, the Jewish authorities bound Jesus and led him to Pilate. The Jewish guards and the Roman soldiers mistreated Jesus after the trials. The soldiers led Jesus to Golgotha to crucify him, compelling a passerby, Simon of Cyrene, to carry his cross. Some modern Passion plays and films are too dramatic, erroneously depicting Jesus as carrying it. The charge against Jesus, "the King of the Jews," was inscribed on the cross, and the soldiers crucified him. Two rebels were crucified with him, one on each side. Some women who had followed Jesus from Galilee watched from afar; the disciples apparently were too frightened to do so. Soon after Jesus died one of his disciples, Joseph of Arithmathea, "who was also looking for the kingdom of God, took courage and went to Pilate, and asked for the body of Jesus" (Mark 15:43). He wrapped the body in a linen shroud and laid it in a tomb hewn in the rock.

The Passion story illustrates the gospel writers' practice of altering and creating traditions. For example, because Judas had committed such a despicable deed as betraying his master, early Christians felt that God must have punished him by a terrible death. Consequently we have the story in Matthew 27 that Judas was so ashamed that he returned the money and then hanged himself, while in Acts 1 Judas kept the money and bought a field with it, then fell headlong, his abdomen burst open, and he died. Bursting open was a popular method with Jewish writers of depicting the death of the wicked. In Bel and the Dragon 27 in the Apocrypha Daniel feeds pitch to the dragon that gentiles have been worshiping: the dragon bursts open and dies. In *Ahiqar* in the Jewish Pseudepigrapha the treacherous Nadin swells up and dies.[12] Eusebius, as well as the author of Matthew, liked the idea that enemies of Christianity must have committed suicide. He erroneously reported that Pilate did so (2.7). John 18:10 illustrates the tendency to add names and other details later to make accounts look authentic, even though they were unknown. Here, at the arrest of Jesus, the anonymous man who drew a sword becomes "Simon Peter," and the anonymous slave whose ear was cut off becomes "Malchus." In our earliest source, Mark, the ear is simply "his ear," but in Luke and John, written later, the story becomes more specific: it was "his right ear."

Many other features in the gospels, including some in the Passion story, will be discussed below in relation to the early church.

8

RESURRECTION AND ASCENSION

FLIGHT TO GALILEE

Although Peter followed Jesus as far as the high priest's courtyard when Jesus was arrested, he as well as the other disciples from Galilee soon fled in fear to their homeland. This event is alluded to in words ascribed to Jesus in Mark 14:27-28: "You will all fall away; for it is written, 'I will strike the shepherd, and the sheep will be scattered.' But after I am raised up, I will go before you to Galilee." This "forecast" is expanded in Mark and Matthew in a statement of an angel at the empty tomb: "He is going before you to Galilee; there you will see him, as he told you." A variant is in John 16:32: "Behold, the hour is coming (and has come [redactor's insertion]) that you will be scattered, each to his own (home) and you will leave me alone." Matthew states that "the eleven disciples went to Galilee" (28:16). The flight of the disciples to Galilee was embarrassing to the early Christian communities, and the author of Luke-Acts eliminated it by depicting the disciples as remaining in Jerusalem.

Fear was not the only motivation for the disciples' return to Galilee. Disillusionment was also a major factor. Their hopes were dashed by Jesus' death; he evidently was not the Christ after all, and the kingdom of God was not about to appear. The disciples' discouragement is reflected in the story of the two who saw the resurrected Jesus while they were walking to the village of Emmaus. Before they recognized him and became convinced that he was alive again, they were sad and told him, "We had hoped that he was the one to redeem Israel" (Luke 24:17-21). Contrary to some passages in the gospels, Jesus clearly had not predicted his death and resurrection; the disciples did not expect them to happen.

THE RESURRECTION[1]

Soon after the disciples had returned to Galilee, Simon Peter had a vision that changed the course of history. Without it, Christianity would have died with Jesus' crucifixion. Peter's vision of Jesus convinced him that Jesus was alive again and that in spite of the crucifixion, Jesus was indeed the Christ who would usher in the kingdom of God. Peter succeeded, with some difficulty, in convincing the other disciples. The event is summarized in words ascribed to Jesus: ". . . when you [Simon] have turned again, strengthen your brethren" (Luke 22:32). Paul, in 1 Corinthians 15, argued earnestly that God had raised Jesus from the dead. His evidence consists of visionary appearances of Jesus to believers of whom the first was "Cephas," that is, Peter. A verse in Luke also testifies to the primitive tradition that Peter was the first to see the risen Jesus: "The Lord has arisen indeed and has appeared to Simon" (24:34). Whether later others besides Paul had visions of the risen Lord is uncertain but possible, considering how contagious visions can be, even in modern times: for example, visions of the Virgin Mary. At least it is certain that Peter was the first. The empty tomb stories are fiction, and we know that the resurrection faith began with Peter's vision, not an empty tomb (see below).

Were feelings of guilt for denying Jesus a psychological factor in causing Peter's vision? Later Paul had a vision of the risen Jesus, and he felt guilty because he had persecuted the church (1 Cor. 15:8-9).

Peter's vision had two personal consequences for him. First, it made him a hero in the church, in spite of the fact that he had denied knowing Jesus. In Mark 8:29 he is honored as *the* disciple who recognizes that Jesus is the Christ. Matthew expands this with Jesus' telling him that he is "the Rock" (Greek: *petros*), "and on this rock I will build my church" (16:18). "Church" here refers to Christianity in general and not to the church at Rome. The second personal result of Peter's vision was that it changed his name, which originally was Simon. Because he was, in effect, the founder, or foundation stone of the Christian faith, he was called "Simon the Rock." Because the disciples' language was Aramaic, the title "Rock" was in Aramaic, *cephas*. When the Christian movement spread to Greek-speaking Jews and gentiles, "Cephas" became

"Petros" (Peter in English translations). Eventually the title was used as a personal name; thus "Simon" became "Simon the Rock" which became "Simon Peter," or simply "Cephas" or "Peter." Jesus' name underwent a similar change: "Jesus" became "Jesus the Christ" which became "Jesus Christ" or "Christ."

At first the disciples did not believe in Jesus' resurrection; several allusions to that fact are in the gospels. According to a story in Matthew 28 the eleven disciples saw the risen Jesus on a mountain in Galilee. "And when they saw him, they worshiped him, but they doubted" ("some" is not in the original Greek text). The risen Jesus criticizes the two disciples on the road to Emmaus for being "slow of heart to believe" (Luke 24:25). When women reported the empty tomb to the apostles, "These words seemed to them as idle, and they disbelieved them" (Luke 24:11). In John 20 we have the famous story of doubting Thomas, who would not believe that Jesus was raised until he saw Jesus' hands and felt his side.

To counteract doubts about Jesus' resurrection, some "proofs" were created. Not only did Thomas see and feel a physical Jesus (even though "the doors were shut, but Jesus came and stood among them" (John 20:26), but Jesus also ate and drank after his resurrection (Acts 10:41).

The supreme effort to support the faith in a physical resurrection is the empty tomb story. It originated later than Paul's first letter to the Corinthian church, for if Paul had known of it, he surely would have used it as evidence to support his argument that God raised Jesus and therefore there will be a general resurrection of the deceased Christians (1 Cor. 15). Paul personally knew Peter and some other leaders of the Jerusalem church, and if there had been an empty tomb, they certainly would have told him about it. It is not in the early preaching in Acts. Thus the foundation of the resurrection faith was not an empty tomb attended by angels, but Peter's vision.

The argument with the doubters ran as follows: "Maybe it was not the same tomb." "Yes, it was, for Jesus' burial cloths were still in it" (John 20:6-7). "How do you know that the tomb was empty?" "Witnesses saw it." "If the tomb was empty, someone must have entered it and removed the body." "No, the stone covering the entrance was a huge one [Matt. 27:60], and the first visitors to the tomb were women, who could not have removed it." "The disciples must have stolen it; they could have rolled the stone away." "No, because the chief priests and Pharisees induced Pilate to post a guard of soldiers at the tomb [utterly implausible] and the soldiers sealed it." "If such a miraculous event occurred, why didn't the soldiers tell us?" "The Sanhedrin bribed the soldiers to tell people that the disciples stole the body while they were asleep" (Matt. 27 and 28). The *Gospel of Peter* expands the story by having Jewish elders and scribes guard the tomb along with the Roman soldiers, after they seal it with seven seals.

Acts 1:3 adds another proof of a resurrected Jesus: To the apostles "he presented himself alive after his passion by many proofs, appearing to them during forty days." Yet another argument set forth was the claim that Jesus' resurrection fulfilled Old Testament prophecy. Acts 2:27 quotes Psalm 16:10 (15:10 LXX) as proof: "For you will not abandon my soul to Hades, nor let your holy one [i.e., "saint"] see corruption." Actually, the Psalmist was referring to himself, not Jesus. Translators who capitalize "holy one" are begging the question in favor of traditional Christian misinterpretation of the verse; there are no capital letters in ancient Hebrew, the language in which the Old Testament was written.

Why was the resurrection dated on "the third day"? Was that the date of Peter's vision, or was the date chosen to counterbalance Moses' receiving the Law on the third day (Exod. 19:16) or (the most probable) to fulfill Hosea 6:2, "After two days he will revive us; on the third day he will raise us up." The *Apocalypse of Zephaniah* in the Jewish Pseudepigrapha suggests that there may have been a Jewish belief that on the third day after death, souls enter heaven;[2] was that belief a factor?

Why was Jesus' resurrection set at sunrise (Luke 24:1)? That was the most sacred hour in many ancient religions, especially in the cults of sun gods, but not confined to them. Melqart was the national sun god of Tyre, a city-state in Phoenicia. Like numerous other vegetation deities in Greece and the Near East, he descended each autumn into the underworld in the earth, but each spring, at the vernal equinox, he arose from the underworld and arrived at Tyre *at sunrise*, returning from the dead as a youthful god again. Upon arrival he entered his temple and ascended his throne. Although there are differences between this myth and the story of Jesus' resurrection, they would not prevent early Christians from selecting a few useful features to incorporate in their own stories.[3] We should also observe that Jesus' resurrection occurs "on the first day of the week," Sunday, the day sacred to sun gods. Whoever originated the story of Jesus' resurrection on Sunday must have known the myths of a Near Eastern sun god, who may have been Melqart.

The belief that God had raised Jesus while leaving the other dead in their graves required explanation. The disciples must have thought, "If Jesus is raised from the dead, then the general resurrection has begun. But where are the others? God has raised Jesus first." Paul refers to this belief in 1 Corinthians 15:20 when he says, "Christ has been raised from the dead, the first fruits of those who have fallen asleep," that is, died. "But why did God raise Jesus first?," asked the disciples. One answer was that God did it to honor Jesus as the Messiah. Colossians 1:18 expresses this view concisely: The Son is "the firstborn from the dead, that in everything he might be pre-eminent." Another answer attaches even more significance to God's act, for thus he has empowered Jesus as the Messiah, the Christ; God has thus designated him as the "Son of God in power according to the Spirit of holiness by his resurrection from the dead" (Rom. 1:4).

Belief in Jesus' resurrection was crucial for the disciples and for the birth of the Church. Paul wrote: "If Christ has not been raised, then our preaching is in vain and your faith is in vain" (1 Cor. 15:14). Why was that faith so important? It was not a part of Jesus' basic message. Nevertheless the belief was vital for the disciples. While Jesus was alive, they believed that he would usher in the kingdom of God, but when he died without accomplishing that goal, they abandoned hope. The belief that he was alive again, however, restored their faith that he was the Christ and that the new kingdom was near. Other reasons were conceived later for the necessity of Jesus' resurrection. One was that Jesus' death and resurrection were necessary to atone for sins: "If Christ has not been raised, your faith is futile, and you are still in your sins" (1 Cor. 15:17). In the same chapter Paul argues that Jesus' resurrection demonstrates that there will be a general resurrection of the dead. Another claim was that it was necessary to fulfill prophecy (but there was no prophecy that the Christ would be raised from the dead!).

Belief in the resurrection of the body had presented a

problem in Judaism, namely, that since bodies die and decay, how can bodies raised from the grave live forever on earth? Pharisees solved the problem theoretically with the doctrine that at the resurrection the body will be transformed into an incorruptible body that will never decay. Some Hellenistic Jews, however, believed in the immortality of the soul, or spirit, in heaven. As Christianity expanded, both concepts of immortality existed among the churches, causing much debate. Although most Christians today believe in the immortality of the soul in heaven, many repeat—without realizing the inconsistency—"I believe in . . . the resurrection of the body" in the Apostles' Creed. Paul formulated a compromise doctrine: The human body "is sown [like seed sown in the ground] a physical body; it is raised a spiritual body" (1 Cor. 15:44).

By the second century the dualistic philosophy of spirit versus body had created disagreement on the nature of Jesus' resurrection. By then the empty tomb story was accepted by Christians generally, and it implied that Jesus had had a physical resurrection with his body transformed into an imperishable form. But dualism suggested a further development: his body must have been a spiritual body, just as Paul implied in his remarks on the general resurrection. But belief in the resurrection of any kind of body, even a spiritual one, was rejected by Gnostic Christians, whose thorough dualism would accept the immortality of only the soul, or spirit. Consequently they believed that Christ was a spirit and was never raised from a grave.

THE ASCENSION

Very soon after the disciples became convinced that Jesus was alive once more, another crisis of faith must have occurred. "Where is Jesus? Why don't we see him?"

The disciples concluded that God must have taken Jesus to heaven temporarily. The author of Acts sets the origin of the belief at the occasion of Jesus' ascension. As a cloud takes Jesus out of sight, two angels come to the disciples and say, "This Jesus, who was taken up from you into heaven, will come in the same way as you saw him go into heaven" (Acts 1:11). A similar belief about Elijah as an eschatological prophet was already in Judaism. As we have seen, the Bible teaches that Elijah was taken to heaven in a whirlwind and that he will return "before the great and terrible day of the Lord comes." Other Jewish heroes of the past were also thought to have ascended to heaven. Enoch pleased the Lord and was taken up from the earth (Sirach 44:16). Others so honored were Moses, Isaiah, Jeremiah, Baruch, and Ezra. These popular beliefs suggested a solution to the problem of the disappearance of Jesus: God has taken him to heaven too, but will soon send him back to complete his messianic task.

The early Christians did not agree on how soon Jesus ascended after his resurrection. In Acts he stays on earth for forty days (a popular number). In the *Gospel of Peter* and *Epistola Apostolorum* (2d c.) Jesus ascends on the day of his resurrection. *Epistle of Barnabas* 15:9 and the original Gospel of John (chapter 21 was added later) indicate that Jesus ascended a week after his resurrection ("on the eighth day" after something is a week later, for the days were counted at both ends of the span). The Valentinian and Ophite Gnostics claimed that the Christ remained on earth eighteen months to give them secret knowledge which he did not impart to other Christians. *Pistis Sophia* (3d c.) asserts that Jesus remained for eleven years teaching his disciples and stayed one more year to give secret knowledge to Gnostics.

In addition to explaining Jesus' disappearance, his ascension seemed to make Jesus superior to everyone except God. Ephesians 1:20-22 states that God raised Christ from the dead and made him sit at his right hand, "far above all rule and authority and power and dominion, and above every name that is named, not only in this age but also in the age to come; and he has put all things under his feet and has made him the head over all things for the church." This idea is also in Hebrews and 1 Peter. A related idea is in Acts 5:31: "God exalted him [Jesus] at his right hand as Ruler and Savior, to give repentance to Israel and forgiveness of sins" to Jews. In Romans 8:34 the ascension has enabled Jesus to be "at the right hand of God" where he now "intercedes for us"; that is, by sitting beside God in heaven, Jesus is now in a position to plead with God to forgive the sins of Christians.

Belief in Jesus' ascension created a new problem: The ascension of the Messiah was not in accord with Scripture or Jewish expectations of the Messiah. Consequently non-Christian Jews raised objections to the belief. In John 12:34 the crowd says, "We have heard from the Law that the Christ remains forever. How can you say that the Son of Man must be lifted up?" This was still a Jewish objection in the middle of the second century, when Trypho the Jew said to Justin the Christian: "Give us full reasons why he who you say has been crucified and has ascended into heaven, is the Christ of God . . . prove to us that this is he" (*Dial.* 39:7). Trypho also said: "You say many blasphemous things . . . that this man who was crucified . . . has ascended into heaven and comes again on earth, and is to be worshiped" (*Dial.* 38:1).

Jews asked for scriptural evidence, and Christians searched diligently for proof, but had difficulty in finding any. The best they could find at first was Psalm 110:1 (109:1 LXX):

> The Lord says to my lord:
> "Sit at my right hand,
> Until I make your enemies your footstool."

"My lord" in the psalm is the Israelite king, but early Christians interpreted the phrase as a reference to the Messiah.[4] The scribes and rabbis of the Pharisees interpreted the psalm very differently from the Christians, however, and better "proof" was needed. Some Jewish Christians thought that they had found it in the Jewish sectarian belief in a Son of Man Messiah. We will examine that subject in chapter 12.

THE PRIMITIVE CHURCH

Our main sources for the history of the founding of the earliest Christian communities, or churches, are the Book of Acts and Paul's letters to the Galatians and Corinthians. When both Paul and Acts report the same incident, they sometimes disagree. In such cases Paul's account is to be preferred because it is first-hand (he was there) and because the author of Acts employed some literary devices that can easily mislead us. He composed speeches which he put in the mouths of Peter, Stephen, and Paul that represent later views in the churches more than those of the alleged speaker. Composing speeches and putting them in the mouths of historical persons was a practice of some ancient writers. Paul's accounts of his conversion and of his conference with leaders of the Jerusalem church are more trustworthy than the accounts in Acts. Comparison of Acts with Paul's accounts give us insight into the techniques and tendencies of the author of Acts, which in turn aid us in evaluating the rest of Acts.

THE JERUSALEM CHURCH

When the disciples became convinced that Jesus was alive again, they returned to Jerusalem because it was expected to be the capitol city of the new kingdom of God. At first the disciples and the women who had followed Jesus met in the upper room of a house in Jerusalem and "with one accord devoted themselves to prayer" (Acts 1). They were awaiting the imminent appearance of Jesus and the kingdom of God. Under those circumstances we would not expect that in the very earliest days of the church the disciples would engage in much missionary work, and the first speech ascribed to Peter in Acts is addressed "to the brethren," not to potential converts. Acts mentions Jesus' mother and brothers as among those who gathered in the upper room; eventually they (or at least his brother James) did believe that Jesus was the Messiah, but did they change their opinion so soon? We also wonder how many followers Jesus had. The meeting in an upper room indicates a small number, but Acts 1:15 gives the number of brethren as about 120. Jesus probably had had more followers, but some were disillusioned by the crucifixion, some temporarily, some permanently. We must remember too that the author of Acts, writing at least fifty years after the crucifixion, lacked sufficient information.

When the disciples resumed their missionary work, which had ceased temporarily after the crucifixion, they called listeners to repentance (Acts 2:38; 3:19). Listeners' doubts that Jesus was the Christ and that he had been raised from the dead forced the apostles to shift their preaching toward putting the doubts to rest. According to Acts the function of the Twelve was to be "a witness to his resurrection" (1:22). More and more, the preaching stressed that Jesus was and *is* the Messiah. "And every day in the Temple and at home they did not cease teaching and preaching Jesus as the Christ" (Acts 5:42). The preaching included the belief that he will come again (Greek: *parousia*) soon; it continued to emphasize the choice between eternal salvation and eternal punishment. The *kerygma,* or proclamation of the apostles, according to Acts 2, included the claim that God had performed "mighty works and wonders and signs" through Jesus and that Jesus was delivered to be crucified according to God's plan and foreknowledge. This developed form of the gospel must have taken several years to formulate. The preaching was effective, and many Jews in Jerusalem joined the apostles. Priests joined (Acts 6:7), and some of them probably were Essenes. Some Pharisees also joined (Acts 15:5), and surely uneducated "people of the land" as well.

"And all who believed were together and had all things in common; and they sold their possessions and goods and distributed them to all [members] as any had need" (Acts 2:44-45; cf. 4:32-37). Food was distributed daily (6:1-2). Why did the Jerusalem church adopt the practice of communal living, the oldest and simplest form of communism? As far as we know, Jesus did not teach it and the disciples did not practice it during his lifetime.

The Essenes at Qumran practiced sharing all things in common. They who join "shall bring all their mind and their strength and their property into the Community of God" (1QS

1:11-12). Josephus states that the Essenes live the same kind of life as the Pythagoreans,[1] and we know that both groups had two categories of membership: trainee, and full member.[2] Essenes lived elsewhere in Palestine too, for Josephus says "many live in every city."[3] In fact, the very city in which the first Christian community arose probably had a major section inhabited by Essenes, for Josephus mentions an "Essene gate" in the First Wall of Jerusalem.[4] That gate probably was the entrance to an Essene quarter in Jerusalem, as some modern archaeologists are convinced. Archaeologists have excavated a gate in the First Wall near the southwest corner of that wall; it could be the Essene gate.[5] If so, the Essenes in Jerusalem could easily have heard and been persuaded by apostolic preaching. Since the Essenes at Qumran practiced common ownership, the Essenes in Jerusalem very probably did too. There was a special reason why Essenes would be attracted to Jewish-Christian preaching: they too believed that they were living in the "end of days" (CD 4:4; 6:11) and that God would soon establish his rule over the earth. Both the Jerusalem Christians and the Essenes punished members who refused to donate to the commune their property or the cash from its sale. Acts 5 reports that Ananias and his wife Sapphira withheld a portion of the proceeds from the sale of land, and God caused them to fall down and die. If an Essene lied about his wealth, he was demoted for a year and deprived of one-fourth of his food allowance (1QS 6:25).

Other similarities between the two groups also indicate probable Essene influence on the Jerusalem church. Both groups referred to their own beliefs and practices as "the Way." The Essenes called themselves "the poor" (1QpHab 12:3; 1QM 11) and Paul referred to the Jerusalem Christians in that manner (Gal. 2:10). The whole congregation, or membership, is called "the many" repeatedly in the Essenes' Manual of Discipline, as is the Jerusalem Christian community in Acts 6:5 (though often translated as "the whole multitude," the literal Greek is "all the many"). Matthias was chosen by lot to replace Judas, and at Qumran the lot determined a candidate's admission into the community (1QS 6:16). The formulas introducing Old Testament quotations in the part of Acts that describes the Jerusalem church are very similar to those in the Dead Sea scrolls, as Father Joseph Fitzmyer has observed.[6] Examples are "it is written" and "the prophet says." Both sects were especially devout in offering prayers. Both groups, contrary to the

Pharisees, believed that God's Holy Spirit was again active in the world as it had been in the days of the prophets.

Although Essenes joined the Christian community in Jerusalem in sufficient numbers to influence it considerably, they did not convert it into an Essene camp or community. Essenes became Christians, and not vice versa. The Christians differed from the Essenes in that they expected the return of one Messiah, Jesus, not the coming of two Messiahs (a priest and a king). Unlike the community at Qumran, the church lacked complex organization. Although priests and Levites joined the church (Acts 6:7), they no longer functioned as such; no priest blessed the bread and wine at meals, contrary to the practice at Qumran. Unlike the Christians (Acts 2:42), the Essenes did not refer to their meals as "breaking bread," as far as we know.

Communal sharing in the Jerusalem community may not have lasted long, for Paul had to collect a fund from his churches to help "the poor" in that church. The arrangement in Jerusalem was impractical because the Christians there consumed the funds instead of investing them in production. In contrast, the Essenes at Qumran owned and farmed land. Wealthy Christians may have been few at Jerusalem, and sharing was not popular with some of them, as the story of Ananias and Sapphira illustrates.

Apparently at least a portion of members' wealth was shared in Rome a century later. Justin wrote that Christians "now bring what we have into common (koinon), sharing to all in need" (1 Apol. 14). He also said: "And they who are well to do and willing, give what each thinks fit; and what is collected is deposited with the president, who succors the orphans and widows and those who, through sickness or any other cause, are in want, and those who are in bonds, and the strangers sojourning among us, and in a word, takes care of all who are in need" (1 Apol. 67).

Herod Agrippa I persecuted some leaders of the Jerusalem church in A.D. 44. He killed James, a son of Zebedee, and imprisoned Peter. The reason given in Acts 12 is that "it pleased the Jews." Eventually Peter and James' brother John became martyrs too. James' and John's martyrdom is alluded to in Mark 10 where Jesus is represented as telling them that they will drink the cup that he drinks and will be baptized with the same baptism as he; here both cup and baptism symbolize martyrdom. The early martyrdom of Peter and the two sons of

Zebedee is the probable reason that they are named together so often in the synoptic gospels. As martyrs they became heroes in the early church.

Another James, Jesus' brother, became a leader in the Jerusalem church (Gal. 1:19; 2:12). He strictly observed the Law, opposing Paul's policy of eating with gentiles and not requiring the circumcision of male converts. Peter yielded to James, but Paul did not. In A.D. 62 the high priest Ananus accused James and some others before the Sanhedrin, charging that they were breaking the Law. For this the accused were stoned to death;[7] the accusation seems strange considering James' previous zeal to enforce the Law. Was Ananus' charge false, or had James become less observant of the Law as a result of contact with Paul and his churches?

The Jerusalem church did not join the Jewish revolt against Rome in A.D. 66-70, probably because its members expected that with God's help, Jesus at his return would dispose of the Romans. Instead it fled to Pella, a gentile city east of the Jordan River.[8] Evidently it migrated to be safe from Jewish nationalists, especially the Sicarii, who murdered their Jewish brethren who refused to join the rebellion.

"THE HELLENISTS"

We now return to the early days of the Jerusalem church. Its members divided into two groups: "the Hebrews" and "the Hellenists" (Acts 6:1). The Hebrews, with the twelve disciples as leaders, were Jewish Christians who spoke Aramaic, and the Hellenists were Jewish Christians who spoke Greek.[9] The Hebrews included the disciples of Jesus and evidently controlled the Christian community. The Hellenists complained that the widows in their group were not given a fair share of the food that the Hebrews distributed daily. So "the Twelve" called a meeting of "the many of the disciples" (literal Greek text) and said, "It is not right that we should give up preaching the word of God to serve tables" (Acts 6:2). At their request the Hellenists selected seven members of their own group to perform the chore. The Hellenists preached too, however.

The preaching of Stephen, one of the seven, was so unorthodox in Jewish sight that non-Christian Jews had him arrested and tried by the Sanhedrin. It condemned Stephen and had him stoned to death.

> And on that day a great persecution arose against the church in Jerusalem, and they were all scattered throughout the region of Judea and Samaria, except the apostles. . . . Now those who were scattered went about preaching the word (Acts 8:1, 4).

"The apostles," who evidently were "the Hebrews" in Acts 6, were not persecuted. Thus the disciples who had personally known Jesus evidently preached a gospel that was not too offensive to Jewish officials. On the other hand, the Hellenists, who had not known Jesus and had been influenced by Greek culture, were too radical in their views for Jerusalem leaders to tolerate. What were their radical beliefs?

According to Acts 6 the main charge against Stephen was that he spoke against the Law. Did the Hellenists assert that the Law no longer need be observed because the Messiah has come? If so, that belief could cause persecution and could be the source of Paul's similar stance—after all, Paul evidently heard Stephen preach (Acts 8:1). In Judaism observance of the Law was generally regarded as absolutely essential.

Did Stephen believe that Jesus was the supernatural Son of Man, as Acts 7:55-56 indicates with its story of his heavenly vision? The belief did not come from Jesus, as we will find later. Is it the basis of the charge that Stephen spoke "blasphemous words against . . . God" (Acts 6:11)? That is possible, for in the Jewish background the Son of Man is a divine figure; identifying the human Jesus with him would be seen as a threat to monotheism. The belief may have originated later, for Paul does not mention it. On the other hand, Stephen was the leader of the Hellenists, and the belief is prominent in Mark and Q, which were written by converts of the Hellenists.

The "speech" ascribed to Stephen in Acts 7 has nothing to do with the charge against him. It is a condemnation of non-Christian Jews and their ancestors for persecuting prophets, including Jesus. It places on Jews all the responsibility for Jesus' death, a later idea, and many New Testament scholars rightly regard it as a composition by the author of Luke-Acts.

Marcel Simon, while Dean of the Faculty of Letters at the University of Strasbourg, pointed out six similarities between the story of Jesus' trial and death and the story of Stephen's passion.[10] Dean Simon rightly saw the six parallels as evidence that the author of Luke-Acts deliberately portrayed

Stephen's martyrdom as similar to that of Jesus, and that therefore we should be wary of some details in his account.

The first doctrinal division within the church saved Christianity from early extinction. Considering that the Jerusalem church lasted only a few decades, the Christian movement would have died if it had not spread outside of the city. The Hellenists, however, founded new churches elsewhere that survived after the Jerusalem church disappeared. If Paul had not heard Stephen preach and observed his stoning, he might never have become a Christian and established numerous gentile churches.

The second major consequence of the Hellenists' separation from the Jerusalem church was that their converts—not Jesus' disciples—produced the synoptic gospels. We wish that the Jerusalem church had written a gospel. If it had, what would its contents be?

THE HELLENIST CHURCHES

The Hellenist Jewish Christians who were scattered because of the persecution that arose over Stephen carried their version of the Christian gospel into cities in Judea, Samaria, and Galilee. They established Christian communities there and also in Antioch and Damascus in Syria and in Phoenicia, Cyprus, and even in Cyrene in northern Africa;[11] this suggests that some of the Hellenists may have originally lived in those cities before coming to Jerusalem. Little is known about the founding of these churches.

At first "the word" was proclaimed only to Jews (Acts 11:19), but Philip converted Samaritans (Acts 8:5). The Jerusalem church became concerned when it learned that Samaritans "had received the word of God," so it sent Peter and John to investigate. The reason given in Acts is that Peter and John came to pray that they might receive the Holy Spirit. A major reason, however, probably was that Samaritans were being brought into membership in the Jewish-Christian movement. Palestinian Jews regarded Samaritans as outsiders to be shunned, and did not want to accept them as religious brothers.

Antioch was the first church to accept gentiles into membership, thanks to the missionary work of some Jewish Christians who came there from Cyprus and Cyrene (Acts

11:19-26). Thus the mission to gentiles originated not with Jesus (contrary to Mark 16:15, a third-century creation added to the text), not with the church his disciples founded in Jerusalem, not with the Hellenists, but with Jewish-Christian converts from outside of Palestine. The Jerusalem church was astonished at this further expansion of the Christian mission, for gentiles were even farther outside of Judaism than the Samaritans, who at least shared some Jewish traditions, including the Torah as their Bible. When news of the admission of gentiles reached the Jerusalem church, it sent Barnabas to Antioch to investigate. He was pleased with what he saw, and thereafter he was attached to the church at Antioch instead of the one at Jerusalem.

The story in Acts 10:1--11:18 depicts the conversion of some gentiles at Caesarea in Samaria. According to it, Cornelius, a Roman centurion, had a vision in which an angel told him to send men to bring to him Simon Peter, who was at Joppa. Cornelius was "a devout man who feared God with all his household, gave alms liberally to all the [Jewish] people, and prayed constantly to God" (10:2). He was a God-fearer, a gentile who worshiped the Jewish God, Yahweh, and attended synagogue services, but did not become a Jew. Peter came and preached to Cornelius and his assembled kinsmen and friends. The Holy Spirit fell upon them, causing them to speak in tongues and extol God. Therefore Peter ordered that they be baptized, even though they were gentiles.

Just how much credence we should give to this story is debatable, for it contains legendary elements and Christian apologetics, namely, a rationale for the admission of gentiles and an effort to promote Christian unity by reconciling Peter to the mission to the gentiles. The conversion of a God-fearing Roman centurion and his household at Caesarea is probably historical, however, but it must have occurred after, and not before, the admission of gentiles at Antioch, since gentiles were first converted there according to Acts 11. Also, if Peter had converted gentiles at Caesarea, why would the Jerusalem church be disturbed when gentiles were admitted at Antioch? Into the story about Cornelius another story (Acts 10:9-16) has been inserted. In it a heavenly voice tells Peter three times that he should eat all kinds of animals, reptiles, and birds (gentile meats), for God has made them all clean.

The purpose of the stories is to counteract three conservative tenets based on the Law: Jewish Christians should not associate with gentile Christians; they should not eat gentile foods; they should not accept uncircumcised male gentiles into church membership. The story's solution to these problems is to assert that Christian possession of the Holy Spirit replaces the need to observe the Law. Another purpose is to depict Peter as completely won over to Paul's position on the Law; that picture of Peter is contrary to his withdrawal from eating with gentiles at Antioch, reported in Galatians 2. The author of Acts tried to counteract that incident by relating that the angel told Peter to eat all kinds of meat. Presumably the Jerusalem church would not object to the admission of gentiles provided they became Jews and obeyed the Jewish Law. The Antioch church was lenient in respect to observing the Torah, and its Jewish sectarian background was probably mainly responsible, though its early admission of gentiles may have been a factor.

Judging from the favorable portrayal of the tax collectors, or publicans, in the synoptic gospels, some of them must have been among the early converts to Christianity. They were local men, including Jews, who collected taxes for the Romans. They were often corrupt and were generally hated. The typical Jewish attitude toward them is expressed in the Mishnah: "If taxgatherers enter a house, [all that is in it] becomes unclean" (*Tohorot* 7:6).

PAUL

For knowledge of Paul we shall rely more on his letters than on the Book of Acts.[12] Saul, later called Paul, was a Hellenistic, Greek-speaking Jew who grew up in Tarsus, a city in Cilicia in Asia Minor. Judging from his letters he was well educated in Jewish Scriptures and Greek philosophy. He was a Pharisee (Phil. 3:5), and he may have gone to Jerusalem to study the Law under a rabbi (cf. Acts 22:3). Motivated by zeal for the Law,[13] he energetically persecuted the church.[14] Contrary to Acts, Paul could not have obtained letters from the high priest authorizing him to arrest Christians in synagogues in Damascus and bring them to Jerusalem, for the high priest and the Sanhedrin had no jurisdiction outside of Jerusalem.

Paul describes his conversion as a visionary experience in which he thought he was carried up to the third heaven, where he "heard things that cannot be told, which man may not utter" (2 Cor. 12:1-4). He also describes the experience as the time when God "was pleased to reveal his Son to me" (Gal. 1:16). Paul may have been referring to that experience when he wrote that he had seen "Jesus our Lord" (1 Cor. 9:1). The three accounts in Acts of his conversion [15] differ from Paul's and from each other. This event, which occurred around A.D. 35, transformed Paul from a zealous opponent to a zealous proponent of Christianity. Subsequently he believed that he had an "abundance of revelations" (2 Cor. 12:7), in which either God's Spirit (1 Cor. 2:10) or the spiritual Jesus (2 Cor. 12:8-9; Gal. 1:12) spoke to him.

Soon after his conversion Paul went to Arabia and then returned to Damascus, where the Nabatean governor tried to seize him, but he escaped (2 Cor. 11:32). (Acts 9:23 substitutes "the Jews" for the governor in order to place the blame on them.) Three years later Paul spent fifteen days with Peter in Jerusalem and saw James, Jesus' brother, but none of the other apostles. Next he spent about ten years in missionary activity in Syria and Cilicia. After the church at Antioch began to accept gentiles into membership, Paul was a member of it and stoutly defended its policies regarding gentiles and the Law.

Descriptions of the missionary journeys of Paul, Barnabas, and others are abundant in current literature and will not be repeated here. Both Paul and the Jerusalem church regarded his work as mainly a mission to gentiles, whereas the mission of Peter and the Jerusalem church was to Jews (Gal. 2:9). According to Acts, however, Paul and Barnabas began their first mission by preaching in the synagogues of the Jews (13:5). The congregations included "Greeks" as well as Jews; the Greeks were God-fearers. The gentile God-fearers must have played an important role in the growth of Christianity in the first century. They were already acquainted with Jewish messianic beliefs and the Jewish Scriptures, so they could more readily understand and accept Christian preaching than could other gentiles. They were an important bridge between the Jewish and gentile worlds. Three main factors prepared the way for Christianity's transition from a Jewish sect to an international religion: (1) the assimilation of Hellenistic ideas by some Jews; (2) the assimilation of Jewish thought by some gentiles;[16] Paul's freeing gentile converts from obeying the Jewish Law and its requirement of circumcision. At first Paul and Barnabas preached primarily to Jews; the preaching to gentiles occurred merely because gentiles happened to be in the congregation in the synagogue. The unorthodox preaching of Paul and Barnabas aroused so much Jewish antagonism that the apostles "turned to the gentiles" (13:46), preaching to them outside of the synagogues.

After Paul and Barnabas returned to Antioch from their missionary journey, some men from Judea came there and taught the brethren, "Unless you are circumcised according to the custom of Moses, you cannot be saved." This precipitated vigorous debate, and the Antioch church sent Paul and Barnabas to Jerusalem to settle the issue. On the way they reported their conversion of gentiles to the brethren in Phoenicia and Samaria, and no doubt explained their position on the Law. At Jerusalem they explained their policy to the church leaders, Peter and the two sons of Zebedee, James and John. (Gal. 2; Acts 15). Paul and Barnabas had brought with them Titus, a Greek convert, and the Jerusalem leaders did not require him to be circumcised. However, some Pharisees who were Christians (Paul calls them "false brethren" and "the circumcision party") argued that all male gentile Christians must be circumcised. Paul did not submit to their pressure, and the Jerusalem leaders decided at this "Apostolic Council," as the meeting has been called, that Paul and Barnabas should continue their mission to the gentiles, while the Jerusalem church would continue its mission to Jews. They requested that Paul take up a collection in his churches for the poor members of the Jerusalem church. He agreed and subsequently took up a collection for them (Rom. 15:25-26).

Later Peter came to Antioch and ate with gentile Christians, just as Paul and Barnabas—and presumably the other Jewish Christians at Antioch—were doing. But James sent a delegation from the circumcision party condemning such transgression of the Law. This James was not the son of Zebedee, but the brother of Jesus. He had succeeded the three disciples of Jesus as leader of the Jerusalem church after Herod Agrippa I persecuted it during his reign over Judea (41-44). Under pressure from the delegation, Peter and Barnabas withdrew from the table fellowship with gentiles. For this Paul scathingly denounced Peter.

Paul had never known Jesus and had even persecuted Christians before his conversion. How could he be so bold as to disagree with Jesus' brother and with the church Jesus' disciples had founded? The answer is that Paul got his courage from his conviction that his beliefs were founded on spiritual messages he had received from the risen Jesus. He even boasted that he had received his gospel not from man, but through "a revelation of Jesus Christ" (Gal. 1:12).

Some of Paul's churches failed to adhere to the gospel he preached to them, and he felt compelled to redirect them to the proper course. Members of the church in Corinth were divided into parties saying "I belong to Paul" or "I belong to Apollos" or "I belong to Cephas"; Paul appealed to them to stop thinking that way and to be united (1 Cor. 1). The divisions apparently were caused by other traveling apostles who proclaimed a different form of the gospel than Paul's (2 Cor. 11:4). We have seen that "Judaizers," as scholars have called them, came to Antioch to persuade the church there to require circumcision; they succeeded in Galatia, causing Paul to write Galatians to them and scold them for yielding. Some Corinthian Christians preferred "wisdom" to Paul's gospel; the wisdom may have been preached by itinerant Cynic philosophers. Paul's response was to attack "the wisdom of the world" and to extol spiritual wisdom from the Spirit of God. He boasted that "the spiritual man judges all things, but is himself to be judged by no one" (1 Cor. 2:15)!

The converts in Corinth retained some of their pagan practices, and Paul wrote 1 Corinthians to correct them. Some members were still eating meat that pagans had sacrificed to their gods, for such meat was available at meat markets, and some ate and drank too much at the Lord's Supper. Paul rebuked them in chapters 8, 10, and 11. The tension over meat sacrificed to "idols" (pagan gods) was a natural consequence of having gentile converts who still thought as pagans, just as tension over the observance of the Law was the result of members who still thought as Torah-observing Jews.

Paul, the Torah, and Ethics

Whether Stephen spoke against the Law as a whole or only parts of it (Acts 6:11-14) is not known. Paul, however, states plainly his own position on the Torah. In Galatians he concedes that it has been useful in the past, for "the Law was our custodian until [the] Christ came. But now that [Christian] faith has come, we are no longer under a custodian" (3:24-25). (The sectarians who wrote the The Testaments of the Twelve Patriarchs had in effect, already broken away from the Jewish Law by adopting the Stoic universal law.) Regardless of whatever was Stephen's opinion of the Law, it was Paul's influence that transformed Christianity by separating it from the Law. Paul thereby opened the door to the influx of gentiles and the eventual establishment of Christianity as a new religion instead of merely a new Jewish sect. Paul himself, however, regarded the Christian faith as a movement within the fold of Judaism.

Paul's theology is difficult to state concisely and with certainty, for some of his statements seem ambiguous. Basic in Paul's theology is the Greek word *pistis*, which has various meanings. In some passages it refers to belief. "The faith" is something that Paul preaches (Gal. 1:23). Hearing the gospel with "faith" causes Christians to receive the Spirit (Gal. 3:2); "faith" is something that has been revealed (Gal. 3:23). Justification by faith makes Christians righteous and ensures their salvation; faith includes belief in Jesus' atoning death and his resurrection (1 Cor. 15:14, 17). *Pistis* followed by the preposition *pros* probably meant "trust" in God in 1 Thessalonians 1:8, although in verses 9-10 it is associated with certain beliefs. A debated question is whether *pistis tou Christou* means Christ's faithfulness to God or Christians' belief in Jesus.

In addition to spiritual and doctrinal matters, Paul gave advice on many aspects of Christian conduct, especially in 1 Corinthians. He opposed sexual sins, preferred celibacy, opposed taking into pagan courts the disputes among Christians, and gave advice on conduct and worship in the church. The basic missionary message he had preached to these gentiles is indicated in 1 Thessalonians 1:9-10, where he has received reports "how you turned to God from idols, to serve a living and true God, and to wait for his Son [who will come] from heaven, whom he raised from the dead, Jesus who saves us from the wrath to come." Paul believed that ethical conduct is required in order to enter the kingdom of God: "We exhorted each one of you [Christians at Thessalonica] . . . to lead a life worthy of God, who calls you into his own kingdom and glory" (1 Thess. 2:11-12).

Paul's primary basis for ethics is not the Torah; this is a logical result of his breaking away from it. In Paul's theology the Christian does not become righteous ("justified") in God's sight by doing good deeds ("works") commanded by the Law. Instead, it is "faith in Jesus Christ" that does this (Gal. 2:16;

Rom. 3:23-26). And how does faith accomplish this? By belief that Jesus is the Christ and that his death atones for one's sins. But if one does not believe this, he is still a sinner. Faith, not works, is the basis of salvation.

Even faith is not the guide for daily moral conduct in Paul's theology; it is dualistic mysticism. Other forms of dualism were applied to ethics in Judaism: God versus Satan (Old Testament); the good inclination versus the evil inclination within each person (Essenes and Pharisees). To Paul, the dualism is between the human physical body, or "flesh," and the Holy Spirit of God. This idea is an adaptation of the philosophic dualism in the Hellenistic world, especially in Pythagoreanism, Platonism, and Gnosticism. The Spirit is a moral guide because it dwells within each Christian: "Do you not know that you are God's temple and that God's Spirit dwells in you?" (1 Cor. 3:16). The best way to describe Paul's theory is to let him speak for himself:

> But I say, walk by the Spirit, and do not gratify the desires of the flesh. For the desires of the flesh are against the Spirit, and the desires of the Spirit are against the flesh; for these are opposed to each other, to prevent you from doing what you would. But if you are led by the Spirit, you are not under the Law. Now the works of the flesh are plain: immorality, impurity, licentiousness, idolatry, sorcery, enmity, strife, jealousy, anger, selfishness, dissension, party spirit, envy, drunkenness, carousing, and the like. I warn you, as I warned you before, that they who do such things shall not inherit the kingdom of God. But the fruit of the Spirit is love, joy, peace, patience, kindness, goodness, faithfulness, gentleness, self-control; against such there is no law. And those who belong to Christ Jesus have crucified the flesh with its passions and desires. If we live by the Spirit, let us also walk by the Spirit. Let us have no self-conceit, no provoking of one another, no envy of one another (Gal. 5:16-26).

Paul's spiritual, non-Law basis for moral conduct is the very antithesis of the Law basis of Jesus and the synoptic gospels.

ALEXANDRIA AND ROME

The Book of Acts does not mention the founding of the

churches in Alexandria and Rome, but it does imply that a Christian community existed early in Alexandria. It reports in chapters 18-19 that Apollos, a Jewish Christian who was a native of Alexandria, came to Ephesus and Corinth when Paul too was an itinerant missionary. Presumably Apollos was from the Alexandrian church. Like Philip's converts in Samaria, they knew only "the baptism of John," which did not bestow the Holy Spirit.

The earliest document we have from the Alexandrian church is the Epistle to the Hebrews written to a church that was suffering persecution, probably the church at Rome. The date may be that of Nero's persecution (A.D. 64), for the Temple is described as currently functioning (10:1; etc.), or that of Domitian's persecution in A.D. 95. It cannot be later because *1 Clement* quotes from it. It employs the Alexandrian allegorical method of interpreting the Bible, and it reveals that the church's theology and christology have been influenced by the Alexandrian type of mysticism. The Gospel of John probably was written in Alexandria too, around A.D. 100. It combines some traditional Jewish-Christian ideas with semi-Gnostic mystical thought. Professors Martyn at Union Theological Seminary and Culpepper at Southern Baptist Theological Seminary have called attention to the fact that this gospel was produced in a Christian community in severe conflict with the local synagogue, which had excommunicated members who became Christians, thereby forcing them to form their own religious community, a church.[17] A similar process must have occurred in some other cities also.

A thriving Christian community already existed in Rome when Paul wrote to it around A.D. 56. Judging from Paul's letter to it, the Roman church was composed of Jewish and gentile Christians, with the latter predominant. Paul tried to unite the two groups. It was not founded by Peter nor, as fond tradition would have it, was he ever bishop there; in fact, no church had a bishop during Peter's lifetime, for the office was a later development.[18] We have mentioned that the Roman church suffered some persecution under the emperors Nero and Domitian. In Domitian's persecution Flavius Clemens, a Christian who was a Roman consul and belonged to the Flavian family, was executed and his wife banished from the city. The fact that these preeminent Romans were Christians then tells us that, although Christianity began with poor, uneducated disciples, before the end of the first century it had influential members in Rome. Persecutions did not stop the conversion of wealthy and prominent men and women, a significant step in the direction of the eventual triumph of Christianity over paganism. 1 Peter, a letter written from the church at Rome to churches in Asia Minor that were suffering persecution under Emperor Hadrian (A.D. 112), shows some concern for ethical teaching (3:8-9) and no interest in encouraging spiritual ecstasy.

Although reliable evidence is scarce, we can see that Christianity developed differently in the various Christian communities in the first century. The Jerusalem church, with disciples who had accompanied Jesus, must have held some beliefs close to his, but it has left no records. The Hellenists and their converts founded other churches in Palestine and Syria; in many of them ecstasy, spiritual revelations, and speaking in tongues added to the variety of beliefs. Paul combined that practice with his own rationale of Christianity and promoted his beliefs in the gentile churches he founded in Asia Minor and Greece. In the next few decades after Paul some Jewish-Christian churches in Palestine and Syria combined some Christian traditions dealing with church problems with ideas and ethics inherited from sectarian Judaism; these churches produced the synoptic gospels and the Q source material in Matthew and Luke. The author of Matthew, and probably his local church too, sought to restore observance of the Written and Oral Law, which Paul had tried to discard. The Roman church became famous for its more rational and more highly organized approach to religion.

Although we speak of "the church at Antioch," "the church at Ephesus," and so on, in the larger cities Christians must soon have had several congregations, which met separately in house-churches. The house of Prisca and Aquila, for example, was used as a church (Rom. 16:3-5). The practice of meeting in houses occurred also in pagan religions. At least two houses in Rome had a chapel in them for the worship of the mystery cult god Mithras; their remains exist today under the churches of San Clemente and Santa Prisca.

Jewish Christians later built churches, which probably were in the form of synagogues. In James (end of first century) the "church" (*ekklesia*, 5:14) is also a "synagogue" (*sunagoge*, 2:2).

BAPTISM AND SPIRIT

BAPTISM

At first Christian baptism must have been similar to that of John the Baptist. In chapter 5 we concluded that Jesus probably baptized, continuing the Baptist's practice. And if Jesus baptized, his disciples would naturally do so too after his death. In fact, that is the only reasonable explanation of the practice in the Jerusalem church, where the disciples baptized and associated the ritual with repentance.

Function

As early Christianity grew, the nature and function of Christian baptism changed, with considerable variation among the churches because of the influence of different members with different backgrounds.

If at its initial stage it was like John's, the theory underlying it was that it cleansed the body at the same time that repentance cleansed the soul. Repentance caused God to forgive one's sins. In a more developed stage, however, baptism as well as repentance is needed to cause God to forgive one's sins, as in a speech ascribed to Peter: "Repent, and be baptized every one of you in the name of Jesus Christ for the forgiveness of your sins, and you will receive the gift of the Holy Spirit" (Acts 2:38).

The belief that baptism conferred the Holy Spirit is a later idea. It was not a function of baptism with John, and if Jesus continued John's mission, his baptism did not include that feature either. Also, if Jesus baptized, he surely must have baptized his own disciples, but according to Acts 2, they did not receive the Holy Spirit until the day of Pentecost, and then baptism was not involved in the process. It is true that Acts 2:38 depicts baptism as having this function, but that verse represents Christian thought later than the primitive days of the Jerusalem church.

Further evidence is supplied by churches established by the Hellenists. According to Acts 8, the Samaritan Christians at first did not believe that baptism conferred the Holy Spirit, and they were converts of Philip, one of the Hellenists who had been converted by Jesus' disciples in Jerusalem.

> Now when the apostles at Jerusalem heard that Samaria had received the word of God, they sent to them Peter and John, who came down and prayed for them that they might receive the Holy Spirit; for it had not yet fallen on any of them, but they had only been baptized in the name of the Lord Jesus. Then they laid their hands on them and they received the Holy Spirit (Acts 8:14-17).

The church in Alexandria has left additional evidence. Like the Samaritan church, it was founded by Hellenists (or converts of the Hellenists); it was not founded by the Jerusalem church which apparently founded no new churches. At first it too did not practice spiritual baptism. Evidence: Apollos came to Ephesus from there and he "had been instructed in the way of the Lord" and he "taught accurately the things concerning Jesus." Yet "he knew only the baptism of John," which did not confer the Spirit, so the Christians Priscilla and Aquila took him aside and "expounded to him the way of God more accurately" (Acts 18:24-26). Previously Apollos had made some converts in Ephesus, and they too had been baptized into John's baptism and had not received the Holy Spirit. So Paul baptized them and laid his hands on them "and they spoke in tongues and prophesied" (Acts 19:1-7). Since "the baptism of John" here is Christian, this evidence indicates that the baptism practiced by the Hellenists was the same type as John's, which did not transmit the Spirit. After Christians added that feature to baptism, they separated the new form from the original by calling the latter "the baptism of John"; i.e., it was like John's. Apollos also had converts in the Corinthian church (1 Cor. 1:12).

The Jerusalem church provides evidence too. The Pentecost story in Acts 2 depicts it as receiving the Holy Spirit apart from baptism. The recipients are disciples of Jesus. We will examine the story when we discuss the Spirit. The point to note here is that the author of the story did not think that the original apostles received the Spirit through baptism.

The author of Acts tries to connect baptism figuratively

with the reception of the Spirit on Pentecost by referring to that event as a baptism of the disciples. He ascribes to the risen Lord Jesus these words: "For John baptized with water, but before many days you will be baptized with the Holy Spirit" (1:5). The author also assigns to Peter a saying in which "baptism" refers metaphorically to descent of the Spirit while Peter is preaching (11:16). These waterless "baptisms" are really independent of the Christian baptisms with water, but the author of Acts tried to reconcile with each other two different ideas of how the Spirit was received. Therefore he labeled any reception of the Spirit a "baptism."

The earliest certain appearance of the belief that baptism bestowed the Holy Spirit is in Paul: "For by one Spirit we were all baptized into one body," the body of Christ (1 Cor. 12:13). Where did Paul get this concept of baptism? The author of Acts depicts the apostles at Jerusalem as teaching it, but this is probably an anachronism. The idea was not in the Jewish environment or taught by John the Baptist or Jesus. One theory is that some Christians introduced it because of the pericope in the synoptic gospels that Jesus received the Spirit when he was baptized. This theory is weak because the story of Jesus' baptism is late in origin and is the result of the use of the *Testament of Levi*. Another possible source is the influence of the Mithraic religion. Baptism was a feature in its initiation rites too, and the ancient *Mithras Liturgy* reveals that initiation into that cult was accompanied by the reception of the Spirit of the god Mithras. In the *Liturgy* the initiate prays that "I may be born again in thought and the sacred spirit breathe in me."[1] The cult was popular with Roman soldiers, and we know that Roman soldiers joined Christianity early (Cornelius, the Roman centurion, Acts 10; friendly mention of Romans in Mark).

The belief that Christians always received the Spirit as a result of baptism had a serious flaw; namely, sometimes they did not receive it and begin to prophesy and speak in tongues. In the third century the church father Origen lamented that "not all who are bathed in water are forthwith bathed with the Holy Spirit."[2]

In the next change in the function of baptism, repentance was omitted, and baptism itself made one a new sinless person, guaranteed a blessed immortality.

In order to understand this new interpretation of Christian baptism, we turn to the gentile environment with its mystery religions. Many Hellenistic mystery cults existed all around the Mediterranean. In some, water played an important role in their initiation rituals. In the cult of Demeter and Kore (Persephone), also known as the Eleusianian Mysteries, there were five stages of initiation; the first consisted of ritual purification. This was performed by a priest who sprinkled the *mystes* (initiate) with water, or poured water on his head from a pitcher, or immersed him or her in the Ilissos River near Athens. This stage was in the Lesser Mysteries, a preparation for the annual Greater Mysteries, in which, on the second day, the *mystai* rushed into the sea. The salt water of the sea was thought to have greater purifying power than fresh water, and this immersion in the sea was believed to purify a *mystes* from all sin,[3] a precondition for attaining blessed immortality. Each one carried along a young pig to sacrifice later, and was accompanied by a personal tutor or guide. The Isis-Sarapis (Latin: Serapis) cult initiation apparently included a baptism by immersion. In some locations a baptismal tub stood outside the front entrance to the temple; at other sites a baptismal chamber was inside the temple.[4] These were large enough for immersion.

The cult of Mithras apparently practiced baptism by sprinkling in at least one of its seven stages of initiation of converts. The Mithraic chapels at Carnuntum (near Bad Deutsch Altenburg, Austria) and Saalburg, Germany, had a font just inside the entrance; at other sites basins were built into the front edge of the podia inside the chapels. In the Mithraeum under the Santa Prisca church in Rome, however, there is a built-in tub for baptism by immersion. As with other mystery cults, the rites were secret, and therefore our knowledge of details is slight. At Santa Prisca an inscription states that the initiate "is piously reborn."[5] In a graffito found there a worshiper says that he was "born at the first light,"[6] that is, reborn at sunrise, the hour sacred to sun gods such as Mithras. In Mithraism the converts (all were males) were naked in at least one stage of initiation; we have learned this from the frescoes in the Mithraeum excavated at Santa Maria Capua Vetere in Italy.[7] In the cult of Dionysus, too, initiates were naked. The nakedness symbolized the rebirth of the initiate, who has been born again, pure like a new-born baby.

In the mystery cults that practiced some form of bathing or baptism in their initiation rituals, two different methods were employed, immersion and sprinkling. Also, two different rationales were involved. One view was that the ceremony was a cleansing of the soul from sin, a view developed from the practice of bathing to cleanse the body. Either sprinkling or immersion could accomplish the cleansing. Another view was that baptism effected the death of the old self and one's rebirth as a new sinless self, or soul, assured of blessed immortality. We suspect that the origin of this idea was the interpretation of immersion as the drowning of the old self, with the worshiper emerging from the water as the reborn self. Considerable exchange of ideas occurred among the mysteries, and sprinkling, too, came to be interpreted as the death of the old self.

Christian parallels to these cultic beliefs occur in the New Testament and the church fathers. Justin expressed the concept of baptism as a cleansing from sin when he wrote: "Baptism, which alone can cleanse them who have repented, even this is the water of [eternal] life."[8] Baptism as the death of the old self and rebirth in the form of a new, sinless self, however, soon became the predominant view of baptism among the churches. Titus 3:5 calls baptism "the washing of rebirth" ("regeneration" in some Bibles is simply a different translation of the same Greek word meaning "rebirth"). Justin, too, called Christian baptism "rebirth," as well as "illumination."[9] The earliest Christian expression of this doctrine is in Romans 6:2-4:

> How can we who have died to sin still live in it? Do you not know that all of us who have been baptized into Christ Jesus were baptized into his death? We were buried therefore with him by baptism into death, so that as Christ was raised from the dead by the glory of the Father, we too might walk in newness of life.

Here Paul has carried the death/rebirth doctrine a step farther by connecting it with Jesus' death and resurrection. The same connection is in Colossians 2:12 and 1 Peter 3:21.

Baptism in the cultic sense of rebirth theoretically made converts sinless *permanently* and insured eternal salvation. Small wonder that this doctrine became popular. The nature of rebirth is stated succinctly in 1 John 3:9: "No one born of God commits sin, for God's nature abides in him, and he cannot sin because he is born of God." Those who are baptized for the remission of sins "live without sin henceforth," wrote Justin (*Dial.* 44:4). This doctrine of baptism had a serious flaw; namely, some Christians (and mystery cult devotees too, no doubt!) did sin after baptism and rebirth. That situation created a doctrinal problem for the early Christians. If Christians sin after becoming new, pure persons, can they repent again and be baptized again? Some Christians believed that they could; some disagreed. The author of the Epistle to the Hebrews, writing at a time when some Christians were abandoning the faith during a persecution, felt that the sin of apostasy was unpardonable. "For it is impossible to restore again to repentance those who have once been enlightened [baptized], . . . and have become partakers of the Holy Spirit, . . . if they then commit apostasy" (6:4-6). The main concern of the author of the *Shepherd of Hermas* was the problem of sins in general, not just apostasy, committed after repentance and baptism. He decided that Christians could repent once more—and only once more—for their sins. [10] The danger of committing sin after baptism was of great concern to some church fathers. Therefore some thought that baptism should be postponed until adulthood (Augustine delayed it until he was about 30) or even until one is near death.

The pagan Hermetic cult in Egypt (2d c. A.D. or earlier) believed in a spiritual baptism. According to its mythology God filled a large vessel with "mind" (Greek: *nous*) and sent it down to earth for men to baptize themselves in so that they can ascend to God as immortal souls. [11] In John 3 Christians must be born again of the Spirit. This similarity is support for the conclusion that John too was written in Egypt.

Special Features

Originally Christian baptism must not have mentioned Jesus, for that would be pointless in a cleansing ritual concerned only with the relations between man and God. But as the churches attached increasing importance to the person of Jesus, that trend was supported by baptizing in his name. Paul refers to the formula in 1 Corinthians 6:11: "But you were washed [i.e;., baptized], you were sanctified, you were justified in the name of the Lord Jesus Christ and in the Spirit of our God." Baptism "in the name of Jesus Christ" occurs in Acts 2:38. What was the rationale behind the practice of baptizing in the name of Jesus?

In ancient thought one's name is part of oneself. "Particularly in the case of such powerful persons as deities, the name is regarded as part of the being of the divinity so named and of his character and powers." [12] As a part of the deity, the name contained divine power. Hence the name of the deity was invoked to use its power to accomplish what the worshiper desired. This notion survives today in prayers in the name of Jesus, especially those for healing in his name. The power of a divine name could be used for evil as well as good, including putting a curse on someone. Jewish prohibition of pronouncing the divine name Yahweh rested not only on awe of it, but also on the desire to keep heathen from learning it and misusing it. The names of humans with power were potent too; for example, the names of kings.

Belief in the importance of personal names is demonstrated in the New Testament; for example, "hallowed be thy name" in the Lord's Prayer and "blaspheming his [God's] name" in Revelation 13:6. Prayers in Jesus' name will be granted (John 15:16), and demons may be exorcised in his name (Mark 9:38-39). The fullest New Testament statement of the awesomeness of Jesus' name is in Philippians 2:10: "that at the name of Jesus every knee should bow, in heaven and on earth and under the earth." The significance of "baptized in the name of" (1 Cor. 1:12-15) included the belief that the baptized person is thought of as the property of, or under the protection of, the bearer of the name.[13]

By the middle of the second century Jewish Christians in Syria were baptizing in the name of the Triad: "Baptize in the name of the Father and of the Son and of the Holy Spirit" (*Didache* 7). (The Triad [Father, Son, and Holy Spirit] did not become a Trinity until Christian doctrine asserted that the three are one.) At the same time gentile churches in Rome were also baptizing in the name of the Triad.[14] The passage at the end of Matthew portrays the risen Jesus as commanding his disciples to make converts of all nations, baptizing in the name of the Triad. This passage must be a later addition, for it is contrary to the way the author of Matthew himself describes Jesus as sending the disciples out on their mission: "Go nowhere among the gentiles" (10:5). Also, setting forth to convert gentiles is just the opposite of what the disciples did after Jesus' death: they stayed in Jerusalem and preached only to Jews. Dean M'Neile of Cambridge University, commenting on the present ending of Matthew, recognized the later Christian tendency to universalize the Christian mission as one to gentiles as well as Jews:

> The universality of the Christian message was soon learnt, largely by the spiritual experiences of S. Paul,

which are authoritative for the Church. And once learnt, they were easily assigned to a direct command of Christ. It is impossible to maintain that everything that goes to constitute even the essence of Christianity must necessarily be traceable to explicit words of Jesus.[15]

When worshipers believe that their religion bestows blessed immortality upon them, but they have loved ones who have died without becoming members of the religion, they naturally are sorrowful because they believe that the loved one will not be with them in the hereafter. Some religions devised ways to save the deceased. The Orphic and Dionysiac cults had rites that were performed for that purpose.[16] Some Christians had similar rites. Paul implies that it was common in his churches: "If the dead are not raised at all, why are people baptized on their behalf?" (1 Cor. 15:29). Later the church fathers Chrysostom, Epiphanius, and Tertullian mentioned Christian vicarious baptisms to save the souls of the dead. Today, in the Temple in Salt Lake City the Church of Jesus Christ of Latter-Day Saints (Mormon) still practices baptism for the dead.[17]

Martyrdom was sometimes referred to metaphorically as "baptism." The martyrdom of Jesus and of James and John, the sons of Zebedee, is alluded to in Mark 10:39: " . . . with the baptism with which I am baptized, you will be baptized." That Jesus' baptism here is not his past baptism by John the Baptist, but his future martyrdom, is indicated by the reference to his future baptism in Luke 12:50: "I have a baptism to be baptized with, and how I am constrained until it is accomplished." Why was martyrdom called "baptism"? Probably because both involved the death of the old self.

SPIRIT

In Judaism

Many of ancient man's ideas about deity have their roots in his ideas about himself. The saying, "Man created God in man's own image," is not without some foundation. In the Old Testament God has human form and human emotions. Even the belief in God's Spirit has its origins in human experience. Man observed that when he and animals breathe, they have life and energy, but when they cease breathing, they lose them. In the later Creation story (Gen.2: 4b-25) the Lord God breathed "the breath of life" into man who then became a living being. Breath was called spirit, which was identified with life. If man has spirit, then deities also must have it. Further, if God created the universe, he created the natural spirit that is in man. In addition, God has a Spirit of his own, which he can share with mankind. And somewhere along the line of religious development, spirit, both human and divine, became connected with mind, which in turn led to association of spirit with speech, knowledge, and—eventually—with wisdom.

Possessed with a divine spirit, groups of prophets wandered around and prophesied, dancing like dervishes to the accompaniment of music, sometimes speaking words, but more often uttering gibberish which had to be interpreted to find its meaning. They were prevalent in ancient Canaan, Mesopotamia, and Anatolia. These ecstatic prophets were in Israelite society too. Saul, Israel's first king, became one of them (1 Sam. 10). Israel's earliest prophets were religious and nationalist zealots.[18] In the eighth century more rational prophets began to appear, the writing prophets; they also were eager to promote the worship of Yahweh and believed that they were inspired by his Spirit. Amos combined prophecy with his anguish over the social and economic injustice rampant in Israel. In the following centuries numerous other prophets arose. They believed that Yahweh told them what to say: "And the Spirit of the Lord fell upon me, and it said to me, 'Say, Thus says the Lord'" (Ezek. 11:5). The Spirit of the Lord is rarely called "the Holy Spirit" in the Old Testament, but it often is in rabbinical writings, where it usually refers to the source of prophetic inspiration.

The Spirit of the Lord could produce other effects besides prophecy. It could make a man a powerful warrior and guide him in his activities (Judg. 3:10), or give him great strength, as it did Samson (Judg. 14:6). It came upon David (1 Sam. 16:13) and made him a great king; this tradition is the ultimate source of the later tradition that the Spirit of the Lord will rest upon the Son of David Messiah.

When the New Age comes, the Lord will pour out his Spirit on all flesh, says Joel 2:28. Isaiah and Ezekiel limit the recipients to Jews: "But now hear, O Jacob my servant, Israel whom I have chosen. . . . I will pour my Spirit upon your descendants" (Isa. 44:1, 3). "I will put my Spirit within you, . . . and you shall be my people, and I will be your God" (Ezek. 36:27, 28). In the second century B.C. the author of the

Testament of Judah predicted that God will pour out his Spirit of grace on Jews and they will thus become sons of God in truth (24:3).

Two contrasting concepts of the Spirit appear. (1) Sometimes the Spirit "comes upon" or "rests upon" someone. The Spirit of God came upon Balaam and he prophesied (Num. 24:2). The Lord "took some of the Spirit that was upon him [Moses] and put it upon the seventy elders; and . . . they prophesied" (Num. 11:25). Similar usage is frequent in the Old Testament, and the typical result is that it causes men to prophesy. The concept of the Spirit being "on" someone appears to be an outgrowth of the old practice of anointing, in which oil poured ceremonially upon the head of a man prepared him to become a king, a prophet, or a priest.

(2) In other cases the Spirit is "in" or enters "into" someone, just as breath does. This comes as a special gift from God, in contrast to the Greek Stoic concept of the natural spirit which is in everyone from birth. When the Lord filled Bezalel with his Spirit, it automatically filled him with ability, intelligence, knowledge, and "all craftsmanship" (Exod. 31:3). Joshua was qualified to be a leader because the Spirit was in him (Num. 27:18). When the Spirit is in people, it can cause them to obey the statutes of the Law (Ezek. 36:27) and can fill them with power and zeal for justice (Mic. 3:8);. In *Testament of Benjamin* 6:4 "the Lord dwells in" the good man.

Wisdom, the knowledge and judgment to choose the best course of action, was honored in ancient Egypt and Israel. "Wise men" in kings' courts and elsewhere wrote wisdom literature, including Proverbs and Job in the Old Testament and Sirach and Wisdom of Solomon in the Apocrypha. In Proverbs 8 Wisdom is personified; she calls to men to learn from her, for she speaks truth, righteousness, and knowledge. Thus Wisdom provides the same virtues as the Spirit and the Law. In the Wisdom of Solomon, Wisdom is described in terms that would fit the Spirit as well: it is "a breath of the power of God" (7:25).

Even in ancient Israel other spirits were believed to exist. Yahweh sent an evil spirit upon the men of Shechem, causing them to deal treacherously with King Abimelech (Judg. 9:23). The Lord also took his Spirit away from Saul and gave him instead an evil spirit to torment him (1 Sam. 16:14). In *1 Enoch* God is the Master of the numerous spirits in the world: "Holy, holy, holy [is] the Lord of Spirits; the spirits fill the earth"

(39:12). The Essenes at Qumran, as we know, believed in the existence in men of "a spirit of truth" and "a spirit of error." In addition they believed in God's Holy Spirit which reveals the truth to man and purifies him (1QS 3:6-7; 4:20-21).

In Christianity

The early Christians generally believed that they had received the divine Spirit, but their particular beliefs about it varied considerably. For instance, the churches apparently became confused as to whether the Spirit is the Holy Spirit of God or the Spirit of Jesus. The Christians began with belief in the Holy Spirit, the Spirit of the Lord God, a heritage from Judaism. The synoptic gospels are consistent in distinguishing between Jesus and the Holy Spirit: The Holy Spirit is Jesus' father in the virgin birth stories; Jesus receives it at his baptism; Jesus speaks of it as a separate entity. The Spirit is God's Spirit in Acts' description of the pre-Pauline churches. On the other hand, in Acts 16:7 it is "the Spirit of Jesus" which did not allow the apostles to go to Bithynia. Paul's letters also are not consistent as to whose Spirit is involved; in many passages it is God's Spirit, but in others it is the Spirit of Jesus or of Christ.[19] Eventually Christians regarded the two Spirits as virtually synonymous, as in Romans 8:9. But did Paul himself really regard the two as identical? We know that Paul's letters were edited after his death (demonstrated by internal linguistic evidence) and phrases and sentences inserted. The few Spirit-of-Jesus passages may have been inserted then. We observe that in 1 Corinthians and 1 Thessalonians the Spirit consistently is God's.

How could the Spirit of Jesus be identified with the Spirit of God? The usual answer is that Christians began to think of Jesus and God as one person, as in the doctrine of the Trinity. But that idea originated much later. The key, I believe, is the use of the word "Lord." In the Septuagint, the Bible of the churches (except at Jerusalem), Yahweh is "the Lord." Some Christians began to refer to Jesus as "Lord Jesus," first in the sense of "Master Jesus" and later as "God Jesus." Mixing the two "Lords" together was an easy step, which occurs in Acts 2: the "Lord our God" (verse 39) has made Jesus "both Lord and Christ" (verse 36). Some references to the Lord in the Old Testament were mistakenly interpreted by Christians as references to Jesus instead of God. A further step was to say that Jesus *is* the Spirit, not that he had the Spirit, as in the *Shepherd of Hermas*: "the Holy Spirit . . . is the Son of God" (*Sim*. 9.1.1). 1 Peter 1:10-11 even goes to the extreme of claiming that the Old Testament prophets had "the Spirit of Christ within them."

How did individual Christians receive the Spirit? There were several ways, but they all had one common denominator: faith. Although the content of the faith varied with the apostle proclaiming the gospel, the belief that Jesus was the Christ became standard, replacing the call to repentance as the central theme. Paul mentions that the Galatian Christians received the Spirit "by hearing with faith" (Gal. 3:2), and in Acts 10:44 Peter's preaching causes the Holy Spirit to fall "on all who heard the word." One method of obtaining the Spirit was by prayer: "the heavenly Father will give the Holy Spirit to those who ask him" (Luke 11:13). Acts repeatedly mentions the laying on of hands as the method by which the Spirit was received. 1 Timothy 4:14 speaks of the reception of the Spirit "when the council of elders laid their hands upon you." (Moses laid his hands on Joshua to transmit to him Moses' authority [Num. 27:23] and Moses' spirit of wisdom [Deut. 34:9]). As we have seen, baptism was the method which apparently became typical. Both baptism and the laying on of hands are employed in Acts 19:5-6.

When did Christians receive the Spirit? Not until after Jesus' death. In fact, according to John 7:39 it could not be given until after Jesus had been "glorified," and in the same gospel Jesus breathes the Holy Spirit on his disciples after his resurrection (20:22). This idea may be intended to explain why the notion that Christians had the Spirit, while others did not, was a belief that originated after the crucifixion.

In Acts a very different account is given of how the early Christians first received the Holy Spirit. When the Jerusalem church was assembled on the day of Pentecost, the Spirit miraculously came upon them:

> And suddenly a sound came from heaven like the rush of a mighty wind, and it filled all the house where they were sitting. And there appeared to them tongues as of fire, distributed and resting on each one of them. And they were all filled with the Holy Spirit and began to speak in other tongues, as the Spirit gave them utterance (2:2-4).

A crowd of Jews from many countries gathered around, and each of them heard the sound as though it was speaking to him in his own language.

Did the disciples and other members of the Jerusalem church really believe that they all received the Spirit simultaneously on the day of Pentecost? At first glance it appears plausible that mass hysteria may have seized the members at a meeting when they eagerly expected the arrival soon of the kingdom of God. A second look raises doubts. First, Acts disagrees with the story in John 20 in respect to how, when, and where the disciples received the Holy Spirit. The only feature the two accounts agree on is that Jesus, not God, is the one who gives the Spirit to the Church, though, unlike the method in John, in Acts Jesus ascends to heaven and receives the Spirit from God and then pours it out from there (Acts 2:33). Secondly, the story contains mythological features. Do we have an event which has been exaggerated, or do we have a myth? A story in Philo's writings helps us to answer that question. It describes God's giving the Law to Jews in similar mythological terms: God gave the Law by means of a "holy miracle," creating a marvelous sound in the air; a rational soul changed the air into "a kind of flaming fire." "And a voice sounded forth from out of the midst of the fire, which had flowed from heaven, . . . the flame being endowed with articulate speech in a language familiar to the hearers."[20] A tradition in the Midrash parallels the idea of different people hearing the noise in different languages: "Although the Ten Commandments were promulgated with a single sound, . . . when the voice went forth it was divided into seven voices and then went into seventy tongues, and every people received the Law in their own language."[21] The similarities in the Acts account to the Jewish stories can hardly be accidental. Another Jewish tradition that is relevant here is that the Lord gave the Law at Mount Sinai on the day of Pentecost.[22]

The primary key to understanding the story in Acts, however, is the early Christian theory that Christianity is the New Judaism which replaces the Old Judaism (we will describe it in another chapter). One aspect of that theory is the belief that the Spirit which Christians have replaces the Law which Jews have. As Paul put it: "But now we are discharged from the Law, dead to that which held us captive, so that we serve not under the old written code but in a new life of the Spirit" (Rom.

7:6). When all this evidence is combined, we can see what the author of Acts was trying to do. He created an event to support the Christian theory. His rationale is that as the Law was given on Pentecost, so the Spirit that replaces it was given to the Jerusalem church on the very same day of the year. As we have seen, the Hellenists, Paul, and the gentiles received the Spirit by other means.

According to Acts 2:33 Jesus poured out the Holy Spirit from heaven on Pentecost, although in the same chapter Joel is quoted as prophesying that God will pour it out (2:18). The G source in John insists that Jesus had to "go away," that is, ascend to heaven, before Christians could receive the Spirit, the Paraclete (16:7); in a different source, however, Jesus breathes the Holy Spirit on the disciples *before* his ascension (John 20:22).

The effects of having the divine Spirit were multiple. Paul recognizes this in 1 Corinthians 12 and 14, and lists some of the Spirit's manifestations. One effect was glossolalia, speaking in tongues, which produced some real problems. Since this gibberish was not in sensible words—even the speaker did not understand it—an interpreter was required, on whom the Spirit had bestowed the ability to give "interpretation of tongues" (1 Cor. 12:10). Since no one understood the gibberish, no one could prove that the interpretation of it was wrong! This gave the interpreter the power to introduce all sorts of ideas into a church, for his or her interpretation was believed to be from the Spirit. Another problem with glossolalia was that if many members indulged in it, the situation became noisy and confusing, and Paul urged that only two or three persons utter it at a meeting, one person at a time (1 Cor. 14:23, 27).

A related effect of the Spirit was prophecy, which also produced noise and confusion in church meetings, and Paul ordered that prophets should "prophesy one by one, so that all may learn and be encouraged; . . . For God is not a God of confusion but of peace" (14:31-33). Women cannot be blamed for the confusion, for Paul indicates that it was customary in all the churches for women to keep silent, a practice he commanded to be continued (14:33-34).

The Spirit serves as a teacher and guide in various ways, giving prophecy, wisdom, knowledge, and faith (1 Cor. 12:8-9). The belief in the Spirit of God as the teacher of the early Christians is stated concisely by Paul in 1 Corinthians 2:9-13.

Jesus' preaching is inspired by the Holy Spirit in Luke 4:17-21. When Jewish Christians are arrested, they should not be anxious about what to say, "for it is not you who speak, but the Spirit of your Father speaking through you" (Matt. 10:19-20). In the Gospel of John "the Counselor [Greek: *parakletos*], the Holy Spirit, which the Father will send in my name, will teach you all things" (14:26). Early in the second century Bishop Ignatius believed that the Spirit controlled his preaching: "I cried out when I was among you; I spoke with a loud voice, the voice of God, . . . It was the Spirit that was preaching, saying this: 'Do nothing without the bishop, . . .'" (*Phil.* 7:1-2). According to Acts the Holy Spirit served as a general guide for the apostles: It told the Antioch church to send Barnabas and Paul on their missionary journey together (13:2), and it forbade Paul, Silas, and Timothy to preach in the province of Asia (16:6).

Both Essenes and the early Christians were very active in reinterpreting Scripture to support their beliefs, and both probably believed that the Holy Spirit guided them. The Spirit told Philip to go to the Ethiopian eunuch, which he did and then interpreted Isaiah to him. Paul regarded the ability to perform healings and other miracles as one of the gifts of the Spirit (1 Cor. 12:9-10). In Matthew 12:28 Jesus casts out demons by "the Spirit of God." The theory of exorcisms was that God's Spirit is much stronger than the evil spirits and therefore could overpower them and cast them out. The Spirit of the Lord even performed miracles directly: It mysteriously transported Philip from the road to Gaza, where he had baptized an Ethiopian, to the town of Azotus (Acts 8).

In Hellenistic Christianity an effect of having the Spirit was that it bestows immortality. This belief was based on philosophic dualism, the idea that divine Spirit is directly opposed to the human body, or flesh. The idea originated in the Greek world and was adopted by some Hellenistic Jews. As we know, Paul believed in the dualism of flesh versus spirit. He was confident that possessing God's Spirit guarantees immortality for the raised body of deceased Christians (Rom. 8:11). Thus Paul combined the Hellenistic concept of a Spirit with the Pharisaic idea of a resurrected body (cf. 1 Cor. 15). The new life in the Spirit was often seen in terms of rebirth. Apart from its Gospel of Signs source and the additions of the redactor, the Gospel of John is thoroughly dualistic. In chapter 3 the doctrine of spiritual rebirth is explicit: "That which is born of the flesh is flesh, and that which is born of the Spirit is spirit" (verse 6). "Truly, truly, I say to you, unless one is born from above, he cannot see the kingdom of God" (verse 3).

The belief that the Holy Spirit of God could rest upon selected individuals was typically Jewish, and the belief that it could dwell within a person also occurred in Judaism. But when some Christians thought that the *Spirit of Jesus* was inside them, they were adapting pagan thought to Christian faith, although the paganism could come indirectly through Hellenistic Jewish Christians. Even Paul was a mystic. "He who is united to the Lord becomes one Spirit with him" (1 Cor. 6:17). "Jesus Christ is in you" (2 Cor. 13:5). Paul, however, did not deify Jesus, but later gentile Christians did. And when some gentile Christians believed that the Spirit of the god Jesus was in them, they had gone all the way in adopting a form of the pagan *unio mystica*, "mystic union" with deity.

The Holy Spirit made Christians sons of God: "For all who are led by the Spirit of God are sons of God" (Rom. 8:14). In Galatians 4:6 the Spirit is that of God's Son. It also made the elders the "guardians of the flock," that is, leaders of the local church (Acts 20:28). After Jesus breathed the Holy Spirit on the disciples after his resurrection, they (that is, the Church) had the power to decide whether or not the sins of other Christians should be forgiven (John 20:22-23).

Considering that early Christians believed that the Spirit bestowed so many powerful, highly desirable effects, it is not surprising that speaking against the Holy Spirit is denounced as blasphemy and an unpardonable sin. It is blasphemy against the Holy Spirit to charge that Jesus did not have it and use it in casting out unclean spirits (Mark 3:28-30). It is also unforgivable to deny that Christians have it; in *Didache* 11:7 the unpardonable sin is to test or question the Spirit by which the Christian prophet speaks.

We have observed that an effect of the Spirit, in the opinion of Paul and his churches, is that the Spirit has replaced the Torah, the Law. Paul states this emphatically in Galatians.

With so much spiritual revelation going on, we should not be surprised to learn that many of the revelations did not agree with one another. The earliest evidence of this is in 1 Corinthians 14:37-38, in which Paul denounces those prophets in the Corinthian church whose teaching evidently disagreed with his (remember, Paul also regarded himself as a prophet, "taught by the Spirit," 1 Cor. 2:13). "If anyone thinks that he is a prophet, or spiritual, he should acknowledge that what I am writing to you is a command of the Lord. If anyone does not recognize this, he is not recognized."

Soon prophets with whom one disagreed were denounced as "false prophets." Matthew 24:11 ascribes to Jesus a forecast that "many false prophets will arise and lead many astray." A warning against them is even in the Sermon on the Mount: "Beware of false prophets, who come to you in sheep's clothing but inwardly are ravenous wolves. You will know them by their fruits" (Matt. 7:15-16). This problem led to various tests to determine who really has the Spirit. Paul stated that "no one speaking by the Spirit of God ever says 'Jesus be cursed!' and no one can say 'Jesus is Lord' except by the Holy Spirit" (1 Cor. 12:3). Decades later, when the heretical docetic Christians claimed that Christ was a spirit, temporarily united with the human Jesus, the author of 1 John wrote in opposition: "By this you know the Spirit of God: every spirit which confesses that Jesus Christ has come in the flesh is of God, and every spirit which does not confess Jesus is not of God" (4:2-3). And in *Didache* 11:8 we read: "But not everyone who speaks in a spirit is a prophet, but only if he has the ways of the Lord."

Spiritual inspiration in the churches produced such a variety of doctrine that it had to be curbed. Elders, the oldest members of the congregation, governed the Jewish-Christian churches (just as elders governed the synagogues) and were a restraining influence. In gentile churches, and eventually in all churches, a local bishop assumed control, but not without considerable resistance. Ignatius strove mightily to assert the authority of the bishop. In his day Gnostic heretics were claiming revelations from the Spirit as the authority for their doctrines. The churches needed a bishop as their head with authority to provide some standardization and stability and to defend themselves from the Gnostics. Doubtlessly bishops sometimes abused their authority, however.

A century later the doctrine of the Trinity began to appear, the doctrine that the Father, Son, and Holy Spirit are really all one. That subject is best postponed until we discuss the origin and development of the belief in the divinity of Jesus.

EXPLAINING JESUS' DEATH

THE CHRISTIAN ENVIRONMENT

The early Christian writers were influenced not only by their Jewish and gentile environments, but also by their Christian environment; that is, the events, issues, and problems in the early Christian communities. Their writings help us to understand church history, and the history helps us to understand the writings. Thus a "continuing conversation" must be maintained between the history and the literature. To understand a book in the New Testament, for example, it is not enough to study that book alone, for other early Christian books may give us a fuller picture of what the author was writing about and why.

The problems within the churches and the issues between Christians and non-Christians were manifold and increased as the religion expanded. The solutions multiplied too and often were inconsistent with one another. Sometimes one idea helped to solve several problems. But sometimes a solution created new problems. The Christian writings were apologetics in the sense that the authors were trying to defend and promote the faith by solving problems that were obstacles to some form of Christian belief or practice. The first problem to arise was that of explaining Jesus' death.

EXPLANATIONS OF JESUS' DEATH

How could a man who died without accomplishing the basic task of the Messiah (the overthrow of foreign rule over the Jews) possibly be the Messiah? Besides, some did not expect the Messiah to die. This view is reflected in the objection of the Jewish crowd in John 12:34, "We have heard from the Law that the Christ remains forever." Paul testifies that Jesus' death was an obstacle to apostolic preaching: "We preach Christ crucified, a stumbling block to Jews and folly to gentiles" (1 Cor. 1:23). Early in the second century the cross was still a problem; Ignatius admitted that it "is a stumbling block to unbelievers" (*Eph.* 18:1). The manner of Jesus' death was a special handicap in apostolic preaching. Jews must have cited Deuteronomy 21:23, "a hanged man is accursed by God," for Paul quotes it as evidence that Christ "became a curse for us" (Gal. 3:13). The Marcan pericope in which Peter rebukes Jesus for predicting his death reflects the problem of Jesus' death (8:31-32).

Death Is According to Divine Will and Plan

Faith in Jesus' resurrection, ascension, and future return enabled the disciples to regain their faith that he was the Christ, but it did not explain *why* he died. One reason conceived by some early Christians was that it must have been according to God's will and plan. In Judaism the suffering and death of an individual or of many Jews had been explained that way. For example, the so-called "suffering Servant" in Isaiah 53 is not the Messiah, not Jesus, not the nation Israel, but an Israelite prophet, a man who has died a martyr's death (verse 9). His death was according to divine will: "And it was the will of the Lord to bruise him" (verse 10) is the explanation of his death.

This explanation of Jesus' death was widely accepted among Christians. "This Jesus [was] delivered up according to the definite plan and foreknowledge of God" (Acts 2:23; cf. 4:28). And what is the evidence that the event was in accord with God's will? Jesus' death was prophesied in Scripture—that was the Christian answer. A concise statement of this view is ascribed to Peter in Acts 3:18: "But what God foretold by the mouth of all the prophets, that his Christ should suffer, he thus fulfilled." In the Last Supper pericope Jesus says, "For the Son of Man goes as it is written of him" (Mark 14:21). The *Epistle of Barnabas* tells us that "his Passion was foretold" (6:7). All of these ideas are summed up in "the Christ must suffer."[1] Another way of representing Jesus' death as according to plan is Mark's technique of having Jesus predict it three times during his career.[2]

Death as a Sacrifice

The very earliest Christian communities, as we have seen, practiced repentance, which causes God to forgive one's sins. Therefore they had no theological need for an atonement doctrine. Consequently the atonement is absent in the earliest speeches in Acts, in Q in Matthew and Luke, and the Epistle of James. The origin of the atonement doctrine is to be found in a different quarter, namely, the need to explain Jesus' death.[3] As the doctrine developed, it tended to replace repentance as the method of canceling one's sins. A few writers combined the two methods, even though the combination was not logical. Jesus' death brought repentance to Israel in Acts 5:31. A forced connection between atonement and repentance is made in *1 Clement* 7:4:

> Let us fix our eyes on the blood of Christ and learn how precious it is to his Father, because it was shed for our salvation and brought the grace of repentance to the whole world.[4]

How could the Christians think that Jesus' death atoned for their sins? What was the background or source of such an idea? There were two sources.

One source was the practice of animal sacrifices. Animal sacrifices for sin were not unknown among Greeks and Romans, and they were routinely practiced by the Israelites. In early Judaism they were performed at the Temple before its destruction. Leviticus 17:11 gives the rationale: "For the life of the flesh is in the blood; and I have given it for you upon the altar to make atonement for your souls." Both Jesus at his crucifixion[5] and animals when sacrificed shed blood; this similarity provided the basis for the concept that Jesus' death was a sacrifice. The author of Hebrews viewed Jesus' death as analogous to the high priest's offering sacrifices in the Holy of Holies in the Temple. Christ "entered once for all into the Holy Place, taking not the blood of goats and calves but his own blood, thus securing an eternal redemption" [for Christians] (Heb. 9:12).

Some writers regarded Jesus' death as analogous to the sacrifice of the lamb at Passover. "Christ, our pascal lamb, has been sacrificed" (1 Cor. 5:7). Jesus is "the Lamb of God" in John 1:29, 36, and in the Book of Revelation he is frequently referred to as "the Lamb." This idea is the basis of dating the crucifixion in John, where Jesus' death occurs at the same time that the pascal lamb is killed (the afternoon of the Day of Preparation).

References to Jesus' death as atonement are numerous in both the New Testament and the Apostolic Fathers. In 1 Peter

3:18 we read: "For Christ also died for sins once for all, the righteous for the unrighteous, that he might bring us to God." Polycarp urges faithfulness to "Jesus Christ, who carried the burden of our sins in his own body on the cross" (8:1). In Romans 3 and 5 Jesus' death reconciles gentiles to God. His death is also interpreted as redemption: "You were bought with a price" (1 Cor. 6:20); "in him we have redemption through his blood" (Eph. 1:7).

One interpretation of Jesus' death as a sacrifice was to regard his blood as "blood of the covenant" (Mark 14:24). This idea was derived from Exodus 24:5-8. After Moses read the Book of the Covenant to the Israelites, they covenanted with Yahweh to obey all the words of Yahweh. Then Moses sprinkled half of the sacrificial blood on the people, saying, "Behold, the blood of the covenant which Yahweh has made with you." In the Last Supper account Jesus' blood, in the form of wine, is the blood of the covenant which God is making with Christians. (This idea was also used as a feature in the New Judaism concept of Christianity.)

Somewhat related to the view that Jesus' death is a sacrifice is the idea that his death is the result of God's love for the world (John 3:16, source G) or Jesus' love for his disciples, or Christians (John 15:12-13, author). In the same vein, Jesus is "the good shepherd" who lays down his life for his sheep (John 10:14-15, G).

Atoning Death of a Righteous Man

The second source of the Christian doctrine of atonement is the Jewish belief that the suffering and death of the righteous can atone for the sins of others. The idea is applied to the death of an unknown righteous prophet in Isaiah. Some Christians thought that they had found a prophecy of Jesus' death in Isaiah 52:13-53:12. Actually that passage refers to the death of a "righteous" man, the Lord's "servant," that had already occurred (observe the past tense and the fact that his burial has already happened.) The author, Deutero-Isaiah, interpreted the man's death as vicarious suffering for the sins of the Israelites: "he was wounded for our transgressions, he was bruised for our iniquities"; "he poured out his soul to death, . . . he bore the sin of many."

Extracts of Isaiah 53 were used frequently[6] to explain Jesus' death. The clause, "he bore the sin of many,' is quoted in Hebrews 9:28 and *1 Clement* 16:14. Although Jesus is depicted as applying the same thought to himself, the Son of Man, in Mark 10:45, the authors of Hebrews and *1 Clement* do not say that Jesus said it. Isaiah 53 is not a major source of the Passion Story in the synoptic gospels, but in the third or fourth century a Christian scribe tried to connect the two accounts. He inserted Mark 15:28, "And the Scripture was fulfilled which says, 'He was reckoned with the transgressors,'" quoting from Isaiah 53:12. Jesus' prayer on the cross, "Father, forgive them" (Luke 23:34), probably was suggested by "he made intercession for the transgressors," which is in Isaiah 53:12. This prayer ascribed to Jesus is a fifth century insertion, however; it is not in the earliest New Testament manuscripts.

In Isaiah 52:14 and 53:2 the Servant's physical appearance was so "marred" and lacking in beauty that people did not want to look at him. Christian apologists ignored such undesirable features in passages they applied to Jesus. Instead, they used the features that seemed to fit, lifting them out of context. They probably were attracted to this Servant Song by its first verse as well as by the suffering and death of the Servant of the Lord. That verse could suggest Jesus' ascension, although that is not what Deutero-Isaiah had in mind.

> Behold, my servant shall prosper,
> he shall be exalted and lifted up,
> and shall be very high (52:13).

The martyrdom of the righteous continued in Judaism to be interpreted as vicarious suffering for the sins of the people. In the *Testament of Benjamin* the father says to his sons, "In you will be fulfilled the heavenly prophecy . . . the sinless one will die for the sake of impious men" (3:8). The deaths of the Maccabean martyrs were regarded as atonement for the sins of Israel. Eleazar prays, "Make my blood their purification, and take my life in exchange for theirs" (4 Macc. 6:29).

In Psalm 22 a righteous man—not David, as the heading added later would lead us to believe—lamented his suffering for the sake of the Lord. The psalmist's enemies have mocked and abused him, and in his anguish he asks God why he has forsaken him. Yet he has faith that the Lord will save and reward him, just as the Lord delivered "our fathers" who trusted him. He does not regard his suffering as atonement for the sins of others, however.

Certain details of the man's suffering appealed to the authors of the synoptic gospels as suitable features to incorporate in the Passion Story. The writers may have been especially attracted to the psalm by the words in verse 16 of the Septuagint version, "they have pierced my hands and feet," which sound like a reference to crucifixion. Even the cry of anguish seemed appropriate because of the psalmist's confidence that God will see to it that all will end well. The use of the psalm in the Passion Story is best seen below.

Psalm 22
1. "They divide my garments among them, and for my raiment they cast lots" (v. 18; 21:19 LXX).
2. "All who see me mock at me, . . . they wag their heads" (v. 7; 21:8 LXX).
3.. "He hopes on the Lord; let him deliver him (v. 8; 21:9 LXX).[7]
4. "O God, my God, why have you forsaken me?" (v. 1; 21:2 LXX).

Passion Story
1. "They divided his garments among them, casting lots for them" (Mark 15:24 par).
2. "Those who passed by blasphemed him, wagging their heads" (Mark 15:29 par).
3. "He trusts in God; let God deliver him now" (Matt. 27:43).
4. "My God, my God, why have you forsaken me?' (Mark 15:34=Matt. 27:46). Note that this is first quoted here in Aramaic, a literary device which gives it the appearance of authenticity.

The details were inserted in the Passion Story to support the claim that Jesus' death fulfilled prophecy; they tell us nothing about what actually happened at Jesus' crucifixion. Many biblical scholars have recognized this (Passion Plays to the contrary). Dr. Lindars has stated the situation succinctly: "From this [Christian apologetic] point of view it [Psalm 22] becomes a quarry for pictorial detail in writing the story of the Passion."[8]

DEATH AS VICTORY

A different type of explanation of Jesus' death was to regard it as a victory. In Acts 2 the total process (death, resurrection, and ascension) has caused God to make him "both Lord and Christ." Professor Nock and others called attention to the fact that in the Greek (and Roman) background outstanding men could be elevated at their death to the rank of hero or demigod.[9] Faith in Jesus' resurrection suggested a related result: his death enabled him to conquer death (2 Tim. 1:10). The *Epistle of Barnabas* adds the idea that by destroying death Jesus demonstrated the future resurrection of dead Christians (5:6-7). In the christological insertion in Philippians (2:6-9) Jesus is a divine figure who "emptied himself" and was born in human form. Then "he humbled himself and became obedient unto death . . . Therefore God has highly exalted him and given him the name which is above every name, . . ." Thus Jesus' death was a triumph for which God rewarded him. Colossians 2:15 expands the triumphant note by claiming that by his death Jesus disarmed the cosmic "principalities and powers." Professor John Knox once remarked that the interpretations of Jesus' death as a victory and as a sacrifice are logically inconsistent.[10] Nevertheless, Hebrews 1:3-4 combines them: After Jesus had made purification for sins, he became superior to the angels and sat down at the right hand of God.

Given the presuppositions concerning life and death in the ancient world, the above explanations seemed reasonable to many, though not to philosophers. Other explanations, however, must have seemed farfetched even in those days. These included the idea that Jesus' death canceled the Law (Col. 2:14), and that Jesus endured the cross so that Jews might complete their sins by persecuting him to death (*Barn.* 5:11-12).

The wildest explanation, however, came from Docetic Gnostic Christians. With their metaphysical dualism, which held that things spiritual are good and things physical are evil, they concluded that there were really two persons who appeared, or seemed, to be one person. The two were the spiritual Christ and the physical Jesus to whom Christ was temporarily united. At the crucifixion it was Jesus who was killed while the invisible Christ stood by and laughed because the executioners thought that they were killing him. After the crucifixion was over, Christ returned to heaven to the unbegotten Father.[11] Thus the docetic solution was to say that it was Christ who was important, and he did not die. In the *Gospel of Truth* Valentinian Gnostics solved the problem another way. In it Jesus is "Jesus the Christ," one person. His death was essential. Because Jesus had taught "the Truth," which was knowledge of souls' previous existence with the Father, "Error" nailed him to the cross. But Jesus took with him to the cross the Book of Life, opened it, and made known the teachings of the Father. He knew that his death meant life for many. Then he stripped himself of perishable garments and put on the garments of imperishability, or immortality.[12]

The early Christians certainly conceived a variety of solutions to the problem of explaining Jesus' death.

THE PROBLEM OF THE CHRIST- A

The basic theme of apostolic preaching was that Jesus is the Christ. The fact that outsiders called the members of the church at Antioch "Christians" is virtual proof that Acts is correct in stating that the apostles proclaimed Jesus to be the Christ.[1]

Even after faith in Jesus' resurrection was established and Jesus' death was explained, many obstacles remained to the belief that he was and is the Christ. Non-believing Jews pointed them out to the Jewish Christians, and the latter were forced to find answers to the criticism to satisfy themselves and try to satisfy the unbelievers.

WHEN DID JESUS BECOME THE CHRIST?

Christians today are generally unaware that this was a serious issue in early Christianity. Let us sketch the main views on this question.

During Jesus' lifetime his disciples became convinced that he was the Christ, but his death caused doubts and disbelief. Faith in his resurrection led to new views about him.

1. Jesus became the Christ at his resurrection or ascension. He had failed to perform the basic task of the Christ (overthrow foreign rule) before his crucifixion, and therefore he must not have been the Christ then. If God has raised him from the dead before other dead are raised, and temporarily taken him to heaven to return to earth later to accomplish his mission, then he must be the Christ now. When did he become the Christ? God must have made him the Christ, the Son of God, by means of the Holy Spirit by raising him from the dead (Rom. 1:3-4). This is the belief too in Acts 13:33. A variation of it occurs in Acts 2:33-36 wherein God has made Jesus both Lord and Christ at his ascension by giving him the Holy Spirit. Observe that apparently it is the possession of the Holy Spirit that gives the

risen Jesus the power to be the Christ.

2. Jesus became the Christ at his baptism. The belief that Jesus *became* the Messiah at his resurrection was not in accord with Jewish prophecy and expectation, which anticipated a Christ who would appear only once. The Jewish belief that the Messiah would receive the Holy Spirit during his one and only earthly life was applied to Jesus at his baptism, as we have seen. There God announces that Jesus is his Son at the same time that he gives Jesus the Spirit; that combination clearly indicates that the synoptic authors believed that this was the time that Jesus became the Christ.

3. Jesus became the Messiah at his very birth. The virgin birth stories in Matthew and Luke, in effect, place the beginning of Jesus' messiahship at that time. The Holy Spirit is the father of Jesus, and therefore he has the Spirit from infancy. Admittedly this does not agree with his later reception of the Spirit at baptism, but we must remember that all four canonical gospels are mixtures of early Christian beliefs. The gospel authors were compilers and apologists; they were not systematic theologians or historians.

4. Jesus is the preexistent heavenly Messiah. The earliest form of this type of Christology is the belief that Jesus was the Son of Man. The Gospel of John contains a later form: the semi-Gnostic view that Jesus is the divine Son of the Father; as a supernatural preexistent being Jesus was the Son and Christ from the beginning of the universe.

WHICH TYPE OF CHRIST?

Son of David

Some Jews did not expect the coming of a Messiah, but among those who did, the concepts of him varied considerably. The most popular belief was that he would be the Son of David, that is, a descendant of King David. Both Pharisees and Essenes anticipated this type of Messiah. The scriptural foundation of the belief is 2 Samuel 7:12-14, wherein the Lord says to David:

> When your days are fulfilled and you lie down with your fathers, I will raise up your offspring after you, who will come forth from your body, and I will establish his kingdom. He will build a house [the Temple, which David's son Solomon built] for my name, and I will establish the throne of his kingdom for ever. I will be

his father, and he will be my son.

This passage is not speaking of a future Messiah, but of Solomon and the uninterrupted line of kings of Judah who were David's descendants. It had been reinterpreted, however, and served as an inspiration for messianic prophecies (see chapter 3).

"Son of David" is the title of this kind of Messiah in *Psalms of Solomon* 17:21 (1st c. B.C.) (described above in chapter 3). He was still expected late in the first century A.D., as *4 Ezra* 12:32 demonstrates: the Messiah "whom the Most High has kept until the end of days, who will arise from the posterity of David, and will come and speak to them." The Essenes expected two Messiahs, "the Messiahs of Aaron and Israel" (1QS 9:11). The Messiah of Aaron will be the new high priest, and the Messiah of Israel will be the king, a descendant of David.

Some Christians too interpreted 2 Samuel 7 as messianic when they claimed that Jesus was the Son of David. "Of this man's [David's] posterity God has brought to Israel a Savior, Jesus, as he promised" (Acts 13:23). To Paul, Jesus Christ is God's "Son, who was descended from David according to the flesh" (Rom. 1:3). In Mark 10:47 the blind beggar Bartimaeus hails Jesus as "Son of David." Matthew emphasizes this belief. Only in that gospel is Jesus hailed as "the Son of David" by two blind men (9:27), the Canaanite woman (15:22), the crowds when Jesus enters Jerusalem (21:9), and children in the Temple (21:15). Another device is to make Jesus' father, Joseph, a descendant of David (1:20). Both Matthew and Luke foster this idea with genealogies of Jesus which allegedly trace his ancestry to David through his father Joseph.

The claim that Jesus was the Son of David had a significant weakness: he was not a descendant of David! This harsh fact is recognized in Mark 12:35-37 par. In this pericope Jesus is portrayed as disagreeing with the scribes who say that the Christ is David's son. Psalm 110:1, which many Christians interpreted messianicly and was assumed to have been written by David, is quoted: "The Lord [God] said to my Lord" [the Messiah, in Christian interpretation]. The conclusion drawn in the Marcan passage is that the Messiah is not David's son because David himself, as the author, calls the Messiah "Lord," not "Son." *Epistle of Barnabas* 12:10-11 specifically rejects the notion that Jesus is the Son of David.

A second kind of evidence that Jesus was not a descendant of David consists of the extremes to which some writers went to try to prove that he was. For example, the two genealogies for that purpose do not even agree on who Jesus' paternal grandfather was (Jacob vs. Heli). Another desperate effort to make Jesus qualify as the Son of David Messiah was the creation of the Bethlehem birth stories. King David was born in Bethlehem, and some Jews expected that the Son of David would be too. Micah 5:2 predicts of Bethlehem: "from you shall come forth for me one who is to be ruler in Israel." In Matthew 2 this passage is interpreted as a prophecy that the Christ, the descendant of David, will be born in Bethlehem. In Luke 2 the angel calls Bethlehem "the city of David." But Jesus apparently was born in Nazareth, a fact that caused critics to ask, "Can any good thing [the Messiah] come out of Nazareth?" (John 1:46).

Therefore in order to get Jesus' parents into Bethlehem in time for his birth there, Luke provides us with the fiction that they went to Bethlehem to register for a Roman census, because Joseph "was of the house and lineage of David." But that would never happen! The Roman procedure was just the opposite, as an ancient papyrus discovered in Egypt reveals. In it a Roman census edict of A.D. 104 states:

> Since the census is approaching, it is necessary to command all who for any reason are out of their own districts to return to their own home, in order to perform the usual business of the taxation.[2]

Then, as now, basic census taking occurred at individuals' own homes. To order people to travel to the homes of their ancestors or tribe for a census would have produced chaos!

Matthew's devices for solving the problem are even more ridiculous. In that gospel Jesus' parents are depicted as already living in Bethlehem, but this creates the problem of getting the family back to Nazareth where they really lived. So Matthew has an angel tell Joseph to take his family to Egypt because Herod wants to kill Jesus. This they do, Herod kills all the male infants in or around Bethlehem (an event that never happened—the author did not like Herod!), then after Herod's death the family follows the angel's further instructions and settles in Nazareth. The author created the journey to and from Egypt in order to use Hosea 11:1, "out of Egypt I called my son," in an effort to make Jesus "fulfill" Scripture. These fables have had a lot of influence, even in the twentieth century (the carol, "O little town of Bethlehem"; tours to Bethlehem to see the very spot "where Jesus was born"; planetarium shows that vainly attempt to demonstrate that a comet might have appeared then over Bethlehem [they ignore the apologetic and mythological motives that produced the story]).

The Son of David Messiah would be a king, which made the Romans suspicious of the idea, for they wanted no rebellions. After all, Pilate had executed Jesus on the charge that he wanted to be king of the Jews. Eusebius reports that the Roman Vespasian, after the capture of Jerusalem, "ordered a search to be made for all who were of the family of David, that there might be left among the Jews no one of the royal family."[3] The early Christians sought peaceful relations with the Romans, and consequently the Son-of-David christology became less popular; another cause of its decline was the increasing number of gentile converts who were not attracted to a Christ who would be king of the Jewish nation.

Son of God
   The phrase "sons of God" had various meanings in early Judaism and early Christianity. In one sense, all humans are children of God, the Father who created them. In another sense, only the people of Israel are "sons of the living God" (Hosea 1:10). In another sense, Christians are the ones because they have the Spirit: "For all who are led by the Spirit of God are sons of God" (Rom. 8:14). In Galatians 4 Christians have received adoption as sons of God, and in the *Epistle of Barnabas* 4:9 they are urged to withstand the evils that are to come "as befits sons of God." Christians are viewed as sons of God when they address him as "our Father," as in the Lord's Prayer.
   Another line of thought was that an individual can be God's son in a special way that others are not. Among both Canaanites and Israelites, kings were thought to be sons of god, El or Yahweh, respectively. In the Ugaritic Keret Text the Canaanite king, Keret, is the son of El, the supreme god of the Canaanite pantheon. The kings of Judah, descended from David, are the Lord's sons (2 Sam. 7:14). In Psalm 2:7, a royal enthronement psalm, the Lord adopts the king as his son when the king ascends the throne: "He [the Lord] said to me, 'You are my son; today I have begotten you.'" On the basis of the later claim that the Psalms were written by David, this psalm was

used to support the belief that the Lord adopted as his sons all Davidic kings on the day they were enthroned. Logically, then, the future Messiah descended from David also would become the son of God. In all of the above the son of God is a human, not divine, person, and the expression is not yet a title.

Many early Christians applied this idea to Jesus and used the same two verses as the scriptural basis. He became the human Son of God when God adopted him at his resurrection/ ascension or at his baptism. Two pericopes in Mark depict the heavenly voice of God as declaring Jesus to be his beloved Son at his baptism (1:11) and at his transfiguration (9:7). The original setting of the transfiguration probably was Jesus' ascension. If that deduction is correct, then the transfiguration agrees with the tradition in Acts 2:34-36 that "God has made him both Lord and Christ" at his ascension. As the Lord had adopted the Israelite kings at their enthronement, so did he adopt Jesus at his enthronement in heaven (in pre-Marcan Christian tradition) or at his baptism (the belief in Mark).

Although "a son of God" remained a term for a righteous person, "Son of God" became a title for the Messiah, as in the synoptic gospels[4] and Acts 9:20. Contrary to popular opinion today, "Son of God" in Paul's letters and the synoptic gospels designate a human, not divine, Christ.

Although the idea that the Messiah would be the anointed Son of God was already in Judaism, biblical scholars have debated whether the actual title was current there, or whether it originated in early Christianity. Fragments of scrolls found at Qumran should settle the debate. In one scroll (4QFlor 10-14) Psalm 2:7 (in which the Lord calls the king "my Son") is interpreted as a prophecy about the coming Messiah,[5] and Christians interpreted it as a prophecy about the Messiah Jesus in Acts 13:33 and in the story of his baptism. Decisive evidence is in another Dead Sea scroll fragment, 4Q246, in which the Messiah is called "the Son of God" and "the Son of the Most High." This text demonstrates that these titles "were part of Christianity's original Jewish heritage," as Hershel Shanks states.[6] Both titles are in Luke 1, where, as in this fragment, the text predicts that the coming king "shall be called" by these names.

With the passage of time the title was taken more literally by some Christians; Jesus was the Son of God not by adoption, but from birth. This point of view led to the creation of the birth

stories in Matthew and Luke, in which Jesus is still of Davidic descent through Joseph, and yet it is the Holy Spirit which impregnates Mary. In Luke 1:35 the angel says that Jesus will be called "the Son of God"; thus Luke explicitly combines Davidic descent with the title Son of God. The Son of God Messiah could be–but was not necessarily–also the Son of David.

Do the virgin birth stories make Jesus a divine being? Not really. In the first place, the authors did not do a thorough job of integrating their material. On the one hand, Joseph did not have sexual intercourse with Mary until after Jesus was born (Matt. 1:25), and it was the Holy Spirit which impregnated her in both gospels. That makes the Spirit the father. On the other hand, Joseph is implied to be Jesus' father wherever he is said to be of Davidic descent (Matt. 1:20 and the genealogies). The confusion is the result of mixing two different views of Jesus' birth. Even the Holy Spirit as his father did not make Jesus divine in the sight of the authors of Matthew and Luke, judging from other aspects of their gospels. Those Jewish-Christian authors were not trying to portray Jesus as divine, but rather wanted to *enlarge the theory that Jesus had the Holy Spirit.* Since *possession* of the Spirit did not make Paul and other Christians divine, would *birth* by the Spirit make one divine?

Greek and Roman myths relate that certain gods had made love to women on earth, producing superior human progeny. The god Zeus and the mortal woman Alcmene were the parents of Hercules; according to Euripides, intercourse was accomplished by "the descent of Zeus's glory."[7] Legends arose that Alexander the Great, Romulus and Remus, Plato, Pythagoras, and others were the sons of gods.[8]

Nevertheless, gentile Christians soon began to interpret "Son of God" as signifying the divinity of Jesus. Rudolf Bultmann once stated this succinctly:

But one must recognize that the title, which originally designated the messianic king, now takes on a new meaning which was self-evident to Gentile hearers. Now it comes to mean *the divinity of Christ, his divine nature,* by virtue of which he is differentiated from the human sphere.[9]

Although "Son of God" occurs in John in the Gospel of Signs source in the early Jewish-Christian sense of a human Messiah, the author of John used it in the divine sense.[10] In

Shepherd of Hermas the Son of God is a supernatural figure who sustains all creation. [11] The development of the idea of a cosmic Christ will be described in the next chapter.

Son of Man

Jesus as the Son of Man has been the most puzzling, the most enigmatic, of all the christologies in the early christian communities. Biblical scholars have spilled many drops of ink over it. Is the Son of Man human or divine? Did Jesus utter the Son of Man sayings? Does this title refer to Jesus or to someone else? The history of the Son of Man tradition is complex and fascinating.

In the Near East the expression "son of man" meant simply "man." This usage occurs in the Old Testament too. The prophet Ezekiel applied the expression to himself many times, and it occurs in Psalm 8:4 and the Aramaic manuscripts from Qumran. [12] When it occurs in the New Testament, however, it denotes a supernatural figure. How could it have that meaning? What is the origin and development of the idea of a supernatural Son of Man?

Sometime, somewhere in the ancient Near East— probably in Iran—a myth arose about a primordial, supernatural Man. Historians have called him Anthropos (Greek for "Man"), Primal Man, First Man, or simply Man. A German term for him is *Urmensch*. The original myth has been lost, but the Parables of *1 Enoch*, *Sibylline Oracles* (Book 5), Philo, 4 Ezra, Gnostic writings, and the Hermetic document *Poimandres* contain enough allusions to "Man" as a pre-existent, supernatural being to tell us that the general idea was floating around in Syria and Egypt at the time of Christian beginnings. "Son of Man" in the Parables in *1 Enoch* is a term for the Man. The idea of the Primal Man is modified by Jewish thought in the Parables, Philo, and 4 Ezra and by Greek and Gnostic thought in *Poimandres*. *Poimandres* is too late to be a source for us, but it retains a primitive feature: the supreme God existed before the Man and gave him authority over the world. [13]

A Near Eastern poem is quoted in Daniel 7:9-10, 13-14, in which "one like a son of man" came "with the clouds of heaven . . . to the Ancient of Days . . . and to him was given dominion and glory and kingdom, that all peoples, nations, and languages should serve him. His dominion is an everlasting dominion, . . . and his kingdom one that shall not be destroyed." Is the one "like a man" here the Primordial Man or a god who looks like a man?

The author of Daniel reinterpreted him as a personification of the people of Israel because he wanted to use this extract from a poem to support the idea that Yahweh is going to give Israel dominion over the whole world. This reinterpretation tells us nothing about the meaning of the original poem, however. "One like a son of man" does not mean Man, but rather that the personage looks like a man. His traveling on clouds suggests that he may be Baal, the Canaanite and Phoenician god who was called "the rider of the clouds."[14] The "Ancient of Days" in Daniel corresponds to the Canaanite "Father of Years," for both titles indicate the god was very old.[15] Ugaritic, or Canaanite, myths have been excavated which tell of Baal defeating his enemies, then coming to the assembly of the gods in the skies and receiving from El, the ancient head of the pantheon of the gods, the worldly dominion. Judging from this evidence, the "one like a man" is not Primordial Man, but Baal. Daniel 7 is the source of "one like a son of man" in Revelation 1:13 and 14:14; it is also the source of the addition of "coming with the clouds of heaven" to the Son of Man pericope in Mark 14:62. But we must look elsewhere for the source of the title and basic characteristics of the Son of Man in the gospels and Acts 7.

We turn to the Parables section of *1 Enoch* to find closer similarity to the Christian Son of Man. The Parables are Jewish and pre-Christian. Here we find features that are probably preserved from the myth of the Primordial Man. In it the Lord of Spirits (God) chose the Son of Man before the creation of the world and has hidden him in his presence (48:6). Even his name was preexistent: his name was named before the sun and stars were created (48:3). The name "Lord of Spirits" suggests an Iranian, or Persian, background.

A general description of the Son of Man in the Parables was given in chapter 3 above. He is a syncretism of the Primordial Man, the Mazdean-Zoroastrian savior Saoshyans (who will come at the end of the present era to resurrect the dead), and Jewish Messiah. Consequently he is a supernatural Messiah. At the end of this age God will reveal him to the holy elect ones—that is, the righteous (62:7). The Son of Man will descend from heaven, depose the rulers of the earth (46:5), who will worship him and beg for mercy, but they will be punished

174

(62:9-10); he will sit on his throne of glory and judge the living and the risen dead (62); only the righteous will live on earth; the Son of Man will reveal the wisdom of the Lord of Spirits to them (48:7); all the righteous will worship him (48:5); he and they will dwell here forever. The parallelism of some of these features with the Son of Man in the synoptic gospels is too close to be accidental. Matthew even quotes a clause from it. In *1 Enoch* 62:3, 5, the Son of Man will "sit on the throne of his glory" and conduct the Judgment, and in Matthew 25 also the Son of Man will "sit on the throne of his glory" and conduct the Judgment. (The exact parallelism that exists is hidden in English translations such as "his glorious throne" in RSV [Matt. 25:31].) He has taken away from Yahweh two functions: raising the dead and conducting the Judgment.

For the earliest Christian use of the name and concept of the Son of Man, we turn to the Q material and to Mark. Of the eight pericopes, or units, in Q that mention the Son of Man, four are about miscellaneous aspects of the Son of Man—all of Christian origin. The other four, however, are about one subject, namely, the return, or parousia, of the Son of Man. In them his coming will be sudden, unexpected, and will bring judgment.[16] None of these sayings display influence from Daniel 7, but the last four pertain to the basic function of the Son of Man in *1 Enoch*; namely, he will come down to earth to conduct the Judgment. This concentration and his title indicate the influence on Q of the Son of Man tradition in sectarian Judaism.

In Mark the title Son of Man occurs in thirteen verses, three of which are concerned with Jesus' future coming.[17] Here too his title indicates the influence of the Parables; in two verses the Son of Man will come "with the clouds of heaven," which indicates the use of Daniel 7. In 14:62 "the Son of Man seated at the right hand of Power" (God) exhibits the use of Psalm 110:1 to support the belief that Jesus is in heaven, and what would seem more logical than to combine it with the Son of Man who is in heaven? Thus Mark combines support of the ascension faith with support of the faith in Jesus' return.

The title "Son of Man" occurs in a source used in the Gospel of John. Let us examine the twelve verses that contain it to see what is going on there. In six of the verses the Son of Man is directly related to the faith in Jesus' ascension.[18] Here, for the first time in Christianity, the belief in the preexistence of

175

the Son of Man is accepted; Jesus has existed in heaven, has descended to earth, and has ascended again. "No one has ascended into heaven except he who descended from heaven, the Son of Man" (3:13). And "what if you were to see the Son of Man ascending *where he was before?*" (6:62). In John Jesus is the semi-gnostic Christ, the Son of the Father, who is a preexistent Savior who has descended to earth and has ascended again. The Son of Man christology, in this respect, is compatible with the Son of the Father christology. But the Johannine christology is not compatible with the belief that the Christ is coming to earth again. Therefore there is no parousia in John; Jesus will send the spirit of Truth instead (15:26). In one verse in John the older idea of the Son of Man as judge on judgment day has survived: the Father has given the Son authority to execute judgment because he is the Son of Man (5:27). This verse clearly is an effort to unite the Son of the Father with the Son of Man. In two verses in John the Son of Man has been (13:31) or will be (12:23) "glorified"; apparently these are references to Jesus' crucifixion as the first step toward his ascension.

In all four canonical gospels miscellaneous features are associated with the Son of Man. The only apparent reason for this is to reinforce belief that Jesus is the Son of Man by frequently repeating the title. There must have been a need for such support. Historical deduction tells us that early tension surely existed within Christianity over belief in two opposing types of Christ: the human Son of David and the supernatural Son of Man. Adherents of the belief that Jesus is the Son of Man must have encountered strong opposition from both Jews and Jewish Christians, and consequently they strove mightily to support their belief. Three pericopes may reflect that situation. In Q we read that whoever says a word against the Son of Man will be forgiven;[19] this indicates that some people were speaking against the Son of Man. Their speech may well have included rejection of the belief that he is Jesus. If not, why is Jesus' title here Son of Man instead of Son of David or the Christ? Disbelief that Jesus is the Son of Man could also be reflected in John 9:35, where Jesus asks the blind man, "Do you believe in the Son of Man?" Also, "whoever is ashamed of me and of my words in this adulterous and sinful generation, of him will the Son of Man also be ashamed, when he comes in the glory of his Father with the holy angels" (Mark 8:38). Why is Son of Man the messianic title chosen to be connected with being ashamed of Jesus?

Since the Son of Man in *1 Enoch* is a supernatural being who lives forever, Jews must have found it especially difficult to believe that a human who had died could be the Son of Man. Mark 8:31 probably was written to alleviate the problem. It represents Jesus as declaring that the Son of Man *must* suffer, be killed, and rise again. Non-Christian Jews evidently regarded as blasphemy the belief that Jesus was the supernatural Son of Man, for that opinion is ascribed to the high priest in Jesus' trial before the Sanhedrin (Mark 14:64).

The author of Mark had a special reason for accepting the Son of Man christology and rejecting the Son of David christology, as he did. Six of the Son of Man sayings in Mark pertain to Jesus' arrest and crucifixion.[20] According to them Jesus taught his disciples that "it is written that the Son of Man must suffer" (a statement contrary to fact), that the Son of Man will be delivered to men who will kill him, and that Judas' betrayal is a case of the Son of Man being "betrayed into the hands of sinners." Why does Mark contain a concentration on this theme? It certainly does not come out of the original Son of Man christology—the supernatural Son of Man would never die!

As we have seen, explaining Jesus' death was a tremendous problem for the earthly Christians. How could he possibly be the Christ when he died without accomplishing the mission of the Christ? One solution was to claim that all is according to divine plan, a mystery which has been kept *secret*. And the Son of Man of the Parables seemed to fit in with this theory, even though, unlike the historical Jesus, he was a preexistent being.

In Mark Jesus' identity as the Christ is generally kept secret from outsiders; therefore he speaks in parables, and after the Transfiguration he commands Peter, James, and John not to tell anyone what they have seen "until the Son of Man has risen from the dead" (9:9). He commands that no one should make known his reviving a little girl from the dead and his healing a deaf man (but people proclaimed it anyway) and a blind man; when he exorcises demons, he orders them not to tell anyone about it.[21] Why does Mark associate his secrecy theme with the Son of Man Christ?

The answer is in the Parables of *1 Enoch*, where the Son

of Man will reveal secrets to his chosen, the righteous.

> And he [the Elect One, the One chosen by God to be the Messiah, who is also the Son of Man] shall choose the righteous and holy ones from among (the risen dead), . . . In those days, (the Elect One) shall sit on my [the Lord of Spirits'] throne, and from the conscience of his mouth shall come out all the secrets of wisdom, for the Lord of the Spirits has given them to him and glorified him (*1 Enoch* 51:2-3).

Thus the Son of Man, whom the Lord of Spirits has secretly kept hidden in heaven, and who will come to earth and reveal "the secrets of wisdom" to the righteous whom he has chosen, was far better suited to Mark's theory of the messianic secret than was the Son of David Messiah. The secrecy features of the Enochic Son of Man seemed to explain why most people did not realize that the Messiah is the Son of Man and that Jesus is he. The same passage also gave support to the idea that the Christ should be a teacher, revealing God's wisdom. Scholars generally have missed the connection between Mark's messianic secret theory and the Son of Man in the Parables.

The basic Christian reason for adopting the Son of Man Christology was the need to find a type of Christ that would be in heaven and then come down to earth. In short, the early Christians needed support for their faith in Jesus' ascension to heaven and return to earth. The German professors Hans Conzelmann and Philipp Vielhauer, among others, recognize this.[22] As Vielhauer realizes, the exaltation of Enoch to become the Son of Man was probably a factor. The compiler of *1 Enoch* added to the Parables the chapters 70-71 in which God takes Enoch up to heaven and appoints him to be the Son of Man. Some Christians adapted the idea to fit their need; they claimed that it was Jesus who was taken up to heaven to become the Son of Man. Hence a source in the Gospel of John emphasizes the necessity of the exaltation of the Son of Man for two reasons: to support the belief in Jesus' ascension and the belief that he was the Son of Man. Neither Enoch nor Jesus was preexistent in heaven, but that discrepancy was ignored except in John, where Jesus is the preexistent Son of the Father.

The Enochic Son of Man provided support for the faith in Jesus' ascension, for Mark's theory that Jesus gave secret teaching to his disciples, and for the general idea that Jesus was a teacher. The statement in the Parables that "the spirit of righteousness has been poured out upon him" (62:2) must have seemed to both the author of *1 Enoch* and the author of Mark to be a clear indication that the Son of Man is the Messiah.

In Mark 8:32-33 Jesus rebukes Peter for objecting to the idea that the Son of Man must "be killed and after three days rise again." This pericope is surely a rebuke, not by Jesus but by some early Christians, of disbelief that the human Jesus, who was killed, could be the supernatural Son of Man.

There is a growing consensus among biblical scholars that the expression Son of Man in the gospels does indeed refer to Jesus, but he never applied it to himself or uttered any of the Son of Man sayings. The belief in his ascension to heaven and return to earth as the Son of Man or any other type of Christ originated in the early Christian communities, not with Jesus. Invariably the Son of Man sayings deal with one or another of the beliefs and problems that first arose in the churches.

In Q the Son of Man is not the suffering Messiah who will die; that idea first appears in Mark. Matthew and Luke incorporate Mark's theory, and Luke adds its author's own support in 17:24-25, stating that the Son of Man "must suffer many things and be rejected by this generation."

The Parables of *1 Enoch* had applied to the Son of Man the idea in Deutero-Isaiah that the messiah would be "the light of the gentiles." [23] This aspect must have appealed to those Jewish Christians who believed that the Christian mission should be extended to the gentiles.

THE PROBLEM OF THE CHRIST- B

WHICH TYPE OF CHRIST, cont.

The Eschatological Prophet

A belief in Judaism was that before the messianic kingdom was established, God would send an eschatological Prophet, that is, a special prophet who would come "in the last days." Several forms of this belief are present in the literature of early Judaism.

1. *A non-Messiah Prophet.* One belief was that a special prophet who is not the Messiah will come at the end of this age. The Maccabees tore down the altar of burnt offering in the Temple because gentiles had profaned it. Then they stored its stones on the Temple hill "until there should come a prophet to tell what to do with them" (1 Macc. 4:46). In the same book "the Jews and their priests decided that Simon should be their leader and high priest forever, until a trustworthy prophet should arise" (14:41). They may, or may not, have thought of the prophet as an eschatological one; apparently his role will include making legal decisions.

The *Manual of Discipline* states that the Essenes "shall be ruled by the first laws with which the men of the Community began to be disciplined until the coming of a Prophet and the Messiahs of Aaron and Israel" (1QS 9:10-11). Evidence of a Jewish belief in an eschatological Prophet who is not the Messiah is also in the Gospel of Signs: When asked, the Baptist confesses that he is not the Christ, or Elijah, or the Prophet (John 1:21); here the Prophet is clearly thought of as a person distinct from the Messiah, the Christ.

2. *Prophet-Messiah, or Prophet-King.* In chapter 7 we found that some self-proclaimed prophets aspired to be the king of Israel, and therefore they tried to start rebellions. Thus they combined in themselves the concepts of the future Prophet and

the future Messiah.

In the synoptic gospels Jesus is the Messiah who is also a prophet. Matthew and Luke, contrary to Mark and John, mix in the idea that Jesus is also the Son of David Messiah. In the synoptics Jesus has the attributes of a Jewish prophet: At his baptism the Holy Spirit descends on him, and in all four canonical gospels God has "sent" Jesus,[1] a characteristic of Jewish prophets. Jesus, the Christ, is clearly a prophet in Luke 4, where he is depicted as reading in the synagogue at Capernaum a passage from Isaiah 61 and applying it to himself:

The Spirit of the Lord is upon me,
Because the Lord has anointed me
To bring good tidings to the poor.
. . .
To proclaim the year of the Lord's favor,
And the day of vengeance of our Lord.

In a post-resurrection story the disciples say that Jesus was "a prophet mighty in deed and word before God and all the people." Then they add, "We had hoped that he was the one to redeem Israel" (Luke 24:19-21). In this passage the disciples clearly think that Jesus is both a prophet and the Messiah. Though not explicitly *the* Prophet, Jesus here is both a prophet and the Messiah.

In the Gospel of Signs, however, Jesus is definitely the Prophet-Messiah; he is the Messiah in John 4:26 and "the Prophet who is coming into the world" in John 6:14. In the latter the people hail Jesus as the Prophet after he performs the miracle of the fish and loaves. In the next verse: "Perceiving then that they were about to come and take him by force to make him king, Jesus withdrew again to the hills by himself." Of interest to us here is the fact that in this pericope the belief that Jesus is the eschatological Prophet causes the people to think that he should be king.

3. *Elijah.* Another Jewish belief was that Elijah would return as the eschatological Prophet. In Sirach 48:10-11 we find:

You who are ready at the appointed time, as it is written,
To calm the wrath of God before it breaks out in fury,
To turn the heart of the father to the son,
And to restore the tribes of Jacob.

Here Elijah is the Prophet Messiah. He is not only a reconciler, but also a restorer; he will restore Israel as a nation, which is a function of the Messiah. (The Servant of the Lord in

Isaiah 49 will also restore the nation by causing the Jews who are scattered abroad (the Diaspora) to return to Palestine.)

The belief that Jesus was Elijah is rejected in Mark 8:27-29 par. Some people wondered if Jesus was one of the prophets of old who had returned (Mark 8:28 par).

4. *Moses.* Another concept of the messianic Prophet that existed in Judaism was of Moses *redivivus*, Moses brought back to life. Moses had prepared the way for the establishment of Israel. Therefore it seemed logical that he would return and reestablish the nation. Moses was hailed as the greatest: "And there has not arisen since in Israel a prophet like Moses, whom the Lord knew face to face" (Deut. 34:10). In his *Life of Moses* Philo portrayed Moses as the ideal king and ideal prophet. In fact, Philo virtually deified him: "He was named [by God] god and king of the whole nation."2 Moses is called a king in some rabbinic traditions. A further step in honoring Moses as a great hero was the creation of the tradition that he, as well as Jeremiah, Isaiah, Baruch, and Ezra, "was taken up to heaven without tasting death." Presumably that tradition was in the lost *Assumption of Moses*. The belief in Moses' assumption, or ascension, of course, prepared the way for the expectation that he would return as the eschatological prophet.

Apparently in some circles Moses and Elijah were expected to return together as eschatological prophets. In Revelation 11 the seer has a vision of the coming of two of God's witnesses who will prophesy for three and a half years. They evidently are Moses and Elijah, for they will have the power to perform the same kind of miracles they did. These "witnesses" are probably Messiahs, for they can kill their enemies by fire from their mouths, an attribute of the Messiah in some apocalyptic literature. Further evidence that they are Messiahs is the fact that they are represented as the two olive trees in Zechariah, which in 4:14 are called "anointed ones" (the same term as "Messiah"). The belief that Moses and Elijah will return is explicit centuries later in the Midrash, *Deuteronomy Rabbah* 3 (ca. A.D. 900).

Early Christians did not regard Jesus as Moses *redivivus*. The situation was different, however, in respect to another concept of an eschatological prophet, to which we now turn.

5. *Prophet like Moses.* The coming in the last days of a prophet like Moses was another idea in limited circulation. It

was derived from Deuteronomy 18:18-19, in which the Lord promises Moses:

> I will raise up for them a prophet like you from among their brethren; and I will put my words in his mouth, and he shall speak to them all that I command him. And whoever will not give heed to my words which he shall speak in my name, I myself will require it of him.

With the passage of centuries Moses acquired a reputation as the supreme lawgiver, and numerous Israelite codes were ascribed to him. In the passage above the prophet like Moses will be like him in that he, too, will speak the Lord's commandments. An Essene *Testimonia* leaf found at Qumran quotes the same passage in Deuteronomy. Whether the Essenes applied this to their founder, the Teacher of Righteousness, or to the future Prophet is not clear. It could fit either person, for the Teacher of Righteousness gave the sect some new rules, or laws, and, as *Manual of Discipline* 9:11 shows, the coming Prophet will too.

The Samaritans believed that the same Deuteronomic passage is a prophecy of the Prophet Messiah they expected.

The Samaritans' Messiah, called *Taheb* or *Shaheb*, meaning "Restorer," would restore the "Second Kingdom," which was their equivalent of the Jewish and primitive Christian messianic kingdom. He will gather the scattered Samaritans, deliver them from persecution, and restore them to freedom, while ruling as their king. He will rebuild their temple on Mount Gerizim and discover the hidden vessels of the old Tabernacle. The Messiah will be the Prophet like Moses promised in Deuteronomy 18:15, a passage which the Samaritans considered to be so important that they included it in their own lengthy Tenth Commandment. On the basis of this Deuteronomic passage the Samaritans called him "the Teacher." Apparently the teaching would not be new law, but rather the instruction of non-Samaritans in the old Samaritan law. The Samaritans maintained also that this Restorer Messiah might be Moses himself come to life again. Thus the Samaritans combined two concepts of the Mosaic eschatological Prophet: the return of Moses himself, and the coming of a Prophet like Moses. This Messiah would be a priestly one, from the tribe of Levi.

While Pontius Pilate was procurator of Judea, a Samaritan arose who claimed to be the Messiah. He assembled a multitude, promising them that if they would follow him up Mount Gerizim, he would show to them the sacred vessels which Moses had hidden there.[3] Since the Samaritans expected their Messiah to be a New Moses, they must have regarded this man in that light, and he probably pretended to be such. . . . Origen relates: "After the time of Jesus, also Dositheus the Samaritan wished to persuade the Samaritans that he was the Christ [Messiah] predicted by Moses, and he appears to have won over some to his views."[4] The phrase, "predicted by Moses," probably indicates that Dositheus claimed to be the prophet of Deuteronomy 18.

The Samaritan miracle-worker, Simon Magus, whose career, according to Justin, was during the reign of Claudius Caesar (A.D. 41-54), apparently was identified by his followers with the eschatological Prophet.[5]

Two passages in Acts represent Jesus as the Prophet-like-Moses type of Messiah. In Peter's speech in 3:22-23 the Deuteronomic passage is quoted as a prophecy about Jesus uttered by Moses. A portion of it is quoted again in Stephen's speech in 7:37.

Two features in the Deuteronomic passage must have appealed to early Christians. In it God will "raise up" (Greek in LXX: *anistemi*) a prophet. This means that God will cause him to be born, but the author of Acts uses the same verb to denote Jesus' resurrection (2:24, 32). Thus the passage could easily be misinterpreted as a prophecy of God's raising Jesus up from the grave. The second appealing feature in the passage is the denunciation of anyone who does not listen to the words of the prophet. This could seem very appropriate at a time when Christians were confronted with Jewish disbelief and persecution, the main concern in Stephen's speech. Samaritan converts seem to be the most probable Christians to be the first to regard Jesus as the Prophet-like-Moses type of Christ. Although this Christology appears early in Acts, it disappeared from Christian literature until the third century, when the Clementine books and some church fathers revived it.[6]

The Cosmic Son

In some early Christian writings Jesus is "the Son" (of God or of "the Father") in a cosmic, semi-Gnostic or even Gnostic sense. Sometimes the Father is not mentioned, and sometimes "the Son" may be the Son of God in a non-cosmic sense. By "cosmic" we mean that the Son is a supernatural, preexistent being who has existed in the heavens from the beginning of time. The Son of Man in *1 Enoch* is a cosmic Messiah, but "the Son" is not one of his titles. The origin of the Son of the Father Christology is to be found in Gnosticism, where the Son knows the Father, the Father knows the Son, and believers seek to know both.

The earliest occurrence of this type of Christology in Christian writings is a pericope from Q in Matthew and Luke:

All things have been delivered to me by my Father, and no one knows who the Son is except the Father, or who the Father is except the Son and anyone to whom the Son chooses to reveal him (Luke 10:22).

In the parallel verse in Matthew 11:27 the text is "knows the Son" and "knows the Father" instead of "knows who the Son [or Father] is." The Lucan version is probably earlier than Matthew, for when Matthew and Luke differ in the reading of Q material, Matthew's version tends to contain that author's own ideas and diction. In short, Matthew has changed Q, and Luke's version is closer to the original. A further indication that Matthew's version is later is that the thought in it is close to that in John 10:15 and 17:25, verses written several decades after Q was formulated. The idea in the Q pericope is semi-Gnostic, quite unlike the rest of the material in the synoptic gospels. Why is the pericope included in Q? A reasonable deduction is that the Son of Man sayings in Q induced the editor who compiled the Q sayings to include this saying about the Son, for both the Son of Man and the Son were supernatural, preexistent figures, and both had the word Son in their titles.

In the first chapter of Hebrews Jesus is God's Son who is the preexistent figure through whom God has created the world. "He reflects the glory of God and bears the very stamp of his nature, upholding the universe by his word of power." He is God's firstborn whom the angels should worship. He has come to earth, made purification for sins by his death, and ascended to heaven temporarily. Elsewhere in Hebrews Jesus is called "the Son of God." Here in Hebrews 1 we have a transformation of the Son of God Christology under the influence of Hellenistic mysticism.

The first chapter of Colossians too has an early stage of the Son of the Father Christology. God is "the Father" and Jesus is "his beloved Son."

> He [Jesus] is an image of the invisible God, the firstborn of all creation; for by [not "in"; this is the instrumental use of *en* in the Greek text] him all things were created, in heaven and on earth, visible and invisible, whether thrones or dominions or principalities or authorities. . . . For in him all the fullness [Greek: *pleroma*, a Gnostic term; "of God" is not in the Greek text] was pleased to dwell (Col. 1:15-16, 19).

This passage, not written by Paul, rests on advanced Hellenistic mysticism that had not yet developed into real Gnosticism. It lacks the basic element of Gnosticism, namely, the necessity of "knowing" the Son and the Father and whence one's soul is from and whither it is going. The beloved Son here has come to earth and suffered as a human, for he has reconciled all things to himself, "whether on earth or in heaven, making peace through the blood of his cross." In both Hebrews and Colossians Jesus is the Son of God, but "the Son" has not become a title, as it has in the Q passage cited above. In the *Shepherd of Hermas*, Jesus is supernatural and preexistent and is called "the Son of God." "The Son of God is much older than all his creation, so that he was the Father's counselor in his creation." "The name of the Son of God is great and incomprehensible and sustains the whole world."[7]

Ignatius, bishop of Antioch, also regarded Jesus as God's preexistent Son.[8] In the greeting of his letter *To the Romans* Ignatius refers to Jesus as "the Son of the Father." Ignatius uses the titles "the Son of God" and "the Son" once each.[9] God is frequently "Father." These facts may seem insignificant at first, but actually they are evidence of a process that was underway in the churches at the close of the first century and beginning of the second, namely, a reinterpretation of Jesus in terms of Hellenistic mysticism. Philo, the Alexandrian Jew, had reinterpreted Judaism in those terms, and apparently some Alexandrian gentiles created some philosophy and the Hermetic cult along similar lines. (It is tragic that the great Alexandrian library was destroyed by fire; if it had survived, it would have given us a much fuller view of the contemporary world.)

Jesus is preexistent, but not called "Son," in 2 Tim. 1:9, John 1:9-11, and insertions Phil. 2:6-11 and Col. 1:15-19.

Within the New Testament the most developed Cosmic Son concept of the Christ is in the Gospel of John. Here the title "the Son" occurs twenty times, always in passages written by the gospel's author or from a semi-Gnostic source. Here the Son is developed in a Gnostic fashion. He is the Revealer sent to the earth by the Father to make known to the chosen ones the secret knowledge that will enable souls to return to heaven whence they came and whither they should go to escape this sinful world. The noun *gnosis*, "secret knowledge," does not occur in the text, but the corresponding verb does often; more important, the teaching that the Son makes known in John is of the Gnostic type (see chapter 24 below):

1. Jesus is the Son: (3:16-18).

2. The Son knows the Father, who has sent him to make known what the Father has taught him:

"He who has sent me is true, and him you do not know. I know him, for I come from him, and he sent me" (7:28-29).

"The Father knows me and I know the Father" (10:15).

"All things which I have heard from my Father I have made known to you" (15:15).

"Righteous Father, even the world did not know you, but I knew you" (17:25).

"My teaching is not mine, but his who sent me" (7:16).

3. Knowing the Father is vital, and the way to know the Father is to know the Son:

"You know neither me nor my Father; if you knew me, you would know the Father also" (8:19).

"I am the way, and the truth, and the life; no one comes to the Father, but by me" (14:6).

4. The teaching that the Son gives to those whom he has chosen includes knowledge of whence the Son has come and whither he is going:

"I know whence I have come and whither I am going, but you [Pharisees] do not know whence I come or whither I am going" (8:14).

5. The cosmos is divided into two opposing regions: "above" and "below", heaven and "this world":

"You [Jews] are from below; I am from above. You are of this world; I am not of this world" (8:23).

"You [disciples] are not of the world, but I chose you

out of the world; therefore the world hates you" (15:19).

6. Directly related to the two regions is the belief that it is necessary for humans to be born from above in order to enter the kingdom of God.

The Word

"By the word of the Lord the heavens were made, . . . For he spoke and it [the earth] came to be; he commanded, and it stood forth" (Ps. 33:6,9, Hebrew text; 32:6,9, LXX). In the Septuagint version of the passage the Greek term for "word" is *logos*. This belief continues in Wisdom of Solomon 9:1, where God has made all things by his word (*logos*). That book probably was written in Alexandria. Philo, who lived in Alexandria, virtually personified God's Word, and wrote that the Logos was with God at the Creation, and he even calls it "God."[10] He also associates the Logos with light.[11] Similar ideas were in Greek-Egyptian syncretism, as Émile Bréhier has observed.[12]

The Prologue of the Gospel of John (1:1-18) contains a Christian Gnostic hymn into which the author of the gospel has made a few insertions of his own composition, especially about John the Baptist. This Gnostic hymn itself, moreover, contains a Jewish poem which was not Gnostic, but is reinterpreted along Gnostic lines in the hymn.[13] The poem is an interpretation of Genesis 1, where God created the cosmos by uttering commands, thus creating by his word. The poem is in verses 1, 3-5, and 11; I have reconstructed it as follows:

> 1 In the beginning was the *Word*, and the *Word* was with *God*, and the Word was *God*. 3 All things *came to be* through it, and without it nothing *came to be*. 4 In it was *life*, and the *life* was the *light* of men. 5 And the *light* shines in the *darkness* and the *darkness* did not overcome it. 11 It came to *its own*, and *its own* did not receive it.

Observe the stylistic repetition: Word, Word; God, God; came to be, came to be; life, life; light, light; darkness, darkness; its own, its own. (The English phrases "came to be" and "its own" are single words in the Greek text.) The thought in the poem comes out of Hellenistic Judaism, especially that in Alexandria. Like Philo, the poem associates the Word, Logos, with light. Like Philo, it personifies the Word and states that it was with God at the Creation. The poem is also similar to some features in the Wisdom of Solomon. In order to recognize this, we must realize that God's Word and God's Wisdom are synonymous in Wisdom 9:1-2, and therefore what the book says about Wisdom applies also to the Logos. "With you [God] is Wisdom who knows your works and was with you when you made the world" (9:9). Another parallel which indicates the Jewish origin of the poem is the rejection of God's Word/ Wisdom. In the Wisdom of Solomon wicked men ignored Wisdom (10:8). The writer may have had Proverbs 1:20-22 in mind, for there Wisdom calls to men in the streets and markets, but the simple and scoffers pay no attention. This idea must be behind the poem's statement that the Word's own did not receive it. The logic is that because the Word created humanity, humanity is the Word's own; tragically humanity did not receive it.

A Christian composed a Gnostic hymn and incorporated the Jewish poem, which he reinterpreted by identifying the Word of God with Jesus. Why did he make this reinterpretation? Because as a Gnostic he believed that Jesus was a heavenly figure before he appeared on earth, and by using the poem the way he did, he obtained support from Jewish literature for his Gnostic view of Jesus. This reinterpretation of the poem makes Jesus a preexistent figure, God's agent at the Creation. It elevates him to equality with God—he performed God's task of creating the universe. This interpretation appealed to the author of John, so he attached the hymn as a prologue, with his insertions in it, because Jesus as the preexistent Word fits in with his own belief that Jesus is the preexistent Son of the Father. Considering his attacks on Jewish disbelief in Jesus, the evangelist must have also been attracted to the poem's sentence, "It came to its own, and its own did not receive it," with "its own" reinterpreted as "his own." Some biblical scholars have stated that in John the main doctrine of Jesus as the Christ is the Logos christology, in which Jesus is the Word of God. That view is an error, for Jesus is never called the Word in the rest of the gospel. Thus the source of the notion that Christ is the Word of God is not the author of John, but the Gnostic hymn he incorporated in the gospel's Prologue.

The early Christians were slow to adopt "the Word" as a title for Jesus. In the Apostolic Fathers the Word is usually not Jesus, but God's Word at the Creation, as in 1 Clement 27:4. In the second and third centuries some church fathers occasionally referred to Jesus as the Word, the Logos, but the expression did not become a major title like Christ, Son of God, and Lord. Justin mentions only incidentally that Christ, the Son of God, is also "the Son" of "the Father" and "the first-begotten Word of God."[14] Irenaeus states that Christ was the Word who existed with God from the beginning (3.18.1). Clement of Alexandria wrote: "Our Instructor is the holy God Jesus, the Word, who is the guide of all humanity."[15] Origen wrote: "He whom we regard and believe to have been God from the beginning, and the Son of God, is the very Word, and the very Wisdom, and the very Truth."[16]

The Servant

In the ancient Near East virtually all worshipers of a deity were regarded as the god's slaves or servants. Persons who performed special service to the deity, such as being his or her priest or prophet, could be regarded as particularly a servant. Prophets, patriarchs, and kings in the Old Testament are called "servants of the Lord." In the "Servant Songs" in Deutero-Isaiah[17] a prophet is the Lord's servant. At the close of the *Manual of Discipline* the Essene author of a hymn to God calls himself "your servant." Numerous psalmists said to the Lord, "I am your servant." "Servant of the Lord" and "the Servant" were not titles for the Messiah in Judaism or in primitive Christianity.

Jesus, whom God has anointed, is called God's servant in Acts 3:26 and 4:27, but so is David in 4:25. Both Jesus and David are God's servants in *Didache* 9:2, and both Jesus and Moses are in *1 Clement* (51:3; 59:2). In these instances Jesus is God's servant in the same sense as Moses and David.

Certain features in the Servant Songs in Isaiah appealed to Christian writers. "I have put my Spirit upon him" (42:1) seemed to fit the story of Jesus' baptism, and the synoptics' "with you I am well pleased" may be based on "my chosen, in whom my soul delights" (Hebrew text; LXX reads "Israel, my chosen, my soul receives him favorably") in the same verse. Matthew 12:18-21 loosely quotes the first Servant Song, but revises it. Matthew's source (one of the *testimonia*?) is quoting from the Septuagint, for only it has "and in his name will the gentiles hope." If the passage was a *testimonium*, or proof text, it must have been used to support the mission to the gentiles. The author of Matthew, however, has used it very illogically as a prophecy fulfilled by Jesus' healing the sick!

Christians treated the fourth Servant Song as a prophecy of Jesus' suffering and death, as we observed in chapter 11. This interpretation is explicit in Acts 8 where a passage in Isaiah 53 is quoted. The Ethiopian eunuch is reading it and Philip asks him about whom it is speaking. "Then Philip opened his mouth, and beginning with this Scripture he told him the good news of Jesus." This caused the eunuch's conversion.

The early Christians found the Servant Songs, as well as certain Psalms, to be very useful in their efforts to solve their intellectual problems and promote their faith. Isaiah 53 was an important force in shaping the synoptic accounts of Jesus' death. But the Servant in the Songs is not the Messiah. The Suffering Servant type of Messiah was not a concept in Judaism; Jewish Christians created it to help explain Jesus' death and to justify their mission to the gentiles.

The Messianic Priest

Jewish priests as well as kings were anointed with oil when they took office. Therefore when the belief arose in some quarters that a new high priest would appear in the new age or kingdom, it was only natural that he too would be called "Anointed One," or Messiah. The Jewish writers of *Testaments of the Twelve Patriarchs* believed in a dual messiahship: a king Messiah from the tribe of Judah (*Judah* 24) and a priest Messiah from the tribe of Levi (*Levi*18). The Essenes, too, expected a priest-Messiah and a king-Messiah as we have seen. The Essenes had a special reason for wanting a priestly Messiah. They were very unhappy with the priesthood in charge of the Temple in Jerusalem. They believed that Jews needed a new high priest who would conduct religious matters correctly.

Early Christians did not adopt a belief in two Messiahs but one New Testament writer believed that Jesus fulfilled both offices. Was there any precedent in Judaism for such a belief?

The Hasmonean kings, beginning with Simon in 142 B.C., had combined the office of high priest with the kingship (1 Macc. 13:42), a policy followed by Simon's son and successor, John Hyrcanus I. This policy, together with the Hasmoneans' shift from concern for religious freedom to emphasis on worldliness and territorial expansion angered the orthodox party, the Hasidim. Nevertheless, these kings had their followers, and someone in the king's court composed Psalm 110, a royal psalm sung at the coronation of either Simon or John Hyracanus. It sanctions the union of the kingship and the priesthood; in it the Lord has sworn that the king is "a priest forever after the order of Melchizedek."

The Christian author of the Epistle to the Hebrews combined the offices of high priest and king in his interpretation of Jesus as the Messiah. He applies the title "High Priest" to Jesus ten times. He describes Jesus as "having become a high priest forever after the order of Melchizedek. For this Melchizedek, king of Salem [i.e., Jerusalem], priest of the Most High God, met Abraham returning from the slaughter of the kings and blessed him" (Heb. 6:20-7:1). Why did the author choose Melchizedek? Because he was both a priest and king. But why interpret Jesus as a priestly Messiah? The author's reason is quite apparent. Christ, he states, became "flesh and blood. . . so that he might become a merciful and faithful high priest in the service of God, to make expiation for the sins of the people" (2:17). Jewish high priests had offered sacrifices for the sins of the people; Jesus was both the high priest and the sacrifice, for he had offered himself. The author's motive for this view is to enhance and support the doctrine of atonement as an explanation of Jesus' death.

This priestly Christology does not occur elsewhere in the New Testament, and it never became very popular in the early churches. The destruction of the Temple and the growing opposition to things Jewish (except the Old Testament—and some Gnostics rejected that) surely must have discouraged it.

COMPARISON OF THE TYPES

Much confusion and many arguments resulted from the early Christian efforts to decide what kind of Christ Jesus is. The original basic definition of the Christ that prevailed in both Judaism and primitive Christianity was that he would be a prophet-king anointed by God with the Holy Spirit. But the concept was revised by various Jews as the result of the influence of Iranian and Greek cultures. Various early Christians too revised and even replaced it with new concepts, produced partly by efforts to solve problems of belief, partly by the growing separation from Judaism, and partly by contact with other cultures as Christianity expanded. The main types of early christologies, or concepts of Jesus as the Christ, are in two categories: those that were already in Judaism, and those created by the Christians. For the sake of clarity let us here repeat by briefly listing the types and the reasons that they appeared in Christianity.

We begin with the types that were already in Judaism. The earliest in Christian faith was the general concept of the Prophet-King, who would become the Messiah when the Lord anointed him with the Holy Spirit.[18] The prevalence of this concept in contemporary Judaism would be enough cause for the disciples, who were Jews, to adopt it, but this belief probably has some foundation in Jesus' actual life. One form of this type of Christ was the Son of David. This was applied to Jesus by some Christians because they thought Jesus should fit Jewish expectations and prophecy, but it was rejected by other Christians because they and Jews knew that he was not a descendant of King David.

The belief that Jesus was a Prophet-like-Moses type of Christ was a short-lived minority view. A few Christians adopted it because it seemed to be prophesied in Deuteronomy, which thus gave support to the claim that the early Christians in general regarded as vital, namely, the claim that Jesus fulfills messianic prophecy.

A third type is the idea that Jesus became the Son of God by adoption. This has roots in the Jewish belief that Israelite kings were adopted by the Lord when they assumed the kingship (Ps. 2:7). This was not really a separate type of Christ in Judaism, but only an aspect of the Prophet-King. In effect, however, this became a separate concept in Christianity, when in the synoptics Jesus is anointed at his baptism.

The fourth type of Christ derived from Judaism is the Son of Man. Some Jewish Christians who came from a sectarian background chose it because the Son of Man was expected to descend to earth from heaven when the kingdom of God came, and that fit and supported the Christian faith that Jesus would soon do the same. Such support was needed, for the Christian claim that Jesus has died, ascended to heaven, and will return was a serious obstacle to Jewish acceptance of the Christian belief that he is the Messiah. The Son of Man christology did not solve the problem, however, because non-Christian Jews knew that he was not a supernatural, preexistent person. At first Christians overlooked the fact that Jesus had not previously existed in heaven; later they claimed that he had.

The second category of types of Christ consists of those created by the Christians. The earliest is the belief that Jesus became the Son of God at his ascension when God adopted him then as his Son and gave him supernatural power. The Messiah's adoption by God as his Son at his resurrection and ascension was, of course, unknown in Judaism, where there was no prophecy or expectation that the Messiah would be raised from the dead and ascend to heaven. This concept served to explain why Jesus had not overthrown Roman rule: God did not empower him during his earthly career.

The belief that Jesus became the Son of God by means of a virgin birth is completely Christian. It must have originated in a mixed Christian community of both Jewish and gentile converts; it served to compete with rival pagan hero cults whose gods were born of a divine father and human mother.

The idea of a cosmic figure in heaven who was created by God at the beginning of time is found in Judaism, but the figure was not a type of Messiah, except as the Son of Man. Under the influence of Gnosticism the figure became the Son of the Father who saves souls by revealing knowledge of the Father.

The Suffering Servant Messiah was created by some Christians to explain Jesus' death and support the mission to the gentiles. By identifying Jesus with the Servant in Deutero-Isaiah, the explanation was given scriptural support.

Jesus as the High Priest in Hebrews was another explanation of Jesus' death, suggested by the Jewish background. Nevertheless, the High Priest was not a definite type of Christ in other Christian literature of the first two centuries.

Christian doctrines did not originate systematically. No one drew up a set of beliefs that were in harmony with each other and were generally accepted. Christologies were no exception. If Jesus was the human Prophet-King, he could not be the divine Son of the Father. If he was a descendant of David, he could not be the preexistent Son who has existed in heaven from the beginning of time. If he was the Son of Man, he will help God set up his kingdom on a rejuvenated earth, but if he was the Son of the Father, he will not come back to earth, and immortality will be in heaven, not here on earth. Some efforts were made to combine the various titles and concepts of the Christ. In early Christian writings some titles given to Jesus were soon used interchangeably. "Christ," "Lord," "Son of

God," and "the Son" were applied to any or all concepts. Some writers combined several types, whether they fit together or not. The author of Mark combines the titles and some attributes of the Son of God and Son of Man and some features of the Suffering Servant. Apparently he was not trying to unify them systematically, but happened to combine them because he liked some aspects of each. Ignatius deliberately combined titles in his letter *To the Ephesians* 20:2: "Jesus Christ, who was physically descended from David, the Son of Man and Son of God." Reconciling the Incarnation with the Virgin Birth is impossible, but some enterprising church fathers tackled it as early as the second century:

Apology of Aristides: Jesus the Messiah . . . is called the Son of God Most High. And it is said that God came down from heaven, and from a Hebrew virgin assumed and clothed himself with flesh; and the Son of God lived in a daughter of man (2).[19]

Epistula Apostolorum: On that day, when I [the Lord Jesus Christ] took the form of the angel Gabriel, I appeared to Mary and (spoke) with her. Her heart received me and she believed; I formed myself and entered into her womb; I became flesh (14).[20]

Irenaeus, Bishop of Lyons: The Word, who existed in the beginning with God, by whom all things were made, who was also always present with mankind, was in these last days, according to the time appointed by the Father, united to his own workmanship, inasmuch as He became a man liable to suffering, [it follows] that every objection is set aside of those who say, "If our Lord was born at that time, Christ had therefore no previous existence." For I have shown that the Son of God did not then begin to exist, being with the Father from the beginning; but when He became incarnate, and was made man, He commenced afresh the long line of human beings, and furnished us, . . . with salvation.[21]

The different christologies created an interesting but incompatible variety of journeys of the Christ:
Son of David: earth to heaven to earth.
Son of Man: heaven to earth to heaven to earth.

Johannine Son of Man and Son of the Father: heaven to earth to heaven (no Second Coming).

ATTRIBUTES OF THE CHRIST

Righteousness
In Judaism the Messiah was generally expected to have certain attributes. Both the Son of David and the Son of Man would be completely righteous, and the early Christians naturally thought that Jesus was too. Jesus is "the Righteous One," or "the Righteous," in Acts 7:52 and 1 John 2:1. The author of the Gospel of Matthew inserted into the Marcan account of Jesus' trial before Pilate the story that Pilate's wife advised him to "have nothing to do with that righteous man, for I have suffered much over him today in a dream." The story is quite implausible as history, but is very understandable as the author's effort to exonerate Jesus, the "righteous" Messiah.

Knowledge and Wisdom
Another attribute of the Messiah in Judaism was that he would possess great knowledge and wisdom. Luke states that the child Jesus grew, "filled with wisdom, and the favor of God was upon him" (2:40). Luke also depicts Jesus at the age of twelve as astonishing the teachers in the Temple with his learning and understanding; then Luke adds that Jesus "increased in wisdom and in stature and in favor with God and man" (2:52). Philo told an equally fictional story about Moses in which teachers from many countries came to train him, but Moses soon "advanced beyond their capacities; his gifted nature forestalled their instruction, so that his case seemed to be one of recollection rather than of learning, and indeed he himself devised and propounded problems which they could not easily solve."[22] According to Mark 6:2 the people hailed Jesus' teaching in the synagogues as a display of astonishing "wisdom." Portraying Jesus as a man of great wisdom probably resulted from a desire to make him fit the description of the Messiah, although Acts 6 and 7 ascribe "wisdom" to others also.

FUNCTIONS OF THE CHRIST

King

At first the basic function of the Christ was the same in Christian thought as it was in Jewish expectation. He would restore the Jewish nation and assist God in establishing his kingdom. In one sense or another, both Jesus and God would be king. The concepts were vague and inconsistent. Christ will reign for a thousand years and then deliver the kingdom to God, according to the Book of Revelation. As Son of Man, Jesus' reign may have been expected to be permanent. The variety of the concepts is confusing.

The Son of Man christology contributed the function of judge at the Judgment.

The Christian atonement doctrine provided a new function, one that the Christ had already accomplished by his death.

The Jewish functions of the Christ decreased as gentile membership increased and the Great Controversy between Christians and Jews grew. More and more, Jesus became a deity whose primary function was to save the souls of the righteous and punish the wicked.

Teacher and/or Lawgiver

The Prophet-Messiah was expected to teach messages from God, even as other prophets had taught what the Lord had revealed to them. The coming Son of David in the *Psalms of Solomon* will teach, at least in his role as judge of the peoples in the assembles; "his words will be as the words of the holy ones" [angels] (17:43). The Son of Man will reveal God's wisdom to the righteous on earth (*1 Enoch* 48:7). Thus in the earliest churches members naturally thought that Jesus had been a teacher in the past, was continuing to be one by means of spiritual revelations in the present, and would teach in the future after his return to earth. That would be their conviction whether they believed that Jesus was the eschatological Prophet, the Son of David, or the Son of Man.

The Prophet like Moses would automatically be expected to be a lawgiver, for the belief was widely accepted that Moses wrote the Torah. Some Christians interpreted portions of the Servant Songs in Isaiah as prophecies of Jesus, and the Servant is a lawgiver ("and the coastlands wait for his law," 42:4). Paul wrote: "Bear one another's burdens, and so fulfill the law of Christ" (Gal. 6:2); he mentions "the law of Christ" again in 1 Corinthians 9:21. Whether Paul was influenced by the idea that the Messiah will be a lawgiver is uncertain. We are not surprised that Jesus is seldom portrayed as a lawgiver, for that messianic function is a minor theme in early Judaism compared with the theme that the Messiah will be a teacher. Also, the belief that the Messiah will be a Prophet like Moses was a minority view in both early Judaism and early Christianity.

The function of the Christ as a miracle worker is discussed in the next chapter.

14

MIRACLES

ANCIENT MIRACLES

Belief in miracles was prevalent in the superstitious ancient world, in both Near Eastern and Greek cultures. Sometimes a deity or a demon (either good or evil) performed the miracles directly, and sometimes a human being did something to make them act. Sometimes a miracle was called an act of "power" (Greek: *dunameis*), as in the synoptic gospels and Acts, where *dunameis* is often translated as "mighty work." The basis of the term was the belief that the miracle worker accomplished the deed by using a superior power, either his own or, typically, that of a deity. From the viewpoint of Jews and Christians, the human was a genuine miracle worker if he was a member of their own religious group, but only a magician if he was an outsider. Both Judaism and Christianity had miracle workers; both denounced magicians.

Some modern anthropologists maintain that in primitive societies personal experience is the source of miracle stories. The extent to which the theory is valid may be debatable, but it certainly does not explain the origin of the bulk of the biblical miracles. Neither the Near Eastern world of the Old Testament nor the Greco-Roman world of early Christianity were primitive societies. Instead, they were cultured societies in which heroes, miracle workers, and deities played a large role and were expected to perform miracles. If they were unable to do so, they were not accepted as superior beings by the populace. Both tellers of oral folk tales and writers of literature responded to the need.

Ancient miracles can be divided into two broad categories: general, including nature miracles, and healings. Restoring the dead to life can be viewed as the ultimate in healing. Various means could be used to perform miracles: commands, use of the name of a powerful being, laying on of hands, prayer, faith, and uttering magic formulas.

The canonical gospels ascribe numerous nature miracles to Jesus. This type may be defined as events in which supernatural power overrides the laws of nature. Perhaps the story of Jesus' stilling "the great storm of wind" in Mark 4 was suggested by an act of the Lord in the Psalms: "Then they cried to the Lord in their trouble, and he delivered them from their distress; he made the storm be still, and the waves of the sea were hushed" (107:28-29). (We must remember that the early Christians often erroneously interpreted "the Lord" in the Old Testament as a reference to Jesus.)

Healers and healing miracle stories were especially popular in ancient times. War injuries, accidents, and prevalence of disease on the one hand, and lack of scientific knowledge of methods of healing on the other hand, created a tremendous yearning for health and an eager demand for healing. Anyone who was thought capable of healing others was immensely popular. A few such persons were even deified after their death, including the Egyptian physician Imhotep, a vizier of the pharaoh Zozer (ca. 3000 B.C.), and the Greek physician Asklepios (before 700 B.C.). At the time that Christianity began, itinerant healers traveled around plying their trade in the Mediterranean world. Apollonius of Tyana, a Pythagorean philosopher (1st c. A.D.), is reported to have healed various ailments. For centuries before and after Christianity arose, the cult of Asklepios (Latin: Aesculapius) healed and claimed to heal many who were ill, lame, paralytic, blind, dumb, and deaf, as inscriptions and votive gifts found at its cult centers (especially at Epidauros, Greece) testify. The cult mixed sheer superstition (the god took the form of a serpent and healed while the patient slept at the center) with rational means (surgery, exercise, and rest in the center's sanitarium). Temples and health centers of Asklepios operated from Spain to the Near East.

The New Testament contains several summary statements about Jesus as a healer. "And he healed many who were sick with various diseases, and cast out many demons" (Mark 1:34). "He went about doing good and healing all who were oppressed by the devil, for God was with him" (Acts 10:38). Jesus stood on a level place with "a great multitude of people from all Judea and Jerusalem and the seacoast of Tyre and Sidon, who came to hear him and to be healed of their diseases, and those who were troubled with unclean spirits were cured" (Luke 6:17-18). Observe how the author of Luke-Acts has expanded Mark's "healed many" to "healing all" and has enormously enlarged the geographical scope of the crowd.

Similar sweeping claims were made for the apostles. "The people also gathered from the towns around Jerusalem, bringing the sick and those afflicted with unclean spirits, and they were all healed" (Acts 5:16).[1] In fact, according to the Bible and apocryphal Christian literature, the apostles equaled Jesus in the number and variety of miracles they performed. Paul states that he did among the Corinthian Christians the signs of a true apostle, namely, "signs and wonders and mighty works" (2 Cor. 12:12). To win gentiles to faith in Christ, he wrought "signs and wonders by the power of the Holy Spirit" (Rom. 15:18-19), and he worked miracles among the Galatian Christians (Gal. 3:5). Other apostles, too, performed miracles.[2] Their methods are often the same as those ascribed to Jesus: by taking by the hand (Acts and Mark); by faith (Acts 14:8-10; Mark 5:34); by touching the healer's clothing (Acts 19:11-12; Mark 5:27-29). Jesus revived the dead Lazarus (John 11), and Peter restored Tabitha to life again (Acts 9). Sometimes miracles were performed through the name of Jesus (Acts 4:30).

A special type of healing was exorcism, the casting out of demons or unclean spirits. The belief that demons or unclean spirits can enter a person and cause illness is a notion that can be traced to ancient Sumer in the third millennium B.C. In Sumer and Babylonia a demon could be removed by uttering incantations and placing beside the sick person an object that the demon could be induced to enter. Then the object was destroyed, killing the demon in it. By New Testament times exorcism of demons was performed by various means, one of which was by the command of a superior person or by invoking the name of a deity stronger than the demon. In the synoptic gospels—but never in John—Jesus repeatedly exorcises demons, or unclean spirits, by command.

Mark contains evidence that the attempts to perform miracles did not always succeed. In his own country (Galilee) Jesus "could do no mighty work there, except that he laid his hands on a few sick people and healed them. And he marveled because of their unbelief" (Mark 6:5-6). When Jesus exorcised an unclean spirit from a boy, "his disciples asked him privately, 'Why could we not cast it out?' And he said to them, 'This kind cannot be driven out by anything but prayer'" (Mark 9:28-29). Also, some exorcisms apparently were not permanent. A pericope from Q (Matt. 12:43-45=Luke 11:24-26) states that the unclean spirit that has been cast out of a man returns with seven other evil spirits and they enter the man, "and the last state of that man becomes worse than the first." The gospels attempt to connect the apostles' miracle-working with Jesus by depicting him as delegating to them the authority and power to perform miracles.[3]

LITERARY PARALLELS

The parallelism between the New Testament miracle stories and similar non-Christian ones shows that the Christian writers were much influenced by their literary environment, both Jewish and pagan. Even when they did not adapt a particular story, the writers made use of attitudes and literary forms that were popular in their day.

For example, in Acts when Peter is in prison, he "was sleeping between two soldiers, bound with two chains, and sentries in front of the door were guarding the prison; and behold, an angel of the Lord appeared, and a light shone in the cell; and he struck Peter on the side and woke him, saying, 'Get up quickly.' And the chains fell off his hands." The angel led him out. "When they had passed the first and second guard, they came to the iron gate leading into the city. It opened to them of its own accord, and they went out" (12:6-10).

Miraculous escape from prison as the result of divine intervention was an old theme in the Greek world. In his drama *The Bacchae*, Euripides tells what happened when Pentheus, king of Thebes, dared to imprison a stranger, who is none other than the god Dionysus. A servant leads the god to the king and speaks: "As for his votaries [i.e., worshipers of Dionysus] whom you yourself did arrest, seizing and binding them hand and foot in the public jail, all these have loosed their bonds and fled into the meadows where they are now playing, calling aloud on the Bromian god [Dionysus]. Their chains fell off their feet of their own accord, and doors flew open without man's hand to help. Many a marvel has this stranger brought with him to our city of Thebes" (443-448). Also, a story was told that Apollonius (1st c. A.D.) was arrested and put in bonds by the guardians of the temple of Dictynna. "But about midnight he loosed his bonds, and after calling those who had bound him, so that they might witness it, he ran to the doors of the temple, which opened wide to receive him; and when he had passed within, they closed again."[4]

Form critics (Martin Dibelius, Rudolf Bultmann, and others) observed that the literary form of popular healing stories in the Hellenistic and Roman worlds has three basic parts: (1) identification of the ailment, (2) the act of healing and its method, and (3) proof of the cure. The same three parts are in the gospel healing stories too, as the form critics also observed. Sometimes additional themes are woven into the story, as in the case of the healing of the paralytic in Mark 2, where the clause "the Son of Man has authority on earth to forgive sins" is an extra feature. The story of the healing of Simon's mother-in-law is a simple story consisting of only the essentials. Part 1: "Now Simon's mother-in-law lay sick with a fever, and immediately they told him of her." Part 2: "And he came and took her by the hand and lifted her up, and the fever left her." Part 3: "And she served them" (Mark 1:30-31). The statement, "she served them," is intended as proof that she is well again, just as the healed paralytic in Mark 2 picks up his bed and walks (in contrast to his being carried in on a pallet before the healing).

Various healings are reported to have been accomplished by Apollonius and his disciple Damis:

> There also arrived a man who was lame. . . . A lion had sprung on him and dislocated his hip so that he limped with one leg. However, when they massaged his hip with their hands, the youth immediately recovered his upright gait. And another man had had his eyes put out, and he went away having recovered the sight of both of them. Yet another man had his hand paralyzed, but left their presence in full possession of the limb.[5]

Apollonius also cast out demons. In one story a youth burst into loud laughter while Apollonius was speaking:

> The youth was, without knowing it, possessed by a demon, for he would laugh at things no one else laughed at, and then he would start weeping for no reason at all, and he would talk and sing to himself. . . . Now when Apollonius gazed on him, the phantom in him began to utter cries of fear and rage, such as one hears from people who are being burned alive or stretched on a rack. And the demon swore that he would leave the young man alone and never take possession of any man again. But Apollonius addressed him with anger, . . .

and ordered him to leave the young man and to show by
a visible sign that he had done so. "I will cast down
yonder statue," said the demon, and pointed to one of
the images which were in the king's portico, for that was
where the scene occurred. When the statue began by
moving gently, and then fell over, one cannot describe
the hubbub which arose among the people and the way
they clapped their hands in amazement. But the young
man rubbed his eyes as if he had just woke up, . . . no
longer did he stare madly about, for he had returned to
his own self, . . . he gave up his fancy garments . . .
and fell in love with the austerity of philosophers and
donned their cloak, and stripping off his old self, he
modeled his life upon that of Apollonius.[6]

In Mark 1 and 5 also demons talk before they are cast
out. In the latter passage a man has been living among the
tombs and on the mountains, crying out night and day, cutting
himself with stones. He ran to Jesus, who recognized that he
had an unclean spirit, or demon. Jesus commanded, "Come out
of the man, you unclean spirit," and asked his name. The
unclean spirit replied, "My name is Legion, for we are many,"
and then implored Jesus not to send them out of the country.

Now a great herd of swine was feeding there on the
hillside; and they [the spirits] begged him, "Send us to
the swine; let us enter them." So he gave them
permission. And the unclean spirits came out and
entered the swine; and the herd, numbering about two
thousand, rushed down the steep bank into the sea, and
were drowned in the sea. (Mark 5:11-13).

The unfriendly attitude toward the swine suggests that
the story originated in Jewish Christianity, not gentile Christianity. Observe that just as the fall of the statue in the Apollonius
story is proof that the demon is cast out, so in this story about
Jesus the insane conduct of the swine is proof that the unclean
spirits have come out of the wild man. Mark adds further proof
to remove all doubt: people now see the man sitting clothed and
in his right mind, and Jesus told him, "Go home to your
friends, and tell them how much the Lord has done for you."

Exorcisms were known in Syria too. Lucian reports the
following conversation:

"You act ridiculously," said Ion, "doubting everything.
I would like to ask you what you say about those who

free demoniacs from their fears, thus plainly exorcising the ghosts. I do not need to go into it: everyone has known of the Syrian from Palestine, an adept in these things; whomever he received, those who were moon-struck and roll their eyes and fill their mouths with foam, they arose, and he dispatched them away healthy, when they were free of the terror, for a large fee. When he stands by them as they lie there he asks from whence they came into the body. The sick man is silent, but the demon answers in Greek or some barbarian tongue, or in the language of the country from which he comes, how and from whence he came into the man. The Syrian levels oaths at him, but if the demon is not persuaded, he threatens and expels the demon. I actually saw one coming out, black and smoky in color."[7]

Two stories in Mark portray Jesus as using spit in healing a deaf and dumb man and a blind man.[8] Tacitus reports that Emperor Vespasian also healed a blind man by means of his spit. While the emperor was in Alexandria, the man came to him because the god Sarapis had ordered him to pray to the emperor to heal him. The blind man asked Vespasian to moisten his cheeks and eyeballs with the emperor's spit. After some hesitation, Vespasian did so and the blind man saw the light of day again.[9]

The Gospel of John relates that Jesus raised Lazarus from the dead, and Luke 7 tells the story that he raised the widow's son at Nain. This type of miracle was alleged to have occurred in the pagan world too. Pliny describes Asclepiades' raising of the dead, and Philostratus makes the same claim for Apollonius.[10]

In summary, literary and archaeological evidence shows clearly the prevalence of the demand for and expectation of miracles—especially healing miracles—in New Testament times. That was the situation among Christians as well as among their neighbors. The parallels between Christian and non-Christian miracle stories demonstrate that Christians employed some of the ideas and literary features of Jewish and pagan accounts.

WAS JESUS A MIRACLE WORKER?

This question has been much debated in modern biblical scholarship. The old view that the miracles must be true simply because they are in the Bible is a belief properly rejected by historians. Too many features in the Bible are demonstrably erroneous for us to hold on to the old view. Another old view is that, even though some miracles strain our credulity, they still occurred, because "with God all things are possible." They who make this assertion forget another rule: "With human imagination all things are possible."

Many of the gospel miracles are utterly impossible, so they are not evidence that Jesus was a miracle worker. Apart from the healings, these are nature miracles. Examples in the canonical gospels are the miraculous multiplication of the loaves and fishes, walking on water, changing water to wine, stilling the wind, cursing the fig tree which made it wither to its roots the same day, the miraculous draught of fish in Luke 5 and John 21, and the raising the dead. Most of the healings are impossible too. In real life patients are not healed by touching the healer or his garments, nor by his declaring, whether he is nearby or afar, that the patient is healed. Demons are not seen, are not heard, nor do they even exist. Blindness, deafness, dumbness, lameness, and epilepsy cannot be cured by any of the methods used in the stories in the gospels and Acts. It is true that some ailments can be cured—at least temporarily—by psychology, by faith that the cause is removed and one is therefore well again. When an epileptic's fit ended, people could easily believe that he was well. But whether that was the case in any of these stories, we may well doubt. When demons or unclean spirits speak sensible words as in the gospels, we are dealing with superstition, not history. We observe that what the demons say often is just what the author would want them to say! (See next section of this chapter).

A second kind of evidence against the historicity of these miracle stories is their similarity in content and literary style to non-Christian legendary and mythological stories, an aspect we have just observed. The similarity shows that the gospel stories are of the same type as non-biblical stories, which no one today regards as accounts of events that actually occurred. Why should we persist in claiming that the biblical stories are different? Contrary to the traditional view, the fact that they happen to be in the Bible does not make them true historical records.

In the third place, details in the stories are rarely evidence that they are authentic, for creating details to make a story more interesting and appear to be true was a standard practice among ancient storytellers, whether the story was told orally or in writing. That is one of the laws of folklore. The practice of adding details is demonstrated by the treatment of Marcan stories when they were copied by the authors of Matthew and Luke. Although at times they shortened the pericopes in Mark, the authors often added details. Here is an example:

> Mark 1:40. And the leper came to him beseeching him, and kneeling said to him, . . .
> Luke 5:12. While he was in one of the cities, there came a man full of leprosy; and when he saw Jesus, he fell on his face and beseeched him, . . .

The tendency to add details continued when scribes copied the manuscripts. In fact, this happened in the example above. "And kneeling" in Mark is not in Codex Vaticanus, the earliest manuscript we have of the text; the phrase was inserted into manuscripts in the fourth century to add detail.

If Jesus had performed miracles, we would expect Paul to allude to them as antecedents of apostolic miracles, but he never does. This is important evidence, for as we will see below, Paul made wide-ranging claims about his own miracle-working powers.

Does the admission of Jesus' failure in Mark 6 indicate that he tried to perform miracles, but failed in Galilee? We cannot trust that story, for its phrase, "because of their unbelief," is suspiciously similar to early Christian apologetics.[11] The apostles' failure to perform some miracles is here ascribed to Jesus.

Morton Smith has written that the gospel authors wished to defend Jesus from the charge of being a magician, and therefore they probably minimized evidence of it.[12] There is no valid evidence that they were reluctant to portray him as a miracle worker; in fact, all four canonical gospels abundantly portray him in that fashion. In Mark 3:22-30 par the scribes from Jerusalem accuse Jesus of casting out demons by using the power of Beelzebub, or Satan. The charge, according to this pericope, amounts to blasphemy against the Holy Spirit of God, for Jesus has and uses the power of the Holy Spirit, not that of an unclean spirit, to cast out demons. This story does not suggest that Jesus was criticized for performing exorcisms, but rather for the spirit by which he did it. (Actually, this controversy probably was between the scribes and the apostles; see chapter below, "The Great Controversy.")

In the pericope in Mark 1:38 Jesus says to his disciples, "Let us go on to the next towns, that I may preach there also; for that is why I came forth." If these are authentic words of Jesus—and they could be—they imply that he regarded preaching rather than miracle-working as the essential function of his mission. If the words are not authentic, they indicate that some apostles regarded preaching as more important than performing healings and other miracles. The author of Mark adds in the next verse one of his own generalizing sentences that includes exorcisms: "And he went throughout all Galilee, preaching in their synagogues and casting out demons" (1:39). The source material in verse 38, however, does not mention the casting out of demons; it is consistent with our conclusion that Jesus performed few, if any, healings or other miracles.

THE DEMAND FOR MIRACLES

If Jesus did not actually perform miracles, why did the gospel authors assign them to him? And why did some apostles try to work miracles? One reason was the attitude toward miracles in the ancient world. The apostles lived in an environment in which miracles were not only readily accepted, but even expected and demanded of religious leaders. "Everybody was doing it," and the new religion needed miraculous accomplishments in order to be accredited. Professor S. J. Case once summarized the situation thus:

> The ancients knew no other way [than supernaturalism] to validate religion. . . . The appeal to supernaturalism was a very valuable method for interpreting Christianity to the ancients. This mode of thinking was not only widely current but was most highly esteemed by ordinary people. Had Christians been unsuccessful in this area of expansion, their religion never would have become the prevailing faith of the Roman Empire. As a means of defending Christianity against its critics, or of presenting it appealingly to prospective converts, the assertion of its unique otherworldly validity was the

most powerful apologetic that could be imagined.[13]

The competition with other religions and other miracle workers was enough to force the early Christians to think that surely Jesus and the apostles must have accomplished miraculous deeds. Simon Magus, or Simon the Samaritan Magician, was a competitor reported in Acts.

There was a man named Simon who had previously practiced magic in the city and amazed the nation of Samaria, saying that he himself was somebody great. They all gave heed to him, from the least to the greatest, saying, "This man is the power of God which is called Great." And they gave heed to him, because for a long time he had amazed them with his magic (8:9-11).

According to Acts, Simon was so impressed with the apostles' bestowing the Holy Spirit by the laying on of hands that he offered them money if they would give him the same power. Simon Magus illustrates the importance that some people attached to miracles.

Further evidence of the competition with other miracle workers is a story in Acts 13. In it a Jewish magician, a "false prophet," Elymas or Bar Jesus by name, tried to prevent Barnabas and Paul from preaching the Christian faith to the Roman proconsul. Paul denounced the miracle worker as a "son of the devil" and told him that the Lord would make him temporarily blind, which, of course, happened "immediately."

THE SIGNIFICANCE OF MIRACLES

The performance of miracles by Jesus and the apostles had varied significance in the faith of the Christian communities. First, as a result of the general demand for miracles by the ancient world, they were regarded as "testimony," or "witness" (both are same word in Greek), of the validity of the Christian faith. This is a major theme in Acts. At Iconium Paul and Barnabas spoke boldly for the Lord, "who bore witness to the word of his grace, granting signs and wonders to be done by their hands" (Acts 14:3). Paul viewed miracles as essential testimony in converting gentiles:

In Christ Jesus, then, I have reason to be proud of my work for God. For I will not venture to speak of anything except what Christ has wrought through me to win obedience from the gentiles, by word and deed, by the power of signs and wonders, by the power of the Holy Spirit (Rom. 15:17-19).

Related to the view that miracles testify to the truth of Christianity was the belief that they witness to the imminent arrival of the kingdom of God. Jewish opponents demanded evidence that the kingdom was about to appear. They evidently asked, "Where are the signs that it is near at hand? What testimony, or evidence, can you give us?" Jewish Christians turned to a prophecy in Isaiah:

Behold, your God will come with vengeance, . . .
Then the eyes of the blind shall be opened,
And the ears of the deaf unstopped;
Then shall the lame man leap like a deer,
And the tongue of the dumb sing for joy (35:4-6).

Miracles of healing were a logical accompaniment of the arrival of the kingdom, for conditions, including health, would be ideal there. Although in Q Isaiah's prophecy is cited as proof of Jesus' messiahship, the original Christian use of it may well have been as proof that the kingdom was near at hand. This is closer to the prophecy, for in it God, not the Messiah, will perform the miracles. Regardless of this particular prophecy, the apostles clearly viewed their own miracle-working as evidence of the approach of the kingdom, and not of proof of Jesus' messiahship. In a pericope in Q miracles should cause persons who see them to repent;[14] the logic is that they indicate that the kingdom and the Judgment are imminent, so people should repent immediately. In another pericope in Q Jesus is depicted as having the view that his exorcisms are proof that the kingdom has already arrived: "But if it is by the Spirit of God that I cast out demons, then the kingdom of God has come upon you."[15]

Exorcisms are related in a special way to the coming of the kingdom of God. A Jewish belief was that the coming of God's rule over the earth would put an end to Satan's rule over it. In the *Testament* [or *Assumption*] *of Moses* 10:1 we read: "Then his [God's] kingdom will appear throughout his whole creation. Then the devil [Satan] will have an end" [i.e., he will no longer exist]. In the New Testament this concept of the advent of the kingdom is applied to the healings performed by Jesus and the apostles. When the disciples report that they have cast out demons, Jesus says, "I saw Satan fall like lightning from heaven" (Luke 10:17-19). Jesus' exorcisms too are a sign that Satan's kingdom is coming to an end; the situation is analogous to binding a strong man (Mark 3:22-27 par). The logic of this belief is that the demons or unclean spirits which cause illness are Satan's agents, and conquering them amounts to conquering Satan himself, and when Satan is conquered, God's kingdom will come.

Miracles attributed to Jesus came to be regarded as witnesses of his messiahship. That belief is implicit in this statement: "Jesus of Nazareth, a man attested to you by God with mighty works and wonders and signs which God did through him" (Acts 2:22). Why were miracles seen as evidence of messiahship? Did Jews expect the Messiah to perform miracles?

In some Jewish prophecies the Messiah is expected to destroy miraculously the world's rulers and other wicked people. In Isaiah the Son of David Messiah will "smite the earth with the rod of his mouth, and with the breath of his lips he shall slay the wicked" (11:4). In the *Psalms of Solomon* this Davidic Messiah "will destroy the unlawful nations [i.e., the gentile nations, which do not obey the Jewish Law] with the word of his mouth" (17:24). Isaiah 11 apparently is the basis of that passage. In *4 Ezra* 13 the Messiah is the Man who rises from the sea, and the seer has a vision of him in which the nations are gathered together to fight him, but he destroys them with a stream of fire from his mouth. Slaying multitudes with fire from one's mouth is certainly a miraculous deed, but is quite unlike the New Testament miracles and cannot be their source. Nor was the expectation of a Prophet like Moses the source, for Jesus' miracles are not the Mosaic type.

Two factors were the main sources: the need to compete with non-Christian miracle-workers, and the Jewish expectation that God would perform miracles when the kingdom came. The latter was developed into the belief that God would perform his miracles by acting through the Messiah; this idea is expressed in Acts 2:22, which refers to Jesus' mighty works "which God did through him."

The belief underlies Q's interpretation of the passage we cited from Isaiah 35, which predicts that the blind, deaf, and dumb will be healed when the kingdom comes. Q views healing miracles by Jesus as fulfillment of Scripture and proof that Jesus is the Messiah. In Q disciples of John ask Jesus if he is the

Messiah ("Are you he who is to come, or look we for another?"):

> In that hour he cured many of diseases and plagues and evil spirits, and on many who were blind he bestowed sight. And he answered them, "Go and tell John what you have seen and heard: the blind receive their sight, the lame walk, lepers are cleansed, the deaf hear, the dead are raised up, and the poor have the good news [or gospel] preached to them" (Luke 7:21-22; parallel in Matt. 11:4-5).

The clause, "the poor have good news preached to them," is adapted from Isaiah 61:1, where the prophet says, "the Lord has anointed me to bring good news to the poor";[16] the word "anointed" suggested that this is a reference to the Messiah. The combining here of the two different passages from Isaiah reveals plainly the desire to portray Jesus as the Messiah who fulfills Old Testament prophecy by performing miraculous healings and by preaching the gospel.

In the story in Luke 7 of Jesus' raising from the dead the son of the widow at Nain, Jesus' feat causes the crowd to hail him as a prophet type of Christ: "A great prophet has arisen among us!"

In Mark some of the stories of Jesus' exorcisms have an added feature that provides explicit testimony that Jesus is the Messiah; with their supernatural insight demons or unclean spirits recognize that Jesus is the Christ. An unclean spirit calls him "the Holy One of God" (1:24). "He cast out many demons, and he would not permit the demons to speak, because they knew him" (1:34); Luke's version makes the identification explicit by concluding "because they knew he was the Christ" (4:41). Whenever the unclean spirits beheld him, they fell down before him and cried out, "You are the Son of God" (Mark 3:11). The unclean spirit(s) in the Gerasene demoniac also recognizes Jesus as the Messiah: "And when he saw Jesus from afar, he ran and worshiped him; and crying out with a loud voice, he said, 'What have you to do with me, Jesus, Son of the Most High God?'" (5:6-7). Mark connects this idea with the theory of the messianic secret. Although the demons recognize Jesus, they do not make him known to the public because he commanded them to be silent: "And he strictly ordered them not to make him known" (3:12).

The Gospel of Signs in John presents miracles assigned

to Jesus as authentication of his messiahship. His miracles are "signs" that testify to it; they should cause people to believe in him. "This [changing water into wine], the first of his signs, Jesus did at Cana in Galilee and manifested his glory, and his disciples believed in him" (John 2:11). In the same source in John the chief priests and the Pharisees say, after Jesus has restored life to the dead Lazarus, "What are we to do? For this man performs many signs. If we let him go on thus, everyone will believe in him" (11:47-48). The emphasis on miracles in this gospel demonstrates the importance early Christians attached to them.

The story of Jesus' healing a paralytic in Mark 2 has a feature which needs special explanation. The story is that when four men brought a paralytic on a pallet to him to heal, Jesus said to the man, "My son, your sins are forgiven." The scribes who heard thought that this was blasphemy, for only God can forgive sins. Jesus perceived in his spirit what they were thinking, so he said to them, "But that you may know that the Son of Man has authority on earth to forgive sins," he said to the paralytic, "I say to you, rise, take up your pallet and go home." This the man did, for he was now healed.

The story raises two questions. First, what is the connection between the forgiveness of sins and healing? The key to the answer is the ancient Jewish belief that illness is the Lord's punishment for sin, a belief that is one of the explanations of suffering in the Book of Job. In such cases, then, a cure for illness is forgiveness from God for one's sins. This theory of illness is understood in a description of the coming kingdom, or New Age, in Isaiah: "And no inhabitant will say, 'I am sick'; the people who dwell there will be forgiven their iniquity"—and thereby will be in good health (33:24).

The second question is, Why is Jesus called the Son of Man here? Why not Son of David or Son of God? The probable explanation is this: The Parables section of *1 Enoch* says nothing of the Son of Man's power to forgive sins, but if any type of Messiah is to be given that authority, the Son of Man is the most likely candidate. He is the only Messiah in Judaism who is supernatural and will be the judge on Judgment Day. In Mark 2 the authority of the Son of Man has been expanded by giving him a function traditionally limited to God.

Not all early Christians were enthusiastic about miracles.

Even they who believed in them viewed them only as testimony, as support for belief in Jesus' messiahship and the nearness of the kingdom; miracles were not the foundation of religion. No one in the first century—unlike the twentieth century—said, "If you don't believe in the miracles, you are going to hell, because the miracles are in the Bible, and the Bible is the Word of God, so you have to believe all of it." Jesus' resurrection, however, was viewed as a necessary miracle, not because it was a miracle, but because without it Jesus could not return to perform the functions of the Christ, and therefore could not be the Christ.

The belief that Jesus performed miracles which demonstrated that he was the Messiah was a belief with an inherent flaw. The Christians who held that belief also believed that the apostles performed miracles, and they were not Messiahs! Apostolic miracles must have diminished the significance of Jesus' miracles in the opinion of many.

In fact, some Jewish Christians, at least, rejected the idea that Jesus had to perform miracles in order to be the Messiah. The mythological Temptation Story in Q[17] depicts a conversation between Jesus and the devil. In two of the three temptations the devil challenges Jesus to perform a miracle "if you are the Son of God." Jesus refuses and regards such demands as cases of tempting God. The church or churches that produced this story did not share other churches' zeal for miracles. There probably were two reasons for this point of view in Q. (1) Q's churches may have realized that Jesus did not perform miracles and that the miracle stories are only legends. (2) The Q material often displays a rational streak with special interest in ethics.

A passage in Matthew minimizes the importance of Christian prophecy, exorcisms, and other miracles:

Not everyone who says to me, "Lord, Lord," shall enter the kingdom of heaven, but he who does the will of my Father who is in heaven. On that day many will say to me, "Lord, Lord, did we not prophesy in your name, and cast out demons in your name, and do mighty works in your name?" And then I will declare to them, "I never knew you; depart from me, you evildoers" (7:21-23).

Apparently the author of Matthew was not very favorably impressed by apostolic prophecies, exorcisms, and miracles. He believed that doing the will of God was more important.

THE LORD'S SUPPER

The origin of the Lord's Supper, or Eucharist, is cloaked in mystery. Is it founded on a last meal Jesus had with his disciples or not? Although the synoptic gospels and a tradition in 1 Corinthians depict the Lord's Supper in that manner, the Gospel of John and the *Didache* do not. Also, certain features in the synoptic accounts raise our doubts. In the synoptic setting the occasion is the celebration of the Passover, but the meal is not a paschal meal, either in the words spoken or the procedure followed. Further, Jesus and his disciples were Jews, and it is utterly improbable that they would drink his blood and eat his flesh, even symbolically. (And the texts do not state that it is symbolic; the bread IS his body and the wine IS his blood.) The Jewish Law is very explicit in prohibiting the eating of any blood, for "the blood is the life; and you shall not eat the life with the flesh" (Deut. 12:23). Also, the idea of eating Jesus' flesh surely would have seemed to the disciples to suggest cannibalism. Finally, the Last Supper accounts contain features which originated in the life of the early churches, as we will see.

Let us search for possible sources and causes of the Christian Lord's Supper tradition. It is in two of the three earliest Christian sources we have, Paul's letters and Mark, but it is not in Q.

JEWISH BACKGROUND

One theory is that the forerunner of the Lord's Supper was a Jewish meal which either Jesus or Jewish-Christian churches transformed into the Christian rite. To investigate that possibility we must examine various Jewish meals.

One theoretical meal, hoped for in the future, was "the messianic banquet," which the righteous would eat with the Messiah in the new kingdom. The source of the idea may be Isaiah 25:6, which states that (on the day of the Lord) Yahweh will make a feast for all peoples on Mount Zion. In *1 Enoch* 62:14 the righteous will eat with the Son of Man Messiah forever in the new kingdom, but no particular meal is mentioned. In fact, none of the Jewish Pseudepigrapha describe a particular meal. Some of those writings mention that the righteous will eat abundantly in the new age, but they do not refer to a specific meal or ritual, nor is the Messiah necessarily involved. Three New Testament passages may possibly be references to a messianic banquet. In Mark 14:25 par Jesus says, "I shall not drink again of the fruit of the vine until that day when I drink it new in the kingdom of God." In Luke 22:15-16 Jesus says, also in connection with the Lord's Supper, that he will not eat "this Passover" again "until it is fulfilled in the kingdom of God." "Blessed are those who are invited to the marriage supper of the Lamb" (Rev. 19:9). It is doubtful that these passages are speaking of the messianic banquet, but even if they are, they tell us nothing of the procedure. No sound evidence exists that the Lord's Supper began as a preview of the messianic feast. The idea of eating and drinking the Messiah in the kingdom of God would be weird, and the gospels do not say that the disciples will partake of the wine or meal in the future kingdom—only Jesus is mentioned.

Is the Lord's Supper a Passover meal? In Jesus' day lambs were slaughtered and eaten in the Passover; the bread was unleavened bread; the Hallel, consisting of certain Psalms, was recited; and God was blessed. The Passover was celebrated at the Temple; after it was destroyed in A.D. 70, the Seder meal was substituted for the lamb, enabling Jews to celebrate the Passover at home. The biblical accounts can hardly be authentic reports of how Jesus celebrated the Passover, for the meal is not at the Temple, and none of the distinctive features of the Passover are mentioned. Also, unlike the Passover procedure, Jesus gives thanks instead of a blessing over the cup and he blesses the bread instead of blessing God. None of the words spoken at the Lord's Supper are those of the Passover.

Sanhedrin 43a in the Talmud states that Jesus was hanged on the eve of the Passover. In the Quartodeciman controversy in the churches in the second century, the Quartodecimans held that Jesus' crucifixion instead of his resurrection should be celebrated as the date of Christian redemption. And what date did they maintain was the time of Jesus' crucifixion? The eve of Passover. Further, Mark, the earliest gospel, con-

216

tains several pericopes that also indicate that Jesus was arrested and crucified before, not after the beginning of Passover. If that is correct, then Jesus' last meal clearly was not the Passover meal. Mark 14:1-2 plainly states that the chief priests and scribes planned to arrest and kill Jesus, but they said, "Not during the [Passover] feast, lest there be a tumult of the people." In Mark 15:42 Joseph of Arimathea asked Pilate for the body of Jesus on "the day of Preparation," which was the day *before* the Passover began, the day on which the lambs were slaughtered and prepared for the paschal meal. John 19:14, 31, depict Jesus' Roman trial and crucifixion as occurring on "the day of Preparation"; these statements in John are insertions by the redactor.

Some scholars are convinced–rightly–that Mark 14:12-16, which places the Lord's Supper in a Passover setting, is a later idea. It is inconsistent with the rest of Mark's Passion story. Verse 12 reveals the writer's ignorance of Jewish customs. It states: "And on the first day of Unleavened Bread, when they sacrificed the Passover lamb, . . ." But the Jewish custom was that the lambs were sacrificed on the 14th of the Jewish month of Nisan, and the first day of Unleavened Bread was the 15th. The story in Mark 14:12-16 has features similar to the story in Mark 11:1-7. In both Jesus sends two disciples on a mission and forecasts what they will find. Martin Dibelius once commented that such features were characteristic of legends in the Greco-Roman world.[1]

Why did Mark (copied by Matthew and Luke) represent the Lord's Supper as a paschal meal? The reason was to represent the Christian ritual meal as replacing the Jewish ritual meal. The Lord's Supper is the New Passover. As the blood of the sacrificed paschal lamb atoned for Jew's sins, so did the blood of Jesus atone for Christians' sins.[2] Further evidence that the Lord's Supper was an element in the Christian claim that Christianity was the New Judaism is the statement, "This is my blood of the covenant" in Mark and Matthew ("new" is not in the earliest manuscripts of these gospels). As the Passover celebrated the divine covenant with Judaism, the Lord's Supper was regarded as a celebration of the divine covenant with Christianity.

Some New Testament scholars have sought the origins of the Lord's Supper in the Jewish kiddush, a ceremonial blessing pronounced over bread or wine on the Sabbath or holy days, before the morning and evening meals. It is a benediction on the holiness of the day. But the similarities between the two rituals are slight. Like the Lord's Supper, bread and wine are the foods involved. Bread and wine, however, were the foods in many other ritual meals in the ancient world. In the kiddush the wine cup was called "the cup of blessing" (archaeologists have found Jewish wine cups with the word "blessing" inscribed on them), and in 1 Corinthians 10:16 the Lord's Supper cup is called "the cup of blessing," though this may be a judaizing of the Christian tradition. This expression occurs also in the Passover feast, where the third cup is called by that name.

But in contrast to the Lord's Supper, the words spoken in the kiddush are very different. Psalms are recited, instead of identifying the bread and wine with body and blood. In the kiddush the term associated with the cup of wine is "bless"; in the Lord's Supper it is "give thanks." In the kiddush as well as the Passover, God is blessed, not the food. Also, the kiddush was spoken before meals, not during them as in the Lord's Supper in the synoptics.

GENTILE BACKGROUND

Six passages in the New Testament describe or mention the Lord's Supper.[3] In each passage the bread and wine are identified with body and blood. Another feature of the passages is that thanks are given over the bread or wine. Neither of these features is characteristic of Judaism, so we must look elsewhere to find the background of these two basic elements in the Eucharist. We turn to the pagan world.

Why would anyone identify bread with the body of either a human or a deity? The notion has its roots in the worship of grain deities. Grain-raising peoples in the ancient world honored grain because their lives depended upon it, and they usually worshiped a goddess or god of grain. In some cultures the grain itself was virtually deified. Thus eating the grain was, in a sense, eating the deity. Sacramental meals based on grain occurred in ancient Greece, but they were not necessarily a common, or group, meal; only two persons were needed, a priest and a worshiper. In the Eleusinian mystery cult, which spread around the Mediterranean, the grain goddess Demeter and daughter Kore, or Persephone, were worshiped. *Mystae*, or initiates, partook of a sacrament in which they ate holy bread and drank the *kukeon*, a sacred drink of barley mixed with water flavored with mint. An archaic vase-painting in Naples depicts two *mystae* of the cult seated before a table under which is a basket full of bread; a priest standing before them hands them the cup of sacred drink. In the Samothracian mysteries its priest broke sacred bread and poured out drink for the initiates, according to an ancient Greek inscription.[4] Professor Willoughby and others called attention to the fact that in the liturgy of the Cybele and Attis cult, Attis himself was addressed as a "reaped ear of corn" ("corn" is not maize, but wheat or barley). Willoughby commented: "It is not unlikely that a corn product, or some other vegetable food in which Attis was believed especially to dwell, formed a part of the sacred repast. In partaking of this meal, the devotee was enabled to share in a materialistic manner the life of the god."[5]

These mystery religions have not transmitted to us their specific interpretation of their rituals, which may or may not have regarded the grain as the mystery "body" of the deity. The mystery cult of Mithras in the first and second Christian centuries, however, may be a different matter. Judging from Justin's comment on it, in the Mithraic ritual the Lord Mithras too took bread and said that it was his body.[6]

Why would anyone want to drink the blood of a human or a deity, either the blood itself or in the form of wine? This notion has a long, complex history too. In primitive societies a man's blood seemed to be his very life, for when he was severely wounded and lost it, he died. Therefore if a man drank another's blood, he believed that he acquired the power and attributes of the other man. For example, drinking the blood of a great warrior made one a great warrior too. This idea was easily applied to animals also; to be strong like a bull, drink some of the bull's blood. The next step was the belief that the animal was divine. Of special interest to us is the tendency of ancient cattle raisers to worship a cow-goddess or, more frequently, a bull-god. This occurred among the Hittites, Egyptians, Cretans, and Canaanites. At an early period the Israelites apparently worshiped a bull-god; this is indicated by archaeology and reflected in the story that Aaron made a molten calf to which the people offered sacrifices (Exod. 32).

In its early phase the worship of the Greek god Dionysus involved the eating of the raw flesh of bulls, calves, goats, and fawns, in which the god was believed to be temporarily incarnate. Sometimes the flesh was torn from an animal while it was alive and then eaten. The raw flesh and hot blood were devoured quickly while the essence of the god was still in them.[7] Cultured Greeks rejected this crude form of religion. When some devotees substituted the drinking of wine for the drinking of blood, they refined the cult somewhat while enhancing its ecstatic, orgiastic nature. The stimulating effects of the wine aided the belief that the life, or spirit, of the god was in the wine just as it was in the physical blood. Thus drinking the wine was, in effect, the act of drinking the blood of the god.

Eventually wine was substituted for blood in the rites of some other religions also. Wine was explicitly identified with the blood of some gods. In a magical papyrus written around the time of Paul, the writer identifies the wine he pours into a cup with "the blood of Osiris," an Egyptian god.[8] Justin's statement we have mentioned also indicates that in Mithraic ritual wine was viewed as the blood of the god Mithras.

The result of eating the flesh of a god and drinking his blood was union with the god—a physical mysticism. Because he had consumed some of the god, the worshiper was now of the same nature as the god, was like the god, was one with the god.

In some ancient religions the deity was present at the communion, or fellowship, meal. The belief occurs as early as the Hittites in Asia Minor in the second millennium B.C. Archaeologists have uncovered Hittite representations of a goddess seated opposite her priest or a warrior devotee; a communion table stands between them with wafers of bread and a chalice of wine on it. The goddess is drinking from a cup.[9] The ancient belief in the deity's presence at a sacred meal continued in the ancient mystery religions. In the Eleusinian mysteries the goddess Demeter partakes of the sacred cup in the Homeric Hymn to Demeter.[10] In the papyri found at Oxyrhynchus, Egypt, are two invitations to worshipers of Serapis to dine "at the table of the Lord Serapis" in the god's temple, the Serapeum.[11] Historians believe that the expression "table of the Lord Serapis" indicates belief that the god was not only present, but was the host. This apparently was a dinner, but may have been a sacramental ritual meal as well. In the case of Dionysus, the god was believed to be invisibly present at the dances in his orgiastic festivals, according to Euripides (5th c. B.C.), who had witnessed them in Macedonia.

A characteristic of ancient communion meals was that all participants drank from the same vessel. Some Egyptian and Hittite representations of the communion with a deity show a jar of wine in which two tubes have been inserted, one for the deity and one for the devotee. They also show a stool between the devotee and the deity with a cone-shaped loaf of bread on it.[12] By Christian times, however, participants drank from a common cup or bowl which was passed around. In the Stadtmuseum in Linz, Austria, I saw a common cup of the cult of Mithras.

IN CHRISTIANITY

In early Christianity various expressions were used to refer to the Lord's Supper, but they could also refer to other things. Although the term "Lord's Supper" is customary in many Protestant churches today, it occurs in the Greek text of the New Testament only in 1 Corinthians 11:20, and a similar expression, "table of the Lord," occurs in verse 21 of the preceding chapter. Although "Eucharist" is the standard term in Roman Catholicism today, the Greek noun, *eucharistia*, which means "giving thanks," or Eucharist, is never applied to the Lord's Supper in the Bible. That usage first appears in Christian literature in the second century. The Greek verb *eucharisteo*, which means "to give thanks," occurs in the Last Supper accounts in the synoptic gospels and 1 Corinthians 11; this verb is also used frequently in the New Testament in the general sense of giving thanks to God, unrelated to the Eucharist. "To break bread" is used in Acts to refer to ordinary meals: whether in 20:7 it refers to the Lord's Supper is debated. The Greek word *koinonia* can be translated as "sharing," "participation in," "communion," or "fellowship." In 1 Corinthians 10:16 it indicates the Lord's Supper, where consuming the wine and bread is declared to be a sharing in the blood and body of Christ. (In the benediction in 2 Corinthians 13:14 the word signifies the sharing in the Holy Spirit.)

The New Testament contains several traditions about the Lord's Supper, and we must find and study them separately to understand the growth of the idea and practice. On the surface 1 Corinthians 11:23-26 appears to be the earliest, for Paul seems to be quoting an earlier tradition he has received. A close examination, however, discloses that such is not the case. Its first feature that makes us suspicious is the claim that it was "received from the Lord." Although elsewhere in his letters Paul states that he has revelations from the Lord, their content consists of ideas, not narratives of past events. This tradition, however, purports to be what Jesus said at the Last Supper. Also, it interrupts the flow of thought, a characteristic of later insertions into ancient texts. A third type of evidence that this passage was not written by Paul is that the style of its Greek is more developed than Paul's style, as Robert Hawkins, for example, once noted.[13]

We can see several reasons why an editor would want to insert it. Unlike the other Lord's Supper passages in Paul's letters, it places the Lord's Supper in Jesus' last meal, and thereby brings Paul into harmony with the synoptic gospels by making Jesus the founder of the sacred ritual. Another reason is that the editor wanted to make the Lord's Supper a memorial of Jesus, which he did by inserting "Do this in remembrance of me," another feature not in Paul's references to the Lord's Supper. Meals in memory of deceased loved ones were held in antiquity by some Egyptians and Romans. Some Christians at Rome combined that idea with the Lord's Supper by celebrating it in the catacombs in honor of deceased members of *their family*.[14] The editor of Corinthians, however, has made the Eucharist a memorial of *Jesus himself*. To give the impression that this passage is a primitive Christian tradition earlier than Paul's letters, he composed the introduction, "For I received from the Lord what I also delivered to you." This editorial insertion and Luke 22:19b-20 have four features in common not found elsewhere in the New Testament.[15] This suggests that either they had a common source, or more probable, that the insertion in 1 Corinthians was derived from the Lucan passage.

The earliest traditions that have been transmitted to us, then, are elsewhere in Paul's letters. In 1 Corinthians 10:14-22[16] Paul refers to the Lord's Supper in this manner: "The cup of blessing which we bless, is it not participation in the blood of Christ? The bread which we break, is it not participation in the body of Christ?" Therefore Christians should not partake of similar meals in paganism, for: "I do not want you to be partners with demons [pagan gods]. You cannot drink the cup of the Lord and the cup of demons. You cannot partake of the table of the Lord and the table of demons." In this passage Paul accepts belief in the existence of the pagan deities, for otherwise how could anyone be a partner with them? (Verse 19 and chapter 8 contradict this by denying the existence of such gods, which there are called "idols" instead of "demons." Apparently these statements are editorial insertions made by others to uphold the doctrine of monotheism; Paul was not as inconsistent as the editors of his letters have made him appear.) Participants were consuming the essence of other divine lords besides that of the Lord Jesus and coming into mystical union with them, which is why the act seemed so sinful.

The other genuine Pauline eucharistic tradition we have is 1 Corinthians 11:20-22, 33-34a, which reads as follows (verses 23-32 may be Pauline):

> When you meet together, it is not the Lord's Supper that you eat. For in eating, each one goes ahead with his own meal, and one is hungry and another is drunk. What! Do you not have houses to eat and drink in? Or do you despise the church of God and humiliate those who have nothing? What shall I say to you? Shall I commend you in this? No, I will not. . . . So then, my brethren, when you come together to eat, wait for one another—if anyone is hungry, let him eat at home—lest you come together to be condemned.

Here Paul is taking the Corinthian Christians to task for eating and drinking too much. After celebrating the Lord's Supper they went ahead with a full meal in which some overindulged. The gluttons were disgracing the church. The later insertion of verses 23-32 adds another shameful consequence: the gluttony profaned the body and blood of the Lord which they have just eaten. For that offence the Lord has and will judge and punish them.

What was the nature of the full meal? Some scholars have suggested that it was an agape, a love feast, which occurred in the Greco-Roman world as public, or communal, feasts at which the poor were fed. Some Christians celebrated an agape, for in Jude 12 false teachers are denounced who "are blemishes on your love feasts [agapai], as they boldly carouse together, looking after themselves." However, Paul's statement that "you humiliate those who have nothing" suggests that the meal was not an agape, for in an agape the poor could eat and drink as much as the rich. Paul's advice to the hungry to eat at home first also indicates that the meal was not an agape, which all partakers ate together.

Nevertheless, the agape was practiced in some churches until Augustine's day, when Bishop Ambrose banned it because of its excesses. It was widely practiced, including in the atrium of St. Peter's Cathedral in Rome, where it honored Christian martyrs. At the Christian catacombs at Rome in the second to fourth centuries it was a funerary feast in honor of the dead.

1 Corinthians 11:21 indicates that the Lord's Supper came first, and the Corinthians spoiled it by each going ahead with his own meal and overindulging. Given the theory behind the ritual, that would be the natural order; the Lord's Supper created the unity of the participants, which was followed by joyously celebrating it with a fellowship meal.

After Paul, our next early source of information is Mark 14, copied in Matthew 26. Here the Lord's Supper has become the Last Supper, placed in the setting of Jesus' last meal with his disciples. The purpose of this change was to support the ritual by portraying it as instituted by Jesus. Here he takes bread and blesses it and takes the cup and gives thanks. He says that the bread and wine are his body and blood, that the blood is "my blood of the covenant, which is poured out for many," and that he won't drink wine again until "I drink it new in the kingdom of God."

The original Lord's Supper pericope in Luke apparently consisted of Luke 22:15-19a. It differs from the Marcan tradition in that the cup (wine) precedes the breaking of the bread, and before Jesus breaks the bread, he gives thanks instead of a blessing. We accept the manuscript evidence that 22:19b-20 is a later accretion.

Next we turn to the Gospel of John, where the Lord's Supper is unrelated to the Passover or to a final meal of Jesus. The text is complex because several writers are involved. The author of the gospel quotes from a semi-Gnostic source, "G," which presents Jesus as proclaiming: "I am the living bread, which has come down from heaven. If anyone eats this bread, he will live forever" (6:51a-b). In the preceding verses and in 58a, E, the editor, expands this idea by contrasting Jesus as "the Bread of Life" that has come down from heaven, with the manna that came down from heaven to the Israelites during the Exodus. Judging from the point of view of both E and G elsewhere in the gospel, both writers are using the verb "eat" (*esthio* in Greek) in a figurative, spiritual sense. From a different source, verses 51c-53 introduce the eucharistic doctrine that one must eat the "flesh" and drink the blood of Jesus, who is called "the Son of Man." Here, too, the verb for eat is *esthio*.

The redactor who later made insertions in John was not satisfied that the book was explicit enough in supporting the Lord's Supper. Therefore he inserted verses 54-57, which state emphatically that one must eat Jesus' flesh and drink his blood to have "life eternal." He uses a different Greek verb for "eat": *trogo*.

When we examine these traditions of the Lord's Supper, we are impressed with the fact that invariably the bread and wine are identified with the body and blood of Jesus, and that consuming them has a mystic effect. When the Christian eats and drinks them, he participates, or shares, in Jesus' body and blood because some of it is now inside him. Therefore any abuse of his own body, such as sexual sins (1 Cor. 6:9-20), overindulgence, and eating meat that has been sacrificed to pagan gods, profanes the very body and blood of Jesus, and those guilty will be punished. "For anyone who eats and drinks [the Lord's Supper] without discerning the body [of the Lord], eats and drinks judgment upon himself" (1 Cor. 11:29).

And how do the elements, bread and wine, become the body and blood of Jesus? The earliest Christian sources do not tell us, and Jews, Christian Gnostics, and some pagans said it was impossible. Eventually bishops produced the change. Irenaeus said it occurred when the elements "receive the Word of God."[17]

MYSTERY CULT SOURCE

What is the source of such a strange notion as consuming the body and blood of Jesus? There is nothing like it in early Judaism, and it would surely be completely foreign to the mind of Jesus, a Jew. Paul and the Gospel of John do not ascribe it to Jesus, nor do two other early Christian sources, the Q material in Matthew and Luke, and the Gospel of Signs in John. Q and the Gospel of Signs do not even contain the idea. Early in the second century Ignatius in his letters to the various churches repeatedly emphasized the vital importance of the Eucharist, but he never claims that Jesus instituted it. Also, Acts never states that the "Lord's Supper" or the "Eucharist" was practiced in the primitive church; in Acts "breaking bread" refers to ordinary meals, not a ritual.

The only parallels to eucharistic thought were in the gentile world, as we have seen, where in some religions bread and wine were identified with deity and partaking of them has the same effect, namely, mystic union with the deity. John and Ignatius emphasize a related aspect of the Eucharist: it bestows immortality, "eternal life." This effect logically follows from the belief that Jesus was divine. If a person has physical union with a god, then, like the god, he will live forever; this was the belief in some mystery cults. It is not an accident that the belief that the Eucharist bestows immortality first appears in the writings of authors who regarded Jesus as a god. Paul, who regarded Jesus as the human Messiah, did not proclaim that belief; he regarded faith, baptism, and possession of the Spirit as the means of achieving a happy immortality. A feature common to all the Last Supper accounts is that Jesus "gave thanks" over the cup, and in Luke and in the tradition inserted in 1 Corinthians 11, he gave thanks over the bread too. Gentile literature and inscriptions abound in examples of "giving thanks" to a god or gods. At least one inscription gives thanks "to the Lord Serapis."[18] Giving thanks to God was prevalent in Hellenistic Judaism too, but blessing rather than giving thanks was characteristic at meals.

Justin Martyr remarked on the similarity of the Eucharist to the ritual in the cult of Mithras. He cites the Last Supper tradition in which Jesus says, "Do this in remembrance of me." Then he states:

> Which the wicked demons have imitated in the mysteries of Mithras commanding the same thing to be done. For, that bread and a cup of water are placed with certain incantations in the mystic rites of one who is being initiated, you either know or can learn (*1 Apology* 66).

Justin wrote to promote and defend the Christian faith, so he blamed imitation by "wicked demons" for the similarity of the two rites. Actually, if there was imitation, it was Christianity that did the borrowing, for Mithraism became a mystery religion in the first century B.C., before Christianity was born.[19] Archaeologists have never found any evidence of Christian symbolism among Mithraic remains, so there is no reason to think that the Mithraists borrowed from the Christians. They have found clear evidence that there were seven degrees of initiation in Mithraism and the cult connected initiation with a ritual meal of bread and wine. Justin mentions only water, but wine was surely in it, for Mithraic iconography displays numerous cultic representations of bunches of grapes. Some pagan cults and some early Christian churches mixed water with the wine to reduce expense and drunkenness; an expression for the mixture was "the mingled cup."

Further evidence of a mystery cult source is the fact that only Christians were allowed to partake of the Eucharist, a policy still followed in churches. In the cults, too, only members could partake of the rituals. Justin explains:

And this food is called among us Eucharist, of which no one is allowed to partake but the man who believes that the things we teach are true, and who has been washed with the washing [baptism] that is for the remission of sins and unto rebirth, and who is so living as Christ enjoined (*1 Apology* 66).

Also, Christians celebrated the Lord's Supper weekly, on Sunday, the day sacred to the Lord Mithras and other sun gods. They referred to Sunday as "the first day of the week" and "the Lord's day"—the latter term was borrowed from the cult of a sun god, probably that of Mithras. The numerous close similarities of the Lord's Supper to the thought and practices in pagan religions, especially Mithraism, indicate that the beginning of the Eucharist was a Christian adaptation of a ritual in the gentile world. How did this happen? And especially, we wonder, how could Hellenistic Jewish Christians accept it, with its barbaric notion that Christians consumed Jesus' body and blood? The fact that they did is astonishing. Let us try to reconstruct the probable process.

Gentile converts—perhaps in Syrian churches, perhaps in Paul's—brought the Lord's Supper into Christianity as a means of worshiping the "Lord Jesus" in a manner similar to the way they had worshiped a pagan Lord. They wanted assurance that their new Lord, whom they clearly regarded as a god, would give them the blessed immortality promised them in pagan religions. Some even continued to worship a pagan Lord too, for pagan religions were not exclusive. Some gentiles played it safe and belonged to two mystery cults. We catch a glimpse of the background when Paul refers to the belief that eating food offered or sacrificed to pagan deities makes one a partner with them—a physical mystical union. In the same passage Paul gives us a view of the initial stage of the Christian

227

Lord's Supper: it produces mystical union with the body and blood of Christ (1 Cor. 10:16). And as we saw in John 6, the effect of that is immortality.

Why did Paul adopt the Lord's Supper? One explanation is that his gentile converts brought it into his churches, and he accepted the practice and its theory. A different explanation seems more probable. Gentiles were first converted to Christian faith in Antioch, and before Paul began his missionary journeys, he and Barnabas worked with the Antioch church (Acts 11:26; cf. Gal. 1:21). There Paul surely must have become acquainted with gentile Christians and their ideas, and that experience may have induced him to accept some of their paganizing ideas and to become an apostle to the gentiles. This is a more plausible explanation of the origin of Paul's acceptance of the cultic ideas than the theory that he suddenly learned them from his converts. Also, considering that he was trained as a Pharisee, it is improbable that he held such notions before his conversion, even though he was raised in Hellenistic Tarsus.

But how could the Jewish Christians in the churches that produced the synoptic gospels accept the Lord's Supper? The following scenario seems probable. The Christian ritual must have originated in mixed churches such as Antioch. There gentile converts brought in the basic idea from their own pagan background and adapted it to their new Lord, the Lord Jesus. The Jewish-Christian members in the mixed churches were generally Hellenistic Jews who were not strict in observance of the Law, including its prohibition of eating or drinking blood. They were able to accept the Lord's Supper, with its wine substituted for blood, by connecting it with Jesus' life (his last supper), by associating it with the blood of Jesus' sacrificial death, and by adapting the ancient belief in the mystical union of the participants in a sacred communal meal.

In the Jewish background, sacrificed animals could atone for sins, and eating the meat created a mystic union among the worshipers. (But they did not become one with the animal or god.) Paul regarded the Jewish practice as a reason for accepting the belief that partaking of the Lord's Supper united Christians into "one body": "Consider the practice in Israel: are not those who eat the sacrifices partners in the altar?" (1 Cor. 10:18). Belief in mystic union with each other among the partakers of a sacrificial meal was prevalent in both Jewish and Greek thought.

The connection with sacrifice appealed to Jewish Christians, and they made it explicit. The wine is Jesus' blood "which is poured out for many" in the Last Supper accounts in the Synoptic gospels. Matthew makes it clear by adding "for the forgiveness of sins." Thus the rite was made to support the explanation of Jesus' death as an atonement for Christians' sins. Those accounts omit the pagan idea that consumption of the body and blood makes one immortal. Also, in those accounts the Lord's Supper is "judaized," that is, connected to elements in the Jewish background. The wine is the blood of a covenant between God and Christians, and Jesus' drinking it at the Last Supper is connected with his drinking it at his return in the future kingdom of God; thus it is connected to two Jewish ideas: covenant and eschatology.

The Lord's Supper was also made still more acceptable by placing its institution in Jesus' life; he commanded his disciples to partake of his body and blood. Now it has his authority behind it; the Lord's Supper has become the Last Supper. Eventually it was further modified by interpreting it as a memorial meal.

The Lord's Supper—here called the Eucharist—is thoroughly judaized in the *Didache* in mid-second century:

> First about the cup, "We thank you, our Father, for the holy vine of your servant David, which you have made known to us through your servant Jesus. Glory to you forever." And about the piece of bread, "We thank you, our Father, for the life and knowledge you have made known to us through Jesus your servant. Glory be yours forever" (9:2-3).

Nevertheless, *Didache* retains an original feature: only Christians should partake of it.

Some Jewish Christians, however, rejected the Lord's Supper altogether. We observed that it is not in Q or in the Gospel of Signs incorporated in John.

Biblical scholars, often for conservative reasons, tend to find the origin of the Lord's Supper in either Jesus' last meal or else in a Jewish-Christian meal. But those interpretations are based on later traditions, namely the gospels or the insertion in 1 Corinthians 11. A better procedure is to follow the earliest evidence we have, Paul's own words in 1 Corinthians 10.

In summary, the probable history of the Lord's Supper in the early churches is as follows. Gentile converts in Syria and Palestine introduced the ritual into the mixed (Jewish and gentile) churches to which they belonged. Paul learned it from them and transmitted it to his churches. Jewish Christians accepted it by connecting its blood/wine with the blood of Jesus' sacrificial death, by associating it with other Jewish ideas, and making Jesus the founder. (If the Lord's Supper began with Paul and his gentile churches, why would Jewish Christians adopt it? If Jewish Christians originated it, why would they do so? If it began as a memorial meal, why is that idea not in the earlier sources?)

The original belief that partaking of the Lord's Supper conferred immortality continued in gentile Christianity. Ignatius called the Eucharist "the medicine of immortality."[20]

The docetic Christians early in the second century rejected the Eucharist because it was incompatible with their spirit versus flesh dualism. They believed that the divine Christ was a spirit temporarily united with the human physical Jesus, and therefore the flesh and blood of the physical Jesus were unworthy of Christian consumption, even in the form of bread and wine. Ignatius strove mightily to counteract their influence, and described them as follows: "They abstain from Eucharist and prayer because they do not confess that the Eucharist is the flesh of our Savior Jesus Christ which suffered for our sins."[21]

FISH AND BREAD EUCHARIST

Christians today are surprised to learn that there once was a different form of Eucharist, namely, a ritual meal of fish and bread that bestowed immortality. The Christian catacomb frescoes at Rome depict three types of meals consisting of fish and bread: the Eucharist, the funerary banquet in honor of the dead, and the banquet of Christian souls in heaven. A fresco painted around A.D. 200 in the catacomb of Callistus definitely represents the Eucharist. Fish and bread are on a tripod table in the center; a priest standing at the left blesses the holy food; on the right a woman stands with arms uplifted in prayer. Painted around the same date in the same catacomb is a fresco showing seven men, probably priests, reclining in a semicircle behind loaves of bread and two fish. In front of the eucharistic food are seven baskets full of bread.

With some Christians practicing this type of Eucharist, while in most churches the Eucharist consisted of bread and wine, some rivalry between the two customs was sure to result.

Consequently some efforts were made to honor both. In the famous inscription of Abercius of Hieropolis, also dated around 200, he comments on his travels in Syria and Mesopotamia as follows:

> Everywhere Faith was my guide, and gave me everywhere for food the Fish from the spring, the great, the pure, which the spotless Virgin caught and ever puts before the friends to eat; she has also delicious wine, and she offers wine mixed with water together with bread.[22]

In the catacomb of Lucina at Rome symbols of the two types of Eucharist are painted, one on each side of an arched doorway. Each shows a basketful of bread on top of a fish, with a glass of wine inside that can be seen through the side of the basket. These two frescoes, dated about the middle of the second century, plainly combine the two types of Eucharist, satisfying the practitioners of either type.[23] The fish and bread Eucharist must have existed independently before the symbols were combined.

By the end of the second century some Christians called Jesus "Fish." Around A.D. 200 Tertullian wrote in Greek: "But we, little fishes, after the example of our Fish Jesus Christ, are born in water" (i.e., baptism).[24] In the catacomb of Priscilla at Rome a Greek inscription of uncertain date reads "Alexander in" followed by a drawing of a fish; this is one way of saying that Alexander died in Christ. The Greek word for fish is *ichthus*, and its letters are the initial letters of the Greek words for "Jesus Christ, (of) God, Son, Savior." Therefore an acrostic of those Greek words spells in Greek the word "fish." On the gravestone of Licinia Amias, also dated around A.D. 200, the Greek words *Ichthus Zonton*, "Fish of the living," are inscribed, with two fish drawn underneath. The acrostic may be understood here, so that the thought is "Jesus Christ, Son of God, Savior of the living."[25] Many scholars have thought that the acrostic was the source of "Fish" as a term for Jesus. That was a bad guess! Jesus was identified with fish in the fish and bread Eucharist before the acrostic appeared. Besides, the expression "Jesus Christ, Son of God, Savior" was not customary in the early churches and apparently is a forced arrangement to make the acrostic possible.

Some interpreters have suggested that the feeding of the multitude stories in the gospels and the bread and fish Jesus fed his disciples in John 21 symbolize the bread and fish Eucharist.

Perhaps they are right, but the theory will not be discussed here, for the evidence seems inconclusive.

What is the origin of the fish and bread Eucharist? Fish deities were popular in the ancient Middle East, from Babylonia to Egypt to Syria. Some were gods and some were goddesses. Usually the deity was a particular kind of fish. An Assyrian seal of the eighth or seventh century B.C. shows priests dressed as fish worshiping before a sacred tree, with the winged sun-disk of the god Ashur above it. [26] In early Christian times the Syrian goddess Atargatis was especially popular in Palestine, Syria, and Rome. Christianity, too, was popular in those same regions. Atargatis's cult centers had a pool in which her sacred fish were kept. These fish were eaten by her worshipers in ritual meals, which in the West were eaten in a special room in her temples. She was identified with her fish, and ancient writers described her as half woman, half fish—like a mermaid. When devotees ate her fish, they were, in effect, eating her body.

The source of the Christian fish and bread Eucharist, and the identification of Jesus with fish, then, must have been the influence of converts with a background in that type of religion.

16

THE FUTURE - A

Christian eschatology, beliefs concerning "the last things" that would occur "in the last days" at the end of this world, were mainly derived from Judaism and adapted to Christianity. As with other areas of Christian thought, growth of the churches led to much variety of beliefs. The most radical change was from the initial Christian acceptance of eschatology to Gnostic Christians' rejection of it.

KINGDOM OF GOD

Jesus' central theme, the coming of the kingdom of God, was also the central theme of early apostolic teaching; for example, Philip's in Acts 8:12. It was a basic element in Paul's preaching too: "We exhorted each one of you . . . to lead a life worthy of God, who calls you into his own kingdom and glory" (1 Thess. 2:11-12). The arrival of the kingdom was believed to be imminent. "Some who stand here shall not taste death until they see the kingdom of God come with power" (Mark 9:1); whether Jesus uttered these words or not, the author of Mark clearly believed them. Paul and many other early Christians expected that the kingdom and Jesus would come any day soon (see below). Christians prayed for the coming of the kingdom in the Lord's Prayer. At the turn of the century the author of 1 Peter thought that "the end of all things is near" (4:7), and in mid-second century Justin Martyr still believed that the end was imminent (*Dial.* 28:2).

Nature of the Kingdom

Belief that the kingdom was near at hand naturally led to questions and speculation as time passed. "What will the kingdom be like?" was one of the questions asked. Christian answers were largely derived from Judaism.

Jews expected that conditions in the kingdom would be

ideal because, whether the kingdom is governed by a Messiah or directly by the Lord, the Lord will be in control. First, the wicked and the gentile rulers will be punished or destroyed (Isa. 26:21). Reacting against foreign oppression, some writers expected severe punishment of gentiles in general. Isaiah 61:5 predicts that they will be servants of the Jews, but Micah 4 presents a more tolerant view: many nations will come to Mount Zion to learn the ways and law of the Lord. Second, the Lord's rule will be universal, over the whole earth. Jerusalem on Mount Zion will be restored and glorified as the capital of the kingdom (Isa. 60). Third, peace, righteousness, prosperity, good health, and fidelity to Yahweh will prevail. In Isaiah 2:4 the nations shall beat their swords into plowshares, and in Isaiah 11, after the Lord slays the wicked with the breath of his lips, earth will be a "peaceable kingdom" in which even animals are at peace with each other (cf. chap. 65). The earth will produce bountiful crops: "The threshing floors will be full of grain; the vats shall overflow with wine and [olive] oil" (Joel 2:24). Similar ideas are in the Jewish Pseudepigrapha. For example: "And he who plants a vine upon her [the earth] will produce wine for plenitude. And every seed that is sown on her, one measure will yield a thousand (measures) and one measure of olives will yield ten measures of presses of oil" (*1 Enoch* 10:19).

One concept of the kingdom was that it would be on a new earth. "'For as the new heavens and new earth that I will make shall remain before me,' says the Lord" (Isa. 66:22). God makes a similar statement in *1 Enoch* 45:4-5:

I shall transform heaven and make it a blessing of light forever.

I shall (also) transform the earth and make it a blessing.

Some Jewish Christians too held that belief: "Then I saw a new heaven and a new earth" (Rev. 21:1). Also a new Jerusalem: One of the seven angels "showed me the holy city Jerusalem coming down out of heaven from God" (Rev. 21:10).

Early Christians too expected ideal conditions in the kingdom of God. They too expected that the earth will produce bountifully: Papias wrote that Jesus prophesied that each cluster of grapes will consist of 10,000 grapes, and each grape will yield 25 measures of wine.[1] As we have seen, Isaiah's ideals of justice, no poverty, and no sickness or physical disabilities reappear in the synoptic gospels. The righteous dead will not marry or remain married to former spouses, but will be like the angels in heaven (Mark 12:25). There will be no more death.[2] God's whole creation will be set free from its bondage to decay (Rom. 8:21). Satan's reign will end; this idea is in Revelation 20 and Luke 10:18. It too came out of Judaism: "Then his [God's] kingdom will appear throughout his whole creation. Then the devil will have an end" (*T. Moses* 10:1). "There shall no more be Beliar's [i.e., Satan's] spirit of error, because he will be thrown into eternal fire" (*T. Jud.* 25:3).

The new kingdom will be so wonderful, and the alternative in hell so horrible, that it is worth any sacrifice to be able to enter it. This is the point of the parables of the Hidden Treasure and of the Pearl in Matthew 13. In fact, many of the parables in the synoptic gospels are concerned with problems related to the kingdom of God. And who will enter it? Only the righteous. And they will not be numerous: "For many are called, but few are chosen" (Matt. 22:14). Will uncircumcised gentile Christians be allowed to enter? (This question will be dealt with in a chapter below, "The Mission to the Gentiles.")

Where will the kingdom of God first appear? Some expected it to appear in Jerusalem, which will be its capital city. There people will assemble to usher in the new age. Early in the second century the Christian Montanists in Phrygia expected the new Jerusalem to come down to a small town in their country.[3]

A contrasting view was that the kingdom will suddenly appear everywhere at once. This is the case in *Testament of Moses* 10. In Luke 17:20-21 Jesus says that when the kingdom of God comes, people "will not say, 'Lo, here it is!' or 'There!' for behold, the kingdom of God is in the midst of you." This passage has been much debated by biblical scholars. The problem is with the Greek word *eis*, here translated as "in the midst of you," but it can be translated as "in." Late in the nineteenth century some Christian liberals decided that the passage means "in you," and therefore the kingdom is spiritual. That interpretation is very implausible, for the words are addressed to hostile Pharisees, who, from a Christian view-point, would not have a spiritual kingdom of God within them. In this century C. H. Dodd concluded that the passage indicates that the kingdom has already arrived in the person of Jesus—this view is called "realized eschatology." But Luke connects the passage with the three following verses about the coming of the Son of Man (who will come with the kingdom), which is future and not spiritual. People will not say "There it is" because it will be everywhere in their midst. Unlike the other two interpretations, this one is supported by other passages in the synoptics.

Signs

A general belief in Judaism was that some unusual events, or signs, would occur shortly before the arrival of the kingdom of God. "When you see that a certain part of the predicted signs are past, then you will know that it is the very time when the Most High is about to visit the world which he has made" (*4 Ezra* 9:1-2). A manuscript fragment found in Cave 1 at Qumran contains this statement: "This is a sign to you that it will come to pass."4 In the early second century A.D. a Jewish apocalyptist wrote: "After the signs have come of which I have spoken to you before, when the nations are moved and the time of my Anointed One [Messiah] comes, he will call all nations, and some of them he will spare, and others he will kill" (*2 Bar.* 72:2). Some Christians too expected signs before the end.

What will the signs be? The prophet Joel expected cosmic phenomena to occur: "And I [the Lord] will give portents in the heavens and on the earth, blood and fire and columns of smoke. The sun shall be turned to darkness, and the moon to blood, before the great and terrible day of the Lord comes" (2:30-31). This passage is put to Christian use in Acts 2:19-20. The Book of Revelation contains fanciful visions of supernatural things that will appear in heaven and on earth when the New Age comes. In 15:1 one of the marvels, seven angels and seven plagues, is specifically called a "sign" in the Greek text. Here are some extracts from the description of signs in *4 Ezra* 5:1-5:

Now concerning the signs: Behold, the days are coming when those who dwell on earth shall be seized with great terror, and the way of truth shall be hidden, and the land shall be barren of faith. And unrighteousness shall be increased . . . And the land which you now see ruling shall be waste . . . and the sun shall suddenly shine forth at night, and the moon during the day. Blood shall drip from wood, and the stone shall utter its voice; the peoples shall be troubled, and the stars shall fall.

The same kind of cosmic signs that are in Joel and *4 Ezra* are in the "Little Apocalypse" in Mark 13:24-25.

The most prevalent type of signs in Jewish and Christian

apocalypses was that of widespread suffering on the earth. Modern scholars label those conditions as "eschatological woes," or "messianic woes," because they would occur in the last days of this age. The idea is in Daniel 12:1: "And there shall be a time of trouble, such as never has been since there was a nation until that time." Fantastic description of the tribulations was a favorite feature in apocalyptic writing, both Jewish and Christian. The Book of Revelation, or the Apocalypse, is famous for its woes. The "Little Apocalypse" in Mark 13 par is a Jewish-Christian work presented as words of Jesus. It predicts that wars, rumors of wars, earthquakes, and famines will come first, but all this is only the beginning of the sufferings, which will be followed by persecution of Christians and strife within their families. Next will come the "desolating sacrilege" (the phrase was suggested by the prophecy in Daniel 12:11), which apparently was connected with the Roman attack on Jerusalem in A.D. 70, which caused the people to flee hastily to the hills in Judea, as Mark 13 mentions in verse 14. Luke 21:20 describes that situation plainly: "When you see Jerusalem surrounded by armies, then know that its desolation has come near." Thus the list of woes ends with the Roman attack on Jerusalem, just as it was introduced by a "forecast" of the destruction of the Temple in that war. Revelation 11:2 also prophesies that "the nations . . . will trample over the holy city for forty-two months." In the *Sibylline Oracles* (4:125-127) a Jewish writer too prophesies the Roman destruction of the Temple. All of these "predictions" were made after the event—a typical literary device in both Jewish and Christian prophetic and apocalyptic writings. It appears in all four canonical gospels.

The Little Apocalypse contains another post-event "forecast": "False Christs and false prophets will arise and show signs and wonders, to lead astray, if possible, the elect. But take heed, I have told you all things beforehand" (Mark 13:22-23). The false Messiah-prophets had already appeared when Mark was written. *Didache* 16 also predicts the coming of false prophets in the last days, but the author knows nothing of such a forecast by Jesus.

In our chapter on miracles we observed that exorcisms, whether performed by Jesus or apostles, were regarded as signs that the kingdom of God was near at hand. Jewish apocalyptists anticipated that miracles would occur as signs: "The beginnings [of signs of the end] are manifest in wonders and mighty works" (*4 Ezra* 9:6). In Jewish eschatology God will triumph permanently over Satan at the end of this age, and in the synoptic gospels the casting out of Satan's demons is seen as the ending of Satan's reign—the exorcisms caused him to "fall like lightning" (Luke 10:17-18). Other Christian writers, however, believed that Satan was not yet conquered, but he will be when Jesus returns. ". . . the God of peace will soon crush Satan under your feet" (Rom. 16:20). "When the Son comes, he will destroy the time of the lawless one" (Satan; *Barn.* 15:5). Other miracles too were viewed as signs of the approach of the end. This apparently is the case in Acts with its frequent mention of signs and wonders performed by the apostles.[5] Certain passages in Isaiah prophesied that in the new kingdom invalids will be healed, the dead raised, and good news will be preached to the poor. In Q these are combined and used as evidence that Jesus is the Christ (Matt. 11:5=Luke 7:22); thus, in effect, these are signs that the new kingdom has begun to arrive.

When people see these signs, they should be wise enough to recognize them, just as they do with signs in nature. When leaves begin to appear on the fig tree, "you know that summer is near" (Mark 13:28). Hypocrites can interpret the signs in nature to forecast the weather, "but why do you not know how to interpret the present time?" (Luke 12:56 par). In Luke this is addressed to the multitudes, but in the parallel in Matthew 16:1 it is addressed to the Pharisees and Sadducees.

A contrary line of thought was that no signs will be given. Jesus refuses the demand of the Pharisees that he produce a sign from heaven (Mark 8:11-12). In Luke 17:20 we read: "Being asked by the Pharisees when the kingdom of God was coming, he answered them, 'The kingdom of God is not coming with signs to be observed.'" Thus again we encounter a contradiction in thought that would be strange in one man, Jesus, but not surprising in a mixture of ideas drawn from many persons in the early churches.

A middle ground between no signs and many signs is in the Q source: "This generation is an evil generation; it seeks a sign, but no sign shall be given to it except the sign of Jonah" (Luke 11:29 par). And what is "the sign of Jonah"? It is the Christian mission to the gentiles, for the distinctive feature of Jonah (in addition to his being swallowed by "a great fish") was that he was God's agent who (reluctantly) caused the gentile city of Nineveh to repent and be saved.

When Is the Kingdom Coming?
A natural question, asked by both Jews and Christians, was, "When is the kingdom coming?" Jews had been asking this for centuries. When present conditions are so bad, and life in the new kingdom will be so wonderful, why does God delay? Why hasn't the kingdom come?

Then I answered and said, "How long and when will these things be?. . ." He [the angel Uriel] answered me and said, "You should not hasten faster than the Most High, for your haste is for yourself, but the Highest hastens on behalf of many. Did not the souls of the righteous in their chambers ask about these matters, saying, 'How long are we to remain here?. . .' And Jeremiel the archangel answered them and said, "When the number of those like yourselves is completed, for he has weighed the age in the balance, and measured the times by measure, and numbered the times by number; and he will not move or arouse them until that measure is fulfilled" (*4 Ezra* 4:33-37).

The prophet Habakkuk asked the Lord how long must he cry for help while the wicked swallow up the righteous (1:2, 13). The Lord answered, "For still the vision awaits its time; it hastens to the end—it will not lie. If it seems slow, wait for it; it will surely come; it will not delay" (2:3). Centuries later the author of the *Habakkuk Commentary* found at Qumran had to admit that there had been a delay. He made these comments on that verse: "Its meaning is that the last days shall be longer than all the prophets have predicted, for wondrous are the mysteries of God. . . . Its meaning concerns . . . even though the last days shall delay for them [the men of the Truth], for all the appointed times of God shall duly come, as he has established for them in the mystery of his kingdom" (1QpH 7:7-14). (Observe how the writer freely reinterpreted the Habakkuk passage; although it states that there will be no delay, he interprets it as saying the opposite.)

The same problem confronted the early Christians. At first they believed that the coming of the kingdom was imminent, but even with the passage of decades, it failed to happen, and some Christians abandoned the faith. Christian apologists were forced to explain the delay, and Christian thinking had to be revised.

One explanation is in some of the "Parables of the

Kingdom" in the synoptic gospels: the coming of the kingdom takes time. The kingdom of God is like a seed that grows slowly, but when it is ripe, the sower (God) will harvest it (Mark 4:26-29). The kingdom is like a mustard seed, which though it is the smallest of seeds, eventually becomes a tree (Mark 4:30-32). The kingdom "is like leaven which a woman took and hid in three measures of meal until all was leavened" (Q, Matt. 13:33=Luke 13:20-21).

A note on the Parables of the Kingdom. The introductory formula, "the kingdom of God is like," occurs in Marcan parables, and in Matthew the author has added it to other parables,[6] but it is not in the parables peculiar to Luke. In many of the parables it is not the kingdom itself which is described, but features related to it such as the delay in its coming, the Judgment (parable of the Net, Matt. 13:47-50), and the conditions preceding its coming (parable of the Weeds, Matt. 13:24-30).

Who Can Enter?

Who are qualified to enter the kingdom of God? In Judaism the basic answer was that they are those whom God has chosen. They are the "holy ones," the saints, the righteous Jews who are faithful to Yahweh. In sectarian groups their own members will be the eschatological congregation; when the kingdom comes, "the congregation of the righteous shall appear" (*1 Enoch* 38:1). The Essenes at Qumran are the "Congregation," or "Community," of God; only they will inherit the kingdom of God. The early Christians gradually adopted a similar attitude toward themselves, which clearly is closely related to the concept of Christianity as the new and true Judaism. One expression of the idea is "church of God" in Paul's letters, applied not only to local churches (1 Cor. 1:2), but also as a collective expression for the whole Christian movement (1 Cor. 10:32).

Will all Christians inherit the kingdom? Theoretically all who believe that Jesus is the Christ and are baptized in his name will be saved (some churches continued to require repentance, and some did not). The *Shepherd of Hermas* emphasizes the importance of the name of the Son of God: "Whoever does not receive his name shall not enter into the kingdom of God."[7] With the passage of time various other requirements arose.

The synoptic gospels emerged from Jewish-Christian

communities composed mainly of former members of Jewish sectarian groups. Those groups emphasized ethics, so we are not surprised to find in the synoptics the view that ethical conduct also is required for admission to the kingdom. In Mark 12:28 a scribe asks Jesus which is the first commandment. When he agrees with the two commandments—love God and love your neighbor—, Jesus replies, "You are not far from the kingdom of God." In Mark 10:17-22 a man asks Jesus what he must do to "inherit eternal life," that is, enter the eternal kingdom of God. Jesus' response is to quote some of the Ten Commandments and ask the man to sell all that he has and give to the poor.

The author of Matthew makes kindness to Christians a basis of successfully passing the Judgment. In 25:31-46 he states that when the Son of Man comes, he will sit on his throne and judge "all the nations" (gentiles), separating the righteous from the wicked as a shepherd separates sheep from goats.

> Then the King will say to those at his right hand, "Come, 0 blessed of my Father, inherit the kingdom prepared for you from the foundation of the world; for I was hungry and you gave me food, I was thirsty and you gave me drink, I was a stranger and you welcomed me, I was naked and you clothed me, I was sick. and you visited me, I was in prison and you came to me." Then the righteous will answer him, "Lord, when did we see you hungry and feed you, . . ?" And the King will answer them, "Truly I say to you, as you did it to one of the least of these my brethren, you did it to me."

Whereas kindness to Christians could get one into the kingdom, the unbelieving Jewish chief priests and elders will hardly succeed: "Jesus said to them, 'Truly, I say to you, the tax collectors and the harlots go into the kingdom of God before you'" (Matt. 21:31). Children will be in the kingdom, and adults should receive it like a child (Mark 10:13-16).

Wealth is a hindrance to entering the kingdom: "It is easier for a camel to go through the eye of a needle than for a rich man to enter the kingdom of God" (Mark 10:25). Nevertheless, the wealthy can enter, "for all things are possible with God" (v. 27). Some men believed that sex was a hindrance and therefore made themselves eunuchs for the sake of (entering) the kingdom (Matt. 19 :12).

Who Will Establish the Kingdom?
The notion that a god was also a king was prevalent in the ancient Near East. In the Canaanite clay tablets that archaeologists found at Ras Shamra, or Ugarit, both the supreme god El and the god Baal are called "king."[8] The Egyptian god Sarapis is "ruler of the world" in the Leiden papyrus.[9] The Hebrews before the Exodus and the Israelites after it adopted and adapted ideas and practices from their neighbors, especially the Canaanites. Yahweh too became a king. In Psalm 24 he is both king and war-god: "Who is this King of glory? Yahweh of armies [hosts], he is the king of glory!" Here he is Lord of the whole earth, and so is Baal in the Ugaritic tablets.
The belief that God is king of the universe developed into the Jewish idea that when his kingdom comes, he will descend to earth and rule directly: "The Lord of hosts will reign on Mount Zion and in Jerusalem" (Isa. 24:23). The belief continued in the Pseudepigrapha, although in this example the Lord comes to Mount Sinai instead of Mount Zion and Jerusalem: God "will come forth from his dwelling [heaven]. And from there he will march upon Mount Sinai and appear in his camp emerging from heaven with a mighty power"; he will arrive with ten million angels (*1 Enoch* 1:3-4).
Why did many Jews think that God should come down and rule directly instead of indirectly through a human king? Several reasons are apparent: (1) Disillusionment with human kings was widespread. Jewish kings often were too weak to prevent or overthrow foreign dominance, and the personal conduct of some of them was far from ideal. (2) A Kingdom of God logically suggests that its king will be God himself, visibly present. (3) The supernaturalism of eschatology in general was conducive to the notion of a supernatural ruler in the new kingdom.
It is hard to find evidence that the early Christians believed that when the kingdom arrives, God will immediately assume his throne in Jerusalem. Instead, we find statements that Jesus will be the ruler, at least temporarily. That view was virtually inevitable, considering that Christians believed that Jesus is the Messiah, the anointed king who will rule when he returns.

THE SECOND COMING OR PAROUSIA

In early Judaism some writers expected that the Messiah will establish the new kingdom. Generally they thought that his reign will be temporary; he will prepare the way, and then turn the kingdom over to God. Early rabbinic literature divided eschatological time into two periods: "the Days of the Messiah" and "the World to Come"; the latter is the Kingdom of God, or the New Age. Opinion varied as to the duration of the reign of the Messiah. Many writers did not specify; *4 Ezra* 7:28 predicts it will last 400 years. Among the early rabbis the Days of the Messiah ranged from 40 to 1,000 years; later some rabbis extended the time to thousands of years.[10]

With that Jewish background, early Christians naturally thought that Jesus, the Messiah, would establish the kingdom. The duration of the messianic kingdom varied in Christian eschatology as well as in Jewish. Well known to Christians today is "the millennium," Jesus' temporary reign of 1,000 years after he returns to earth, described in Revelation 20-22. At the end of the millennium God will appear, sitting on a great white throne, followed by a new heaven, new earth, and a new Jerusalem. Thereafter God will rule from his throne in the new Jerusalem. "I heard a great voice from the throne saying, 'Behold, the dwelling of God is with men'" (Rev. 21:3). This stream of thought in the Jewish-Christian Book of Revelation comes directly out of Judaism. Papias too believed in a millennium: "there will be a millennium after the resurrection of the dead."[11] Justin wrote: "There will be a resurrection of the flesh, and also a thousand years in a Jerusalem built up and adorned and enlarged."[12]

In contrast to that line of thought stands the Son of Man christology. In Judaism the Son of Man Messiah, not God, will reign forever; at least he will sit on his throne at the Judgment, he will live forever on earth, and *1 Enoch* never states that he will hand the throne over to God. In fact, we have further Jewish evidence that the Son of Man will take over permanently the dominion of the world. Justin reports that Trypho the Jew said that "passages of Scripture compel us to await One who is great and glorious, and as the Son of Man will take over the everlasting kingdom from the Ancient of Days" [God][13] We are not surprised that the Son of Man's reign in *1 Enoch* will be permanent, for he is not human, but divine.[14] The Son of Man's kingdom is evidently permanent in the synoptic gospels too; at least there is no indication that it will be temporary or passed on to God.

With some early Christians the Kingdom of God became the Kingdom of Jesus as the result of at least two factors. Christian deification of Jesus tended to shift to him various attributes of God, and secondly, the Son of Man christology paved the way with its doctrine that the Son of Man will rule the earth indefinitely. Evidence of the latter factor is in Matthew 16:28 where the author copies Mark 9:1, but changes Mark's "until they see the Kingdom of God come with power" to "until they see the Son of Man coming in his kingdom." Other Christian writers broke away from the Son of Man precedent and ascribed the kingdom to Jesus under various other titles. In Colossians 1:13 God, the Father, "has delivered us from the dominion of darkness and transferred us to the kingdom of his beloved Son." In *1 Clement* 50:3 the souls of the godly who have been in the heavenly store-chambers "will be manifest at the visitation of the Kingdom of Christ." Papias said that after the Resurrection "the Kingdom of Christ will be set up physically upon this earth."[15]

How Will Jesus Return?

A brief description is in 1 Thessalonians 4. "For the Lord [Jesus] himself will descend from heaven with a cry of command, with the archangel's call, and with the sound of the trumpet of God." Mark 13 describes Jesus' descent thus: "They will see the Son of Man coming in clouds with great power and glory. And then he will send out the angels, and gather his elect from the four winds, from the ends of the earth to the ends of heaven." The Son of Man will appear suddenly, everywhere: "For as the lightning comes from the east and shines as far as the west, so will be the coming of the Son of Man" (Matt. 24:27).

When Will Jesus Return?

The questions and answers concerning the return of Jesus were essentially the same as those pertaining to the coming of the kingdom of God. In the first and second centuries Christians generally expected that Jesus' parousia was imminent. Paul's letters and the synoptic gospels provide first-century evidence. Mark twice testifies to the belief that the parousia is near.[16] Paul wrote, "The Lord is at hand" (Phil. 4:5). In the middle of the second century Justin warned Trypho that "if Christ comes suddenly, you will repent in vain."[17]

Further evidence that Christians expected the Second Coming soon is found in the numerous statements that they were "waiting" for it. "As you wait for the revealing of our Lord Jesus Christ," wrote Paul (1 Cor. 1:7). Christians everywhere report "how you [Thessalonians] turned to God from idols, . . . and to wait for his Son from heaven" (1 Thess. 1:9-10). Christ "will appear a second time, not to deal with sin but to save those who are eagerly waiting for him" (Heb. 9:28). In fact, some Thessalonians were so sure that Jesus would return soon that they quit working:

> For we hear that some of you are living in idleness, mere busybodies, not doing any work. Now such persons we command and exhort in the Lord Jesus Christ to do their work in quietness and to earn their own living (2 Thess. 3:11-12).

Some Thessalonians even believed a rumor that Jesus had already returned (2 Thess. 2:1-2).

In Mark and Q Jesus is usually the "Son of Man" in statements about his return. This is strong evidence that some Christians decided early that Jesus must be the Son of Man type of Christ because in contemporary Jewish prophetic and apocalyptic writings, the Son of Man is the only Messiah expected to come down from heaven.

Jesus and the kingdom *did not arrive*, however. The delay of the parousia understandably created problems. It caused some Christians to have doubts that Jesus would return and doubts about the validity of the Christian religion as a whole. Apologists were forced to take action to defend the faith. One response was to explain that preparation for the parousia requires time, and therefore members should be patient and wait:

> Be patient, therefore, brethren, until the coming of the Lord. Behold, the farmer waits for the precious fruit of the earth, being patient over it until it receives the early and late rain. You also be patient. Establish your hearts, for the coming of the Lord is at hand (Jas. 5:7-8).

> Let this Scripture be far from us in which he [the Father] says "Wretched are the double-minded, who doubt in their soul and say 'We have heard these things even in

the days of our fathers, and behold we have grown old, and none of these things have happened to us.' O foolish men, compare yourself to a tree: take a vine, first it sheds its leaves, then there comes a bud, then a leaf, then a flower, and after this the unripe grape, then the bunch of ripe grapes." See how in a little time the fruit of the tree comes to ripeness. Truly his will shall be quickly and suddenly accomplished, as the Scripture also bears witness that "he shall come quickly and shall not tarry; and the Lord shall come suddenly to his Temple, and the Holy One for whom you look" (*1 Clement* 23:3-5).

We should observe that these analogies of slow growth are similar to some parables of the kingdom of God ascribed to Jesus in the synoptics, but the authors evidently do not know of any such words of Jesus, for if they had known of any, they surely would have referred to him here as an authority.

Related to the slow-growth explanation, which demands that more time be allowed, is the device of stretching out the time. An example is in 2 Peter:

. . . scoffers will come in the last days with scoffing, following their own passions and saying, "Where is the promise of his coming? For ever since the fathers fell asleep, all things have continued as they were from the beginning of creation." . . . But do not ignore this one fact, beloved, that with the Lord one day is as a thousand years, and a thousand years as one day (3:3-4, 8).

Another type of explanation was the claim that certain events must occur first, a favorite literary device with both Jewish and Christian apologists. Here are some of the explanations:

1. The Christ "whom heaven must receive until the time for establishing all that God spoke by the mouth of his holy prophets from of old" (Acts 3:21).

2. Acts 3:19-20 indicates that the Christ will come after the Jews repent. "Repent . . . so that times of refreshing may come from the presence of the Lord, and that he may send the Christ appointed for you, Jesus."

3. Psalm 110:1, which early Christians quoted to support their faith in Jesus' ascension, suggests another reason for the delay:

The Lord says to my lord,

"Sit at my right hand,
until I make your enemies your footstool."
   4. Justin combined the above idea with the belief that Satan's demons will be vanquished at the end of this age. He wrote that God the Father of all will keep Christ in heaven "until he has subdued his enemies the demons" (*1 Apol.* 45).
   5. In the same passage Justin adds another explanation: God is keeping Christ in heaven "until the number of those foreknown to him as good and virtuous is complete, on whose account he has still delayed the consummation."
   6. *Shepherd of Hermas* explains that the growth of Christianity must be completed first. Hermas in a vision asks "the Lady" about the times, if the end is yet:

> But she cried out loudly, "Foolish man! Can you not see that the tower [the Church] is still being built? When the building of the tower is finished, the end will come. But it will be built quickly. Ask me nothing more" (Vision 3. 8. 9).

   7. 2 Thessalonians 2 provides this explanation: ". . . that day will not come unless the rebellion comes first, and the man of lawlessness is revealed, the son of perdition, who opposes and exalts himself against every so-called god or object of worship, so that he takes his seat in the temple of God, proclaiming himself to be God." This is a reference to Emperor Gaius Caligula's order (not carried out) to have his statue set up in the Temple in Jerusalem in A.D. 40.[18]

   The failure of Jesus to return was disillusioning and caused some Christians to abandon the faith. Consequently members were exhorted to remain faithful, be steadfast. This is the point of the parable of the Unjust Judge in Luke 18, wherein the disciples (Christians) "ought always to pray and not lose heart," and the parable is followed by the question, "When the Son of Man comes, will he find [Christian] faith on earth?" The parable of the Faithful vs. the Unfaithful Steward in Q (Luke 12:42-46 par) condemns the unfaithful steward who thinks he can do as he pleases because his master (Jesus) has gone away and is delayed in coming back.

Jesus' Functions After He Returns
   When Jesus was thought of as the Son of David, his main function after his return would be to govern as king. When he was conceived of as the Son of Man, his role as judge

at the Judgment was emphasized, as in Matthew 19:28. In both concepts, the Jewish background was the guide. In the Gospel of John Jesus himself will not return to earth except in the G source, where his function will be to lead Christian souls to heaven: "And after I go and prepare a place for you, I will come again and will take you to myself, that where I am you may be also" (John 14:3; cf. 17:24, also from G). This idea may have been suggested by gentile religion; in the cult of Mithras and the cult of Isis, for example, a divine person escorted the souls of deceased worshipers to their heavenly home.

THE FUTURE - B

THE GENERAL RESURRECTION

Although in early Christian writings "the resurrection" can refer to the belief in Jesus' resurrection, it refers more frequently to the belief that the dead will be raised from their graves at the end of the present age.

In Judaism

The roots of Jewish and Christian eschatology are in Persian, or Iranian, religion, which spread to Palestine, Syria, and Asia Minor. In Zoroastrian/Mazdean eschatology the souls of the righteous will rise from their underground chambers where they have been stored, separated from their bodies. At the end of the present age Saoshyant, the divine Savior, will call them out and purify them, raise the bodies, and unite the bodies with their corresponding souls.

Jewish apocalyptists adapted some Iranian eschatology to Judaism in the Persian and Hellenistic periods. Belief in a general resurrection appears in Jewish literature in Daniel 12:2: "And many of those who sleep in the dust of the earth shall awake, some to eternal life, and some to shame and everlasting contempt."

In the original Jewish form of the resurrection doctrine, God will raise only righteous Jews. Late passages in Isaiah 26 state it plainly: The Lord's "dead shall live, their bodies shall arise" (vs. 19), but as for the dead gentile rulers, "they will not live; they are shades, they will not arise" (vs. 14). The belief is expressed in *Psalms of Solomon:* "Those who fear the Lord shall rise up to eternal life, and their life shall be in the Lord's light, and it shall never end" (3:12). In this document the deceased sinners, however, will not be raised, and the sinners who are still alive at the time "shall perish forever in the day of the Lord's judgment" (15:12). God will certainly raise the righteous Maccabees who were faithful Jewish martyrs: "The King of the universe will raise us up to an everlasting renewal of life, because we have died for his laws" (2 Macc. 7:9), but there will be no resurrection for gentiles (7:14). The resurrection of only the righteous is the belief also in *1 Enoch* 22:8-13. In that passage souls will be separated from the bodies when the bodies die. The souls of the righteous will be set by a spring of water, but the souls of the wicked will be buried in the earth. On the day of judgment the bodies of the righteous will be raised and reunited with their souls, but the bodies and souls of the wicked will remain in the ground. This arrangement may have been suggested by Iranian religion.

Another view was that both the righteous and wicked dead will be revived. This is the case in the *Testament of the Twelve Patriarchs*. Here too the bodies will be changed into an imperishable state so that they can live forever. The patriarchs will be raised first, and the other Jews next, each according to tribe. "Then all shall be changed, some destined for glory, others for dishonor" (*T. Ben.* 10:8). "All" apparently includes gentiles, for they will be judged too (10:9). In the Parables of *1 Enoch* Sheol will return all the deposits (souls) it has received, and the Elect One (Son of Man) will choose the righteous from among them (51:1-2). This is the belief also in *Pseudo-Philo* (1 c. A.D.), except that here it is God who will "render to each according to his works" (3:10).

Where are the souls while the bodies are in the ground? In ancient Israel the "shades" of the dead were believed to exist forever in Sheol under the earth. They are shadowy remnants of the bodies. They are mentioned in Proverbs 9:18, where the Hebrew word for "shades" is often translated as "the dead": "the shades . . . are in the depths of Sheol."

As the cloud fades and vanishes,
So he who goes down to Sheol does not come up (Job 7:9).

The dead in Sheol are very similar to the dead in Hades in Homer's *Iliad* and *Odyssey*.

The eschatology inherited from late Zoroastrianism and the influence of the Greek belief in the existence of souls combined to produce in Judaism belief in the soul. Now souls replace shades. The soul is distinct from the body; it is imperishable, but the body is perishable. At the resurrection the soul will be raised from Sheol, and the body from the grave, and the two will be reunited. In the interim between death and the resurrection, souls are stored in "chambers"or "treasuries" deep in the earth or—a later idea—up in the heavens. A variant is the belief that the souls of the righteous await in Paradise (a Zoroastrian word), which in the Pseudepigrapha is located in the East on earth or in one of the heavens.[1]

A Hellenistic school of thought in Judaism taught that the souls of the righteous will dwell in heaven, and therefore no resurrection of the body will occur. This view was prevalent in the Jewish Diaspora; it was derived from Syrian astralism and from Greek religions such as Orphism. In *4 Maccabees* the Maccabean martyrs "are gathered together in the choir of their fathers, having received pure and deathless souls from God" (18:23). In *1 Enoch* 91-104 the souls of the righteous will dwell in a new heaven.[2] A new earth logically is not expected because the Hellenistic view has transferred the locale of blessed immortality from a new earth to heaven; a new earth is not needed because no one would be on it!

In Christianity

Most early Christians too believed in a general resurrection. The Sadducees and Temple priesthood were annoyed because the apostles in Jerusalem were proclaiming the resurrection of the dead through Jesus (Acts 4:2). Paul hoped to "attain the resurrection of the dead" (Phil. 3:11), and in 1 Thessalonians 4 he reassures living Christians that deceased Christians will be raised. Belief in the general resurrection appears in all four canonical gospels.[3] Acts indicates frequently that the apostles in general preached the coming of the resurrection. The Gospel of John anticipates the resurrection in 5:29 and 11:24. In the middle of the second century both Justin and the author of *2 Clement* were awaiting the resurrection.[4]

In respect to the details of how it would happen, Christians differed in their opinions about as much as Jews and along similar lines. Who will raise the dead? The Messiah Jesus, or God? Generally Christians believed that God will do it; he had raised Jesus, and he will raise Christians too. This is Paul's view in 1 Corinthians 15, and he states it concisely earlier in the same letter: "God raised the Lord and will also raise us up by his power" (6:14).

Although in Judaism God is usually the one to raise the dead, in the Parables of *1 Enoch* it is the Son of Man Messiah. The synoptic Gospels do not state that Son of Man will raise the dead, but he will conduct the Judgment (Matt. 25) like the Son of Man in the Parables, and probably is understood to be the one to raise the dead too. In a source in the Gospel of John, Jesus is the Son of Man (1:51) who definitely will raise the dead (6:39). In John 5:21 both the Father and Son will raise the dead. Justin combines God and Jesus as responsible for the resurrection: "God will raise us up by his Christ" (*Dial.* 46:7).

Who will be raised? Paul implies that only the righteous will be, for it is Jesus' resurrection that makes possible the resurrection of Christians (1 Cor. 15:21-22). "The resurrection of the just" in Luke 14:14 suggests that only the just are raised. On the other hand, Acts ascribes to Paul the statement that "there will be a resurrection of both the just and unjust" (24:15). Both the good and the bad will come forth from their tombs in John 5:29.[5] The Book of Revelation anticipates two resurrections: first, that of the Christian martyrs, to be followed by the rest of the dead, both righteous and wicked.[6] To Paul, the first stage was the resurrection of "Christ, the first fruits," and the second stage will be the resurrection of "those who belong to Christ" (1 Cor. 15:23). *Didache* states that at the end there will be "the resurrection of the dead, but not of all" (16:7).

What will happen in the resurrection? Paul states concisely that the Lord Jesus Christ "will make our lowly body to be like his glorious body" (Phil. 3:21). A fuller description is in 1 Corinthians 15:

> But someone will ask, "How are the dead raised? With what kind of body do they come?" . . . What is sown [in the ground] is perishable; what is raised is imperishable. . . . It is sown a physical body; it is raised a spiritual body.

Paul adds that the Christians who are still living at the end will be changed instantly into an imperishable body at the sound of the trumpet (15:51-52).

In accord with the Pharisees' concept of the resurrection is the belief that the body will be raised in its original form, "in the flesh," and immediately transformed into an imperishable, incorruptible body. As Justin wrote, "there will be a resurrection of the flesh" (*Dial.* 80:5). Justin also said that if the body died in a mutilated condition, Christ will raise it whole again (*Dial.* 69:7).

The author of *Martyrdom of Polycarp* (2d c.) apparently expected both body and soul to be raised from the earth. He gratefully looked forward to "the resurrection to everlasting life, both of soul and body in the immortality of the Holy Spirit" (14:2).

Those Christians who believed that the souls of the saved will go to heaven, however, did not believe in the resurrection of the body. Martha in the Signs Source in John expresses faith that her brother will arise in the resurrection (11:24). Although the author of John in passages from his sources allows the resurrection pericopes to stand, here (11:25) he corrects it by having Jesus say, "I am the resurrection." Thus he eliminates the general resurrection, which conflicts with his own belief. The Gnostic Christians believed that their souls will ascend to heaven when the body dies, but the souls of non-Gnostics, however, migrate into other bodies until they acquire the *gnosis,* or knowledge, that will save them from the cycle of transmigration. The body is unfit for immortality because everything physical is evil. Irenaeus described as follows the view of the Gnostic Marcion:

> Salvation will be attained only by those souls who have learned his [Marcion's] doctrine; whereas the body, because it has been taken from the earth [Gen. 2:7], cannot participate in salvation.[7]

(The diversity of opinion on the locale of immortality survives today, although most Christians are unaware of it. Many Christians now believe in the immortality of the soul, but are unaware that in the early churches the belief could be seen as heretical. They also are unaware that it is contrary to a feature in the Apostles' Creed they repeat in church: "I believe . . . in the resurrection of the body.")

Not only Gnostics, but also many Hellenized Christians, who were familiar with Greek thought, denied that there will be a resurrection of the body. Outsiders, too, rejected the notion. Numerous early Christians testify to this problem in their literature and try to defend the original doctrine. Paul remonstrates, "How can some of you [Corinthians] say that there is no resurrection of the dead?" (1 Cor. 15:12). According to Acts 26:8, Paul asked Agrippa, "Why is it thought incredible by any of you that God raises the dead?" We saw in 1 Corinthians that Paul, in defence of the doctrine, cited Jesus' resurrection as proof. The author of *1 Clement* also regarded Jesus' resurrection as proof, and added the analogies of seed sown in the ground and the phoenix, the marvelous bird of Arabia and Egypt that dies and comes to life again every five hundred years (24-26). *2 Clement* 9:1 also rebukes the skeptics: "And let none of you say that the flesh is not judged and does not rise again." Justin thought that a Christian is not a true Christian if he does not believe in the resurrection: "so-called Christians . . . who say too that there is no resurrection of the dead but that their souls ascend to heaven at the very moment of their death." The necessity of believing in the resurrection of the dead was insisted on by the rabbis too.[8]

THE JUDGMENT

"The Judgment" refers to the separation of the righteous from the wicked on "the day of the Lord," or "day of judgment," etc., by either God or the Messiah.

In Judaism
The Old Testament prophets predicted that the Lord will pass judgment on the Israelite nation for the deeds of its people. It and the people will be rewarded for faithfulness in worshiping him and obeying his commandments. The wicked Israelites and the gentiles—especially gentile rulers—will be punished. This will happen in historical time.

The admission of eschatology into early Judaism resulted in the development of individualized rewards and punishments; the Lord will reward or punish particular individuals on a particular day at the end of the present age. Eschatology had a double appeal: it brought the hope of immortality, and it solved the problem of the injustice that occurs when the righteous suffer and the wicked prosper.

The righteous will be rewarded with a happy immortal life on a new earth or in heaven, depending on the concept of immortality. For those who believed in a series of heavens, one above the other, eternal life will, of course, be in the highest one, the seventh heaven, where God dwells. This contrasts with Greek Orphism, which held that all souls go down to Hades; the righteous enjoy a blessed life in one section of it, while the wicked endure lashings and perform endless tasks in another section.[9] *1 Enoch* 1 contains the typical view of the Judgment in early Judaism:

> The God of the universe, the Holy Great One, will come forth from his dwelling. . . . And there shall be a judgment upon all, (including) the righteous. And to all the righteous he will grant peace. He will preserve the elect, and kindness shall be upon them. They shall all belong to God and they shall prosper and be blessed; and the light of God shall shine unto them. Behold, he will arrive with ten million of the holy ones [angels] in order to execute judgment upon all. He will destroy the wicked ones and censure all flesh on account of everything that they have done, that which the sinners and the wicked ones committed against him (1:3, 7-9).

The Essenes too believed in a future judgment day; one of their terms for it is "the day of vengeance" (1QS 9:23). They described it in their *Manual of Discipline* as follows:

> At the season of visitation he [God] will destroy it [wrong-doing, or error] forever. . . And then God will purify by his truth all the deeds of men, and cleanse for himself the body of man, in order to abolish every evil spirit from the midst of his flesh, and to purify him with a holy spirit from every wicked deed; and he will sprinkle on him a spirit of truth . . . so as to give the righteous understanding in the knowledge of the Most High and in the wisdom of the sons of heaven [angels], to give the perfect of way understanding (1QS 4:18-22).

The wicked will be punished either by perpetual suffering or by complete termination of their existence. An early view is that the restored bodies of the wicked will be punished forever with fire and with worms eating their flesh. The earliest Jewish occurrence is in Isaiah 66:23-24, which apparently is a later addition to the end of Isaiah. In it those who worship the Lord will look upon and abhor the dead bodies of those who rebelled against him. The Greek text of Sirach 7:17 reads: "Humble yourself greatly, for the punishment of the ungodly is fire and worms." Similarly in Judith 16:17 we find that the Lord will deal harshly with the nations which rise up against his people. He will punish them "on the day of judgment; fire and worms he will give to their flesh; they will weep in pain forever." This apparently will take place on earth, for the righteous will see them and worms will consume their flesh. The torture by fire is an adaptation of punishment by fire in Iranian religion.

A second view of punishment is that the wicked will cease to exist, though usually they are punished first. This belief is expressed in *Psalms of Solomon* 15:12-13:

> And sinners shall perish forever in the day of the Lord's judgment, when God oversees the earth at his judgment. But those who fear the Lord shall find mercy in it and shall live by their God's mercy.

Who will judge the dead? Usually God, as in the examples above. Wisdom of Solomon 3 refers to the Judgment as a day of decision, a time when God examines souls. Where the Son of Man is expected, however, he is the one who will judge, as we read in *1 Enoch*: "And he shall choose the righteous and the holy ones [saints] from among (the risen dead), for the day when they shall be selected and saved has arrived," and "he shall judge the sinners, and the wicked ones shall be driven from the presence of the righteous and elect." The writer has utter contempt for the rulers of the world:

> At that moment, kings and rulers shall perish, they shall be delivered into the hands of the righteous and holy ones, and from thenceforth no one shall be able to induce the Lord of the Spirits to show them mercy, for their life is annihilated.[10]

An interesting feature of the Judgment in this Parables section of *1 Enoch* is that it seems to be related to the Son of Man's act of teaching: "When the secrets of the Righteous One [the Son of Man] are revealed, he shall judge the sinners" (38:3).

How will the divine Judge know who are the righteous and who are the wicked? One solution offered is that a secret record is kept of the names of the righteous and the deeds of the wicked. Daniel states that "at that time your people shall be delivered, everyone whose name shall be found written in the book. . . . But you, Daniel, shut up the words and seal the book, until the time of the end" (12:1, 4). In *1 Enoch* 81 the angel Uriel shows Enoch a tablet of heaven. Enoch says, "I read that book and all the deeds of humanity and all the children of the flesh upon the earth for all the generations of the world"

(81:2). And in *4 Ezra* 14:35, "For after death the judgment will come, when we shall live again; and then the names of the righteous will become manifest, and the deeds of the ungodly will be disclosed." The Essenes apparently held a similar belief, for in the *Thanksgiving Psalms,* or *Thanksgiving Hymns,* found at Qumran a psalmist wrote: "All things are inscribed before you [God] in a recording script" (Gaster's tr.), or "All things are recorded before you with a pen of remembrance" (Burrows' tr.; 1:24-25).

In Christianity

Much of what early Christians said about the coming of the kingdom of God and the return of Jesus fits the coming of the Judgment, for they are all parts of the same great event. The evidence is clear that many early Christians expected the day of judgment to arrive soon. Paul refers to God's pending judgment repeatedly.[11] In a "vision" in Revelation an angel proclaims in a loud voice, "Fear [i.e., worship] God and give him glory, for the hour of his judgment has come" (14:7). Early in the second century Bishop Ignatius wrote: "These are the last times. . . . Let us fear the patience of God, that it may not become our judgment. For let us either fear the wrath to come, or love the grace [of God] which is present" (*Eph.* 11:1). Several decades later Justin expected the Judgment soon; those who believe in Christ will "obtain salvation and be freed from the punishment by fire" (*Dial.* 47:4). The synoptic gospels amply demonstrate the Christian belief that the Judgment was imminent.

At first Christians believed that God will be the judge. Paul frequently speaks of God as the judge. Justin said that God "will set some as incorruptible and immortal and free from all sorrow in an everlasting kingdom that will never cease, and sends away others into everlasting punishment by fire" (*Dial.* 117:3).

But in Matthew 25 the Son of Man is explicitly the judge on judgment day. Polycarp wrote that "our Lord Jesus . . . is to come as judge of the living and the dead," and "we must all stand at the judgment seat of Christ, and each give an account of himself."[12] Other early Christian writers seem confused by the two ideas that originally were distinct. The solution offered in the Gospel of John is that although the Father has had the authority to conduct the Judgment, he has given that authority to the Son because he is the Son of Man (5:23, 27). These verses and Matthew 25 provide clues as to the cause of the shift from God to Jesus as the judge. The cause is the Son of Man tradition derived from *1 Enoch*, or its sources. In John a reconciliation of the two ideas is sought by offering the explanation that the Father gave the authority to the Son; this also preserves God's superiority to Jesus, for the Father *voluntarily* relinquished the authority. (Yet another idea is in John 16:7-8; there the Paraclete, or Counselor, which Jesus will send, will deal with judgment and the issues of righteousness and sin.)

Numerous writings mix together both ideas, God as the judge and Jesus as the judge. Even Paul does this (though the mixture may be the result of redactors' work). In spite of Paul's abundant references to God's judgment, we read in 2 Corinthians 5:10 that "we must all appear before the judgment seat of Christ, so that each may receive good or evil, according to what he has done in the body." In 2 Thessalonians the two ideas are in adjoining passages: God (1:5) and "Lord Jesus" (1:7-8). Romans 2:16 goes a step farther and harmonizes the two ideas in one sentence: "on that day when, according to my gospel, God judges the secrets of men by Jesus Christ." We have observed a passage in Justin's *Dialogue* in which he views God as the judge. In the same book, however, Justin refers twice to Jesus as the judge: "Christ himself is judge of all living and dead" (118:1), and Jesus is "about to come again as judge of all who have ever lived, as far back as Adam himself" (132:1).

Yet another idea was that Christians will be the judges: "the saints will judge the world" (1 Cor. 6:2). This notion is an adaptation of the Jewish idea that the righteous (that is, Jews) will judge the world. The Jewish idea goes back to Daniel 7:22, and appears frequently in early Jewish literature.

How will the Judgment happen? Again we find variety and some similarity to Judaism. The fullest description in the New Testament is in Matthew 25, where the Son of Man is the judge:

> When the Son of Man comes in his glory, and all the angels with him, then he will sit on his throne of glory. Before him will be gathered all the nations, and he will separate them one from another as a shepherd separates the sheep from the goats, and he will place the sheep at

his right hand, but the goats at the left. Then the King will say to those at his right hand, "Come, 0 blessed of my Father, inherit the kingdom prepared for you from the foundation of the world.". . . Then he will say to those at his left hand, "Depart from me, you cursed, into the eternal fire prepared for the devil and his angels."

In Revelation 20 the Judgment occurs at the end of the millennium, Christ's reign of a thousand years. God will sit on "a great white throne," and the dead will stand before the throne. In the seer's vision books were opened and "the book of life" was also. "And the dead were judged by what was written in the books, by what they had done. . . . if anyone's name was not found written in the book of life, he was thrown into the lake of fire."

Certain pericopes in the synoptic gospels imply that the decision between the good and the bad will be made wherever they are, and not necessarily at a grand gathering of all people. For example, "two women will be grinding together; one will be taken and the other left."[13]

What will be the basis of judgment? For what deeds and thoughts will an individual be rewarded or punished? Actually, in the early Christian literature we find not a single basis, but many different bases or criteria of judgment. Initially the main criteria must have been the same three that are understood in Jesus' message, namely, performance of "good works," repentance for sins, and devotion to God. Paul included all three in his comments on punishment. In Romans 2 he threatens those who are wicked and unrepentant, but he promises eternal life to those who are patient in doing good works. "For he [God] will render to every man according to his works" (2:6). The Lord Jesus will inflict vengeance "upon those who do not know God and upon those who do not obey the gospel of our Lord Jesus" (2 Thess.1: 8).

Good works that Christians should do are described in the Sermon on the Mount and elsewhere, as we saw in our chapter "Ethical Teaching." Paul lists some in Romans 12, including "Bless those who persecute you," but he does not attribute it to Jesus. In the next chapter Paul states: "The day is at hand. Let us then cast off the works of darkness . . . let us conduct ourselves becomingly as in the day, not in reveling and drunkenness, not in debauchery and licentiousness, not in quarreling and jealousy." Elsewhere Paul lists other virtues as essential, even though he does not directly connect them with the Judgment. The Book of Revelation associates some sins with eternal punishment:

> But as for the cowardly, the faithless, the polluted, the murderers, fornicators, sorcerers, idolaters, and all liars, their lot shall be in the lake that burns with fire and brimstone, which is the second death (21:8).

Opposition to a double standard in ethics appears often in connection with the threat of judgment; usually it is in Jewish-Christian writings, which is not surprising since this ideal was already in Judaism. "Do you suppose, 0 man, that when you judge those who do such things and yet do them yourself, you will escape the judgment of God?" (Rom. 2:3). "Judge not, that you be not judged. . . . You hypocrite, first take the log out of your own eye, and then you will see clearly to take the speck out of your brother's eye" (Matt. 7:1, 5). The author of James also has no respect for the double standard: "For judgment is without mercy to one who has shown no mercy" (2:13).

Love of God and neighbor is basic for entering the kingdom of God in Mark 12. In a paragraph concerned with the Judgment, James regards as "the royal law" the command to "love your neighbor as yourself" (2:8). Regrettably, "neighbor" here, as in Judaism, refers only to members of one's own religious group. Love within the Christian community in a time of persecution is commanded in John: "This I command you, to love one another" (15:17). In 1 John the relationship between loving God and loving one another is especially close:

> Beloved, let us love one another; for love is of God, and he who loves is born of God and knows God. He who does not love does not know God, for God is love. . . . In this is love perfected with us, that we may have confidence for the day of judgment (4:7-8, 17).

Whoever wrote 1 Corinthians 13 esteemed brotherly love, but he did not base it on fear of punishment nor necessarily restrict it to Christians.

As the Christian communities expanded, the number of criteria for making the divine decisions on judgment day grew. Response to the Christian mission became a criterion. Persons who refuse to listen to apostolic preaching are going to get it on the day of judgment. Towns that are not persuaded by Christian miracles are doomed (Matt. 11:20-24). Another criterion for determining future reward or punishment was based on persecution. Jewish writers had predicted everlasting punishment for those who persecuted Jews, and similarly Christians expected that the same fate awaited those who persecuted them. Christians who have suffered persecution will be rewarded, and the people who persecuted them will be punished. They who have helped Christians are righteous and will go into eternal life, but they who have not helped them "will go away into eternal punishment" (Matt. 25:46).

> But one can find men of every nation, who, because of the name of Jesus, have endured, and do endure, sufferings of all kinds for not denying him. . . . Will he not then most assuredly at his coming in glory destroy all of them who have hated him, and them who have unjustly revolted from him, and give his own people rest, rendering to them all that they are expecting? (Justin, *Dial.* 121:2-3).

Abandoning the Christian faith provided yet another basis for judgment. In the above quotation, "them who have unjustly revolted from him" probably refers to apostates. The Epistle of James states that "he who doubts is like a wave of the sea that is driven and tossed by the wind. For that person must not suppose that a double-minded man, unstable in all his ways, will receive anything [good] from the Lord" (1:6-8). The *Shepherd of Hermas* denounces the "double-minded" who have listened to "false prophets" and consequently doubted the Christian faith (Mand. 11:4). *Didache* 16:5 says of the end: "Then created mankind will pass into the fiery trial and many will fall away [commit apostasy] and perish, but those who endure in their faith will be saved by the curse" [?].

How many will be saved? Only a few. The classic statement on this is Matthew 7:13-14:

> Enter by the narrow gate; for the gate is wide and the way is easy that leads to destruction, and those who enter by it are many. For the gate is narrow and the way is hard that leads to life, and those who find it are few.

Where will the unsaved be punished? In the synoptic gospels it usually is Gehenna, the Valley of Hinnom adjoining Jerusalem; the word is often translated as "hell," but it is *geenna* in the Greek text. In Matthew 13 it is called "the furnace of fire," an idea that may have been suggested by Daniel 3:6. In the parable of the Rich Man and Lazarus (Luke 16) the wicked are in fire in Hades. Opinion varied on the destination of souls at death. Righteous souls will go to Paradise (Luke 23:43), or to heaven (Luke 16:22); wicked souls will go to Hades (Luke 16:23; Rev. 20:13-14); all souls will go to Hades (Acts 2:27, 31).

The delay in the coming of the Judgment created problems. Why has the day of the Lord not come and put an end to the deeds of the wicked? The answer in the parable of the Weeds, or Tares, is that the situation is like wheat and weeds growing together in a field until harvest; similarly, the righteous and the wicked coexist until the Judgment (Matt. 13:24-30). In this and some other parables which say that the kingdom of God "is like" conditions in the parable, the parable fits the situation *before* the kingdom comes, not *after* its arrival. For example, there will not be any wicked ["weeds"] in the kingdom; thus weeds and wheat growing together is not like the kingdom of God! The Book of Revelation gives a direct answer to the question of the delay. The souls of martyrs cry out, "How long before you [the Lord] will judge and avenge our blood on those who dwell upon the earth?" After they were given a white robe, they were "told to rest a little longer, until the number of their fellow servants and their brethren should be complete, who were to be killed as they themselves had been" (6:10-11).

Although a source in John expects a future judgment day, the author of that gospel does not:

> For God did not send the Son into the world in order that he might judge the world, but in order that the world might be saved through him. He who believes on him is not judged; he who does not believe has been judged already because he has not believed on the name of the only-begotten Son of God (3:17-18).

Why does the author personally reject belief in the Judgment, even though the belief is included in one of his sources? Because he has been influenced by Gnosticism and Hellenistic mysticism.

18

THE NEW JUDAISM

Jewish Christians believed that they constituted the New Judaism, which supplanted the Judaism of the past. The roots of this idea go back to the Israelite prophets. They expected that some day the Lord would bring back to Palestine some of his people whom foreign nations, especially Assyria and Babylonia, had taken to their lands. In Micah Yahweh says, "I will gather the remnant of Israel" (2:12). The remnant will be the righteous Jews who worship him; Isaiah sums up that hope thus:

A remnant will return, the remnant of Jacob, to the mighty God. For though your people Israel be as the sand of the sea, only a remnant of them will return. Destruction is decreed, overflowing with righteousness (10:21-22).

The Essenes at Qumran emphasized the righteousness aspect and maintained that they were the righteous few, the true Judaism. Unlike other Jews, they had "held fast to the commandments of God," which consist of the Law and the correct interpretation of it.

In Romans 11:5 Paul claims that Christians are the ones who are the "remnant chosen by grace." That doctrine logically leads to the view that not all Jews are true Jews: "For not all who are descended from Israel belong to Israel, and not all are children of Abraham because they are his descendants" (Rom. 9:6-7). If Christians are the righteous remnant, then Christianity is the New Judaism which differs from the old. That belief is understood in the sayings against attaching the new to the old: One should not put a new patch on an old garment nor put new wine in old wineskins (Mark 2:21-22). Christians developed the New Judaism doctrine by reinterpreting basic features of Judaism.

NEW COVENANT

In the Old Testament Yahweh makes several covenants with his people: with Noah, Abraham, the Israelites at Mount Sinai, and with David. The Jews at Qumran believed that God had established a covenant with them, "revealing to them hidden things in which all Israel had gone astray" (CD 3:13-16). The covenant is a "new covenant" (CD 6:19). The scriptural basis of the new covenant idea is in Jeremiah:

> "Behold, the days are coming," says the Lord, "when I will make a new covenant with the house of Israel and the house of Judah, not like the covenant which I made with their fathers when I took them by the hand to bring them out of the land of Egypt, my covenant which they broke, though I was their husband," says the Lord. "But this is the covenant which I will make with the house of Israel after those days," says the Lord. "I will put my law within them, and I will write it upon their hearts; and I will be their God, and they shall be my people" (31:31-33).

The members of the sect at Qumran viewed themselves as God's "chosen," "the elect of all mankind," whom "God has chosen for an eternal covenant" (1QS 11:16; 4:22). They are "the chosen of grace" (1QS 8:6). Many early Christians adopted a similar attitude. Paul wrote that Christians too are "a remnant, chosen by grace" (Rom. 11:5). God "has made us [apostles] competent to be ministers of a new covenant, not in a written code but in the Spirit" (2 Cor. 3:6). In Hebrews 9:15 Christ "is the mediator of a new covenant."

Christians made special use of the tradition of the Lord's covenant with Moses. After Yahweh revealed to Moses at Mount Sinai the ordinances which Moses wrote down in "the book of the covenant," Moses read them to the people, who vowed that they would obey them all. Then Moses sealed this covenant between the Lord and the people by throwing on the altar and on the people the blood of the oxen he had sacrificed for burnt offerings and peace offerings. When he threw the blood on the people, he said, "Behold, the blood of the covenant which the Lord has made with you in accordance with all these words" (Exod. 24:8). According to *Barnabas* 4:8 the Israelites lost the covenant they received through Moses, but Christians have "the covenant of Jesus."

The Last Supper tradition in Mark and Matthew specifically identifies wine with Jesus' "blood of the covenant." In the form of the tradition in Luke and 1 Corinthians, the wine has become "the new covenant in my blood." A second method of adapting the Lord's Supper to the New Judaism theory was to connect it and Jesus' death with the Passover. This is done in the Last Supper accounts in the synoptic gospels, so that the Lord's Supper becomes the New Passover, as we saw.[1]

NEW LAW

The expectation that God in the messianic age will reveal new interpretations of the Law is an idea that existed in the Jewish environment.[2] Both the Pharisees and the Essenes set forth new interpretations of the Law that they regarded as correct understanding of the cherished Law and definitely not a replacement of it.

A Jewish writing, Book 3 of the *Sibylline Oracles* (2 c. B.C.), however, is much more radical. According to it, God in the starry heaven will establish throughout the whole earth a perfect universal law,[3] an idea derived from the Stoic ideal of the universal law of nature. This idea of replacing the old Torah is clearly a larger break with the past—in theory—than merely reinterpreting it.

Paul, as we have seen, broke away from the authority of Torah.[4] Paul mentions "the law of Christ" in Galatians 6:2, but he does not claim that it replaces the Law; faith and Spirit do that. *The Epistle of Barnabas*, however, goes all the way in claiming that a new law supplants the old Law: The Lord abolished the sacrifices of the Law "in order that the new law of our Lord Jesus Christ, which is free from the yoke of necessity, might have its offering not made by man" (2:6).

The story of Pentecost in Acts expresses symbolically the idea that the Spirit in the churches replaces the Law. The story portrays the Jerusalem church as receiving the Holy Spirit in a manner similar to the way that a contemporary Jewish legend portrays Moses as receiving the Law. Thus the Spirit, not the Law, is central in the New Judaism.

The Torah requires circumcision, and Paul in Galatians 5 rejects it completely. He does not substitute anything that he calls "circumcision." The author of Colossians, however, was interested in substituting a new theoretical circumcision for the old: In Christ "you were circumcised with a circumcision made without hands, by putting off the body of flesh in the circumcision of Christ" (2:11). Using Jeremiah 4:4 as a proof text, *Barnabas* 9 substitutes circumcision of the heart for physical circumcision.

Some Christians viewed Jesus as a new lawgiver, either as giving new interpretations of the Torah or as giving a new law to replace the Torah. This idea probably was included in the notion that he was the Prophet like Moses as in Acts 3:22-23. In the synoptic gospels Jesus reinterprets the Law, but does not discard it, at least not as a whole. Although in Matthew Jesus is portrayed as like Moses in some respects, he does not give a whole new law to replace the Torah. In fact, in 5:17-19 he stoutly upholds the Law. In the same chapter, however, Jesus gives new teachings that reject certain provisions of the Law.[5]

The attribution of the title "Rabbi" to Jesus evidently arose from the desire to represent him as a new interpreter of the Law. Mark's author likes the idea that Jesus was a rabbi, for in his gospel Jesus is addressed as "Rabbi" by Peter, a blind man, and Judas.[6] The authors of Matthew and Luke, however, do not like it. In Luke no one calls Jesus "Rabbi," and in Matthew only Judas, the traitor, does. The authors of those two gospels declined to copy the other instances in Mark. The author of Matthew adds 23:7-8 in which Jesus denounces rabbis and commands the disciples not to be called rabbis.

In the Gospel of Signs incorporated in John, Jesus is addressed as "Rabbi" eight times by his disciples or by persons friendly to him.[7] The Signs author clearly liked the idea, but the other writers in John never used it. They believed that Christianity is free not just from the Law, but from Judaism as a whole. The author of John used the Signs Gospel for its narrative framework, but he never assimilated its Jewish elements into his own thinking and writing. In short, Mark and the Gospel of Signs depict Jesus as a superior rabbi in the New Judaism, but the other gospels are too hostile to rabbis to accept the notion.

NEW TEMPLE

Another respect in which Christians viewed their religion as the New Judaism was their claim that it replaced the Temple and its high priest. This idea probably would have been conceived anyway, but the destruction of the Temple in A.D. 70 certainly encouraged it. In Mark 13:1-2 Jesus is portrayed as predicting that event.

Christian hostility to the Temple is quite evident in Acts. When Stephen is tried by the Sanhedrin, "false witnesses" charge, "This man never ceases to speak words against this holy place [the Temple, or else Jerusalem, which included the Temple] and the Law, for we have heard him say that this Jesus of Nazareth will destroy this place and will change the customs which Moses delivered to us" (6:13-14). This reference to the destruction of Jerusalem clearly displays knowledge of the event in A.D. 70, and does not reflect either Jesus' teaching or the actual charge against Stephen, for both men died before the Temple was destroyed. Hostility to the Temple is ascribed to Stephen in his "speech," where Isaiah 66:1-2 is quoted in support:

> Yet the Most High does not dwell in houses made with hands; as the prophet says, "Heaven is my throne, and earth my footstool. What house will you build for me," says the Lord, "or what is the place of my rest? Did not my hand make all these things?" (Acts 7:48-50).

The same passage in Isaiah is quoted in *Barnabas*, where we read that "wretched men [Jews] went astray and set their hope on a building, as being a house of God, instead of on God who made them" (16:1). (When several authors cite the same Old Testament passage, their source may be a proof text, or testimonium.)

At the moment that Jesus died, the veil, or curtain, in the Temple was torn in two, according to Mark 15:38. The author of Mark was more interested in the symbolic significance of such an incident than its miraculous nature. We need to know the Jewish background in order to understand this feature. A curtain covered the entrance to the Holy of Holies, the room where the Lord dwelled in the Temple. The curtain served to shield the presence of the Lord in the Holy of Holies from human eyes. Only the high priest could legally enter the room, and even he only once a year on Yom Kippur, the Day of Atonement. The tearing of the Temple curtain in Mark symbolizes the belief that the Temple no longer controls access to the Lord; Jesus' death has opened the way for Christians.

This idea is explicit in Hebrews:

> Therefore, brethren, since we have confidence to enter the sanctuary by the blood of Jesus, by the new and living way which he opened for us through the curtain, that is, through his flesh, . . . (10:19-20).

A further development is the idea that Christians constitute the temple of God, replacing the old Temple. Paul may or may not have had this idea in mind when he wrote: "Do you not know that you are God's temple and that God's spirit dwells in you?" (1 Cor. 3:16). In *Barnabas* the belief is explicit:

> But let us inquire whether there is a temple of God. There is, . . . When we received forgiveness of sins and set our hope on the name, we became new, created again from the beginning, and therefore God really lives in us, in the dwelling which we are. . . . This is the spiritual temple that is being built for the Lord (16:6, 8, 10).

Another form of the New Temple is the notion that it is Jesus himself. In Mark 14:57-58 false witnesses at Jesus' trial before the high priest charge that he has said, "I will destroy this Temple that is made with hands, and in three days I will build another, not made with hands." In Mark 15:29-30 people passing by the cross are alleged to have said, "You who would destroy the Temple and build it in three days, save yourself." In John 2:19 Jesus' response to the Jews' demand for a sign is, "Destroy this Temple, and in three days I will raise it up." The phrase "three days" in these statements clearly refers to Jesus' resurrection. The expression "made with hands" is intended as derogatory, for in Judaism the idols that gentiles worship are "the work of men's hands" (Ps. 135:15), in contrast to the eternal God, who was "not made by hands" (2 *Enoch* 33:4). "Something greater than the Temple is here" in Matthew 12:6 apparently refers to Jesus. The Risen Christ is the New Temple.

NEW HIGH PRIEST

To some early Christians Jesus was the new high priest who replaces the high priest of the Temple in Jerusalem.[8] In Hebrews Jesus has "become a high priest forever after the order of Melchizedek" (6:20); the author's source is Psalm 110:4. And who was Melchizedek? We read in Genesis 14 that he was the (Canaanite) king of Salem (Jerusalem) and priest of the Most

High God (i.e., of the various gods in the heavens, this god is supreme because he is higher than the others). Beginning with Simon, the Jewish Hasmonean kings combined the office of high priest with the office of king, an illegal practice. Therefore they found scriptural support for this policy by saying that they were like Melchizedek, who was both a priest and a king. They even called themselves "priests of the Most High God."[9] Psalm 110 was composed for Simon's coronation, as proved by the acrostic in Hebrew which reads "Simon." So why did the author of Hebrews use it? First, to support his theory that Jesus, the king-Messiah, could also be the high priest. Second, the Psalm was already being interpreted by Christians as a prophecy of Jesus (to support the ascension faith). Third, Melchizedek was "without father or mother or genealogy, and has neither beginning of days nor end of life" (Heb. 7:3), and thus resembles the Son of God. That claim is based on the fact that Genesis does not happen to mention Melchizedek's ancestors, birth, or death. Thus the author of Hebrews finds scriptural support for his belief that Jesus is not only a priestly Christ, but is also a supernatural, preexistent Christ, instead of a Christ who is a human descendant of David.

NEW SACRIFICE

Another facet of Christianity as the New Judaism was the view that Jesus' death was a sacrifice that has replaced the Temple sacrifices. This theory is that as the Jewish sacrifices in the past were for the sins of the people, now Jesus' death is a sacrifice that atones for the sins of the people. This theory, as we have seen, originated in the desire to explain Jesus' death, but it also fits into the New Judaism point of view. (In the original Christian view of sin, human repentance causes God to forgive sins; thus no sacrifice is necessary, neither the Temple's nor Jesus'.) Matthew quotes Hosea 6:6 as proof that the Lord rejects the Temple sacrifices: "I desire mercy, and not sacrifice" (12:7). There mercy replaces the sacrifices, but in Hebrews it is Jesus and his death. Unlike the other high priests, Jesus does not need to offer up sacrifices for sins daily, for "he did this once for all when he offered himself up" (7:27). Hebrews 9:11-14 develops this theory.

One application of the idea is to regard Jesus as the New Pascal Lamb who has replaced the lambs sacrificed annually at the Jewish Passover. This thought appears as early as Paul: "Christ, our pascal lamb, has been sacrificed" (1 Cor. 5:7). In John 1 Jesus is called "the Lamb of God" twice, and the crucifixion account demonstrates that the idea of sacrifice is the source of the title. In John 19, thanks to the redactor's insertions, the crucifixion begins on the day of Preparation when the lamb is killed and prepared for the Passover meal which begins after sundown. Thus Jesus' death occurs at the same time that the lamb dies (contrary to the synoptics). The idea of Jesus as the sacrificial lamb is developed further by the redactor of John by his insertion of 19:31-37 where he created the feature that the soldiers did not break Jesus' legs. He found in Exodus 12:46 the command, "you shall not break a bone of it," the pascal lamb; next he created the event as fulfillment of the Scriptures. A similar procedure occurs in various places in all the canonical gospels.

THE TWELVE

Do the twelve disciples in the synoptic gospels symbolize a New Twelve that supersedes the Old Twelve, the twelve tribes of Israel? Do they represent the Church as the New Judaism?

The twelve tribes and their twelve traditional leaders, the sons of Jacob, were much esteemed in Judaism. Numerous lists of the twelve sons are in the Old Testament, most apparently derived from Genesis 49, where Jacob gathers his twelve sons together to bless them. The *Testaments of the Twelve Patriarchs* uses a similar setting to present Jewish teaching. Although the number twelve was a very popular number in the ancient world—mainly because of the twelve signs of the zodiac—, it was especially used in connection with the twelve Jewish tribes to designate Israel. In the *Testament of Judah* 25:1-2 the twelve sons of Jacob will rule over Israel after the Messiah has come.

In the synoptic gospels the disciples in general often represent the Church, and in Jewish Christianity the twelve disciples in particular often symbolized it. In Luke 22:29-30 Jesus says to his disciples—not necessarily the Twelve—, "I appoint for you . . . that you may eat and drink at my table in my kingdom, and sit on thrones judging the twelve tribes of Israel." In the parallel in Matthew 19:28 to this Q pericope, however, Jesus calls himself the Son of Man and promises his disciples that they will "sit on twelve thrones, judging the twelve tribes of Israel." The general idea here is probably a Christian adaptation of the Jewish idea that at the judgment, righteous Jews will punish the wicked, an idea in *1 Enoch* 38:5-6. The description in Matthew of the thrones on which the disciples will sit as "twelve thrones" plainly indicates that the disciples are the Twelve; the New Twelve will judge the Old Twelve at the Judgment Day.

The concept of the twelve disciples as symbolizing the Church continued for some time in Jewish Christianity. We find it in the middle of the second century in the full title of *Didache*: *The Teaching of the Lord to the Heathen by the Twelve Apostles*. The teaching in the book is not that of Jesus, but of Jewish Christians; "the Twelve Apostles" represent Jewish Christianity.

The Epistle of James in the New Testament is addressed "to the twelve tribes of the Dispersion," who are Jewish Christians as the contents of the book reveal. In James, Christianity is directly the New Judaism; the literary device of twelve disciples is not employed.

GENTILES IN THE NEW JUDAISM

The rapid increase in the number of gentile converts raised the question, How do they fit in if Christianity is the New Judaism? Gentile converts are not Jews, either by birth or by observance of the Law (at least not in Pauline Christianity). Non-Christian Jews rejected the claim that Christianity is the New Judaism, and the presence of numerous uncircumcised gentiles in the movement supported their argument.

Paul, as the most vigorous leader of the mission to the gentiles, would logically have to deal with this problem, and this is indeed what we find in his letters. He stoutly argues that gentile Christians are truly Jews; they are "sons of Abraham," or "Abraham's seed." This is the major theme in Galatians 3 and Romans 4 and 9. Paul sets forth many dubious arguments; here are a few:

1. Gentiles become Jews, true sons of Abraham, by faith when they believe in Jesus Christ. How is that? Scripture proves it. In Genesis 15 Abraham complains to the Lord that he has no children. Therefore the Lord promised him that his heirs would be as numerous as the stars. Abraham believed the Lord,

who reckoned his faith as righteousness (Gal. 3:6). Abraham was not yet a Jew when this happened, for he was not circumcised until later (Gen. 17:24). Thus it was Abraham's faith in God's promise that made him righteous and made him and his descendants Jews. Therefore the inheritance of Judaism now comes not from observing the Law or from being born of the Jewish race, but from belief, which now consists of faith in Jesus Christ.

Paul also found other scriptural passages to use to support his thesis that belief in God's promises is what counts, thereby enabling gentiles to become true Jews through faith. God made promises to Abraham and Isaac that their wives would bear a son, and again Jewish sons were produced as a result of God's promises (Rom. 9).

2. Another scriptural argument of Paul's was that though Esau was born before Jacob (and as the elder brother Esau would be the heir under Hebrew law), Jacob was the one who got the birthright (Gen. 25). Thus the elder served the younger (Rom. 9:12), even as Jews according to the flesh (who were Jews before Christians were) are now subordinate to Christians, the new Jews.

3. Paul employs additional Old Testament passages. In Romans 9 he uses Hosea's "I will say to [those] not my people, 'You are my people'" (Hosea 2:23), and Isaiah's prediction (10:22) that only a remnant of the sons of Israel will be saved. The fact that the prophets were not writing about Christians did not stop Paul.

In 1 Peter gentile Christians are not merely included in the New Judaism—they are it. This epistle clearly was written for gentile—Christian readers, and they are described in the same terms that Jews described their own nation. They are "a holy priesthood, to offer spiritual sacrifices acceptable to God" (2:5). They are "a chosen race, a royal priesthood, a holy nation, God's own people" (2:9). The gentile author of *Barnabas* claims that Christians are the Lord's "new people" (7:5).

What was the source of the doctrine that Christianity is the New Judaism? The foundation of the idea was the Old Testament prophecy that the Lord would make a new covenant with a chosen few, a righteous remnant. Jewish Christians eagerly applied the prophecy to themselves. We saw that Paul believed that Christians were recipients of *the* New Covenant.

Thus this Christian doctrine existed within a few decades after Jesus' death. Further, Paul does not argue in its behalf, but merely mentions it in passing. That evidence is significant, for it indicates that the belief was already established in the churches and need not be defended.

Thanks to archaeology and the Dead Sea scrolls, we now know that the Essenes at Qumran had already applied the notion to their sect. They surely must be the Christians' source, for Christians adopted other Essene traits too. Both sects called themselves "The Way," which as a label for a religious group—not just a manner of living—is distinctive enough to suggest that the Essenes transmitted it to the Christians. Both groups claimed to have been "chosen by grace." Other features common to both include their attitude of superiority to the rest of Judaism and their energetic reinterpretation of Scripture to support their beliefs.

We are compelled to conclude that (1) the New Covenant doctrine appeared in Christianity as early as the Jerusalem church and (2) that church received it not from Jesus, but directly from Essene converts. That conclusion is supported by the fact that there is no evidence that Jesus taught communal sharing, but the Jerusalem church adopted that Essene practice. Thus a significant consequence of the discovery of the scrolls is the recognition that the Essenes were a major influence upon primitive Christianity.

Sometimes it is difficult to determine whether a Christian author thought that Christianity was the New Judaism, within the folds of Judaism, or a new religion outside of Judaism. When he speaks of "our father Abraham", he usually is still within; when he denounces Judaism completely, he is usually outside.[10]

19

THE GREAT CONTROVERSY - A

One of the greatest misunderstandings in history arose between Jews and Christians in the first century and continued unabated in the second. In fact, tension between them has continued to the present day, although now it is less heated and the causes are not necessarily the same.

Various events are reported that demonstrate the developing conflict between the two religious groups, beginning with tension between Jews and Jewish Christians. The apostles' preaching in Jerusalem soon caused Jewish authorities to arrest, imprison, and beat them (Acts 5). The Hellenist Jewish Christians in Jerusalem soon came into even sharper conflict with both Diaspora Jews in Jerusalem and the Sanhedrin, which resulted in the stoning to death of Stephen. Acts reports Paul's ejection from synagogues, and Paul himself complains of the abuse he suffered from Jews (see our chapter "Persecution"). Mark 9:14 states that scribes were arguing with the disciples; did this occur during Jesus' lifetime, or after his death? The Gospels of Matthew and John reflect further hostility to the apostles, and the authors of John and the Epistle of Barnabas have abandoned all hope of converting the Jews generally.

Jewish rejection of Christian preaching is manifest in words on Jesus' lips in the gospels. In the story of his sending out the Twelve, he says: "If any place will not receive you and they refuse to hear you, when you leave, shake off the dust that is on your feet for a testimony against them" (Mark 6:11). In Luke 10:16 Jesus says, "He who hears you hears me, and he who rejects you rejects me, and he who rejects me rejects him who sent me." All four canonical gospels portray Jesus as disputing with and denouncing Pharisees and other Jewish leaders. When discussing the issues in the controversy, however, early Christian writings other than the gospels know nothing of such words of Jesus.

The causes of the controversy were manifold, and

invariably involved religious beliefs and practices. Let us examine them.

THE TEMPLE

Jewish-Christian ill will toward the Jewish Temple authorities began when the latter bribed Judas, arrested Jesus, and brought him to trial before the Sanhedrin--actions that led to Jesus' death. According to Mark, armed men from "the chief priests, scribes, and elders" arrested Jesus. The high priest conducted his trial before the Sanhedrin. Thus the Temple officials, the Sadducees, and probably some Pharisees—some of the elders may have been Pharisees—became enemies in the sight of Jewish Christians.

Soon a new source of tension arose. While the apostles were preaching in the Temple, "the priests and the captain of the Temple and the Sadducees came upon them, annoyed because they were teaching the people and proclaiming in Jesus the resurrection from the dead" (Acts 4:1-2). The Sadducees did not believe that there would be a general resurrection, as both Josephus and Mark 12 testify. The Sadducees disagreed with other teachings of the apostles too, for they arrested the apostles and forbad them "to speak in the name of Jesus," which apparently consisted mainly of "teaching and preaching Jesus as the Christ" (Acts 5:40-42).

Christian hostility to the Temple authorities is manifest in the unhistorical story of Jesus casting out the traders and money-changers in the Temple (Mark 11). Mark presents this incident as a reason for the chief priests' and scribes' desire to kill Jesus, but we have observed that the incident is not mentioned in the charges brought against him at his trial. Actually the story is a Jewish-Christian effort to discredit the manner in which the Sadducees were operating the Temple. The criticism is not of the Temple religion; in fact, the story implies a high regard for it—the Temple is "a house of prayer." In Mark 11:27-29 par Jesus' authority to "do these things" is questioned by the chief priests, scribes, and elders. This is not a reference to teaching, but to this story of cleansing the Temple of commerce. Twice in Mark[1] Jesus is represented as teaching in the Temple, which certainly does not indicate hostility to the Temple per se. Jesus' disciples were loyal to the Temple and its religion, for after his death they attended the Temple daily (Acts

2:46) and preached and taught there (Acts 5:42).

After the Romans destroyed the Temple, however, opposition to it and its religion became a popular Christian theme. This first appears in Mark, where the resurrected Jesus replaces the Temple "made with hands."[2] We have just noted that Christian replacement of the Jewish Temple and its priesthood and sacrifices logically accompanied the view that Christianity is the New Judaism. The opposition of the Temple authorities, however, was the beginning of the growing hostility between Christians and Jews. Christians were furious about the role of the priests and the Sanhedrin in causing the death of Jesus, who, they were convinced, was the Messiah, the Christ. How could their fellow Jews be so evil as to aid the Romans in killing God's "Anointed One"? Christians were embittered also by Jewish leaders' subsequent persecution of the apostles in Jerusalem. On the other hand, the Sadducees regarded Jesus and his disciples as revolutionaries who were about to bring war and destruction upon the Jewish people. They also disagreed with much of the apostles' preaching. And after the destruction of the Temple, many Jews must have cherished for many years the memory of the magnificent building and its religious cults, both of which were lost by the war and never regained. Jews must have resented Christian disparagement of the Temple.

JEWISH DISBELIEF

The vast majority of Jews were never convinced that Jesus was the Christ. In the canonical gospels that situation is carried back into the life of Jesus. It is stated explicitly in John: Jesus says to Nicodemus, "a ruler of the Jews" and "a teacher of Israel," "You do not receive our testimony" (3:11). "Our" indicates that the saying originated in the preaching of the apostles, not in that of Jesus. To the Jews Jesus says: "You do not believe" the words of the one whom the Father has sent (5:38); "you do not want to come to me in order that you may have life" (5:40); "I said to you that you have even seen me and you do not believe" (6:36): "there are some of you who do not believe" (6:64). The situation is alluded to in the Prologue: "It [the Word, Jesus] came to its own, and its own did not receive it" (literal translation of 1:11; RSV reads: "He came to his own home, and his own people received him not"). In Luke the historical rejection of Jesus at Nazareth is a prototype of the widespread Jewish rejection of him after his crucifixion (4:24-30).

Related to disbelief in Jesus' messiahship was the Jewish disbelief in his virgin birth and resurrection. (In the first century many Christians, too, did not belief in his virgin birth, but all except the Gnostics believed in his resurrection.) To counteract this Jewish disbelief, Bishop Ignatius urged Christians to "be convinced of the birth, passion, and resurrection" of Jesus Christ.[3]

The Jewish disbelief in Jesus created a problem for the early Christians: How could Jesus be the Jewish Messiah, the Christ, when most Jews did not believe that he was? Christians strove to find explanations for this disappointing reality.

One Christian explanation was that it occurred because Jews did not understand the Old Testament prophecies about Jesus. "Those who live in Jerusalem and their rulers . . . did not understand the utterances of the prophets which are read every Sabbath" (Acts 13:27). A second explanation was that Jewish disbelief itself fulfilled prophecy, and Christians searched the Scriptures for prooftexts. One verse discovered was Psalm 118:22, "The stone which the builders rejected has become the chief cornerstone." Therefore the verse is applied to Jesus in Acts 4:11 and 1 Peter 2:7, where Jesus is the stone and Jews are the builders. The psalmist, however, was writing about himself, not Jesus. In Mark 12:10-11 Jesus applies it, in a parable, to the "beloved son," who clearly symbolizes himself. Did Jesus misinterpret Scripture, or did the early church do so and ascribe it to him? Neither Acts nor 1 Peter mention that Jesus cited the verse. Paul tackles the problem in Romans 9-11 and arrives at several solutions. He too thinks that Jewish disbelief fulfills prophecy, and in 9:33 he cites a conflation of Isaiah 28:16 and 8:14-15.

Another explanation, closely related to the argument from prophecy, was that the disbelief is according to God's will and divine plan. Paul combines the two explanations in the passage in Romans. Not only has God in the past given predictions of the rejection; he is also active in the first century in directing it, according to some writers. In Q the Father "has hidden these things from the wise and understanding . . . for such was your gracious will" (Luke 10:21 par). In John Jews do not believe, but all whom the Father gives to Jesus will come to Jesus (6:36-37). A related idea is in Ephesians, where the conversion of all Christians is determined by God: "For by grace you have been saved through faith; and this is not your own doing; it is the gift of God" (2:8).

A third explanation offered was the defamatory charge that the Israelites have been "a disobedient and contrary people," and therefore God punished them by giving them a spirit of stupor so that their "eyes should not see and ears should not hear" (Rom. 10:21; 11:8), quoting Isaiah 29:10. A similar theme occurs in Isaiah 6:9-10, which Christians quoted for the same purpose.[4] Only a righteous remnant will survive.

The prophets' denunciation of the majority of their fellow-Jews was grist for the mill of Jewish-Christian apologists, who applied the idea to the majority of Jews in their own day who disbelieved the Christian gospel. Convenient, too, was the Jewish notion of a righteous remnant that would be saved. Paul quotes Isaiah 10:22 to represent the Christians as the remnant that will be saved, while the Lord will execute his judgment upon the rest (Rom. 9:27-28). The belief that many Jews will not be saved caused Paul anguish (Rom. 9:1-5). The point of the parable of the Great Banquet (Luke 14), or Marriage Feast (Matt. 22), in Q is that most Jews refuse to accept God's invitation to accept the Christian gospel. The *Epistle of Barnabas* asserts that "the new law of our Lord Jesus Christ" replaces the Jewish Law, but such knowledge was "obscure to them [Jews] because they have not listened to the voice of the Lord" (2:6; 8:7). In the Christian retelling of Jewish history in Acts 7, Jews are portrayed as rejecting Moses (7:35, 39) and persecuting prophets throughout their history (7:51-53). Thus disregard for divinely appointed leaders is a Jewish characteristic.

Paul adds the explanation that the cause of Jewish blindness is that Jews have been zealous for the Law and the good works commanded by the Law; instead, Jews should have pursued righteousness through faith (Rom. 9:30-32). He comments: "I bear them witness that they have a zeal for God, but it is not accurate knowledge. For, being ignorant of the righteousness that comes from God, and seeking to establish their own, they did not submit to God's righteousness" (10:2-3).

A different explanation of Jewish disbelief was derived from the Jewish notion that God kept some of his knowledge secret—it is a "mystery"—, but he reveals some of it to whom he chooses, whether to prophets and apocalyptists (e.g., "the word of the Lord came to Jonah," Jonah 1:1) or to Israelites generally ("From this time forth I make you hear new things, hidden things which you have not known," Isa. 48:6). Concerning God's knowledge, an angel tells Daniel that "the words are shut up and sealed until the time of the end" (Dan. 12:9). The Essenes believed that they should walk humbly "according to the truth of the mysteries of knowledge" that God has revealed to them (1QS 4:6). Many Jews and Christians valued apocalypses because they believed them to be revelations of divine secrets.

The Jewish belief in mystery, divine secret knowledge, was very useful for Christians. When Jews objected that the Christian message does not agree with messianic expectations, a Christian answer, in effect, was that you Jews do not know the mysteries of God that have been revealed to us. Those mysteries include the mystery of the kingdom of God, the mystery of the Christ or Son of Man, and the mystery of the gospel in general.

Paul interpreted the Christian gospel as "a secret and hidden wisdom of God, which God decreed before the ages for our glorification" (1 Cor. 2:7). Thus Paul applied to Christianity an old Jewish idea which the Essenes also applied to their own religion. The idea is also in Colossians 1:25-26: "I became a minister . . . to make the word of God fully known, the mystery hidden for ages and generations, but now made manifest to his saints" [Christians]. The fullest biblical statement of this Christian belief is in Ephesians 1:9-11, where God's "plan for the fullness of time" is explicitly connected to "the mystery of his will."

In the Gospel of Mark Jesus, too, deliberately hides secret knowledge from Jews. The author uses the idea to explain why most Jews did not regard Jesus as the Messiah, both before and after his crucifixion, and why they did not accept the apostles' preaching in general. According to Mark, the reason is that Jesus kept some of his miracles and teaching hidden from them. This theory is called by modern scholars the Theory of the Messianic Secret. Bruno Bauer, a theologian at Bonn, detected it around 1850. In Mark Jesus commands the demons "not to speak, because [as supernatural beings] they knew him"(1:34). "Whenever the unclean spirits saw him, they fell down before him and cried out, 'You are the Son of God.' And he strictly ordered them not to make him known" (3:11-12). After he healed the daughter of the ruler of the synagogue, Jesus strictly charged that "no one should know this" (5:43). Mark treats Jesus' teaching in a similar fashion. Jesus teaches in parables so that outsiders (non-Christian Jews) will not understand, but he explains his parables privately to his disciples, and thus "to you has been given the secret [Greek: mystery] of the kingdom of God" (4:11). Mark is not consistent in this respect, for sometimes Jesus' miracles and teachings are very plain and public. This inconsistency indicates that the author of Mark has combined several sources, or has added his own composition to source material without harmonizing the material with his own writing, or someone has revised the gospel later. In ancient literature inconsistency usually is a sign of composite writing.

In Mark the teaching that is specifically esoteric, given only to disciples, is not about himself, but consists of miscellaneous teaching.[5] Matthew and Luke reproduce some of Mark's esoteric features and add a few more.[6] John 14:22 reflects the explanation that Jesus manifested himself to his disciples, but not to the world.

The Gospel of John often describes Jesus' listeners as misunderstanding his words. Perhaps the motive behind the use of this literary device is to suggest that misunderstanding of Jesus' teaching prevented people from recognizing him as the Christ. For example, Jews misunderstand his statement, "Where I am going, you cannot come" (8:22). The misunderstanding in John often hinges on the double meaning of words. Thus Nicodemus misunderstands "born again"(3:4) as a physical instead of spiritual rebirth; the Samaritan woman misunderstands "living water" as flowing water instead of a metaphysical metaphor (4:11); the disciples misunderstand Lazarus' "sleep" as literal sleep instead of as death (11:12).

A parable could be used to explain the situation. The parable of the Great Supper (Luke 14), or Marriage Feast (Matt. 22), is a story about a man who invited many to a feast, but they refused to come. Therefore he told his servants to bring in others from the streets and highways. The earlier version of this story is the one in Luke, where the point is that the poor and handicapped are the ones who deserve the feast and they are the ones who come. At the end, however, Luke interprets it figuratively as God's inviting Jews, but few respond. Therefore "none of those men who were invited shall taste my banquet." In Matthew the application of the parable to the tension between Jews and Christians is clearer: A king (God) sent his servants (the apostles) "to call those who were invited" (Jews), but they would not come, and some of them mistreated and killed his servants. "The king was angry, and he sent his troops [the Romans] to destroy those murderers [Jews who persecuted Christians] and he burned their city" [Jerusalem in A.D. 70]. After expanding the parable, Matthew concludes: "For many are called, but few are chosen."

THE SCRIPTURES

Reinterpretation

Both Jewish and gentile Christians quoted, misquoted, and misinterpreted the Old Testament to support their beliefs and explain Jesus' death. Jews indulged in the same practice to support Jewish general beliefs or those of their sect. Interpreters were able to do this sincerely because of their ignorance of the original setting and meaning of scriptural passages and because of the prevalence of unsound methods of biblical interpretation.

Christian interpretation of the Old Testament may have begun with the Hebrew-speaking members of the Jerusalem church. We know that Greek-speaking Christians, using the Septuagint, reinterpreted both the Law and the Prophets, and the scribes of the Sadducees and the scribes of the Pharisees strongly disagreed with their interpretations. At first the Christians were Jewish Christians, but later gentile Christians got into the act—for example, Justin Martyr. Everyone was quite capable of quoting Scripture for his purpose, but the wildest interpretations came from those of the gentiles who applied allegorical interpretation—for example, the author of *Barnabas* and later Origen and Clement of Alexandria. The Jew Philo preceded them with his wild allegorical interpretations of the Septuagint.

Jews, even those within the same religious party or sect, often disagreed among themselves in biblical interpretation. This was especially characteristic of the Pharisees and rabbis; the Mishnah and Talmud are full of such variant opinions. More serious were the conflicting interpretations which were partly responsible for the founding of the parties of the Pharisees and Essenes.

Jewish Christians had some heated arguments with the

Pharisees and their scribes over Scripture. Pharisees charged that Christians were wrong in claiming that Scripture predicts the coming of Jesus and that its descriptions of the coming of the kingdom of God fit the current situation.

Some interpretations of the Written Law pertained to personal conduct and ethics. In Matthew 5:21-47 in the Sermon on the Mount we find six examples of that type; they may reflect some arguments between Christians and Pharisees. Here statements in the Law concerning murder, adultery, swearing oaths, and loving one's neighbor are accepted and expanded.[7] Not only should one not kill, as the Decalogue commands, but one should not even become angry with one's brother (a member of one's own religious group, as in the Dead Sea scrolls). Not only should one not commit adultery, but a man should not even look at a woman lustfully. Not only should one not swear an oath falsely, but he should not swear an oath at all. A person should not only love his neighbor; he should even love his enemies.

In that Matthean passage two points of the Law are rejected[8] and a different rule is substituted. First, the Law permits a man to divorce his wife, but Matthew denounces that except in cases of the wife's unchastity.[9] Mark 10 opposes all divorce. Matthew's position is the same as that of the School of Rabbi Shammai, according to the Mishnah: "The School of Shammai say: 'A man may not divorce his wife unless he has found unchastity in her'" (*Gittin* 9:10). Both the School of Hillel and Rabbi Akiba were more lenient in permitting divorce.

Secondly, Matthew rejects the Law's *lex talionis*, direct retaliation with "an eye for an eye and a tooth for a tooth," and substitutes for it the principle of turning the other cheek. Also in this passage in Matthew 5, for "hate your enemy" Matthew substitutes "love your enemies and pray for those who persecute you." Actually, the Law does not command one to hate one's personal enemy, although expressions of hatred of national enemies are certainly there. In fact, the passage in the Law that says "love your neighbor" also states, "you shall not hate your brother in your heart" (Lev. 19:17-18). "Neighbor" and "brother" are synonymous and mean Israelite.

Matthew introduces those six quotations from the Law with "you have heard it said" ("it is said" in 5:31), and follows up by having Jesus say, "But I say to you."[10] Thus the author represents Jesus as opposed to certain rules in the Law—though not to the Law as a whole. Jesus' approach is confrontational;

he is superior (to the Pharisees?) as an interpreter of the Law, and in respect to certain of its provisions, even superior as a lawgiver.

Changes in the Law

Professor Davies called attention to the fact that a minority view in Judaism was that the Law would be changed or enlarged when the Age to Come, or kingdom of God, arrives.[11] Perhaps that was the view held by Stephen. At least Acts 6 states that Diaspora Jews charged that he spoke "blasphemous words against Moses [i.e., the Law] and God" and "against this holy place and the Law," and that he preached that "Jesus of Nazareth will destroy this place [Jerusalem] and will change the customs which Moses delivered to us." To the majority of Jews, who believed that the Law was eternal and unchangeable, such preaching would be a serious matter. Changes or additions to the Law may be implied by the idea that Jesus was a Prophet like Moses (Acts 3:22-23), for Jews and Christians regarded Moses as a lawgiver.

Non-Observance of the Written Law

When King Josiah in 621 B.C. received the "Book of the Law" that the high priest had found in the Temple, he made a covenant with the Lord, which made obedience of the Law mandatory for himself and the people. The content of the Law was greatly enlarged later until it consisted of today's Pentateuch, and the expanded Torah too was exalted as the explicit expression of the Lord's will to which Jews should conform. The Maccabean Revolt in the second century B.C. renewed devotion to the Law, as did the Pharisaic Council of Jamnia in the first century A.D.

The importance of observance of the Law is implicit in the Pharisees' detailed interpretations of it, for the motive behind their careful study was to obey completely and lovingly God's commandments. The Jewish literature known in the first Christian century abounds in statements praising the Law and emphasizing the necessity of observing and meditating on it. Sirach precedes the Mishnah in urging meditation: "Reflect on the statutes of the Lord, and meditate at all times on his commandments" (6:37); "let all your discussion be about the Law of the Most High" (9:15).

In *Pseudo-Philo* the Law is "an eternal light" for Jews

(9:8), and by it God "will judge the whole world" (11:2). "For as many as did not acknowledge me [the Most High], . . . and as many as scorned my Law while they still had freedom, and did not understand but despised it while an opportunity of repentance was still open to them, these must in torment acknowledge it after death" (*4 Ezra* 9:10-12). "To you and to your fathers the Lord gave the Law above all nations. And because your brothers have transgressed the commandments of the Most High, he brought vengeance upon you and upon them and did not spare the ancestors" (*2 Baruch* 77:3-4). "You will bring down a curse upon our nation, because you want to destroy the light of the Law which was granted to you for the enlightenment of every man" (*T. Levi* 14:4).

In contrast to the prevailing Jewish practice, two views arose in Christianity that rejected the observance of the Law: 1. The Law was valid only until Christianity began. 2. The Law never was valid. To most Jews both views were rank heresy.

Paul is famous for his zealous proclamation in Galatians of the first view: "The Law was our custodian until Christ came, . . . but now that faith has come, we are no longer under a custodian." Thus Christian faith has replaced the Law as the essential guide in religion. A similar view is in Luke 16:16, which states: "The Law and the Prophets were until John; since then the gospel of the kingdom of God is preached." The parallel in Matthew modifies that statement, but retains the main idea: "For all the Prophets and the Law prophesied until John" (11:13).

Later many—mainly gentile—Christians developed the idea further and affirmed that the Law never was valid. To them, it was the Jews' Law, not Christian Law. This is plainly the view of the author of the Gospel of John, who depicts Jesus as calling the Law "your Law" when he addresses Jews (8:17; 10:34). The author inserted into the Christian Gnostic hymn in his Prologue this sentence to represent Jesus as superior to the Law: "For the Law was given through Moses; grace and truth came through Jesus Christ" (1:17). The central theme of the Epistle to the Hebrews is that Jesus and Christianity are superior to, and therefore replace, the main elements of Judaism, including Moses and the Law (ch. 3). "The Law made nothing perfect; on the other hand, a better hope is introduced, through which we draw near to God" (Heb. 7:19). The author of *Barnabas*, too, is hostile to the Law: God has abolished animal sacrifices, new moons, and Sabbaths "in order that the new Law of our Lord Jesus Christ. . . might have its offering not made by man" (2:5-6).

In contrast to rejection of the Law, many Jewish Christians remained loyal to it. Although in 5:21-41 he used a source which rejects certain tenets of the Law, the author of Matthew is personally opposed to abolishing or even relaxing any of its commandments; that is the theme of his own composition in 5:17-19. He ascribed both passages to Jesus, but it was he, not Jesus, who was inconsistent. The author of James clearly upholds the whole Law: "For whoever keeps the whole Law but fails in one point has become guilty of all of it" (2:10). In the second century some Jewish Christians, including the Nazaraean sect, remained faithful to the Law.

1. *Circumcision.* With the possible exception of Stephen and the Hellenists, the controversy over the Law probably began with Christian non-observance of certain of its features. Circumcision was the first to be rejected. Perhaps Paul concluded that the Law was no longer needed because the Messiah Jesus has come, and then went on to deduce that therefore gentile converts need not be circumcised. It seems more probable that he thought inductively instead of deductively here. Circumcision is a painful ordeal, which hindered the conversion of gentile males to Judaism and Christianity. As a result of his missionary work, Paul may have decided that the circumcision requirement of the Law was undesirable, so he discarded it, and then proceeded to justify his policy by rationalizing that the whole Law was no longer needed.

Paul's refusal to circumcise gentile converts aroused the wrath of non-Christian Jews and even of conservative Jewish Christians—"the circumcision party"—in the Jerusalem church (Gal. 2). This opposition was to be expected, for Jews regarded circumcision as one of the most basic requirements of the Law; it is a covenant God made with Abraham. "This is my covenant, which you shall keep, between me and you and your descendants after you: Every male among you shall be circumcised" (Gen. 17:10). Therefore uncircumcision was a *very serious* matter: "Any uncircumcised male who is not circumcised in the flesh of his foreskin shall be cut off from his people; he has broken my covenant" (Gen. 17:14). The covenant idea in the Old Testament is derived from the Near Eastern background, in which a covenant is an agreement between two groups or two individuals that should never be broken. Jewish belief in the necessity of circumcision continued through the centuries. *Jubilees* 15:34 says this of the sons of Israel who do not circumcise their sons: "They have made themselves like the gentiles to be removed and to be uprooted from the land [of Israel]. And there is therefore for them no forgiveness or pardon. . ." Needless to say, all male converts to Judaism also had to be circumcised.

Circumcision must have been required generally in the Jewish-Christian communities, but not in Paul's gentile churches. He aggressively opposed the imposition of the commandment upon his converts, as we know from Galatians and Acts. Later the gentile author of *Barnabas* reinterpreted circumcision as a spiritual rather than a physical condition. As support he quoted Deuteronomy 10:16, "Circumcise the foreskin of your heart," and Jeremiah 4:4, "Circumcise your hearts."

2. *The Sabbath.* Before any of the gospels were written, Christians generally—except those in the Jerusalem church—broke another vital feature of the Law, namely, the fourth of the Ten Commandments: "Remember the Sabbath day, to keep it holy. . . . In it you shall not do any work" (Exod. 20:8-10). Like circumcision, Sabbath observance is required by a covenant: "Therefore the people of Israel shall keep the Sabbath, observing the Sabbath throughout their generations, as a perpetual covenant" (Exod. 31:16). Failure to observe the Sabbath was just as reprehensible as uncircumcision: "Everyone who profanes it shall be put to death; whoever does any work on it, that soul shall be cut off from among his people" (Exod. 31:14).

The origin of the Sabbath is cloaked in mystery. It probably began as a day of resting from work, for that is its fundamental characteristic in the early traditions (e.g., Exod. 34:21), and the name probably is derived from the Hebrew verb *shabat*, which means "to cease," and thus could designate a time of ceasing from work. Therefore the essential way to keep the Sabbath holy was to do no work on it.[12] The original theological foundation for the practice was that Yahweh had commanded it and it was a covenant between him and Israel (Exod. 31:16), but soon after the Exile the priests added the notion that he had set the example at the Creation. That idea does not appear in the earlier sources. After the Sabbath was instituted, its observance acquired additional significance as obvious evidence of whether or not a person was still a faithful Jew.

A We-section in Acts testifies that on the Sabbath Paul and his followers went to a place of prayer at the riverside in Philippi (Acts 16:13). Paul in his letters never mentions the Sabbath; this, too, implies that he observed the Sabbath, for if he did, he had no need of defending his position on it. His assertion that the Law is no longer binding, however, must have encouraged his churches to break away from Sabbath observance. The author of Colossians 2:16 warns against those who pass judgment on Christians for non-observance — apparently — of the Sabbath; this indicates that the author did not celebrate the day.

In Mark 2 the Pharisees complain to Jesus that his disciples are breaking the Sabbath by plucking ears of grain as they are going through the fields. The rationale behind the charge is that the disciples are breaking the Law by doing work on the Sabbath. Jesus defends them by saying that David, too, did what was (technically) unlawful when he was hungry and ate the bread of the Presence in the Temple (see 1 Sam. 21).

In Mark 3 Jesus heals a man with a withered hand, and this work on the Sabbath causes the Pharisees to counsel with the Herodians how they might destroy Jesus. Again, the issue is work on the Sabbath, and the Pharisees regard it as a serious offence. Jesus asks if it is lawful on the Sabbath to do good and to save a life. Actually the Oral Law of the Pharisees, which is incorporated in the Mishnah and the Talmud, permits work on the Sabbath to save life. In the Mishnah work is allowed then even if there is doubt that a life really is in danger: "If a man has a pain in his throat, they may drop medicine into his mouth on the Sabbath, since there is doubt whether life is in danger, and whenever there is doubt whether life is in danger, this overrides the Sabbath" (*Yoma* 8:6). The Oral Law, however, does not permit the performance on the Sabbath of less crucial good works; healing a withered hand, for example, would be postponed until the next day.

Luke 13 and 14 add two more stories of Jesus' healing on the Sabbath. Here, too, healing is regarded as work. In both cases healing is seen as an act of mercy; that is the principle in the two illustrations cited: leading an ass or an ox to water to drink on the Sabbath, and pulling out on the Sabbath an ass or an ox that has fallen into a well (it is a sheep in Matthew's insertion [12:11] into Mark's story). The Talmud permits work on the Sabbath to save an animal's life or to save it from pain (*Shabbat* 128b).

In John 5 Jesus heals a man who has been ill for 38 years. "The Jews" criticize the man for doing the work of picking up his bed and walking on the Sabbath after the cure, and then they turn on Jesus for healing on the Sabbath. In fact, states 5:16, "this was why the Jews persecuted Jesus, because he did this on the Sabbath." The defense of this type of healing is not given until 7:22-23, where the reasoning is that the Law permits the work of circumcising on the Sabbath (in order that the commandment to circumcise on the eighth day may not be broken), so why "are you angry with me because I made a whole man well on the Sabbath?" In John 9 Jesus is said to heal a blind man on the Sabbath, and the Pharisees say that Jesus is not from God because he does not keep the Sabbath. The setting of this healing is outdoors as Jesus was passing by. The healings in John are always outdoors, never in a synagogue.

The controversial healings in the canonical gospels generally occur on the Sabbath. Why? Because observance of the Sabbath, not healing per se, is the real issue. The point is that Jesus and the apostles have the right to break the Sabbath. This idea is explicit in the pericope about the disciples' plucking grain on the Sabbath. The theme of the story itself is that the need to satisfy hunger is more important than strict observance of the Sabbath. The statement added at the end gives a new twist to the story. The disciples have the right to break the Law because their master, or lord, the Son of Man, is lord of the Sabbath (Mark 2:28 par). In effect, the Son of Man is a higher authority than Moses. The Son of Man saying indicates that the pericope originated in Jewish-Christian churches and that "the disciples" represent the apostles in the churches.

By the beginning of the second century the Sabbath had become controversial for another reason: Gentile Christians discarded it, substituting Sunday as the holy day of the week. Ignatius attests to the change: Christians are "no longer keeping the Sabbath but observing the Lord's Day," that is, Sunday (*Mag.* 9:1). Gentile Christians preferred Sunday for two reasons. First, it was the day that they were already celebrating. This would be particularly true of converts from the cults of sun gods, to whom Sunday was "the Lord's Day." The second reason was the growing controversy with Jews, and the consequent desire of gentile Christians to distance themselves from Jewish practices. A tradition arose among Christians that they observed Sunday because that was the day of Jesus' resurrection, but that was a later idea to provide a Christian rationale for observing Sunday.

In *Barnabas* 15 misinterpretation of Scripture is employed to eliminate the Sabbath in favor of Sunday. The author reinterprets the Creation story to mean that, since the Lord ended his work in six days, and a day in the Lord's sight is as a thousand years (based on Psalm 90:4), therefore in six thousand years everything will be completed. "'And he rested on the seventh day.' This means that when his Son comes, he will destroy the time of the lawless one . . . and then he will rest on the seventh day"(15:5). Thus *Barnabas* eliminates the Sabbath as the seventh day of the week created by the Lord. Next he uses Isaiah 1:13-14 as the basis for "your new moons and Sabbaths I cannot endure," and concludes: "You see what he [the Lord] means: It is not the present Sabbaths that are acceptable to me, but the one that I have made, on which, having brought everything to rest, I will make the beginning of an eighth day, that is, the beginning of another world. Wherefore we also celebrate the eighth day, on which Jesus rose from the dead." The logic—if any—in all that is a little difficult to follow!

As far as we know, Jesus had no reason to adopt a policy of breaking the Sabbath. On the other hand, the early Christians, both Jewish and gentile, had a strong incentive: they were breaking away from Judaism and its Law.

Barnabas attacks other features of the Jewish Law. In chapter 2 the author quotes from and agrees with Isaiah 1 and Psalm 51 in substituting righteous conduct and a contrite heart for the sacrifices. He rejects fasting by quoting from Isaiah 58, in which the Lord says that the fast that he chooses is to loose the bonds of wickedness, to feed the hungry, and to clothe the naked (3). *Barnabas* discards the Jewish food laws by quoting the commandment against eating swine (Lev. 11:7) and then reinterpreting it allegorically: Moses means "you shall not associate with men who are like swine" (10). The author warns against those Christians who want to remain within Judaism;

they sin by saying that the (Jewish) covenant is "both theirs and ours." Jews lost the covenant, he says, when Moses broke the tablets at Mount Sinai (Exod. 32:19) and thus broke their covenant (4).

The author of Hebrews also rejects major elements in the Jewish Law, but on a different philosophical basis. He sees Christianity as the New Judaism, which has new forms of sacrifice, Temple, covenant, and so on; Christianity is still Judaism, but a superior revelation of it. The author of *Barnabas*, however, sees Christianity as a new religion, distinct from Judaism. Nevertheless even he—like most Christians through the centuries—has not made a complete break, for he retains the Jewish Bible and the Jewish God. Justin insisted that Christians worship the Jewish God: "We have fled for refuge to him who is the God of Jacob and the God of Israel" (*Dial.* 110:2). But Justin's contemporary Marcion rejected the Jewish Scriptures and the Jewish God (see chapter "Gnosticism" below).

20

THE GREAT CONTROVERSY - B

THE ORAL LAW

As the controversy over the Written Law grew and the
Pharisees became more involved in it, the early Christians
rejected the Oral Law of the Pharisees, which consisted largely
of interpretations of the Written Law. The author of Matthew,
however, did not go that far. Although he was angry with the
Pharisees and denounced them as "hypocrites," he urged his
readers to obey their Oral Law: "practice and observe whatever
they tell you, but not what they do, for they preach, but do not
practice" (Matt. 23:3). These words are here ascribed to Jesus,
but the literary characteristics of the passage are those of
Matthew. Few other early Christian writers, however, had much
respect for the Oral Law. Christian opposition to specific
Pharisaic teachings and practices appears in the synoptic
gospels.

Fasting

Abstention from food and drink for religious reasons
was widely practiced in the ancient world. Private fasts and
official public fasts were the two basic categories. In Judaism
the public fast Yom Kippur, or Day of Atonement, is commanded in the Torah, in Leviticus 16 and 23. The command,
"You shall afflict yourselves" on the Day of Atonement (23:27),
was interpreted as a command to fast then. The command is
vital: "Whoever is not afflicted on this same day shall be cut off
from his people" (23:29). After the Exile Jews instituted other
public fasts. Fasts in the ancient world were often followed by
feasts; for example, the Day of Atonement was soon followed
by the Feast of Booths, or Tabernacles (Lev. 23; cf. Lent
followed by Easter in Christianity). Small wonder that such
feasts were thoroughly enjoyed—the participants were starved!

Private fasting in Judaism was practiced for various

purposes. It was used to purify the individual in preparation for close association with a deity (e.g., Moses on Mount Sinai, Exod. 34:28). [1] Fasting could be a way of expressing grief for the dead or for a tragic event. It could be an expression of repentance, either for personal sins or for the sins of the nation as in Joel 2:12. Some individuals fasted regularly primarily to enhance their personal piety. Private fasting is well attested in the Old Testament, the Apocrypha, the Jewish Pseudepigrapha, and the Mishnah. The Pharisees fasted regularly and produced many rules concerning the practice, rules which are incorporated in the Oral Law in the Mishnah. The book *Taanit* in the Mishnah deals with the proper days for fasting.

As faithful Jews, both Jesus and the Jerusalem Christians probably fasted on occasion. The Hellenist Jewish Christians evidently did too, at least in the first few decades, for the church at Antioch commissioned Paul and Barnabas for their missionary journey by "fasting and praying" and the laying on of hands (Acts 13:3). The preceding verse indicates that the Antioch Christians normally combined fasting with worship. On their journey Barnabas and Paul, "with prayer and fasting," appointed elders in every church they founded (Acts 14:23).

As the controversy between Jews and Christians developed, the Christian acceptance of Jewish types of fasting turned to rejection. This was especially the case in the gentile churches.

According to Mark 2:18 par the disciples of the Pharisees and John the Baptist practiced fasting, but Jesus' disciples did not and were criticized for not doing so. The fact that Jesus himself is not accused implies that he fasted and that only the disciples are unorthodox in this matter. But why would the disciples not fast if their Master fasted? The "disciples" here, as often elsewhere, represent the apostles in the early churches when they were separating from the Law and Jewish practices. There is no apparent reason for Jesus' disciples to abstain from fasting, but the reason for the apostles in the churches to do so later is obvious. This conclusion is supported by verses 21 and 22 which teach that new cloth and wine should not be joined to old cloth and wine; that is, the new religion should not be attached to the old (Judaism), [2] and therefore Christians should not fast like their Jewish rivals and opponents, the Pharisees and the disciples of the Baptist.

Although some Jewish-Christian churches and probably

all gentile churches rejected Jewish fasting, the Jewish-Christian church in which the *Didache* was written continued to fast regularly, but made a point of doing so on different days than the Pharisees. A Pharisee is reported in Luke 18:12 as saying that he fasts twice a week. The Mishnah confirms that this was the Pharisaic and rabbinical practice, and specifies the days as Monday and Thursday *(Taanit* 2:9). *Didache* orders Christians to fast on two other days: "Your fasts must not be on the same days as the hypocrites [Pharisees], for they fast on Monday and Thursday, but you must fast on Wednesday and Friday" (8:1).

Table Fellowship with Gentiles

Although prejudice against gentiles often appears in the Torah, a specific law against eating with them does not occur there. In some Jewish Pseudepigrapha, however, the separation from gentiles at mealtime is becoming explicit. In *Joseph and Aseneth* the Genesis story of Joseph in Egypt is retold and expanded. In it we read that Joseph entered the house of Pentephres and sat upon the throne. "And they washed his feet and set a table before him by itself, because Joseph never ate with the Egyptians for this was an abomination to him" (7:1). The author of *Jubilees* set forth the explicit rule: "Separate yourself from the gentiles, and do not eat with them" (22:16). The Jewish insistence on not eating certain gentile foods was emphasized after King Antiochus IV tried to force Jews to eat food such as pork which Jews regarded as unclean.[3] Describing the Jews in the days of Ptolemy IV Philopater (ca. 200 B.C.) *3 Maccabees* 3:4 states that the Jews "kept themselves apart in the matter of food, and for that reason they appeared hateful to some." The food laws prevented Jews from dining in gentiles' homes for fear of eating forbidden foods. Eventually some rabbis extended the rule to unlearned Jews, who were called the *Am-ha-Aretz*, the "People of the Land": "The disciples of the learned [the rabbis] . . . must not sit at table in the society of the *Am-ha-Aretz*" (Talmud, *Berakot* 43). Pious Jews had two reasons for not eating with gentiles: the risk of eating gentiles' ritually "unclean" foods such as pork, and the danger of personal contamination resulting from intimate association with gentiles.

Using the Index in Danby's edition of the Mishnah, I read all the Mishnaic passages containing the word "gentiles." The rabbis who are quoted there and in the Talmud differ from each other in their opinions, but they consistently treat gentiles and Samaritans as separate classes of people, inferior to Jews. The rabbis in the Mishnah do not express actual hatred of gentiles, however, in contrast to *Jubilees*. Condescendingly, *Shebiit* 4:3 states: "Greetings may be offered to gentiles in the interests of peace." The School of Hillel was more lenient in its attitude toward gentiles than was the School of Shammai; for example, it permitted a gentile to eat the firstborn sacrificed animal in the company of a priest, but the School of Shammai did not (*Bekhorot* 5:2).[4] Although the Jewish sources do not prove that the Pharisees taught that Jews should not eat with gentiles, the probability is very high that they did.

Paul freely associated closely with gentile Christians. His philosophical basis was that those who have been "baptized into Christ" are "neither Jew nor Greek, . . . for you are all one in Christ Jesus" (Gal. 3:27-28). Since that was his rationale, we may logically deduce that he probably did not eat with gentiles who were not Christians.

The question of table fellowship among Jewish Christians and gentile Christians arose at Antioch. At first Paul, Barnabas, and Peter ate with gentile Christians, but Peter and Barnabas separated from them when pressured by the circumcision party from the Jerusalem church, and Paul denounced them (Gal. 2). Paul continued to eat with gentile Christians, and table fellowship must have been the practice in the churches he founded. A century later Trypho remarked that Jews were puzzled by the fact that "you [Christians], saying that you worship God, and thinking yourselves superior to other people, do not separate from them, and do not make your life different from the heathen in that you do not observe the feasts, Sabbaths and circumcision."[5]

According to Mark 2:15-17, Jesus ate with tax collectors and "sinners" in Levi's house, and the scribes of the Pharisees criticized him for it. The word "sinners" (Greek: *hamartoloi*) can refer to gentiles, but in Judaism it usually meant sinners literally, and probably does here, as verse 17 implies—but if so, how would anyone know they were sinners?

Burying the Dead

In the ancient world the custom in most places was to bury the body soon after death. Out of respect for the deceased, the body was to be buried before decomposition began, which occurs early in hot climates. Another reason was the belief that a dead body was ritually unclean and defiles those who touch it. The Torah commands that a hanged man must be buried on the same day to prevent his body from defiling the land (Deut. 21:22-23). At the time that Christianity began, prompt burial of all dead on the day of death was a religious duty, in the opinion of the Pharisees, unless the day of death was the Sabbath or a festival, or certain other conditions overrode the rule. "Everyone who allows his dead to remain overnight [without burial] transgresses a negative command; but if he had permitted it to remain because of the honor due to it, to bring for it a coffin and burial clothes, he does not thereby commit transgression" (Mishnah, *Sanhedrin* 6:5).

In Matthew and Luke a pericope from the Q material depicts Jesus as advocating breaking the rule about burying the dead. Following Jesus (Matt.) or proclaiming the kingdom of God (Luke) take precedence over burial. "Another of the disciples said to him, 'Lord, let me first go and bury my father.' But Jesus said to him, 'Follow me, and leave the dead to bury their own dead.'"[6] The point of the next pericope in Luke is that following Jesus is more important than even saying farewell to one's family; this pericope clearly teaches that proclaiming the gospel is more important than family obligations. Is that the only point of the Q pericope too, or is that pericope also saying that the Christian gospel is more important than the Oral Law?

Washing Hands

In a pericope in Mark 7 par, Pharisees and scribes ask Jesus, "Why do your disciples not live according to the tradition of the elders, but eat with hands defiled?" (7:5). Verse 2 defines hands "defiled" as hands "unwashed." "The tradition of the elders" is the Oral Law of the Pharisees, which the Mishnah claims was transmitted through "the elders" (*Abot* 1:1). Once again the Pharisees and scribes are critical of the disciples, not Jesus, which suggests that "the disciples" are really the apostles in the Christian communities. That deduction is supported by the personal attack on the Pharisees and scribes assigned to Jesus: he charges that they "leave the commandment of God [the Written Law], and hold fast the tradition of men" [the Oral Law]. As an example Jesus says that their tradition causes persons to give to God what should be given to their parents for their support, and thus they are breaking the Written Law's command to "honor your father and your mother." This type of reasoning, characteristic of Jewish and Christian scribes, would be surprising in an unlearned prophet. Next Jesus argues that nothing from outside which enters a man defiles him, but that which comes out of him does. Jesus explains this "parable" privately to his disciples—a literary device used in the synoptics to explain why non-Christian Jews did not know that Jesus uttered the teaching. His reasoning is that what goes into a man from outside (dirt from unwashed hands is understood) goes into his stomach and passes out again, but his evil thoughts and deeds come from his heart and defile him.

The author of Luke used a literary device of his own to depict Jesus as opposing Pharisaic teaching and conduct. The device is to place Jesus in a setting of dining in the home of a Pharisee. Professor Tasker, for one, called attention to it.[7] In Luke 7 the sinful woman who loves Jesus and washes his feet with her tears is contrasted with Jesus' Pharisaic host, who lacks the woman's "faith." To a denunciation of the Pharisees in Q (Matt. 23:25-36 par) Luke adds a similar setting (Luke 11:37-38). In this type of setting in Luke 14:1-6 Jesus teaches that it is lawful to heal on the Sabbath.

HOSTILITY TO THE PHARISEES

The disputes over the observance of the Written Law, the validity of the Oral Law, the question of whether signs of the end of this age have occurred, and above all, the validity of the Christian message in general, all produced bitter hostility between the Pharisees and the Jewish Christians. Convinced that the Christian gospel was false, most Pharisees refused to join the Christian sect and by their arguments prevented other Jews from joining. A saying in Q expresses the Christian anger: "But woe to you, scribes and Pharisees, hypocrites, because you shut the kingdom of heaven against men; for you neither enter yourselves, nor allow those who would enter to go in."[8] When the crowd, who did not know the Law (i.e., the unlearned "People of the Land"), were receptive to Christianity, the Pharisees denounced them as "accursed" (John 7:49).

The controversy became nasty as it expanded from a discussion of issues to personal denunciations of the other group. The classic Jewish-Christian attack on the Pharisees and their scribes is chapter 23 in Matthew. Here the author has compiled a list of charges: They lay heavy burdens on men; they do all their deeds to be seen by men; they want the best seats at feasts and in synagogues; they engage in various trivial religious practices, but neglect "the weightier matters of the Law, justice and mercy and faith"; "you are like whitewashed tombs, which outwardly appear beautiful, but within are full of dead men's bones and all uncleanness"; "you are full of hypocrisy and iniquity"; "you snakes, you brood of vipers, how are you to escape being sentenced to hell?" In his additions to Mark 7 he adds the relatively mild accusation that "they are blind guides" (Matt. 15:14). The Pharisees' hostility to the Christians was even sharper, often resulting in persecution (see next chapter).

One product of the Christians' hostility consists of their changes in tradition to enlarge the negative picture of the Pharisees. In a Q pericope John the Baptist denounces "the crowds" as a "brood of vipers" (Luke 3:7); when Matthew retells it (3:7), "Pharisees and Sadducees" are substituted for the crowds. In Q Jesus addresses the crowds as "an evil generation" (Luke 11:29); in Matthew 12:38 the crowds have become "some of the scribes and Pharisees." According to Josephus the high priest Ananus, a Sadducee, caused James, the brother of Jesus, to be stoned.[9] But the Christian version in Hegesippus' account makes the Pharisees the murderers of James![10]

In spite of the controversy, a few Pharisees joined the Christian sect. Acts witnesses to that: "Some [Christian] believers who belonged to the party of the Pharisees rose up and said, 'It is necessary to circumcise them and to charge them to keep the Law of Moses'" (15:5). Paul testifies that he formerly was "as to the Law a Pharisee" in his preconversion days when he persecuted the church (Phil. 3:5). The Gospel of Signs in John portrays Nicodemus, a Pharisee and "official of the Jews," as recognizing Jesus as "a teacher come from God" (John 3:1-2). (Nevertheless, the same source, in John 7:48, depicts the Pharisees as asking rhetorically, "Have any of the Pharisees believed in him?," implying—apparently wrongly—that none did.) A debatable question is whether the author of Matthew had been a Pharisee. Although he hates them as persons, he strongly endorses their teachings (23:3). Did he learn their teachings as a result of being a member of the sect, or merely from attending the synagogues?

Donald W. Riddle's book, *Jesus and the Pharisees*, is a penetrating analysis of the gospel traditions concerning the controversies with the Pharisees. His conclusions deserve to be repeated here:

> Even as one may confidently affirm that there is no possible place in the experiences of Jesus for the conflicts with the Pharisees to have occurred as they are described, it is possible, once attention is directed to the Christian movement, to find exactly the places in the experiences of the Christian leaders and groups for just those conflicts to have taken place. Furthermore, as attention is focused upon the Christian communities, it is possible to perceive how the attitudes which were developed in relation to contemporary Jews might have been read back into the experience of Jesus. This secured for them a sanction whose effect might by no other means have been so great. . . . The traditions of Jesus and the Pharisees, when taken as produced by the necessities of the Christian communities, become at once understandable in themselves and useful in the delineation of the life of the early Christians.[11]

Jewish Christians resented the disbelief of the Jewish crowds as well as that of Pharisees, Sadducees, and their scribes. The Jewish-Christian denunciations of the Jewish masses, citing biblical passages against them, sound anti-Semitic, but actually both groups were Jews. We would be astonished if we had not learned from the Dead Sea scrolls of a similar attitude on the part of the Jewish sect at Qumran. That sect believed that God will destroy all Jews who are not members of their sect, along with the gentiles. Jewish Christians too became self-righteous, hostile to other Jews.

HOSTILITY BETWEEN GENTILE CHRISTIANS AND JEWS

Causes

Both gentile Christians and non-Christian Jews inherited some of the arguments, biblical interpretations, and tension resulting from the disputes of Jewish Christians with the Pharisees and Sadducees. The churches, missionaries, and synagogues preserved and promoted the controversy, but that was not the only cause of hostility.

Both groups also inherited the intense prejudices that already existed between gentiles and Jews in the Greco-Roman world. We have seen the background of this in the Israelite hostility to the idolatry of the Canaanites and various adjacent tribes, Antiochus' IV's decree against the observance of the Jewish religion, the resulting Jewish rebellion and Jewish literature such as *Jubilees*, and Jewish revolts against Rome. After Alexander the Great united the Greek and Near Eastern worlds, Hellenistic rulers encouraged Jews to establish colonies within major commercial centers. As inducements the rulers granted them freedom from military service, protection in exercising their religion, and a privileged judicial status. The consequent relations between Greeks and Jews were far from cordial. "The feeling was reciprocal. Greek disliked Jew, and Jew disliked Greek."[12] In the days of Augustus, Greek city governments suppressed Jewish activities, and Greek individuals stole books and money from the synagogues. Riots often occurred because of the tension. Emperor Gaius tried to impose the imperial cult upon Jews in Alexandria, and he deprived them of their rights and privileges, but Emperor Claudius restored them.[13] The emperors generally protected the special privileges of the Jews and exempted them from certain taxes and, because of their monotheism, from worship of the Roman state and the emperor. Jews who were Roman citizens were exempted from military service. Rome continued to give Jews special privileges, even after they revolted.

Why did Jews and gentiles dislike each other? Jews (except the Hellenistic ones who adopted Greek culture) disapproved of gentile loose sexual habits, "unclean" foods, and polytheism. Even if a gentile worshiped only one god, he was a heathen if he did not worship Yahweh, the Lord. Underlying all was the Jewish philosophy of exclusiveness; they were God's chosen people and liable to be contaminated by close association with gentiles.

For their part, gentiles resented Jewish aloofness. Jews lived in the same cities with gentiles, but did not associate with them beyond what was necessary, and they had their own laws. Jewish aloofness was contrary to the trend of the times, which was toward syncretism in religion and tolerance and assimilation in general. (Nevertheless, many Diaspora Jews did adopt much Greek culture, as their writings reveal.) Josephus quoted the Greek Apion as charging that "The Jews bear no goodwill toward any foreigner, and particularly any Greek."[14] Diodorus also objected to Jews' "dislike of strangers" and their "hostility toward the human race."[15] Strabo criticized Jews for their superstitious practices such as food taboos and circumcision, and Cicero denounced the alien and barbarous superstition of the Jewish colonies.[16]

Christian Hostility to Jews

Hostility between gentile Christians and Jews is reflected in the Gospel of John. The gentile author denies that Jews are the true sons of Abraham, for their father is the devil, not Abraham (8:39, 44).

One form of Christian hostility to Jews was to blame them for Jesus' death. This tactic has its beginnings in Jewish Christianity. The synoptic gospels report that the chief priests and the crowd brought charges against Jesus when he was tried and sentenced by Pilate. At the instigation of the chief priests, the crowd called for Jesus' crucifixion. The author of Matthew enlarged the Jewish crowd's responsibility by composing and inserting this sentence: "And all the people answered, 'His blood be on us and on our children'" (27:25). That the crowd would actually say this is utterly implausible! But how could a Jewish-Christian writer take such a vindictive stance against the Jewish crowd and its descendants?

The author's stance is not so surprising as it may seem. Jewish prophets and apocalyptists had called upon the Lord to punish or destroy wicked Jews and even to destroy most of the nation of Israel. At the time that Christianity began, the Pharisees hoped and expected that God would severely punish those Jews who did not obey the Law; the Essenes regarded Jews who refused to accept their beliefs and practices as among the "Sons of Darkness" who are doomed to perdition. The author of Matthew simply adapted to Christianity an attitude inherited from the prophets, namely, God will punish Jews who do the wrong thing, whoever they are.

In the speech assigned to Paul in Acts 13, the persons responsible for Jesus' death are (only) "those who live in Jerusalem and their rulers" (13:27; cf. 3:17). Jews in general and their descendants are not blamed there, but in Acts 10:39 the Jews are guilty: "They put him to death by hanging him on a tree." Gentile Christians soon seized upon that idea.

The author of the Gospel of John was a gentile Christian

who used both Jewish and gentile sources in writing his gospel. He used both kinds of material because he lived in a mixed Christian community with both Jewish and gentile members. He was hostile to non-Christian Jews because the Pharisees had recently banned Christians from the synagogues. He apparently was not on very friendly terms with Christian Jews either; his semi-Gnostic interpretation of Jesus must have led to heated disputes with them. To him Jesus' enemies are not limited to chief priests, Pharisees, and elders; he adds "the Jews." He depicts Jesus as afraid to go about in Judea "because the Jews sought to kill him" (7:1). In 7:13 they are so hostile to him that "for fear of the Jews no one spoke openly about him."

Blaming the Jews

In the second century the idea grew that Jesus was "crucified by the Jews," as Justin expressed it.[17] In *Apology of Aristides* 2 we read that Jesus "was pierced [on the cross] by the Jews," a switch from John 19:34, where it is a Roman soldier who pierced him. The *Gospel of Peter*, of which only a fragment survives, develops the idea further: "None of the Jews washed their hands" (1) of responsibility for condemning Jesus. The unfriendly actions are here committed by the people: they mock him, scourge him, cast lots for his garments, and give him "gall and vinegar" to drink. "And they fulfilled all things and completed the measure of their sins on their head" (17). After Jesus' death "the Jews and the elders and the priests, perceiving what great evil they had done to themselves, began to lament and say, 'Woe on our sins; the judgment and the end of Jerusalem has drawn nigh'" (25). Non-Jews are portrayed as afraid to report Jesus' resurrection because they are afraid of the Jews. They ask Pilate to command his soldiers to tell no one what they had seen at the tomb. "'For it is better for us,' they said, 'to make ourselves guilty of the greatest sin before God than to fall into the hands of the people of the Jews and be stoned'" (48). When Mary Magdalene and her friends came to the empty tomb, "they feared lest the Jews should see them" (52).[18] The *Gospel of Peter* draws elements from all four canonical gospels and revises them to construct a story to place blame on "the Jews" or "the [Jewish] people" and to exonerate the Romans.

The similar tactic appears in the Christian portions (2nd-4th c.) of *The Ascension of Isaiah*. In it the children of Israel tormented the Beloved (Jesus) because the Adversary (Beliar, or Satan) roused them against him (3:13; 11:19).

Paul testifies that he was persecuted by Jews (2 Cor. 11), and Acts frequently portrays the Jews as witnessing against him in court and plotting to kill him.[19] Paul's account can be trusted as first-hand information; the accounts in Acts probably have some truth behind them, but the "speeches" are unreliable compositions of the author. One incident is plain evidence. Paul reports that "the governor under King Aretas guarded the city of Damascus in order to seize me, but I was let down through a window in the wall and escaped his hands" (2 Cor. 11:32-33). When the incident is retold in Acts, "the Jews" replace the governor as the enemy:

> Saul [Paul] . . . confounded the Jews who lived in Damascus by proving that Jesus was the Christ. When many days had passed, the Jews plotted to kill him, but their plot became known to Saul. They were watching the gates day and night to kill him, but his disciples took him by night and let him down over the wall, lowering him in a basket (9:22-25).

Rejection of Judaism

Christian rejection of the Written Law, the Oral Law, and certain practices they commanded, strained to the limits the original premise that Christianity was a Jewish sect. The early belief that Christianity is the New Judaism permitted the extension of the limits, but eventually the boundaries were exceeded. When combined with the intense animosity between the two groups, the forces for complete separation were overwhelming, and Christians discarded Judaism in general. A full break with Judaism is implied in the story of the wedding at Cana in which the steward says to the bridegroom, "You have kept the good wine until now" (John 2:10). Ignatius had the same thought in mind when he wrote, "Put aside then the evil leaven, which has grown old and sour, and change to the new leaven, which is Jesus Christ" (*Mag.* 10:2). Ignatius clearly regarded Christianity as a new religion: "Do not be led astray by strange doctrines and old fables, which are profitless. For if we are still living according to Judaism, we admit that we have not received [God's] grace" (*Mag.* 8:1). "It is monstrous to talk of Jesus Christ and to practice Judaism" (*Mag.* 10:3). Ignatius continues: "But if anyone expounds Judaism to you, do not listen to him; for it is better to hear Christianity from the circumcised [Jews] than Judaism from the uncircumcised" [gentile Christians] (*Phil.* 6:1).

Some Christians, believing that Christianity should remain in the fold of Judaism, propagandized their fellow Christians accordingly. The author of Colossians warns his readers to withstand criticism for non-observance of Jewish food laws and festivals: "Therefore let no one pass judgment on you in questions of food and drink or with regard to a festival or a New Moon or a Sabbath" (2:16).

Total rejection of Judaism required disregard for its festivals, or Holy Days, which included Passover, Pentecost, and Tabernacles or Booths, and the three pilgrim festivals in which every male was obligated to go to the Temple (while it existed). Other festivals were New Years (Rosh Hashanah), Festival of Lights (Hanukkah), and the New Moon. Although we hear little of the New Moon today, it was an important monthly feast in ancient Israel. The prophets usually associated it with the Sabbath and named it first ("New Moon and Sabbath"). Trading was prohibited on both days (Amos 8:5), and a solemn assembly was held on those and other festival days (Isa. 1:13). As we have just seen in Colossians, the New Moon was one of the features of Judaism that Judaizers tried to persuade Christians to observe. Trypho the Jew demonstrated that the New Moon was still an important Jewish festival in the second century A.D.; he told Justin that he would listen to him if he would first keep the commandments of the Law, including the observance of "the Sabbath and the feasts and God's New Moons."[20]

Angels

Belief in the existence of angels is generally accepted in early Christian literature. Jewish apocalyptic influence is responsible for their strong showing in the Book of Revelation, but general Jewish influence is the source in the synoptic stories about Jesus' birth.

1 Peter states that Jesus Christ "has gone into heaven and is at the right hand of God, with angels, authorities, and powers subject to him" (3:22). The subordination of angels to the risen Christ does not necessarily indicate opposition to them, but it may in the first chapter of Hebrews where the idea is emphasized: The Son has "become as much superior to angels

as the name he has obtained is more excellent than theirs. For to what angel did God ever say, 'You are my Son, . . .' And again, when he brings the first-born [the Son existed before the world, for he created it, v. 2] into the world, he says, 'Let all God's angels worship him.'" If the author has an unfriendly attitude toward angels in general, why? How could anyone who believed in the existence of angels be opposed to all of them? Before we attempt to answer that question, let us look at the Jewish background.

The angels in early Israelite religion were adaptations of secondary deities in Near Eastern religions. In Canaanite texts and inscriptions they are called "holy ones," "Sons of God," and "Sons of the Most High." Mesopotamians, Canaanites, and Jews believed that they were clothed in light. In Israel, as elsewhere, they were messengers for a superior deity; a Canaanite term was "messenger of heaven."[21] In early Judaism angels became intercessors as well as messengers. They stand in the presence of the Lord and intercede with him in man's behalf. For example, "I am Raphael, one of the seven holy angels who present the prayers of the saints and enter into the presence of the glory of the Holy One" (Tobit 12:15). They also became guardians of righteous individuals and of the righteous collectively. An angel said to Levi, "I shall be with you, for the Lord sent me" (*T. Levi* 5:3). During the Maccabean Revolt "two glorious angels" descended, filling the enemy with terror, and bound them with shackles (*3 Macc*. 6:18-19). The chief angels were rulers with dominions; they were "archangels," "princes," or "commanders." In the War Scroll found at Qumran we read, "The Angel of Light you [God] did appoint as our helper; in his lot are all the sons of righteousness, and all the spirits of truth are in his dominion" (lQM 13:10). The angels in the heavens worship the Lord in their assembly (Ps. 89:5-7).

The heavenly gods in Canaanite religion met in an assembly, or council, to deal with problems on earth or in the heavens, and so did the angels in Judaism. The Jews at Qumran regularly held a "council of the community," which they believed was like the "assembly of the holy ones," which they expected to join at death (1QS 11:8). Some of the hymns of praise sung at Qumran may have been intended as duplicates of those sung by the heavenly choir of angels.

The Sadducees did not believe in angels, but the Pharisees did. Sectarian Jews, including the Essenes, were fond of them. According to Josephus, the Essenes swore an oath that they would preserve the names of the angels.[22] In their *Manual of Discipline* they wrote that when the new age comes, God will give the righteous "insight into the knowledge of the Most High and the wisdom of the Sons of Heaven" [angels] (1QS 4:22).

Clearly many Jews held angels in high esteem, for angels were next to God not only in their close association with him, but also next to him in importance in the spiritual world.[23] That point of view explains why Christians who were turning away from Judaism turned against the worship of angels. Hebrews 1:4 emphasizes that Jesus is superior to angels.

By the beginning of the second century, and perhaps earlier, some persons tried to induce gentile Christians to worship angels and observe other Jewish customs. The earliest evidence of this that has been transmitted to us is Colossians 2:16-18, which—contrary to some biblical scholars' opinion— was written later than Paul. Verse 18 reads: "Let no one disqualify you, insisting on self-abasement and worship of angels, taking his stand on visions, puffed up without reason by his sensuous mind." The reference to visions suggests that mysticism may have been involved. In the Syriac version of an apology addressed to Hadrian (117-138) the Christians Aristides and Quadratus accuse Jews of angel worship: "their service is to angels and not to God" (14). A similar charge is in the *Preaching of Peter* (A.D. 100-150) quoted by Clement of Alexandria: "Neither worship him [God] in the manner of the Jews; for they also, who think that only they know God, do not understand, worshiping angels and archangels, the months and the moon."[24]

Thus Christians shook off basic features of Judaism, one after another. Nevertheless, they retained in the New Testament and other writings some minor Jewish features and these three major ones: the Jewish god (though modified by gentile influence, directly or indirectly), the Jewish ethics in the synoptic gospels and the Epistle of James, and the Jewish Scriptures used to support the claim that Jesus was the Christ. The Old Testament was a powerful factor in leading them to worship the God of the Jews, whom Justin admitted they worshiped: ". . . we have fled for refuge to him who is the God of Jacob and the God of Israel" (*Dial.* 110:2). In contrast, the

Gnostic Marcion went almost all the way in discarding Judaism; he rejected its god and its Scriptures, as we shall see later.

The Great Controversy was a major cause of the separation of Christianity from Judaism. The controversy created misunderstandings and deep-seated hatreds that were passed on from generation to generation. Christians were embittered by the persecution they suffered from Jews (see below) and by false charges such as that Christians "eat human beings and wallow in sex."[25] We know that Jews deeply resented Christian rejection of their Law. They must also have been stung by (1) the claim that Christians are the New Elect, God's new chosen people, replacing the Old Elect, the Jews, (2) the shifting of responsibility for Jesus' death to the Jewish people as a whole, and (3) the Christian claim that the destruction of Jerusalem by the Romans was God's punishment upon them for the death of Jesus, the Jewish Messiah. That last claim is the basis of the following remark that Justin made to Trypho: "Although your city has been taken and your land laid waste, you [Jews] do not repent" (*Dial.* 108:3). Citing Isaiah 1:7 and 64:10-11, Justin charged that the destruction of Jerusalem was according to prophecy (*1 Apol.* 47).

After gentiles became predominant in Christianity and it became a separate religion, gentile Christians claimed that they were God's chosen and the Jewish Scriptures belonged to them. This was harder for Jews to accept than the similar claims of Jewish Christians. In Jewish eyes the gentiles were usurping the Jewish religion!

21

PERSECUTION

JEWISH PERSECUTION OF CHRISTIANS

Much has been written about the unethical persecution of Jews by Christians in the Middle Ages and subsequent discrimination against Jews. We have observed that some early Christians unfairly blamed Jews en masse for Jesus' death. But persecution between the two groups began with Jews persecuting Christians, not vice versa. This fact is rarely mentioned today. At first the Christians were Jewish Christians, but that does not alter the fact that Jews persecuted Christians.

The First Stage
Tension first arose in Jerusalem when Jewish authorities arrested the apostles, beat them, and ordered them not to preach in the name of Jesus (Acts 4-5). The Sadducees, high priest, and the Sanhedrin were responsible. Actual persecution began with the execution of Stephen and the attack on other Hellenist Christians in Jerusalem (Acts 6:8-8:3). The apostles were not attacked because they did not seem so dangerous in Jewish sight; only the Hellenists had to leave town. Although the instigators were Diaspora Jews, the final authorities responsible were the high priest and the Sanhedrin. Before his conversion, Saul (Paul) was especially zealous in that persecution (Acts 9:1-2). The next persecution was Herod Agrippa's attack on the Jerusalem church when James, the brother of Zebedee, and probably his brother John were killed, an act which "pleased the Jews" (Acts 12:3).
The next stage was the persecution of Paul and his companions. He endured two kinds of affliction: an unspecified physical ailment, which he called "a thorn in the flesh" (2 Cor. 12:7), and persecution. Four times in 2 Corinthians Paul mentions the persecution he suffered.[1] He states that in Asia "we were so crushed that we despaired of life itself" (1:8). He

faced "great opposition" in Thessalonia and "suffered and was shamefully treated at Philippi" (1 Thess. 2:2). At Philippi Paul feared that he might be killed because of his preaching; he counted his suffering as gain for several reasons, including that "I may share his [Christ Jesus'] sufferings, becoming like him in his death" (Phil. 3:10). Paul was persecuted by both Jews and gentiles; he faced "danger from my own people, danger from gentiles" (2 Cor. 11:26). The Philippian Christians, too, suffered persecution (Phil. 1:29-30). Paul strongly disagreed with some rival apostles who were also Jewish Christians. They too had suffered persecution, but he asserted that he had endured more (2 Cor. 11:22-23).

Acts presents a more detailed picture,[2] with Jews stirring up the people and the authorities to arrest, beat, and even try to kill Paul. Jewish hostility appears to have been especially strong in the province of Asia, judging from Paul's mention of it and some references in Acts.[3] Persecution of Paul involved also a plot of more than forty Jews in Jerusalem to kill him (Acts 23:12-15). Acts reports the Jewish beating of Sosthenes, the ruler of the synagogue in Corinth, who had been converted to the Christian faith (1 Cor. 1:1; Acts 18:17). The charges against Paul, according to Acts, included the accusations that he was acting against the decrees of Caesar by teaching that there is another king, Jesus, that he persuaded men to worship God in ways contrary to the Law, and that he defiled the Temple by bringing Greeks into it.

Jews persecuted the churches in Judea too (1 Thess. 2:14). In the year 62 the high priest Ananus persecuted the Jerusalem church by stoning to death some of its members, including Jesus' brother James on the grounds that he did not obey the Law.[4]

Numerous references to Jewish persecution are made in the synoptic gospels. A major block of Q, ascribed to Jesus, urges Christians not to be afraid.

> But take heed to yourselves; for they will deliver you up
> to councils, and you will be beaten in synagogues, and
> you will stand before governors and kings for my sake,
> to bear testimony before them. . . . And when they bring
> you to trial and deliver you up, do not be anxious
> beforehand what you are to say; but say whatever is
> given to you in that hour, for it is not you who speak,
> but the Holy Spirit. And brother will deliver up brother

to death, and the father his child, and children will rise against parents and have them put to death; and you will be hated by all for my name's sake. But he who endures to the end will be saved (Mark 13:9, 11-13).

The "councils" (Greek: *sunedria*) are local Jewish councils. Such courts must have been the ones that five times ordered Paul to receive "forty lashes less one" (2 Cor. 11:24). A pericope in Q also refers to trials of Christians: "And when they bring you before the synagogues and the rulers and the authorities, do not be anxious how or what you are to answer, for the Holy Spirit will teach you . . ." (Luke 12:11-12). In Luke 21:12 we read: "They will lay their hands on you and persecute you, delivering you up to the synagogues and prisons." Luke 4:29 depicts Jewish people as putting Jesus out of the city of Nazareth. The evidence suggests that this is yet another example of writers assigning to Jesus the experiences of the apostles in their missionary work (see chapter 25 below). The author of Luke was well acquainted with the nature of synagogues in his day, as his knowledge of their services reveals (4:16, 20). He probably knew too about the treatment Christians received there.

The Roman writer Suetonius reports that friction between Jews and Jewish Christians in Rome caused so much public disturbance that the emperor Claudius had to take action (ca. 49): "Since the Jews constantly made disturbances at the instigation of Chrestus [Christ], he expelled them from Rome."5 The expulsion must have included Jewish Christians along with the Jews, for at that time Romans viewed Christianity as a Jewish sect.

The Book of Revelation also testifies to Jewish persecution of Jewish Christians. In it an angel gives this message to the church at Smyrna: "I know your tribulation . . . and the slander of those who say they are Jews and are not, but are a synagogue of Satan. Do not fear what you are about to suffer. Behold, the devil is about to throw some of you into prison" (2:9-10). The writer's claim that the Jewish persecutors are not true Jews is consistent with the belief that Christianity is the True Judaism and that Christians are the real Jews.

Hostility between Jews and Jewish Christians grew rapidly. Christian laxity in observing the Torah developed further as a major factor. The claim that Jesus was the Messiah was a source of dispute, but probably not a cause of persecution. Certain other beliefs about Jesus, however, appeared

309

blasphemous to Jews. Jews had applied the title "the Lord" to Yahweh as a substitute for his holy name, but Christians began to use it as a title for Jesus. Further, some Christians began to think of him as fully divine (see chapter below on deification). The late insertion in Philippians (2:6-11) goes "about as far as they can go" in that direction: "at the name of Jesus every knee should bow, in heaven and on earth and under the earth." If that isn't a violation of Jewish monotheism, what is?

The destruction of the Temple in 70 was a severe shock to Jews, including those outside of Palestine, for it left them without their traditional religious and pilgrimage center. With the Romans in control, Jews could not rebuild it. Johanan ben Zakkai saved Judaism from possible extinction by founding a rabbinic academy at Jamnia (Jabneh), west of Jerusalem. He died around A.D. 80, when he was succeeded by Rabbi Gamaliel II. Under Zakkai the school standardized Judaism along Pharisaic lines by issuing a series of enactments which were binding on all synagogues. One of the enactments was the Benediction Against Heretics. About A.D. 85 Gamaliel revised its twelfth benediction to include "the Nazarenes." As revised, it reads as follows:

> For the apostates let there be no hope, and do thou quickly uproot the proud kingdom [Rome] in our days. And let the Nazarenes [Christians] and the Minim [heretics] be destroyed in a moment, let them be wiped out of the Book of Life, and [in it] let them not be written with the righteous [i.e., let them not have a blessed immortality]. Blessed art thou, O Lord, who humblest the proud.[6]

The Jamnia Academy sent messengers to the synagogues in various countries instructing them to enforce that benediction. Jews who accepted Christian teaching were excommunicated, banned from the synagogues. The Gospel of John ascribes to Jesus forecasts of such events: "They will put you out of the synagogues" (16:2).

The Gospel of John was written in a city in which the controversy between the Pharisees and Christians was intense. It probably was written about fifteen years after Gamaliel's version of the Benediction Against Heretics was issued. Professors J. Louis Martyn and Alan Culpepper have examined John in detail in respect to its setting.[7]

As Martyn expresses it, the stories in John 5, 7, and 9

are on two levels. On the surface level they appear to be about Jesus during his lifetime. On the other level, under the surface, some features reflect what was happening in the author's community when he wrote. (This is not a new idea, and the same literary device is employed throughout the canonical gospels.) The author arrives at the sub-level both by his interpretations of the Signs Source and by inserting his ideas independently of that source. Martyn and Culpepper did not recognize the Signs Source in their studies, and therefore the following reconstruction is partly theirs and partly the present author's.

Jewish-Christian evangelists came to Alexandria and persuaded some Jews to believe the Christian gospel. The evangelists may have brought with them the Gospel of Signs, or Signs Source, for, unlike much of the rest of John, it lacks Alexandrian thought and it emphasizes Samaria. "We have found the Messiah" (John 1:41) in the Signs Source surely reflects the evangelists' basic belief. By the time the Benediction Against Heretics was promulgated by Gamaliel, the number of Jewish converts in Alexandria and elsewhere was alarming. The Benediction was enforced, and Jewish Christians were tried in the local Jewish court, the *Gerousia*, and expelled from the synagogue.

Excommunication is mentioned three times by the author of John.[8] In the Gospel of Signs he found material that he used to deal with the situation. In it some of the crowd say that Jesus "leads the crowd astray" (7:12), and the Pharisees have the same opinion (7:47). Even in the source the accusation fits the Christian apostles, and the same charge must have been made against the evangelists who came to Alexandria. The source also contains a story of Jesus' healing a blind man which merely demonstrates that Jesus is a miracle-working Prophet-Messiah (9:13-17). In it the man born blind symbolizes Jews who receive their "sight" by becoming Christians. The gentile-Christian author of John reinterprets the story in accord with his situation and changes the opponents from Pharisees to "the Jews" (9:18-23).

Excommunication did not stop the conversions to Christianity, so a further step was tried. "They will ban you from the synagogues. But the hour is coming when whoever kills you will think he is offering service to God" (16:2). ". . . in the light of John 16:2 we have no alternative but to conclude that this step was the imposition of the death penalty on at least

311

some of the Jews who espoused the messianic faith"[9] The persecution caused some evangelists and their converts to go underground, a situation reflected in 9:12, 22; it caused others to abandon the Christian faith (16:1). Martyn reconstructs the probable process of detecting covert Christians in a congregation: When a member was suspected of having become a heretic, the president *(archisunagogos)* of the synagogue asked the overseer *(huperetes)* of the congregation to appoint the suspect to stand before the Torah ark in the synagogue service and read aloud all of the Eighteen Benedictions. If he faltered on No. 12, the Benediction Against Heretics, he was taken to court.[10] The persecution forced the Jewish Christians out of the synagogues, so they met separately and thus formed a church. In Alexandria they must have met with gentile Christians in the safety of the gentile section of the city. The author of John was a gentile Christian in a racially mixed church.

The Second Century

Jewish persecution of Jewish Christians came from an additional source in the second century. Christians refused to join in the Second Jewish War against Rome, led by Bar Kokhba, just as they had refused to join in the First War and for the same reason, namely, they were waiting for Jesus' return, which would end Roman rule. In the Second War there were two more reasons: the Jewish leader was a false Messiah, and the excommunication of Christians had left them with no desire to be under Jewish rule. Justin reports that Bar Kokhba had ordered cruel punishments for Christians.[11]

The church fathers Justin, Epiphanius, and Jerome attest to the practice among Jews of pronouncing curses against Christians in the daily prayers. Further evidence is in the ancient Jewish manuscripts which Solomon Schechter found in the Geniza in Cairo.[12] Although Justin's personal relations with the Jew Trypho were relatively friendly, he testifies repeatedly to Jewish hostility to Christians: "you [Jews], cursing in your synagogues them that believe on Christ"; "you chose selected men from Jerusalem and then sent them out into all the earth, saying that a godless sect, namely of Christians, had appeared, and saying what all who do not know us are accustomed to say against us"; "the priests and teachers of your people have caused his [the Son of God's] name to be profaned and blasphemed throughout the whole earth. These falsehoods are, as it were, filthy clothing, . . ."[13] Justin states that Jews confiscate Christians' property (*Dial.* 110:5). He also says that proselytes were especially zealous: "But the proselytes not only do not believe, but utter blasphemies against his [Christ's] name doubly more than you [who were born Jews] and wish both to kill and to torment us who believe on him" (*Dial.* 122:2).

Combined Jewish and Gentile Persecution

Sometimes Jews and Greek or Roman authorities cooperated against Christians. This process began with the high priest and the Sanhedrin in Jerusalem when they arrested and tried Jesus and turned him over to Pilate. The process continued after the crucifixion as various Jews tried to stop the apostles from preaching. The Book of Acts testifies to that development. Jews in Thessalonica incited the rabble against Paul and Silas, and when they could not find them, "they dragged Jason and some of the brethren before the city authorities" (Acts 17:6). Jews turned Paul and Silas over to Roman magistrates in Philippi, who released them when they learned that the two were Roman citizens (Acts 16). Jews brought Paul to the tribunal of a Roman proconsul, Gallio (18:12). The high priest and some elders journeyed from Jerusalem to Caesarea and presented to the Roman governor Felix their case against Paul (24:1). When Festus replaced Felix as governor, chief priests and other Jewish leaders tried to involve Festus in their secret plot to kill Paul (25).

Riots and the threat of riots naturally led to arrests, beatings, and imprisonment or expulsion from the city, for maintaining law and order was a major responsibility of Greek and Roman governments alike. Fear of authorities' reaction was expressed by the town clerk of Ephesus when gentile silversmiths stirred up a crowd against Paul and his companions: "We are in danger of being charged with rioting today, there being no cause that we can give to justify this commotion" (Acts 19:40). In Jerusalem Jews from Asia:

> . . . stirred up all the crowd and laid hands on him [Paul], . . . all the city was aroused, and the people ran together; they seized Paul and dragged him out of the Temple, . . . and as they were trying to kill him, word came to the tribune of the cohort that all Jerusalem was in confusion. He at once took soldiers and centurions, . . . and when they [the crowd] saw the tribune and the

soldiers, they stopped beating Paul. Then the tribune . . . arrested him and ordered him to be bound with two chains. . . . he ordered him to be brought into the barracks. . . . the mob of the people followed, crying, "Away with him" (Acts 21:27-36).

Why did Roman authorities become involved? Sometimes it was because they feared that Christians might start a political revolt, as Jesus may have tried to do. At Thessalonica Jews aroused a crowd against Jason for housing Paul and Silas, and they tried to alarm the city authorities by charging that the apostles "are all acting against the decrees of Caesar, saying that there is another king, Jesus" (Acts 17:7). A second cause was that the Romans took very seriously their duty to maintain law and order, and therefore acted quickly to put an end to riots or potential riots.

Why were Jews so opposed to the preaching of Paul? We have seen that his attitude toward the Law was the major cause, judging from his letters, and Acts agrees. Jews charged, "This man is persuading men to worship God [in ways] contrary to the Law" (18:13; cf. 21:21). They also charged that he had defiled the Temple by bringing Greeks into it (21:28). The Roman authorities were not interested in matters of the Jewish Law and Temple, for those were strictly Jewish concerns. The proconsul Gallio illustrates that by saying to the Jews, "Since it is a matter of questions about words and names and your own law, see to it yourselves; I refuse to be a judge of these things" (18:15).

Did Jews Actually Persecute Christians?

Jews and Christians in modern times have generally glossed over the Jewish persecution of Christians. Even Jewish and Christian scholars are reluctant to admit it. The Jewish scholar, Israel Abrahams, argued that Jewish opposition consisted only of argument and teaching; he denied that it ever consisted of violence and persecution, except for a possible mob action.[14] The Christian scholar, Donald Riddle, concluded that the traditions of Jewish persecution in Acts are not valid because of the apologetic motivation of the author, and therefore all the persecution came from the Romans.[15] I used to think that myself, but now I am certain that that opinion is wrong, on the basis of the following evidence:

    1. Although Acts exaggerates, contains unhistorical

speeches, miracle stories, and errors, and the author does have some apologetic motives, it nevertheless contains considerable factual information. Many elements ring true; other elements are not accurate in details but reflect actual history. To separate the wheat from the chaff, we must examine the book carefully.

2. The instances in Acts of Jewish efforts to harm Paul are so numerous, varied, and plausible that one suspects that where there is so much smoke, there must have been some fire.

3. The We-source in Acts was not written by Paul, for it mentions him by name, but it was written by someone who accompanied him and thus provides first-hand information. It reports that a prophet named Agabus came to Paul and his companions in Caesarea and made a prediction. "And coming to us he took Paul's girdle and bound his own feet and hands, and said, 'Thus says the Holy Spirit, 'So shall the Jews at Jerusalem bind the man who owns this girdle and deliver him into the hands of the gentiles'" (21:11). Evidently the prophet, who had just come down from Judea, had reason to believe that some Jews in Jerusalem were planning to capture Paul and turn him over to the Romans. This Agabus incident must be historical not only because it is reported in the We-source, but also because the prediction—like many in real life—was not accurate; Jews did not bind Paul in Jerusalem, but instead the Roman tribune arrested him and ordered that he be bound in chains (21:33). The story was not created later as a prophecy of what actually happened.

4. Paul himself wrote that he was in danger from his own people as well as from gentiles (2 Cor. 11:23-26).

Paul was not the only Christian who suffered. Other Christians endured Jewish persecution in both the first and second centuries. Eusebius quotes a Christian writer who visited the church at Ancrya in Galatia in the latter half of the second century. He found it "talked deaf by this New Prophecy" [Montanism, a charismatic Christian sect]. The writer denounces the Montanists, and one reason that he regards them as inferior to other Christians is that none were ever "persecuted by Jews." "Nor was any one of the [Montanist] women ever scourged in the synagogues of the Jews or stoned."[16] This passage is evidence that (1) in contrast to the Montanists, some other Christians had been persecuted by Jews, and (2) that the Christians who had suffered persecution were Jewish Christians, for scourging in the synagogues and stoning to death were

Jewish punishments of Jews.

Did Jews persecute Christians? The evidence shows that they did. And let it not be said that the Jewish Christians were not Christians, for they, more than any other group, shaped the early Christian faith.

ROMAN PERSECUTION OF CHRISTIANS

History
Pilate's crucifixion of Jesus can hardly be called persecution because Pilate was merely doing his duty as a Roman administrator to prevent political rebellion. He did not punish the disciples for being followers of Jesus. Applying the death penalty to anyone believed to be attempting to overthrow the government is not labeled persecution in any age. The method of execution, crucifixion, was unnecessarily cruel, but so was stoning, the Jewish method of execution for blasphemy that Stephen suffered. The Romans treated Jesus the same way they treated various rebels against the state.

When Romans arrested Jews and Christians for creating riots and other disturbances of the peace, they were not persecuting them. They were merely preserving law and order. When Emperor Claudius expelled Jews and Jewish Christians from Rome for creating disturbances over Christ, he was trying to preserve the peace.

Apart from Paul, the earliest literary reference to a clash between Christians and gentile government authorities, including Roman governors, is in Mark 13:9, where Jesus says to the disciples, "You will stand before governors and kings for my sake, to bear testimony before them." The Book of Acts reports Paul's standing on trial before Roman governors.

In Mark three disciples are singled out for special honors: Peter and two sons of Zebedee, James and John. Only those three accompany Jesus at the Transfiguration and into the Garden of Gethsemane (9:2; 14:33). Why did Mark assign them such honor? Apparently because all three were martyrs: James and probably John at the order of Herod Agrippa 1, and according to ancient church tradition Peter (and Paul) at Rome in Nero's persecution.

The first official Roman persecution of Christians was by Emperor Nero in the year 64. Although it did not continue long, it was a nasty, barbaric affair. A great fire burned much of Rome then, and a report circulated among the populace that Nero had ordered the fire to be set. He tried to shift the blame on to the Christians. The Roman historian Tacitus wrote a brief account:

> Consequently, to get rid of the report, Nero fastened the guilt and inflicted the most exquisite tortures on a class hated for their abominations, called Christians by the populace. . . . a deadly superstition, . . . an arrest was first made of all who confessed [to being Christians]; then, upon their information, an immense multitude was convicted, not so much of the crime of arson, as of hatred of the human race. Mockery of every sort was added to their deaths. Covered with the skins of beasts, they were torn by dogs and perished, or were nailed to crosses, or were doomed to the flames. These served to illuminate the night when daylight failed. Nero had thrown open his gardens for the spectacle, and was exhibiting a show in the circus, while he mingled with the people in the dress of a charioteer or drove about in a chariot. Hence, even for criminals [Christians] who deserved extreme and exemplary punishment, there arose a feeling of compassion; for it was not, as it seemed, for the public good, but to glut one man's cruelty, that they were being destroyed.17

Conceited, capricious, and cruel by nature, Nero was still young at the time. Blame for the fire was placed on Christians because they were unpopular with the masses. Educated Romans regarded Christians as superstitious, but why did the masses dislike them? "Hatred of the human race" was an accusation made also against Jews for their attitude toward gentiles. But soon the majority of Christians were gentiles. They too separated themselves from others in that they believed that they were God's new chosen people; they refused to support or participate in the official Roman cults, and they excluded outsiders from their meetings when they celebrated the Lord's Supper. The latter policy led to the false charges that at their gatherings they ate children and plotted against their pagan neighbors and the government.

The second official Roman persecution of Christians occurred under Emperor Domitian. To understand this and subsequent Roman persecutions, we turn to the background.

The kings of Egypt had been worshiped as living gods since the third millennium B.C. Deification of the kings augmented the power and authority of both the priests and the kings, so both promoted it. Mesopotamian kings, however, were not deified. Alexander the Great permitted the Egyptian priests to honor him as a god, and after his death he was widely regarded as a hero-god.

Julius Caesar had sought divine honors for himself and for the Julian family to which he belonged. The Senate voted him honors with divine implications, including his statues in temples (one statue was inscribed "To the Invincible God") and the title "Jupiter Julius," which combined his name with that of the god Jupiter. In 42 B.C., two years after his death, the Senate bestowed on him the title *Divus Iulius*. Thereafter the Latin word *divus* meant "man-become-god," distinguished from the word *deus*, "god." Man-become-god, as we know, was the basic idea in the Greek hero cults. A comet appeared at the time of Caesar's funeral, and some Romans believed that it signified his apotheosis, his divinization by the gods and the ascension of his spirit to them. Caesar's aim was to change the Roman nation from a republic to a monarchy, and with a divine monarch, such a government was more likely to be accepted, at least in the Greek East.

When Octavian (later called Augustus) became the first Roman emperor, he assumed no divine titles, but he did allow temples to be built in Asia Minor dedicated "to Roma and Augustus." *Dea Roma*, "Goddess Rome," had been honored for two centuries in Greek cities as a sign of alliance with Rome. This new development in Asia Minor was significant in two respects: It set a precedent for the deification of an emperor during his lifetime (instead of after his death), and it was the beginning of combining the worship of Roma and the worship of the emperor as the symbol of loyalty to the state. Augustus established the official cult in some places in the provinces, but not in Italy.

The emperor Domitian claimed divinity for himself, and in the last few years of his reign courtiers and court poets addressed him as "Lord and God." This antagonized philosophers and probably astrologers too, for he twice (in 89 and 93) expelled both groups from Rome. (Emperor Vespasian had expelled astrologers and philosophers from Rome in A.D. 70 because they were critical of his exercise of imperial power.) In

95 Domitian accused the consul Flavius Clemens of "atheism" and had him put to death. Domitian's reign is the beginning of the official Roman view that Christians and pagan philosophers were atheists because they refused to worship the emperor and the state. Jews were spared because Judaism was an old, established monotheistic religion, but new religions were suspect as unpatriotic and rebellious. Dio Cassius, referring to the charge of atheism in Domitian's persecution, said: "On this many others who made shipwreck on Jewish customs were condemned, of whom some were put to death, while others were at the least deprived of their property."[18] *1 Clement* begins: "Because of the sudden and repeated misfortunes and calamities which have befallen us," an apparent reference to the current persecution.

Rome had considered Christianity to be a branch of Judaism and granted it the same privileges as a legal religion, a *religio licita*. But a new development tended to reverse Christians' status. A new temple of Jupiter was built on the Capitoline Hill in Rome and dedicated in 81. The Roman government required Jews to pay to it the half-shekel tax which they had formerly paid to their Jerusalem Temple. Domitian exacted the tax with severity (his successor Nerva abolished it). To escape the tax, gentile Christians must have wanted to prove that they were not Jews, but that cost them their legal status. Thus for practical reasons, Christians were torn between the desire to remain within Judaism and the desire to separate from it.

Domitian required the worship of his statue in the coastal cities of Asia Minor too, as Revelation indicates. There persons who complied were stamped with an official mark on the forehead or right hand; people who lacked the mark could not buy or sell (Rev. 13:16-17).

While Pliny the Younger was governor of the remote province of Bithynia in northern Asia Minor, the populace there raised the question of Christians' loyalty to the state. The resulting official persecution was a local affair, aimed not at the religion but at unpatriotic attitudes which might lead to armed revolt. Pliny reported to Emperor Trajan, asking for guidance in dealing with the situation (ca. 112). In his letter he wrote:

> This is the course I have taken with those who were accused before me as Christians. I asked them whether they were Christians, and if they confessed, I asked them a second and third time with threats of punishment.

If they kept to it, I ordered them for execution; for I held no question that whatever it was that they admitted, in any case obstinacy and unbending perversity deserve to be punished. There were others of like insanity; but as these were Roman citizens, I noted them down to be sent to Rome [this Roman policy explains why Paul appealed to Caesar, Acts 25:11]. . . . several distinct cases arose. An unsigned paper was presented, which gave the names of many. As for those who said that they neither were nor ever had been Christians, I thought it right to let them go, since they recited a prayer to the gods at my dictation, made supplication with incense and wine to your statue, which I had ordered to be brought into court for the purpose together with the images of the gods, and moreover they cursed Christ—things which (so it is said) those who are really Christians cannot be made to do.[19]

In his reply Trajan modified Pliny's policy:

They are not to be sought out, but if they are accused and convicted, they must be punished—yet on this condition, that whoever denies he is a Christian, and makes the fact plain by his action, that is, by worshiping our gods, shall obtain pardon on his repentance, however suspicious his past conduct may be. Papers, however, which are presented unsigned ought not to be admitted in any charge, for they are a very bad example and unworthy of our time.[20]

Two features in Trajan's letter are noteworthy. Trajan apparently is more concerned with the worship of the Roman gods than of himself, and he opposes anonymous accusations. In A.D. 125, while Hadrian was emperor, some informers were making charges against Christians in the province of Asia. Hadrian had no objection if the accusers were willing to make the charges before a court of justice, but he was opposed to mere slander and clamorous outcries. He wrote to the proconsul of Asia about the problem and stated: "If anyone demand a writ of accusation against any of these Christians, merely for the sake of libeling them, you should proceed against that man with heavier penalties, in accordance with his heinous guilt."[21]

During Emperor Trajan's reign the Romans condemned Bishop Ignatius to death and took him to Rome, where he expected to be— and probably was— eaten alive by wild beasts.

He eagerly awaited martyrdom, believing that it assured him of eternal salvation. Polycarp's letter to the Philippians tells us that other condemned Christians were sent with Ignatius. Near the end of Hadrian's reign the bishop of Rome became a martyr (A.D. 138). Polycarp, bishop of Smyrna, was burned to death, the twelfth Christian to suffer martyrdom at Smyrna.

Just how many Christians were executed by the Romans by the middle of the second century is unknown, but evidently their leaders were especially targeted. The methods of torture and execution were unspeakably cruel; Justin summed them up thus: "We are beheaded, and crucified, and exposed to beasts and chains and fire and all other forms of torture."[22] The persecutions were sporadic, and they were more or less localized until the empire-wide persecution by Emperor Decius in 250-251.

Specific persecutions are reflected in various Christian writings. A Christian insertion in the Jewish *Ascension of Isaiah* identifies Nero with Beliar (Satan) and predicts (after the event) that he will persecute some of the Church. He is "a king of iniquity, a murderer of his mother [a clear reference to Nero]—this is the king of this world—and will persecute the plant [the Church] which the twelve apostles of the Beloved will have planted; some of the twelve will be given into his hand" (4:2-3). The last clause evidently is a reference to Peter and probably Paul too; although the Twelve in the synoptic gospels do not include Paul, it soon symbolized the apostles as a whole.

Domitian's persecution underlies several early Christian books: Revelation, Hebrews, and 1 Peter in the New Testament, and *1 Clement* and *Shepherd of Hermas* in the Apostolic Fathers. His persecution is meant in Revelation 13:15 where a beast will "cause those who would not worship the image of the beast to be slain." After Nero's death a popular belief arose that some day he will return to earth from the heavens and rule again. The myth is mentioned in the *Sibylline Oracles.*[23] In Revelation 13 that myth is the basis of the interpretation of Domitian as Nero *redivivus,* that is, that Domitian is Nero, alive again. Nero is "the beast which was wounded by the sword and yet lived" again as Domitian (13:14).

EFFECTS OF PERSECUTION

Encouragement of the Persecuted

When persecuted, Christians needed encouragement. They questioned why God had allowed it to happen, and they had doubts about the Christian faith. Explanations of the adversity provided one type of reassurance. Christians found several reasons for persecution.

1. Persecution is the will of God. "Blessed and noble therefore are all the martyrdoms that have occurred by the will of God."[24] If martyrdom is God's will, it is therefore according to divine plan. Polycarp prays that he be an acceptable sacrifice, just as God "has prepared and foreshown and brought about."[25] The author of Acts may have had this in mind when he ascribed to Paul the remark, "I *must* also see Rome" (19:21).

2. Suffering persecution makes a Christian a real disciple of Jesus. Ignatius wrote, "For when you heard that I was on my way from Syria in chains for our common name and hope, in the hope of being permitted to fight wild beasts in Rome in order that by being permitted I might be able to be a disciple, you were eager to see me."[26]

3. To be a martyr is to follow Jesus' example. "For to this you have been called, because Christ also suffered for you, leaving you an example, that you should follow in his steps" (1 Pet. 2:21). The same idea is in Hebrews 12:1-3. In the *Martyrdom of Polycarp* we find, "We love the martyrs as disciples and imitators of the Lord"[27] and to become a martyr is to "become a sharer with Christ."[28]

4. Enduring persecution is a test of the Christian's faith. "In this rejoice, though now for a little while you may have to suffer various trials, so that the genuineness of your faith, more precious than gold . . . may redound to praise and glory and honor at the revelation [i.e., the coming] of Jesus Christ" (1 Pet. 1:6-7). (See also no. 6 below.)

5. Persecution disciplines the Christian. "It is for discipline that you have to endure" (Heb. 12:7). It develops character and patience: "For what credit is it, if when you do wrong and are beaten for it, that you take it patiently? But if when you do right and suffer for it, you take it patiently, you have God's approval" (1 Pet. 2:20).

6. Persecution is the work of Satan: "Behold, the devil is about to throw some of you into prison so that you may be

tested" (Rev. 2:10). An old Jewish idea was that Satan inflicted evil on people in order to test them. In Job 2 the Adversary, or Satan, afflicts Job to test his faith in God. In Revelation 2 Satan is called the "Devil," the Greek word used to translate Satan in the Septuagint, and his role as tempter and tester is adapted to the problem of explaining Christian persecution.

7. Persecution fulfills Old Testament prophecy. In Romans 8:35 Paul declares that persecution, famine, peril, or sword shall not separate Christians from the love of Christ, and he cites Psalm 44:22 as proof (even though the psalm is speaking of God, not Christ).

8. Persecution of Christians was predicted by Jesus. At least that is the picture in the gospels. Words of encouragement are attributed to Jesus too. In Q we find: "I tell you, my friends, do not fear those who kill the body, and after that have no more that they can do" (Luke 12:4 par).

Those various explanations of their suffering encouraged Christians to endure. Another type of encouragement was the promise of reward. Suffering any type of persecution for being a Christian will be recompensed, but the surest means of attaining blessed immortality is martyrdom: "Whoever loses his life for my sake and the gospel's will save it" (Mark 8:35). "Be faithful unto death, and I will give you the crown of life" (Rev. 2:10). To insure his eternal salvation, Ignatius was eager to become a martyr: "Let me be eaten by the wild beasts, through whom I can reach the presence of God."[29] In the *Shepherd of Hermas* (Vis. 3.1.9) the Lady (the Church personified) asks Hermas to sit on her left, not on her right, because "the seat at the right is a place reserved for others, who have already pleased God and suffered on account of the Name." In *Martyrdom of Polycarp* 2:3 the noble martyrs "despised the world's tortures, [and] at the cost of a single hour [of torture] bought eternal life."

The same view of death caused by persecution was prevalent in Judaism too. The most famous Jewish martyrs were the Maccabees. Philo states the philosophy of persecution thus: "They who desire to consume you will be your unwilling saviors instead of your destroyers."[30]

Further encouragement could be gained by thinking about the eternal punishment awaiting the persecutors. In the *Apocalypse of Peter* the Lord shows his disciples the place of punishment, with different kinds of suffering for different types of the wicked. One group stands in flames up to the waist, scourged by evil spirits, and with worms eating their entrails. They are "those who persecuted the righteous and delivered them up" (27).

Christians varied in their response to persecution. Some believed in resisting to the death. This is the attitude in Revelation and aptly demonstrated by Ignatius. But other Christians, including Paul, advised accommodation with the government:

> Let every person be subject to the governing authorities. For there is no authority except from God, and those that exist have been instituted by God. Therefore he who resists the authorities resists what God has appointed, and those who resist will incur judgment. . . . Pay all of them their dues, taxes to whom taxes are due, . . . honor to whom honor is due (Rom. 13:1-2, 7).

In the synoptic gospels Jesus has a similar attitude toward paying taxes: "Render to Caesar the things that are Caesar's" (Mark 12:17 par). Although 1 Peter urges readers to hold firmly to their faith, it also advises them to be subject to the emperor and governors; "honor the emperor" (2:13-17).

APOSTASY

Numerous factors have caused Jews and Christians to commit apostasy, that is, abandon their religion. One factor is disillusionment with its doctrines or teachings. Another factor is persecution of the religion's adherents. The canonical gospels attest to the fact that both the Jewish and Roman persecutions caused apostasy. Jewish persecution as the cause appears in John 16:1-2: "I have said all this to you to keep you from falling away. They will put you out of the synagogues; . . . whoever kills you will think he is offering service to God." Apostasy resulting from persecution in general is behind Mark 8:38: "For whoever is ashamed of me and of my words in this adulterous and sinful generation, of him will the Son of Man also be ashamed when he comes."

Early Christian writers tried to prevent apostasy by denouncing it and by urging readers to hold firmly to their faith. Rewards are promised to the faithful, and punishment to the unfaithful. "Hold fast what you have, until I [the Son of God] come. He who conquers and keeps my works until the end, I will give him authority over the nations [gentiles], and he shall rule them with a rod of iron" (Rev. 2:25-27).

> If we have died with him, we shall also live with him;
> If we endure, we shall also reign with him;
> If we deny him, he will also deny us (2 Tim. 2:11-12).

These words may have been sung as a hymn to bolster loyalty to the faith in a time of persecution. The classic statement of loyalty is in 2 Timothy 4:7-8: "I have fought the good fight, I have finished the race, I have kept the faith. Henceforth there is laid up for me the crown of righteousness, which the Lord, the righteous judge, will award to me on that Day, and not only to me, but also to all who have loved his coming."

Threat of punishment accompanied promise of reward. We have just observed that the Son of Man will be ashamed of those who are ashamed of him, and Christ Jesus will deny those who have denied him. There is no hope for apostates, even if they repent: "For it is impossible to restore again to repentance those who have once been enlightened, . . . if they then commit apostasy" (Heb. 6:4-6). Christians who have betrayed other Christians have also committed an unpardonable sin. No repentance is allowed for "apostates and betrayers of the church, and men who blasphemed the Lord through their sins, and besides have been ashamed of the Lord's name by which they were called."[31] The "betrayers" evidently were informers such as Pliny mentioned.

The persecutors naturally were regarded as hopeless cases too. Mark 9:42 depicts Jesus as denouncing "whoever causes one of these little ones [Christians] to stumble" [i.e., apostasize; "sin" is not a literal translation].[32]

One explanation of apostasy is that it is the work of the devil:

> Your adversary the devil walks around like a roaring lion, seeking someone to devour. Resist him, firm in your faith, knowing that the same experience of suffering is required of your brotherhood throughout the world (1 Pet. 5:8-9).

In spite of the strenuous efforts made to prevent apostasy, many persons evidently did forsake the faith. That explains why faithful Christians denounced apostasy so sternly.

MARTYROLOGIES AND APOLOGIES

The increasing number of deaths resulting from persecution led to a special type of Christian literature. A martyrology is an account of the suffering, courage, and death of one or more martyrs.

This type of writing had already appeared in Judaism. *4 Maccabees*, written in the first half of the first century A.D., extols the martyrdom of the Maccabees. *Martyrdom of Isaiah*,[33] written in the second century B.C., tells a story of Isaiah's death as a martyr. Both narratives are legendary. The latter half of the Gospel of Mark, beginning with Peter's Confession in chapter 8, is, in effect, a martyrology, for it emphasizes Jesus' Passion.[34] The earliest Christian document that is strictly a martyrology is *Martyrdom of Polycarp* written in mid-second century. Martyrologies served the dual purpose of honoring the martyrs and inspiring the persecuted to endure.

A second special type of Christian writing was the apology. It was written to promote pagan tolerance of Christianity and at least implicitly reassure the Roman government of Christians' loyalty to the state.

When Hadrian came to Asia Minor during the persecution there, Quadratus presented him with an apology. Only a fragment has been preserved in Eusebius' *Ecclesiastical History* (4.3.2). In the fragment Quadratus tries to persuade the emperor of the truth of the Christian religion, demonstrated by "the works of our Savior" consisting of acts of healing and raising the dead. (The latter claim may have only reinforced the Roman view that Christianity is a superstition.) The Athenian philosopher Aristides also addressed an apology to Hadrian. His theme is that the religion of the Christians is much superior to that of the other three "races": barbarians, Greeks, and Jews. Christians have the true concept of God and are distinct in the purity of their morals.

In mid-second century Justin wrote two apologies; the first was addressed to Emperor Antoninus Pius. In the first twelve chapters he states that if Christians refuse to worship the Roman gods, they do so because such worship is foolish. He maintains that fear of eternal punishment makes Christians moral people and reliable supporters of the government. Their moral character suddenly improves after they are converted. In the remainder of his *1 Apology* he defends Christian doctrines and religious practices. In his 2 *Apology*, addressed to the Roman Senate, he blames the persecution of Christians on demons, which hate truth and virtue. God permits that to happen so that Christians can prove by their endurance the superiority of their faith to pagan religion.

Although the Roman persecutions were sporadic and were not empire-wide until the persecution by Decius, many Christians died in them. Nevertheless, their courage and virtuous lives contributed immensely to the rapid growth of the Church. As Tertullian expressed it: "The more we are mowed down by you, the more we grow in number; the blood of Christians is seed."[35]

THE MISSION TO THE GENTILES

IN JUDAISM

Attitudes varied in ancient Judaism in respect to the desirability of winning gentile proselytes. Conservative tradition, with its belief that Jews are God's chosen people and therefore non-Jews are inferior, discouraged the practice. After all, doesn't Yahweh himself regard gentiles as wicked people headed for eternal punishment? Rabbi Shammai was unenthusiastic about converts; Rabbi Eliezer ben Hyrcanus felt the same way because they were prone to revert to their old ways and as gentiles they were naturally bad and inclined to idolatry. Some proselytes were insincere and joined for practical reasons. Also, some abandoned the Jewish faith when conditions were perilous or because they were attracted to Christianity.

On the other hand, a liberal strain in Jewish thought encouraged a Jewish mission to gentiles. If gentiles are liable to spend eternity in hell, then human compassion demands that Jews try to save them. Another cause of proselytizing by Jews and Christians alike was religious pride; success in winning converts was regarded as evidence of the superiority of one's religion.

The roots of the Jewish mission to gentiles are in the Old Testament. In the story of Jonah the people of the pagan city of Nineveh repented and "believed God" when the Lord sent Jonah to preach to it. Jonah is unhappy that God did not punish them, and thus he represents the narrow, exclusive attitude in Ezra and Nehemiah. The author of Jonah, however, held a broader view. The story ends with the people repenting and God forgiving them, much to Jonah's disappointment. Second Isaiah too envisions the salvation of non-Jews, for in it the Lord says to his Servant, "I will give you as a light to the nations, that my salvation may reach to the end of the earth" (Isa. 49:6). Jewish writers held various views somewhere between full acceptance and non-acceptance of gentiles. In Ezekiel 47 the aliens who have resided among the tribes of Israel shall be allotted an inheritance of land among the tribes, but in *Psalms of Solomon* 17 gentiles will no longer live in Palestine after the Messiah comes, because they pollute the land (this idea goes back to Nehemiah's expulsion of gentiles from Palestine, Neh. 13:3).

Hillel and his school gladly accepted proselytes and did not insist on their full knowledge and observance of the Law. Famous is the story of the gentile who came to Hillel and offered to become a convert if "you teach me the whole of the Law while I stand on one foot." Hillel replied, "What you do not like to have done to you, do not do to your fellow. This is the whole of the Law; the rest is commentary on it.'"[1] The Pharisees were noted for traversing "sea and land to make a single proselyte" (Matt. 23:15). Judging from the rabbinic literature, the number of proselytes was considerable and they came from various races and levels of society. Some outstanding rabbis were proselytes themselves, as was Aquila, who translated the Hebrew Scriptures into Greek. Some rabbis were descendants of proselytes, as were Akiba and his disciple Rabbi Meir.

Some proselytes were won over by Jewish missionaries, but others came in through the influence of synagogues, operated by the Pharisees. The services were open to everyone, and a gentile could first attend out of curiosity, then might become interested enough to attend regularly without joining (these were the "men who fear God"); some followed through and joined. Gentiles were attracted by fear of the future judgment day, by the moral standards in Judaism, and by the nature of the synagogue service with its hymns, Scripture reading, and sermon based on an interpretation of the reading. Because a considerable number of the proselytes changed their minds and committed apostasy, the rabbis increasingly emphasized testing them for sincerity of motive when they queried the candidates.

IN CHRISTIANITY

Mission to the Samaritans

The Samaritans had long rejected the Jewish claim that Mount Zion in Jerusalem is the holy mountain on which the Lord should be worshiped and to which he will come and rule when he establishes his kingdom on earth. They maintained that Mount Gerizim in their district is the holy mountain, and therefore they built a temple there in the fourth century B.C. Deuteronomy 12:5-6 instructs the Israelites to "seek the place which the Lord your God will choose . . . to put his name and make his habitation there; . . . and thither you shall bring your burnt offerings and your sacrifices, your tithes . . ." To Jews "the place" is Mount Zion; to Samaritans it is Mount Gerizim. Other disagreements were over the priesthood, ritual, interpretation of the Torah, and the canon. Like the Sadducees, the Samaritans accepted only the Pentateuch as Scripture. The tension between Samaritans and Jews is reflected in John 4:9, 20 and 8:48. Further evidence of it is that Samaritans are classed with gentiles in the Mishnah (*Tohorot* 5:8).

The first non-Jews to join Christianity were Samaritans. Philip and perhaps other apostles, after they fled from Jerusalem, preached to the Samaritans (Acts 8). The mention of Samaria in Acts 1:8 is also evidence of the apostles' success there. The willingness of the Samaritans to believe the apostles' proclamation caused the author of Luke-Acts to portray Samaritans in a very favorable light.[2] In the story in Luke 17:11-19 Jesus heals ten lepers, but only the Samaritan leper is grateful. And who is the man who, in a parable attributed to Jesus, is the model "neighbor" to someone in need? The Good Samaritan, Luke 10. The Gospel of Signs portrays the Samaritan woman as very favorably impressed by Jesus (John 4:29), and the author of John inserted verse 39, "Many Samaritans from that city believed in him . . ."

Considering the background of antipathy between Jews and Samaritans, we logically would expect that the Hellenist apostles' friendly approach to the Samaritans might be questioned by other Jewish Christians. And that is what happened. The Jerusalem Christians sent Peter and John to investigate, but they were soon convinced of the merits of the mission to the Samaritans (Acts 8). The author of Matthew, however, was not persuaded. He portrayed Jesus as teaching the disciples, "Enter not into any city of the Samaritans" (10:5). Mark and Q are noncommittal, for they never mention Samaria or Samaritans. Apparently some Samaritan villages were unfriendly to the apostles because they were Jews, a situation reflected in the story in Luke 9 in which a Samaritan village refuses to receive Jesus because he was going to Jerusalem.

Mission to the Gentiles
1. *Historical beginnings.* Jesus preached to Jews, but not to gentiles, a fact recognized by Paul and the authors of the synoptic gospels. If Jesus had ministered to gentiles, Paul surely would have referred to it as support for his position in his controversy with the Judaizers. Instead we find Paul saying, "Christ became a servant to the circumcised [Jews] to show God's truthfulness" (Rom. 15:8). In the synoptics Jesus does not preach to gentiles. John, written later, does depict Jesus as doing so, but the motivation for the change is clear: to support the gentile mission.

As we have seen, the first apostles to convert gentiles were not Jesus' disciples nor even the Hellenists who were scattered by the Jerusalem persecution. Instead, they were Jewish Christians from Cyprus and Cyrene who came to Antioch (Acts 11). This new development aroused consternation in the Jerusalem church, just as the inclusion of the Samaritans had, and the church sent Barnabas to investigate. Barnabas was converted to the new policy, but he did not return to Jerusalem, and the church there never adopted the new practice.

The conversion of some gentiles in the coastal cities of Palestine is represented in Acts 10 in the story of Cornelius, a Roman centurion. The fact that Cornelius was a "God-fearer" is significant. Gentiles such as the "men who fear God" and the proselytes were familiar with Jewish ideas because they attended the synagogues. In the first few decades of the church, when the apostles were proclaiming that Jesus is the Jewish Messiah, those gentiles who were already devoted to Judaism would be the ones to whom the proclamation would be meaningful.

The fact that Cornelius was a Roman soldier is also significant. The references to Roman soldiers in Mark indicate that they were among the early converts to the Christian message. The presence of the essentially pagan Lord's Supper in Jewish-Christian communities also suggests the inclusion of Roman soldiers in the churches, as we have remarked.

In Galatians 1 and 2 Paul clearly regards his mission as one to the gentiles; he is "entrusted with the gospel to the uncircumcised" (2:7). He says that he is "an apostle to the gentiles" (Rom. 11:13).

Was that the nature of his apostleship from the beginning, or did he first preach in synagogues to mixed audiences? Acts depicts him as preaching in synagogues until, in exasperation, he says at Corinth, "From now on I will go to the gentiles" (18:6). But in the next chapter Paul is preaching in a synagogue again, this time in Ephesus, but again he withdrew because of Jewish opposition (19:9). That some apostles won converts by preaching to mixed congregations is surely true, and especially considering Paul's Pharisaic training, that would be natural for him too. In Acts 9:15 the Lord tells Ananias in a vision that Paul is his chosen instrument "to carry my name before the gentiles and kings and the sons of Israel"; here Paul is seen as an apostle to both gentiles and Jews. Is this picture of Paul in Acts a reflection of history, or is it the result of trying to promote unity between Jewish and gentile Christians?

Did Paul decide at his conversion that his mission would be to gentiles? Hardly. Although the account of Paul's conversion in Acts 26 depicts Jesus as telling him that he will send him to the gentiles, Paul's own account of his ecstatic conversion does not sound like an occasion for such a rational message. Paul says that he "was caught up to the third heaven—whether in the body or out of the body I do not know; God knows," and that he then "heard things that cannot be told, which man may not utter" (2 Cor. 12:2-4). In Galatians 1 Paul does say that God "revealed his Son to me, in order that I might preach him among the gentiles." This is not necessarily a reference to his conversion, however, for Paul states that he had an "abundance of revelations" (2 Cor. 12:7).

When and why did Paul decide that he should be an apostle to the gentiles? Paul and Barnabas taught in the Antioch church for a year before they began their first missionary journey (Acts 11:26). Perhaps the close contact with gentile Christians in that church convinced him that they were worth saving. That experience and the rough treatment he received from Jews probably combined to cause Paul to change from going to Jews and gentiles to appealing to gentiles directly.

How was the mission conducted? By preaching in the synagogues (until the Christians were expelled) and by preaching outdoors wherever anyone would listen. The preaching by Cynic philosophers on street corners may have been a model for apostles. Some apostles, including Paul (Rom. 15:18-19), performed signs and miracles to persuade potential converts, as we have noted. Judging from 1 Corinthians 9, traveling apostles generally were treated as guests by the Christian communities they visited (the Essenes and some pagan religions had a similar practice). Wives who accompanied apostles also were entitled to free food and lodging. Paul boasted that, though he and Barnabas had the right to such support, they earned their own living. Although converts to Judaism and Jewish Christianity had to learn and observe the Law, Paul's gentile converts had to make little intellectual effort to become Christians. In the second century, however, churches were requiring the learning of a catechism.

In the synoptic gospels, including Luke 6, Jesus chooses 12 disciples to be apostles to preach, but in Luke 10:1 he chooses 70 others. Both numbers, 12 and 70, are probably symbolic here, for some scholars have concluded that 12 represents the mission to the Jews (12 disciples replace the 12 tribes of Israel), and 70 represents the gentile mission. The basis for the latter conclusion is that in Judaism 70 represented the gentile world. Using Genesis 10 as the basis of computation, Jews decided that there are 70 nations. Therefore some rabbis thought that when the Law was revealed to Moses, it must have been given in 70 languages.[3]

2. *Support for the gentile mission.* The decision of Paul and some other Jewish Christians to make a special effort to convert gentiles met with strong opposition from some Jews, both Christian and non-Christian, as we have seen. An example of such an opponent is the author of Matthew, who portrays Jesus as follows: "These twelve Jesus sent out, charging them, 'Go nowhere among the gentiles'" (10:5), and in 15:24 Jesus says, "I was sent only to the lost sheep of the house of Israel." Prejudice against gentiles, again placed on Jesus' lips, appears in Matthew 6:7 and 18:17. Even Mark 7:27 portrays Jesus as reluctant to heal the daughter of a gentile.

Paul directly opposed such prejudice by his words and deeds. He eagerly accepted gentiles without requiring their observance of the Torah, and he often stated that gentile Christians and Jewish Christians are equal. "There is no distinction between Jew and Greek; . . . everyone who calls upon the name of the Lord will be saved" (Rom. 10:12-13), and "in Christ Jesus you are all sons of God, through faith. . . . There is neither Jew nor Greek" (Gal. 3:26, 28). Also, if people are Christians, they are sons of Abraham, heirs to the promises God made to Israel (Gal. 3:29); that is, as Christians they have become true Jews. Pauline Christians continued this theme (Eph. 3:6).

Certain pericopes in the gospels portray Jesus as asserting the necessity of the gentile mission. In Mark 13:10 he says that before the end comes "the gospel must first be preached to all nations." In a post-resurrection tradition in Matthew 28:19 Jesus commands the disciples to "Go therefore and make disciples of all nations." See also Matthew 24:14. Thus the synoptic gospels are made to fit the historical situation that Jesus did not preach to gentiles, but some apostles did. At the same time, they depict Jesus as supporting the apostles' mission to the gentiles.

Jewish Christians had to adjust to the new situation. The gentile mission had to be justified, and a rationale for it had to be found. Why has God turned to the gentiles? Paul answers in Romans 9 that it is because Israel wrongly pursued the righteousness that is based on the Law and works, but gentiles have rightly pursued the righteousness that comes through Christian faith. A similar argument is in Galatians 3. The explanation in Ephesians 3:4-6 is that this is "the mystery of Christ" which God did not make known to other generations, but he has now revealed by the Spirit; the "mystery" is that "the gentiles are fellow heirs" with Jews. The author of Ephesians also states: "Remember that at one time you gentiles . . . were alienated from the commonwealth of Israel, . . . having no hope and without God in the world. But now in Christ Jesus you who once were far off have been brought near in the blood of Christ" (2:11-13).

Another explanation was that God has turned to the gentiles because Jews have rejected Jesus, their Messiah. Acts 13:46 ascribes to Paul the statement that "since you thrust it [the word of God, the Christian gospel about Jesus] from you, . . . we turn to the gentiles." This is the point of the parable of the Great Supper in Q.[4] In the parable a man invites many people to a banquet, but they refuse to come; therefore he invites strangers instead. The two groups symbolize the disbelieving Jews and the believing gentiles.

A Jewish argument against the gentile mission was that Jews have been serving God (Yahweh) for centuries, but gentile Christians are only newcomers. Is it not then unfair for God to give the kingdom to gentile Christians equally with Jews or Jewish Christians? Not so, was a Christian answer, because God is like the householder in the parable of the Laborers in the Vineyard (Matt. 20). God, like the householder, has a right to reward equally those who have served him for a long time (Jews) and those who began serving him much later (gentile Christians).

3. *Methods of supporting the gentile mission.* A pericope from the Q source exalts the coastal gentile cities of Tyre and Sidon (where apparently some gentiles were converted) above three Jewish towns, which were not persuaded by the apostles' miracles performed in them.[5] Old Testament analogies were employed too: Elijah and Elisha did not minister to the needy in Israel, but to gentiles (Luke 4:25-27). The gospel stories of Jesus' healing gentiles—and only gentiles—from afar may symbolize the fact that Jesus did not come into direct contact with gentiles.[6] In the case of the centurion who was sure that Jesus could heal his son without seeing him, Jesus says, "Not even in Israel have I found such faith." Numerous scholars have concluded that the gospel stories of Jesus' healing gentiles[7] are intended to foreshadow the gentile mission.

A major method of supporting the gentile mission was to quote and misinterpret the Old Testament, a method used to try to solve so many other apologetic problems of the early Christian communities. Let us look at some examples. Acts 13 represents Paul and Barnabas as saying to hostile Jews that since they thrust the word of God from them, the apostles now turn to the gentiles, as the Lord has said, "I have set you to be a light for the gentiles" (Isa. 49:6). A complicated way to use the Old Testament is in Acts 15, where elements from Amos and Isaiah[8] are combined to state that God will rebuild the dwelling of David so that all the gentiles will seek the Lord, who "made these things known from of old." In their original setting the themes of all these passages are entirely Jewish and have nothing to do with Christianity. The Christian interpretation, however, is that the gentiles will seek the Lord by becoming Christians. Paul misquotes and reinterprets Hosea[9] to claim that gentiles are the ones who were not God's people, but now are his people, "sons of the living God" (Rom. 9:25-26). Paul also uses Old Testament persons as typologies, namely, Abraham (Gal. 3) and Sarah and Hagar (Gal. 4).

The Old Testament was often cited for the same purpose in the second century. In *2 Clement* 2 the author quotes Isaiah 54:1, "For the children of the desolate one will be more than the children of her who has a husband." He interprets that passage by saying, "It meant that our people [the gentiles] seemed to be deserted by God, but now that we have believed, we have become more numerous than those who seemed to have God." Justin too cites that verse. [10] He also cites [11] Psalm 72:17, "all the nations shall bless him" (LXX). He changes the text, however, to read, "all the nations shall be blessed in [or by] him," and then interprets "him" as Christ, whereas in the psalm "him" refers to "the Lord God, the God of Israel."

4. *Gentile vanity.* Paul cautioned gentile Christians against thinking that because God has turned to them, they are better than Jews. You gentiles are only a wild olive shoot that has been grafted on to the olive tree, "so do not boast over the branches" (Rom. 11:17-18). On the other hand, says Paul, you Jews should not imagine that you are superior to gentiles, for "both Jews and Greeks are under the power of sin" (Rom. 3:9).

He cites the Lord's word to Abraham, "I have made you the father of many nations" (Gen. 17:5), to show that the uncircumcised too are descendants of Abraham, and have received righteousness through faith, not circumcision (Rom. 4). Paul also sees hope for the unbelieving Jews (Rom. 11:23-24).

5. *Gentile Christians' adjustment to Judaism.* The Christian missionaries insisted that gentile converts accept certain basic Jewish-Christian beliefs. One of these was the belief that the Jewish Scriptures, as contained in the Septuagint, were inspired by God's Holy Spirit and foretell the coming of Jesus.

Contrary to the polytheistic background of many gentile converts, Jewish-Christian apostles, including Paul, forced them to believe in the existence of only one God, the Lord, Creator of heaven and earth. A Jewish expression of the belief is in *2 Enoch*, "Do not worship unreal gods who made neither heaven nor earth" (2:2). The apostles preached the same belief: "We bring you good news, that you should turn from these vain things to the living God who made the heaven and the earth and the sea and all that is in them" (Acts 14:15). The *Shepherd of Hermas* teaches it also: "First of all, believe that God is one [i.e., there is one God], and he created all things." [12] This monotheism was accompanied by theistic exclusiveness, the belief that it is a sin to worship any other gods, for they are only idols anyway. The one living God was presumed to be the Jewish god, Yahweh, the Lord.

Gentile Christians generally accepted the Jewish idea that Jesus is the Messiah, or Christ, but usually his Jewish nature was diminished or removed. Similarly, Jewish eschatology, with its beliefs in a resurrection of the dead and a judgment day, was modified by some gentile Christians and discarded by others, especially the Gnostics. Gentile Christians adopted the Jewish practice of blessing God, according to Justin.[13] The Jewish practice of repentance was adopted by the Jewish-Christian churches that produced the synoptic gospels and by many gentile Christians. The gentile Justin wrote, "We believe that those who live wickedly and do not repent are punished in everlasting fire."[14]

In the so-called Apostolic Decree in Acts James gives as his judgment that "we should write to them [gentile Christians] to abstain from the pollutions of idols and from unchastity and from what is strangled and from blood" (15:20). This decision was probably made later, for it disagrees with Paul's report in Galatians 2. The features from which gentiles should abstain are typical of Jewish restrictions. Meat from animals which have been strangled is taboo because the blood has not been drained from it. Whether "blood" in the decree refers to eating blood or to shedding blood (murder) has been debated by biblical scholars; it probably refers to eating blood.

Many gentile Christians refused to accept the most nationalistic beliefs of Jewish Christians. In Mark 12 and in *Epistle of Barnabas* 12:10-11 Jesus is not the Son of David, who in Judaism would be a national king. And it was inevitable that many gentiles would throw out the narrow, nationalistic Jewish concept of the kingdom of God. The need to explain and reinterpret the kingdom of God to gentiles may be a factor in the apostolic creation of some gospel parables of the kingdom.

Gentile converts generally had to adjust to the life-style of the Jewish Christians, with its rigorous moral and ethical standards and strict sexual code. Furthermore, those standards were enforced by the churches, as they had been in the synagogues. Gentiles with previous knowledge of and experience with Stoic and Cynic philosophies, with their noble ethical principles, would have little difficulty in adjusting to the Jewish ethics, however. Certain mystery cults had some ethical standards—particularly Orphism and the cults of Mithras and Isis—, but the standards were not so high or broad in scope as in those philosophies and in Judaism. But the Eleusinian mystery cult of Demeter required purity of hand and heart before joining the cult or entering a temple and participating in its ritual.

Gentile Christians were even taught the Jewish and

Jewish-Christian notion that before conversion they were wicked nobodies. 1 Peter 4:3 lists vices alleged to be typical of gentiles, especially licentiousness, drunkenness, and idolatry. Colossians teaches, "You [gentiles], who once were estranged [from God] and hostile in mind, doing evil deeds, he [the Son] has now reconciled in his body of flesh by his death" (1:21-22).

Many disagreements over beliefs and practices existed in early Christianity, and often the disagreements were between Jewish and gentile Christians. Consequently several writers tried to foster unity among various churches and within individual churches. Acts smooths over some of the tensions. The desire to unite Christians is evident in the "new commandment" to "love one another" in John 13:34, inserted by the redactor. Why is it called "a new commandment"? Perhaps the reason is that the gentile-Christian writer intended that this commandment should supplement or even replace the two commandments in Jewish Christianity, namely, to love God and to love your neighbor. The author of Ephesians used material from Paul's letters to write his tract intended to help unify gentile and Jewish Christians.

Some features of Jewish Christianity were reinterpreted by the gentiles. The conspicuous literary example in the New Testament is the Gospel of John. The recent recognition of the Gospel of Signs source in John provides new insight into the process. In Signs Jesus is the Jewish-Christian Messiah, but in the Gnostic sources and in what the author of John wrote, Jesus is a universal Savior, a non-Jewish spirit from heaven, without a Jewish father or mother, temporarily incarnated in a physical body. Instead of being the human Son of God, in John he becomes the spiritual Son of the Father. Also, the kingdom of God no longer has anything to do with Judaism; it is spiritual and is Jesus' kingdom which is not of this world (18:36). Other Christian writers made less drastic changes in the concepts of the Christ and the kingdom of God, but the trend was away from the Jewish concepts. The gentile change in the meaning of the word "Lord" will be described in the next chapter.

6. *Gentile Christians and paganism.* Early Christianity was influenced by its Greek, Roman, and especially Hellenistic environments. "Hellenistic" culture combined Greek and Near Eastern elements. Some Greek and Hellenistic expressions entered Christianity through Hellenistic Jews, Jews who had already combined Hellenistic culture with their Judaism. An

example is the word and concept "conscience," which originated in Stoic philosophy; it appears frequently in the New Testament, including Paul's letters.[15] Another term from the Hellenistic world is "gospel," or "good news" (Greek: *euaggelion*, the source of the English word evangelical). For example, it occurs in a decree of a Greek assembly in the province of Asia (ca. 9 B.C.): "The birthday of the god Augustus was the beginning for the world of the good news [or gospel] that came by reason of him."[16] The expression "eternal salvation" may have been introduced either by Hellenistic Jews or by gentiles.[17] Gentile Christians, however, brought in directly more pagan ideas and practices, which often clashed with the ideas and practices of the Jewish Christians. In 1 Corinthians Paul has preserved for us evidence of the clash; there the problem is the continuation by gentile Christians of the practice of idolatry and eating meat that had been sacrificed to "idols."

Gentiles gradually changed the type of church organization. In contemporary Judaism each community had its council of "elders," or "presbyters," (its oldest men) to supervise its affairs. Jewish Christians passed this arrangement on to the early churches (1 Pet. 5:1-3). Paul and Barnabas appointed elders "in every church" on their joint missionary journey (Acts 14:23). But a bishop, or overseer, was the head of some pagan organizations, and gentile Christians introduced this type of leadership into the churches—1 Timothy 3:1 testifies to this system. At this stage (early second century) some churches still had a council of elders as well as a bishop (1 Tim. 4:14; 5:17; Ignatius, *Phil.* 7:1).

Gentile Christianity exhibits numerous parallels with the Hellenistic mystery cults, especially Mithraism. We have observed that the cult of Mithras was prevalent among Roman soldiers, who were among the converts to Christianity. We should note too that the only Mithraic chapel that archaeologists have found in Palestine was located at Caesarea, and according to Acts, that town early became an important Christian center.[18]

The theology of the Christian Lord's Supper is similar to a ritual in Mithraism. By mid-second century some gentile Christians had adopted other cult features. Justin refers to Christian initiation as "rebirth" and "illumination,"[19] and the same terms were applied to initiation in the cult of Mithras. A graffito written near the baptism basin in the mithraeum under the Santa Prisca church in Rome states that the worshiper was "born at the first light" (*natus prima luce*), that is, at sunrise. When Christians began to have a priest as head of a church, he was called "Father," which was the case in the cult of Mithras.

Even Jewish Christians shifted from Sabbath to Sunday observance: "Those who lived in ancient ways attained a new hope, no longer keeping the Sabbath but observing the Lord's Day."[20] Sun cults existed in the Near East at the time that Christianity began. The planetary week, in which a day of the week was holy to each of the seven planets and the sun god was worshiped on the first day of the week, "already existed in the first century A.D. in the Graeco-Roman world."[21] As Christians, especially gentile Christians, separated from Judaism, they replaced the Sabbath with Sunday, but worshiped Jesus instead of the sun. (Some identified Jesus with the sun, however; for example, in some frescoes in the catacombs at Rome.) The fact that Sunday was sacred to sun gods such as Lord Mithras probably is the source of the practice of calling the first day of the week "the Lord's Day."

The vast majority of the devotees of Mithras, however, did not join Christianity. Instead, Mithraism became a strong rival religion. The story of the three magi (Greek *magoi*) — loosely translated as "wise men" — who follow a star and come to worship Jesus at his birth is designed to represent either Mithraic or Zoroastrian priests, who were called "magi," as recognizing the superiority of Jesus. The story is propaganda against a rival religion. The device is used against the sect of John the Baptist in John 1, where two of John's disciples leave him to follow Jesus.

Pagan influence surely was the cause of the change in the significance of Christian baptism. Instead of being accompanied by repentance, it became an initiation ritual and a means of obtaining divine forgiveness of sins. Tertullian reported that "washing is the channel through which they [Greeks] are initiated into some notorious Isis or Mithras. . . . [also] at the Apollinarian and Eleusinian games they are baptized, and they presume that the effect of their doing that is their rebirth and the remission of the penalties for their sins."[22] Acts 2:38 depicts the new Christian view of baptism as appearing as early as Peter in the Jerusalem church; it is far more probable that it began in a mixed church, just as, we believe, the Lord's Supper did.

7. *Gentile promotion of the faith.* Gentile Christians

were zealous in promoting their religion among non-Christian gentiles. They inherited from Judaism an intolerant attitude toward paganism: its people are wicked and their gods are idols. The attitude was of great assistance in winning converts, especially since it was supported by two other views inherited from Judaism: monotheism and the imminence of a judgment day. The prevalence of pagan mystery cults in the Mediterranean world was a major aid to promotion too. A wide variety of beliefs existed among the pagans, but here is the way the apostles appealed to those gentiles who belonged to mystery religions:

"You are right to believe that it is possible to have a happy eternal life after death, but you won't achieve it the way you are headed. You base your hope on gods that do not exist. We preach the living God, who does exist and who has sent his Son who died for you so that you can have eternal salvation. But God's judgment may come *any day*, so join *now* before it is too late." A powerful, scary message, if you believed it, and it was readily believed in a superstitious world, especially by mystery cult devotees, who were already conditioned to accept it. Later, as church fathers incorporated some Greek and Roman philosophy, the message had more appeal to educated classes.

In the speech he ascribed to Paul at Athens, the author of Luke-Acts appeals to the educated reader by writing a philosophical apology in the style of Aristides and Athenagoras. He also beguiles the Greek reader by quoting Acts 17:28 from the Greek poets Epimenides and Aratus. Monuments have been excavated that read "To the unknown gods." The author of Acts adapts the inscription to fit his purpose by changing the text to read, "To an unknown God" (verse 23).

Other early Christian writers made earnest efforts to win gentiles. The canonical gospels are a modification of a literary format in paganism used to lure converts, namely, the format of a traveling preacher and healer. An example is *The Life of Apollonius of Tyana*, by Philostratus. In it the Pythagorean philosopher, Apollonius, travels about, accompanied by his disciples, teaching, prophesying, casting out demons, healing the sick, and awakening the dead. The Book of Acts and the gospels were written to attract new members by combining history and fiction to demonstrate that Christianity is the best religion. In the second century the volume of Christian promotional literature increased rapidly.

THE DEIFICATION OF JESUS

The early Christian concept of Jesus as the Christ changed from a human Jewish Messiah to a universal divine god. How did this happen? The process was complex, and the development was not in a straight line. The results were more inconsistency in the Christian faith and more controversy.

In the pagan world the masses readily deified humans. In Judaism monotheism usually prevented it, although the Hellenistic Jew Philo went so far as to refer to Moses as a god. An example of gentile eagerness to deify is reported in Acts 14: When Paul healed a cripple at Lystra, the crowds proclaimed, "The gods have come down to us in the likeness of men!" They thought that Barnabas was Zeus and Paul as chief speaker was Hermes. Deification of a human had occurred in the hero cults. Alexander the Great was worshiped in Egypt. Egyptian kings and some Roman emperors claimed divinity for themselves. It was a superstitious world, which philosophers tried to counteract.

IN JEWISH CHRISTIANITY

Certain features in Jewish Christianity helped to prepare the way for Jesus' deification.

Beliefs
Whether faith in Jesus' resurrection was much of a factor is debatable. Being revived from death does not make a person divine in the numerous miracle stories in paganism, Judaism, and Christianity. On the other hand, Near Eastern vegetation deities annually came up from the underworld, and the gods Osiris and Adonis had died and lived again. Nevertheless, death and revivification were not generally characteristic of pagan deities.

The faith that Jesus had ascended to heaven after death would suggest to many gentiles an apotheosis, an elevation by the gods of the deceased to divine status, as in certain hero cults. Some Romans believed that the spirit of Julius Caesar ascended to the heavens at his death and became divine. A Roman declared under oath that he was an eyewitness to the ascension of the spirit of Augustus from the funeral pyre to heaven.

Jewish Christians believed that Jesus performed miracles, as the synoptic gospels and the Gospel of Signs attest. Performance of miracles alone did not prove that one was divine, but deities were generally expected to have the power to accomplish them. The stories in which Jesus performs miracles must have facilitated his deification later. The Jewish-Christian expectation that Jesus as the Christ will do miraculous deeds when he returns could have a similar effect. That expectation resulted partly from the Jewish heritage of the role of the Messiah and partly from the Jewish-Christian belief that God gave Jesus special power at his resurrection/ascension.

Some Jewish Christians believed that Jesus was born from the union of a virgin woman and God's Holy Spirit. Such an event apparently did not necessarily make Jesus divine in their sight, for Jesus is a human Christ in the synoptic gospels. In pagan mythology, however, some deities as well as some outstanding humans were fathered by a god or a divine spirit.

Titles

Jewish Christianity assigned some titles to the human Jesus that suggested divinity to gentile ears.

1. *Son of God.* This title is probably the first of that nature. In Judaism all righteous Jews are sons of God and he is their Father. An Aramaic Pseudo-Daniel text found in Cave 4 at Qumran states: "He shall be hailed the Son of God, and they shall call him Son of the Most High."[1] This manuscript is very fragmentary, but the text is probably speaking of the future Messiah. The same language is applied to Jesus in Luke. In Luke 1:32 Jesus "will be called the Son of the Most High," and in 1:35 he "will be called holy, the Son of God." In 1:32 he is a king to whom "the Lord God will give the throne of his father David." Thus the human Son of David is also the Son of God. In Romans 1:3-4 Jesus is God's Son, and he is human because he has descended from David. References to God as Jesus' Father do not necessarily imply Jesus' divinity, for Paul often

wrote "God our Father,"[2] and thus God is the Father of humans too.

The doctrine that Jesus became God's Son, either at Jesus' baptism or resurrection/ascension, was a Jewish-Christian adaptation of the Israelite notion that Yahweh adopted a new king as his son at the king's coronation. The doctrine was prevalent among Jewish Christians in the first and second centuries and continued even among some gentile Christians, especially in Rome, Syria, and Armenia.

Although in Jewish Christianity "Son of God" generally denoted the human Christ, the author of Hebrews viewed Jesus as a supernatural Son of God. In 4:14 Jesus has that title, and in chapter 1 he is God's Son through whom God created the world. The author probably was an Alexandrian Jewish Christian, as we have remarked. He has moved the title in a supernatural direction more than most other Jewish Christians of his day.

2. *Lord.* The Greek word *kurios*, "lord" or "master," could apply to any man who controlled something, as "the master of the house" (Mark 13:35), "the owner of the vineyard" (Mark 12:9), "the master of the servant" or slave (Luke 12:46), and "Lord of the Sabbath" (Mark 2:28). *Kurios* was used also as a respectful form of address, equivalent to our "Sir" (Mark 7:28), including use by disciples to address their teacher (Acts 1:6 and often in the synoptic gospels).

In Near Eastern languages and in Greek the term "Lord" was readily applied to kings, who were masters of their nations. The title was easily given to gods, who were masters of kings, of various aspects of human life, and even of the whole world. The god of the Assyrian kings was "Lord Assur" (or Ashur). The Syrians gave the Greek god Apollo the title *Mara*, "Lord."[3] Gods of some Hellenistic mystery cults were called "Lord": for example, "Lord Mithras" in the *Mithras Liturgy* and "Lord Sarapis" in papyri.[4] In inscriptions various Greek gods are called *kurios.*[5] The name of one Near Eastern god, Adonis, was simply "Lord," for Adonis means Lord.

Matthew, written by a Jewish Christian, never refers to Jesus as "Lord" in a religious sense. But James, a Jewish-Christian epistle written a few years later in a different Christian community, freely refers to Jesus as "our Lord" and "the Lord." The *Doctrina* and *Didache* are also Jewish-Christian writings (A.D. 100 and 150, resp.) that refer to Jesus as "our Lord."[6]

Jesus is first called Lord in a religious sense on the lips of Stephen, but that may be an anachronism. Paul not only applies the title to Jesus in a religious sense, but regards the belief as basic Christian faith: "We preach . . . Jesus Christ as Lord" (2 Cor. 4:5); "If you confess with your lips that Jesus is Lord and believe in your heart that God raised him from the dead, you will be saved" (Rom. 10:9); "No one can say, 'Jesus is Lord,' except by the Holy Spirit" (1 Cor. 12:3). In a non-Pauline insertion in Philippians Jesus Christ is Lord. Jesus is Lord frequently in Acts. In Revelation 17:14 the Lamb (Jesus) is "Lord of lords and King of kings." Jesus has the same title in the Apostolic Fathers.

What is the source of "Lord" as a title for Jesus in a religious sense? One theory is that the source is the use of Old Testament quotations by Christians to support their claims for Jesus. Psalm 110:1 is especially suspect as a source because it is quoted in Acts 2:34 to support the claim that Scripture prophesies Jesus' ascension, and in Mark 12:36 it is quoted in an ingenious attempt to prove that the Christ is not the Son of David. In both cases the words, "the Lord said to my lord" is misunderstood as meaning that the Lord God spoke to the Lord Jesus, ignoring the setting of the Psalm. In Acts 2:36 the quotation is interpreted as proving that God has made Jesus Lord as well as Christ. Paul in Romans 10:13 cites Joel 2:32, "Everyone who calls upon the name of the Lord will be saved," and treats it as a reference to Jesus.

The theory that the Old Testament is the source of Jesus' title "Lord" has serious weaknesses. Christians never treated consistently the passages there in which the Lord speaks. They accepted "Lord" as referring to God, not Jesus, in the vast majority of instances, and often quoted them as words of God. Also, when they did apply passages to Jesus, they freely chose verses in which the Lord was not speaking. The overall pattern of early Christian use of the Old Testament indicates that the belief that Jesus was Lord came first, and afterwards the belief became a basis for selecting prooftexts.

Since Paul's letters are the earliest Christian writings that have come down to us, let us look for clues in his use of the title. First, we find that he too usually accepts the term in his scriptural quotations as meaning God. He quotes the Old Testament most in Romans, and there the term denotes God in four passages and Jesus in only one.[7] Second, we find in Paul that

"Lord" is often associated with ideas that are similar to those in some pagan religious cults. "The Lord's Supper" (1 Cor. 11:20) reminds us of the sacred dinner to which the Lord Sarapis invited his worshipers. As in some cults, mystic union with the deity at the meal is understood in 1 Corinthians 10:21: "You cannot drink the cup of the Lord and the cup of demons. You cannot partake of the table of the Lord and the table of demons." Also, Paul associates the title with his spiritual mysticism: "He who is united to the Lord becomes one spirit with him" (1 Cor. 6:17). "While we are at home in the body we are away from the Lord, . . . we would rather be away from the body and at home with the Lord" (2 Cor. 5:6-8). "Now the Lord is the Spirit, and where the Spirit of the Lord is, there is freedom" (2 Cor. 3:17).

Paul's repeated association of "Lord" with this gentile type of physical and spiritual union with Jesus can hardly be accidental. He has provided an important clue to the origin of "Lord" as a religious title for Jesus. It is an adaptation of pagan mystery cult usage that he and especially his gentile converts knew.

After the title had been assigned to Jesus, Christians found it easy to select Old Testament verses in which the Lord [God] was speaking and interpret them as prophecies made by Jesus. Even acts of the Lord in the Scriptures could inspire stories about Jesus' life. A passage in the Psalms apparently suggested the narrative of Jesus' stilling the storm (Mark 4:37-41):

> Then they cried to the Lord in their trouble,
> And he delivered them from their distress.
> He made the storm be still,
> And the waves of the sea were hushed (Ps. 107:28-29).

Gentile Christians varied in regard to the application of Lord as a title. Justin limits it to "God the Father and Lord of all" (*1 Apol.* 40). *Barnabas* applies it to both God and Jesus. In *Hermas* "the Lord" occurs often as a name for Jesus.

3. *Son of Man.* This title was given to Jesus by some — and accepted by only some — Jewish Christians, as the synoptic gospels and Acts 7:56 demonstrate. We have described this development in our discussion of the Christian problem of Jesus as the Christ. The concept of Jesus as the Son of Man prepared the way for Jesus' deification by adding such supernatural features as his preexistence with God from the beginning of the universe and his future immortal existence on earth after

he descends to conduct the Judgment. In the synoptic gospels, however, the Son of Man is not preexistent. That is to be expected, for a Jesus who has existed in the heavens since the creation of the cosmos would be inconsistent with a Jesus born on earth. The synoptists and their sources selected from the Jewish Son of Man tradition only those features that served to support their belief that Jesus will come down from heaven.

4. *Savior.* In both the Jewish and gentile environments the idea and often the title of Savior were applied to kings and gods who saved their people from adversities. In the Old Testament the Lord is often "the God of my salvation," as in Isaiah 12 and Psalm 25; he is Israel's "Savior" (Jer. 14:8). God is the Savior in the Apocrypha (e.g., Wisd. 16:7). But humans too can be Saviors in the Old Testament and elsewhere.[8] Although the Jewish Messiah's role will be that of a savior, Jews in Hellenistic times tended to reserve the title for God. In the gentile world both kings and gods could be called "Savior."[9]

"Savior" as a title for Jesus appeared slowly in Jewish Christianity. It does not occur in Paul (except in Phil. 3:20), Mark, and Q, which are our earliest sources. In Luke-Acts Jesus is a Savior of Israel, which fits the human Messiah.[10] In the Gospel of Signs source in John, Jesus is "the Savior of the world" (4:42).

IN GENTILE CHRISTIANITY

Gentile Christians tended to interpret the virgin birth, miracles, resurrection, and ascension of Jesus as evidence of his divinity. In Jewish Christianity these features did not automatically make Jesus a god, but gentile Christians knew of gods and hero-gods who had done such things. Many gentiles had even worshiped such deities.

Titles

Titles of Jesus underwent a similar process. Titles used in Jewish Christianity became in gentile Christianity marks of divinity.

In our first chapter on Jesus as the Christ we pointed out that in paganism legends arose in which certain famous men were literally sons of gods. The Roman emperors Augustus and Domitian accepted for themselves the titles "Son of the Divine" and "Son of God," respectively. We are not surprised that

347

gentile Christians soon reinterpreted the messianic title, "Son of God," as a title of a divine Jesus. In John 20:31 the author of the Gospel of Signs confesses that he wrote "that you may believe that Jesus is the Christ, the Son of God." In the light of verse 28, in which the doubting Thomas acknowledges Jesus as "My Lord and my God," the gentile author of the Gospel of John regards both "Christ" and "Son of God" as divine titles. The *Shepherd of Hermas* states that "all creation is sustained by the Son of God,"[11] hardly the act of a human Messiah. The authors of John and 1 John describe Jesus as "the only begotten Son of God."[12] This clearly distinguishes him from any other alleged Son of God or any human son of God.

The title Lord in a cultic sense had been applied to Jesus by some Hellenistic Jewish Christians, especially Paul, and we are not surprised that some gentile Christians made it definitely a divine title. In John 20:20 Jesus is "Lord," and in verse 28 Thomas's confession is the climax of the original Gospel of John. The insertion in Philippians 2 may well have been made by a gentile Christian. It goes as far as anyone can go in its view that the Lord Jesus is a god:

At the name of Jesus every knee should bow, in heaven and on earth and under the earth, and every tongue confess that Jesus Christ is Lord, to the glory of God the Father (2:10-11).

Nevertheless, Justin, although a gentile, follows the Old Testament practice of reserving the title Lord for God himself. That must have been the practice in his church as well, for he states that Christians are baptized "in the name of God the Father and Lord of the universe, and of our Savior Jesus Christ, and the Holy Spirit" (*1 Apol.* 61).

Gentile Christianity in the second century often assumed that in many Old Testament passages "the Lord said" refers to the Spirit of the Lord Jesus speaking to the ancient prophet. This is stated explicitly in *Barnabas:* "For the Master [Greek: *despotes*; the author uses it synonymously with *kurios*, Lord] made known to us through the prophets things past and things present and has given us the first fruits of the taste of things to come" (1:7). Justin quotes some Old Testament passages as "spoken from the person of the Father" (*1 Apol.* 37), but in others "the words are spoken as from the person of Christ" (*1 Apol.* 49).

In the pagan world the cult deities Asclepios, Sarapis,

and Isis were Saviors.[13] The deified Julius Caesar and the emperors Augustus and Nero were called "Savior." Some gentile Christians bestowed the same title on Jesus; it is in Ignatius, *Philadelphians* 9:2. The title occurs often in the Pastoral Epistles and 2 Peter; in two instances the authors go so far as to claim that Jesus is "our God and Savior."[14] Whether the Pastorals and 2 Peter were written by Jewish or gentile Christians may be debatable, but the extreme position that Jesus is "our God" points to gentile-Christian authorship.

THE NAME

The belief was prevalent in the ancient world that the essence of a person resided in his name. The name was virtually identical with the person; in ancient Egypt, if a pharaoh's name was erased from all his monuments, he ceased to exist.[15] By invoking the name of a deity, an individual secured the deity's power for his own benefit. Also, calling on the name of a god could be an essential aspect of devotion to him. When Abram built an altar to Yahweh, he called on his name (Gen. 12:8); when Israel rebelled against Yahweh, it failed to call on his name (Isa. 65:1-2). Devotion to the Lord's name continues in the Apocrypha: "Bless the name of the Lord" (Sirach 39:35); "they sang hymns, O Lord, to your holy name" (Wisd. Sol. 10:20). In *1 Enoch* 39:7 the righteous "will praise the name of the Lord of Spirits" (God).

Devotion to God's name continued in Jewish Christianity. We are all familiar with "Hallowed be your name" in the Lord's Prayer, which is from the Q source.[16] The author of *1 Clement* asks God that "we may be obedient to your almighty and glorious name" (60:4). And in *Didache* 10:2: "We give thanks to you, O Holy Father, for your holy name which you have caused to dwell in our hearts."

Hellenistic Jewish Christians soon attached so much importance to Jesus' name that it rivaled the power of God's name. The apostles preached in the name of Jesus (Acts 5:40); they baptized in the name of Jesus (Acts 2:38). Jesus' name was even basic for salvation: "There is salvation in no one else, for there is no other name under heaven given among men by which we must be saved" (Acts 4:12). In the Old Testament Naamen thought that the proper way to cure leprosy was to call on the name of the Lord, Yahweh (2 Kings 5:11). In the New

Testament the disciples cast out demons (Luke 10:17), the apostles heal the lame (Acts 3) and perform signs and wonders (Acts 4:30)—all through the name of Jesus. Matthew too witnesses to the practice: "On that day [of judgment] many will say to me, 'Lord, Lord, did we not prophesy in your name, and cast out demons in your name, and do mighty works in your name?'" (7:22; those people will not enter the kingdom of God, however, if they have not done the will of Jesus' Father in heaven). Colossians 3:17 goes so far as to advise: "Whatever you do, in word or deed, do *everything* in the name of the Lord Jesus."

Gentile Christians too regarded a name as a powerful force. In parts of John it is the Father's name that is vital: Jesus says he has come "in the name of my Father" (5:43); "the works which I do in the name of my Father, these witness concerning me" (10:25). In chapter 17 the Father has given his own name to Jesus, who in turn has made it known to the men whom the Father gave to Jesus from the world. But in other passages in John it is Jesus' name which is important: He who has not believed in the name of the only-begotten Son of God is already condemned (3:18); "whatever you ask the Father in my name, he will give it to you" (15:16; Jesus gives it in 14:14). The author wrote so that "believing you may have [eternal] life in his [Jesus'] name" (20:31).

Justin states that "many of our Christian men [are] exorcising them [demons] in the name of Jesus Christ."17 *Hermas* testifies that baptism at Rome was "in the name of the Lord," that Christians there "know the name of the Son of God"; and that "a man cannot enter the kingdom of God in any way other than through the name of his Son."18

PREEXISTENCE

Preexistence of Jesus in General

Jesus, though the Son of Man, is not preexistent in the synoptics. Paul too did not believe in a preexistent Jesus, either as the Son of Man or as any other type of Christ (see Romans 1); three later insertions into his letters give us a false impression of his christology, for they represent Jesus as preexistent: Jesus, "who, though he was in the form of God, . . . emptied himself, taking the form of a servant, being born in the likeness of men" (Phil. 2:6-7). "He [the Son] is the image of the invisible God [a

Platonic notion], the first-born of all creation; for by him all things were created, in heaven and on earth, visible and invisible, . . . all things were created through him and for him" (Col. 1:15-16). "Yet for us there is one God, the Father, from whom are all things and for whom we exist, and one Lord, Jesus Christ, through whom are all things and through whom we exist" (1 Cor. 8:6).

In sharp contrast to the synoptic gospels is the Gospel of John with its threefold basis for the preexistence of Jesus: As the Son of the Father he prays, "Father, glorify me . . . with the glory which I had with you before the world was made" (17:5). As the Son of Man he asks, "Then what if you were to see the Son of Man ascending where he was before?" (6:62). As the Word "he was in the beginning with God" (1:2). Jesus' preexistence is understood in "before Abraham was, I am" (John 8:58).

In Hebrews 1:2 we find: "In these last days he [God] has spoken to us by a Son, . . . through whom also he created the world," and in verse 6 the Son is God's "first-born." In 1 John 1:1 Jesus is "the Word of life" which was from the beginning. Ignatius too believed in Jesus' preexistence: "Jesus Christ, who from eternity was with the Father."[19]

Belief in Jesus' preexistence required some sort of Incarnation doctrine to explain how Jesus came down and appeared on earth. But the Incarnation conflicted with both the completely human Christ of the Gospel of Mark and the Virgin Birth of the Christ in the other synoptics. How can these beliefs be reconciled? Ignatius boldly combined them in one sentence, ignoring the fact that they are contradictory: Jesus Christ our Lord is "of flesh and of spirit, born and unborn, God become incarnate, true life in death, sprung from Mary and from God" (*Eph.* 7:2). Sometimes church fathers, following Paul, explained similar paradoxes and problems as "a mystery" of God.

Preexistence of Jesus as the Logos

Preexistence did not necessarily imply that Jesus was God's agent at the Creation—at least that function is not mentioned in John outside the Prologue nor in the insertion in Philippians nor in Justin. Although Justin believes that Jesus is the Word, the first-born of God and God's only-begotten Son,[20] he says nothing of Jesus' having a role in the Creation; instead he repeatedly refers to God as "the Maker of the universe."

351

From a non-preexistent Christ in Paul's letters and the synoptics, Christian faith shifted towards widespread acceptance of a Christ who was with God from the very beginning. This development alone was enough to make Jesus divine.

How Jesus Became the Logos

What are the sources of the belief that Jesus is God's Word, or Logos, through whom God created or made the universe? Apparently the sources are to be found in two different streams of thought:

1. *A god created the universe by his speech or word.* The earliest example is in the theology of the priests in Memphis in ancient Egypt (second millennium B.C.). They taught that the god Ptah is "the Creator of All." He created by conceiving ideas in his heart and expressing them with his tongue. Thus his words objectified his ideas and made them become reality. The god Atum was the agent of his will in accomplishing the creation; later the gods Horus and Thoth replaced Atum as the agent.[21] The text of the Memphite Theology was inscribed on a granite block in the eighth century B.C. by the order of King Shabako. We speculate that the myth may have been known in a Hellenized form in Egypt when Christianity arose. (Who knows what may have been in the large libraries at Alexandria, which regrettably have not survived?)

Jewish priests composed the Creation story in Genesis 1, probably during the Exile, for it has numerous features paralleled in the Babylonian Creation Epic. In this story God creates the cosmos and all that is in it by uttering commands such as "Let there be light." His speech is not called "Word," and it is not personified nor regarded as his agent; God creates directly. Jewish writers later tended to say that God made everything by his "word," as in Psalm 33 and Wisdom of Solomon 9.

2. *The material world is inferior to the spiritual world, so God, who is spirit, must have made the world indirectly through an intermediary.* In philosophic dualism spirit is superior to matter, and therefore God is Spirit and the world is inferior or even evil, and the body is inferior to the soul. The roots of that dualism are in certain ancient Greek philosophies: Orphism, Platonism, and Neopythagoreanism. Plato wrote that if anyone could rise up above the air and see both worlds, "the things in that world above would be seen to be superior to those

in this world of ours."[22]

Philo combined dualism and traditional Judaism, to some degree. He said that God made the material world in the pattern of the immaterial world, and accomplished this by means of the Logos. His Logos is not just speech, but God's Thought or Reason.[23] Thus the Logos is a philosophical concept. It is the intermediary between God and the world. Philo calls the Logos "Son of God," "Paraclete," "Mediator," and even "God."[24]

Poimandres is a semi-Gnostic, non-Christian tractate written in Egypt, probably in the second century A.D. Some of its ideas likely were in the environment in which John was written. It too unites the two streams of thought, adapting a few elements of Genesis 1 to its Gnostic framework. In *Poimandres* God is Mind and Light, "and the luminous Logos which came out of Mind is the Son of God" (6). *Poimandres* contains a hymn with this line: "Holy are you [God], who by Logos has constituted all existing things" (31).

This line of thought appears in Christianity in the Christian Gnostic hymn in John's Prologue. The hymnist reinterpreted the Logos at Creation as Jesus himself. Now it is Jesus who was the Word with God at the beginning and through whom God caused all things to come into existence. The Incarnation doctrine is the result. "And the Word became flesh and dwelt among us, . . . the only begotten from the Father" (1:14). Jesus is now even called "God," not only by the new interpretation of the Jewish poem (verse 1), but also by the hymnist's direct statement in verse 18, where Jesus is "the only-begotten God" (not Son) in the earlier manuscripts. Deification has gone as far as it can go. And thus the Christian Logos doctrine was born!

Why did the Gnostic hymnist interpret Jesus in that manner? As a Gnostic believing in the dualism between the spiritual and physical worlds, he was glad to put distance between the physical world and God: God thus made the world through a Mediator, without having direct contact with it, and Jesus is that spirit which was temporarily in a human body, but without human parents.

A related Jewish idea was that the first thing that God created was Wisdom, which too was virtually personified. This concept is in Proverbs: "The Lord created me at the beginning of his work, the first of his acts of old. . . . When he established the heavens, I was there. . . . When he marked out the foundations of the earth, then I was beside him" (8:22-30). Late in the first century B.C. in the Wisdom of Solomon, God's Word and God's Wisdom are synonymous:

O God of my fathers and Lord of mercy,
who has made all things by your Word,
and by your Wisdom has formed man (9:1-2)

Here Wisdom acquires the basic attribute of the Word: it was God's agent at the Creation.

The Jewish poem in the Prologue in John says this about the Word: "It came to its own and its own did not receive it." What does that mean? The poet's reasoning is clear in John 1:10-11. The world is the Word's own because the world was made through the Word, but (tragically) the world did not receive God's Word.

DIVINE ATTRIBUTES AND FUNCTIONS

As time passed, more and more divine attributes and functions were assigned to Jesus. For example, exorcists usually cast out demons in the name of someone more powerful than themselves, but in Mark Jesus does it on his own authority (5:8; 9:25).

Omniscience was a characteristic of ancient deities. Justin believed that "foreknowing all that shall be done by all men" is a characteristic of God (*1 Apol.* 44). In John Jesus is omniscient: "He himself knew what was in man" (2:25); his disciples said, ". . . we know that you know all things and need none to question you; by this we believe that you came from God" (16:29-30).

To most Jews and early Christians, God will be the judge when the new kingdom comes, but in Matthew's parable of the Last Judgment (25), the Son of Man (Jesus) will be the judge. Generally in biblical traditions God and angels have glory, but in that parable the Son of Man will come in his glory and sit on his glorious throne. Also as the Son of Man, Jesus has the authority to forgive sins (Mark 2), a claim which automatically raised the opposition of the scribes, for that was a function of God. The claim probably was suggested by the role of the Son of Man as judge, as the story's identification of Jesus with the Son of Man suggests. The same theme occurs in Luke 7:48-49, however, where Jesus is not called the Son of Man; in this pericope, later than Mark, the connection with the Son of Man has dropped out. Cf. James 5:9.

The kingdom of God tended to become the kingdom of Jesus. Jesus does not proclaim the kingdom of God in John; instead he announces, "MY kingdom is not of this world" (18:36). Paul in Colossians 4:11 mentions the kingdom of God, but in someone's insertion the kingdom has become "the kingdom of his beloved Son" (1:13).

Three times in John Jesus says "I AM" (*ego eimi* in Greek) in a special sense that indicates divinity.[25] The English translation "I am he" is erroneous and conceals the significance of the expression, which in these passages is a title. Jesus' announcement of it causes Jews to want to stone him (8:59) and those who came to arrest him to fall to the ground in awe (18:6). Why? Exodus provides the answer. There it is a term for God in his epiphany at the burning bush. God said to Moses, "Say this to the people of Israel, 'I AM has sent me to you'" (3:14). In one of the passages in John, Jesus says, "Before Abraham was, I AM." Here Jesus' age, in addition to the title, is important. The belief was prevalent that age bestowed authority, so the most powerful gods were the oldest. Therefore myths and genealogies were created to establish a deity's antiquity; John's method is to have Jesus declare it.

John also depicts Jesus as a boastful god (unlike the synoptic portrait). Jesus proclaims: "I am the light of the world"; "I am the good shepherd"; "I am the resurrection and the life"; "I am the door of the sheep; all who came before me are thieves and robbers" (chaps. 8-11). Those assertions remind us of the boasts of the goddess Isis in one of her aretalogies: "I gave and ordained laws for men"; "I made strong the right"; "I broke down the governments of tyrants"; "I made an end to murders"; "I overcame Fate."[26]

Worshiping or praying to Jesus was a major development; it definitely made Christianity a religion separate from Judaism. When Stephen was dying, he prayed, "Lord Jesus, receive my spirit" (Acts 7:59). Whether Stephen said this is uncertain, but Christians who read it were certain to regard it as evidence of Jesus' divinity. Worship of Jesus reaches a definite climax in the Philippians insertion wherein every knee should bow at the name of Jesus and every tongue confess that he is Lord (2:10-11). That passage surely draws upon Isaiah 45:22-23, where the Lord says that there is no other God than he and that "To me every knee shall bow and every tongue shall swear." Clearly the author of the hymn insertion knew that he was assigning to the Lord Jesus honor that the Old Testament assigns to the Lord God.

Jesus is first called God in the Gnostic hymn used as a source in the Prologue of John. John also contains the post-resurrection story of the confession of faith by the doubting Thomas, "My Lord and my God," even as Emperor Domitian's courtiers were instructed to address the emperor as "Lord and God."

In the second century Jesus was called God with increasing frequency. In Titus 2:13 Christians are "awaiting our blessed hope, the appearing of the glory of our great God and Savior Jesus Christ." 2 Peter is addressed to those "who have obtained a faith . . . in the righteousness of our God and Savior Jesus Christ" (1:1). Ignatius repeatedly calls Jesus "God."[27] Justin asserts that the Scriptures prove that Christ suffered, is worshiped, and is God.[28]

When gentile Christians honored Jesus as God and worshiped him, he was fully deified. Only the Christian Gnostics carried the process farther.

RESULTS OF DEIFICATION

Deification raised Jesus from the status of future Jewish national king to present universal god offering salvation to the whole world. It enabled Christianity to prosper as an international religion instead of a Jewish sect. It definitely separated Christianity from Judaism and made it a new religion, with a broader theological basis and wider appeal.

Nevertheless, deification caused some serious problems. First, among the more sensible persons, both Jewish and gentile, it added to doubts about the truth of the religion. How can a religion be valid when it is so superstitious as to believe either that a man has become a god, or was born a god, or that Jesus was a divine spirit which descended from heaven and took the form and appearance of a man?

As apostles had been asked for signs that Jesus was the Christ, now Christians in general were asked for evidence that he was divine. The author of John made a strenuous effort to find "testimony" that Jesus is the Son of God the Father, and he found a variety: "These works which I do testify concerning me that the Father has sent me" (5:36). "The Father who sent me has testified concerning me" (5:37). "You search the Scriptures, . . . and it is they that testify about me" (5:39). "You sent to John, and he has testified to the truth" (5:33). The Paraclete, or Counselor, the Spirit of Truth, "will testify concerning me" (15:26). "And you [disciples/apostles] also testify, because you have been with me from the beginning" (15:27). Actually, none of the above was evidence of Jesus' divinity; valid evidence was lacking.

Deification caused some crucial theological problems. Christianity began as a monotheistic religion, and belief in only one God was as mandatory in Jewish Christianity as it was in Judaism. Not only the worship of two gods, but even the belief in the existence of two was blasphemy and utterly reprehensible. Jewish consternation at the claim of Jesus' divinity is reflected in John. In 5:18 Jews sought ways to kill Jesus not only because he broke the Sabbath, but also because "he called God his Father, making himself equal with God." "The Jews answered him, 'We stone you for no good work, but for blasphemy; because you, being a man, make yourself God'" (10:33). Here, as elsewhere, experiences of the early church are set back into Jesus' life.

"I and the Father are one," we read in John 10:30. Many biblical scholars and laymen have interpreted that as meaning that Jesus and God are one person, one god. But two kinds of evidence do not support that interpretation. "One" here is the Greek *hen*, neuter gender, whereas when the word refers to God as a person, it is masculine in gender, *heis*, as in John 8:41. Also, in John 17:21 Jesus prays that the disciples "may be one [neuter], even as you, Father, are in me and I in you, that they also may be in us." And in 17:22 he prays that the disciples "may be one [neuter] even as we are one" [neuter]. Clearly 'one' in the neuter gender in these passages is not referring to being divine, but to being in mystic union with each other: disciples, Father, Son. This is demonstrated by both the neuter gender and the inclusion of the disciples on the same basis as the Father and Son. (But see John 14:9-11 below.)

Even among Christians who believed in Jesus' divinity there was theological disagreement. Is Jesus equal to God or subordinate to him? In some passages in John Jesus has virtual equality: "For just as the Father raises the dead and makes them alive, so also the Son makes alive whom he wishes. For the

Father judges no one, but has given all judgment to the Son in order that all may honor the Son even as they honor the Father. He who does not honor the Son does not honor the Father who sent him" (5:21-23). The doctrine that Jesus is the Logos through whom God made the universe also threatened monotheism by virtually creating a second Creator God. Elsewhere in the New Testament Jesus is subordinate to God.

To believe that Jesus is equal to God is even more unorthodox than simply regarding him as divine. Therefore some writers were careful to make Jesus subordinate. The authors of the synoptic gospels and some of their sources regarded Jesus as human. Consequently they present Jesus as entirely subordinate: "Why do you call me good? No one is good but God alone" (Mark 10:18). The time of Jesus' return is known only to the Father, not to angels or the Son (Mark 13:32). In Gethsemane Jesus prays to the Father, "Remove this cup from me; yet not what I will, but what you will" (Mark 14:36). The supremacy of God is preserved in the early belief that God raised Jesus from the dead—Jesus did not arise through his own power.[29] Paul taught that after Christ returns, he will deliver the kingdom to God, and as the Son he will be subjected to God the Father (1 Cor. 15:24-28).

After Jesus was viewed as divine, the threat to monotheism provided a new incentive for keeping Jesus subordinate; this is a prominent theme in John (except in the passages above). In 14:28 Jesus says, "the Father is greater than I," and in 14:10, "The words that I say to you I do not speak on my own authority." "The Son of Man can do nothing of his own accord, but only what he sees the Father doing" (John 5:19). "I have come down from heaven, not to do my own will, but the will of him who sent me" (6:38). One method of keeping God superior is to emphasize that Jesus is only the mediator: "For there is one God, and there is one mediator between God and men, the man Christ Jesus" (1 Tim. 2:5). Ignatius advised Christians: "Subordinate yourselves to the bishop and to one another, as Jesus Christ in the flesh did to the Father."[30] Justin and others subordinated Jesus by stressing that God existed before Jesus did: God is "unbegotten" and Jesus was "begotten" by him (2 Apol. 6).

The problem of the relationship between God and Jesus—and eventually the Holy Spirit was added—led to grouping them together, one way or another. In Acts 2:38

baptism is in the name of Jesus Christ only; after baptism converts receive the Holy Spirit. In 1 Corinthians 6:11, however, baptism is "in the name of the Lord Jesus Christ and in the Spirit of our God." In Matthew 28:19 baptism is to be performed in the name of three: the Father, Son, and Holy Spirit. Why did the number grow to three, thus forming a triad?

Triads were popular in antiquity; in ancient Egypt the deities Isis, her consort Osiris, and their son Horus formed a triad. Christians gradually began to formulate one of their own, consisting of God the Father, Jesus Christ the Son, and God's Holy Spirit. This triad appears as early as Paul's letters and continues in *1 Clement*, Ignatius, and 1 Peter.[31] The three continued to be grouped together in Jewish Christianity as well as in gentile Christianity: "You will attain the crown through our Lord Jesus Christ, who reigns and rules with God the Father and the Holy Spirit for ever and ever" (*Doctrina* 6:2). Baptism is in the name of the Father, Son, and Holy Spirit in *Didache* 7:1.

The basis of the triad is the close relationship of the three: the Son and the Spirit have both come forth from the Father. Justin is careful to maintain the supremacy of God over the other two. He states that Christians worship the Son, but hold him in second place under God, with the prophetic Spirit in the third place (*1 Apol.* 13). Justin also reports that as the Christian partakes of the bread and wine of the Eucharist, "he gives praise and glory to the Father of the universe, through the name of the Son and of the Holy Spirit" (1 *Apol.* 65).

Gradually some Christian writers began to move toward identifying two or three members of the triad with each other. That process is occurring in at least one strand of the composite Gospel of John. In 14:9-11 Jesus says, "He who has seen me has seen the Father. . . . I do not speak on my own authority, but the Father who dwells in me does his works. Believe me that I am in the Father and the Father in me." (We cannot rely on "dwells in" to indicate either deity or identity, however; Paul believed that the Spirit dwells in Christians, and *Hermas* states that the Lord (Jesus Christ) dwells in them.[32] Another strain of thought is that Jesus as Lord or Son is also the Holy Spirit. This idea is in *Hermas:* "I want to show you what the Holy Spirit, which talked with you in the form of the church, showed you, for that Spirit is the Son of God."[33] The way is prepared for that view by the thought in *2 Clement* 9:5 that "Christ the

Lord . . . though he was at first spirit [but not Holy Spirit], became flesh."

Eventually the church fathers arrived at the doctrine of the Trinity: Father, Son, and Holy Spirit are three in one, three persons in one Godhead. God and Jesus had to be made one in some sense to counteract the charge that Christians were polytheists who worshiped two gods. The doctrine of the Trinity created new problems: for example, are all three of the same substance? In the third century the Modalist Monarchians went all the way in preserving the supremacy of God by claiming that the three in the Godhead are identical with each other, differing only in their modes or operations. They even asserted that since they were really One, the Father suffered on the cross with the Son. Tertullian denounced its leader, Praxeas, and charged that he crucified the Father![34]

Another doctrine was that Jesus was both divine and human. So said Irenaeus and Origen.[35]

Nevertheless, the belief persisted in the second and third centuries, even among some gentile Christians as well as in Jewish-Christian churches, that Jesus was completely human while on earth. The Monarchians adhered to the belief in the Gospel of Mark that Jesus was strictly a man whom God anointed with the Holy Spirit at his baptism and thus became Christ. For such "heresy" popes excommunicated the leaders.

The deification of Jesus was a diverse process, with many different strands produced in numerous Christian communities by a wide variety of causes. Deification enabled Christianity to survive and grow as an international religion, but it also produced many controversies through the centuries.

24

GNOSTICISM

In the second and third centuries Gnosticism split Christianity asunder. Compared to Jesus' own beliefs, those of both Jewish and gentile Christians were heretical, but they were moderate compared to the radical beliefs of the Gnostic Christians. Gnosticism became widespread as its adherents proclaimed it energetically by preaching and writing, and numerous church fathers denounced it vigorously in their writings. Whereas the controversy with Jews had involved mainly Jewish Christians, this controversy involved chiefly gentile Christians.

BELIEFS

What did Gnostic Christians believe? In defining Gnosticism we should look for the beliefs that were basic in the movement and generally shared by its proponents. We should beware of terms and concepts in Gnostic literature that are not basic and occur also in non-Gnostic contexts; those features existed outside of Gnosticism, and some Gnostic writers merely chose to use them.

The following features were essential:

The central feature is a cosmological-anthropological dualism. In simple terms, the dualism consists of the opposition of the spiritual realm, including the soul and the heavens, to the material realm, including the earth and physical bodies. The spiritual is "from above" (the heavens) and is inherently good; the material is "from below" and is inherently bad.

Souls originated in the upper world, but they have been imprisoned in physical bodies. Thus the body (Greek: *soma*) is the tomb (Greek: *sema*) of the soul.

The only salvation for the soul is to acquire secret knowledge (Greek: *gnosis*) consisting of two main features: knowledge of God, "the Father," and knowledge of whence the soul is from and whither it should go. The Father is unknown until the soul acquires Gnosis. The soul must learn that it has come from the upper world and should return to it. Its salvation is achieved only through this secret knowledge, and not by knowledge in general. The soul that does not acquire this knowledge will either perish or be reincarnated in another body.

The supreme God, the Father, is spiritual and transcendent, aloof from matter and the world. Therefore the soul's return to the upper world is a return to God.

Although those features are not stated explicitly in all Gnostic documents, they generally underlie the thinking of the writers.

SOURCES

The sources of Christian Gnosticism have been much debated. Did a pre-Christian Gnosticism exist? If so, where—in paganism or Judaism? If so, was it a system of theological thought, or did it consist of various ideas that Christian Gnostics combined as the foundation of their beliefs? (Not all Christian Gnosticism consisted of a system, however.) To answer those questions, we should search for the antecedents of the basic features listed above; we should not rely on the miscellaneous features added by some Gnostic writers and not by others.

Paganism as Source
The notion that the human spirit or soul can transmigrate into another body—animal or human—was widespread and had existed for centuries. The belief was present in some primitive societies and in Hinduism.

In classical Greece the Orphics believed that souls originated in the heavens and have passed through the air and entered bodies. When bodies die, the souls of humans can transmigrate into animals, and vice versa. People can escape the rebirths, however, by being initiated into the Orphic mysteries and by purifying their souls by being ascetic and ethical. Then the souls will enjoy an eternal blessed life in the section of Hades reserved for the saved. While living on earth, souls have forgotten their past, but acquiring memory of their spiritual origins is essential for their eternal salvation, as a gold tablet (4th or 3rd c. B.C.) found in an Orphic grave in South Italy testifies. The instructions on it tell the soul what to do when it enters Hades. The soul should approach the guardians of the spring which flows from the Lake of Memory and say: "I am a child of Earth and starry Heaven; but my race is of Heaven (alone). This ye know yourselves. But I am parched with thirst and I perish. Give me quickly the cold water flowing forth from the Lake of Memory."[1] The memory is that of the soul's origins, which the body made it forget. The Orphics were ascetics, for they held the body in contempt because it is a hindrance to the soul. Apollonius testified to the popularity of Orphism in Babylon in the first century A.D., for there he saw statues of Orpheus everywhere.[2]

The teachings of the Greek philosopher Pythagoras (6th c. B.C.) were popular and resulted in a widespread movement, but it was persecuted and suppressed around 425 B.C. The movement revived as Neopythagoreanism, and flourished in Rome and Alexandria in the first century B.C. and later. Apollonius of Tyana was a Neopythagorean philosopher in the first century A.D. who traveled and taught in Babylonia, India, Egypt, Asia Minor, and Rome. The Pythagoreans were strongly influenced by Orphism, but revised some of its tenets. They believed in the transmigration of the soul,[3] unless it escapes to the heavens whence it came—not to Hades as the Orphics believed. Babylonian and Syrian astralism caused the change in the soul's destiny from earth to the heavens. They too were ascetic. They refused to drink wine or eat meat—flesh is unclean.[4] They preferred celibacy, but if a man marries, he should not have sexual intercourse except with his own wife.[5] They practiced magic and healings.

Plato (4th c. B.C.) was influenced by the Pythagoreans. In his *Phaedo* he expressly connects his teaching about the transmigration of souls with the teaching of Philolaus, who according to tradition wrote the first exposition of the Pythagorean system (end of 5th c. B.C.).

Plato said: The soul is from the heavenly world, "the Being," but is imprisoned in the body[6] on this earthly world, "the Non-being." The material world is not inherently evil, however. The body is bad, not because it is flesh, but because it hinders the soul from attaining truth and prudence by means of reasoning.[7] The body does that by requiring too much of our attention with its hunger, thirst, diseases, and passions; consequently the soul does not have time for reasoning. In short, the body tends to prevent us from becoming philosophers. The soul has to continue to exist after the death of the body because it must be born (again).[8] The soul can continue to exist because it is invisible and unchanging; the body perishes because it is visible and changeable.[9] When the body dies, the pure soul, which has been reasoning, or philosophizing, ascends to the realm of the good and wise God. Other souls, weighted down by the physical world, are dragged back to earth and enter the bodies of beasts and birds.[10] In the journey after death both good and bad souls are guided by their tutelary genius to the place where the souls of the dead are judged.[11]

God is the Demiurge, "Maker"; he is "the Father and Maker of all things."[12] Plato did not view the world and the Demiurge as evil. In the third century A.D. the Neoplatonist Plotinus upheld that view when he wrote a treatise, *Against the Gnostics, or against those who say that the Creator of the World is evil and that the World is bad.*

Nevertheless, the Middle Platonists held that matter in general, and not just the body, is inherently evil. In a way, Plato had left the door open for the rise of that view. He had affirmed that "the substance or matter out of which it [the universe] came into being did not come to be but was always available to the Maker to whom it submitted itself"[13] [i.e., God did not create it, but merely shaped matter, which already existed]. This idea permitted the later belief to arise that something is wrong with matter, but it is not God's fault because he did not create it. Plato did not quite impugn matter as a whole, for he thought it included both good and bad elements. "For it [the universe] has got from Him who constructed it all the good things, but from its previous state whatever troubles and iniquities occur in the universe—from that source it has these itself—and produces them in its living beings."[14] Plutarch adds that thus Plato was putting "the cause [matter] of evils at the farthest remove from God," that is, he made God transcendent. Yet Plutarch concedes that Plato does not really regard matter per se as evil, but rather "what he calls the cause of evil is the motion that moves matter."[15]

Plutarch (ca. A.D. 46-120) was an eclectic thinker and not an adherent of any particular school of philosophy. He traveled to many countries and read and wrote much. He was initiated into the mystery cult of Dionysos, and in his home town of Chaeronea in Greece he was a priest of the Pythian Apollo.

Both Platonism and Neopythagoreanism contributed heavily to Plutarch's thought. He and the Middle Platonists of the second century A.D. emphasized the transcendence of the supreme God, the divinity of the soul, and the evil nature of the material world. As Plutarch interprets Plato, there are two parts to the universe: body and soul. "The soul, however, when it has partaken of intelligence and reason and concord [all three are from God], is not merely a work but also a part of God and has come to be, not by his agency, but both from him as source and out of his substance."[16] Belief in the transcendence of God and belief that the world is evil tended to support each other.

By the middle of the second century A.D. some Middle Platonists believed in the existence of two major gods: the Father, who is Good, and the Demiurge, who made the universe. Accordingly Albinus distinguished between "the God above the heavens" and "the God in the heavens."[17]

The Hermetica consists of pagan writings which are a synthesis of Greek and Egyptian religious and philosophic thought. They were written in Greek in Egypt—probably Alexandria—in the second and third centuries A.D., but incorporate earlier traditions. They contain many ideas that appeared in Gnosticism. One such idea that they emphasize is the necessity of "knowing God."

In Tractate 1, *Poimandres* (2nd c.), in the Hermetica the writer says to Poimandres, who is "Absolute Sovereignty," or "Authoritative Mind" (Greek: *Nous*), "I want to learn the things that really exist and to understand their nature and to know God" (3). In a hymn of praise to God the Father we read in the same document: "Holy is God, who wills to be known and is known by his own."[18] In Tractate 7, *Ignorance of God*, in the Hermetica the subtitle is: "That Ignorance of God Is the Greatest Evil among Men." In its text we find: "For this evil of ignorance floods the whole earth; it corrupts the soul imprisoned in the body" (1), and ". . . seek a guide to lead you by the hand to the gates of knowledge" (Greek: *gnosis;* 2).

Most of the basic beliefs in Christian Gnosticism were already in paganism. Gnostics could have drawn them from a variety of pagan sources. Here is a list with the probable source or sources.

1. The soul or the divine spark or spirit within it has come down to earth from the heavens and entered a physical

body in which it becomes imprisoned. Plato taught that "our soul [Greek: *psyche*] existed before we were born."[19] Sources: Orphism, Pythagoreanism, and Platonism.

2. When the body dies, the soul transmigrates into another body, unless the soul has been saved. Sources: Orphism and Pythagoreanism.

3. The soul has forgotten where it came from and must relearn that. Source: Orphism. In classical times Orphics taught that the soul must recall this when it enters Hades; we may conjecture that by Christian times the soul may have relearned this information during the body's lifetime by means of initiation into the Orphic mysteries.

4. There is a personal dualism between soul and body. Sources: Orphism, Pythagoreanism, and Platonism. Cosmological dualism exists between the spiritual realm and the physical realm in which matter is inherently evil. Sources: syncretism and Middle Platonism.

5. The supreme God is "the Father." Source: Plato. (Other Christians besides Gnostics used the title, however.)

6. The supreme God is especially transcendent. Source: Middle Platonism.

7. Since God, the Father, is transcendent, he must have made the world through an intermediary. Source: Middle Platonism.

8. The supreme God is "good" or "the Good." Source: Platonism. (It occurs also in the non-Gnostic passage in Mark 10:18.)

9. To know God, or the Father, is vital; he is unknown to non-Gnostics. Source: Hermetic theology.

10. The Father is unbegotten, for he is "the First God." Source: Middle Platonism.

11. The Father is "Truth" and "the source of all truth." Source: Platonism. According to Plutarch,[20] the Middle Platonist Albinus used these expressions. The idea is earlier, for it is in sources used by Philo and in the Gospel of John. Attaining "truth" and "prudence" are the major goals of the soul as early as Plato (*Phaedo* 65).

12. Asceticism logically follows from the inherent evil nature of the body and the material world. Source: Pythagoreanism.

Judaism as Source
For. Moritz Friedlander in 1898 apparently was the first scholar to set forth the thesis that Gnosticism originated in Judaism, from which Gnostic Christians obtained it. In the first half of the twentieth century numerous scholars espoused the theory, but in the second half a growing number have rejected it. What is the evidence, pro and con?

Friedlander's case[21] rested on scant evidence and ample conjecture. He assumed that it must have been Jewish Gnostics that Philo was referring to when he denounced Jewish allegorists who neglected the letter of the Law and Jews who "are disgusted with their ancestral institutions" and those who "blaspheme the Godhead." Friedlander also claimed that Christian Gnostic sects, namely the Ophites, Cainites, and Sethians, were the direct heirs of the Jewish Gnosticism. The argument is extremely weak, for no connection has been demonstrated, and many Jews who were not Gnostics were so attracted to Hellenistic culture that they became very unorthodox and some became apostates. Heretical Jews, including Christian Jews, were numerous enough to be denounced in the Mishnah, but there is no evidence that they were Gnostics.

The modern case for Jewish origin begins with the fact that many Jews, especially in the Diaspora, had combined Hellenistic thought and culture with Judaism, and Philo's synthesis is close to Gnosticism. In his writings he accepts some ideas and uses some terms that are in Gnosticism (but they occur outside of Gnosticism too, in Hellenistic mysticism). Philo regards God as infinite, unchangeable, transcendent, perfect, pure Being. Therefore God does not have direct contact with this imperfect, finite world, but maintains a connection with it by means of mediating Ideas, or Forces. The totality of the Ideas is the Logos, the Reason of God, which was also the spoken Word of God when he created the cosmos. Pure souls have come down from God through airy space and are imprisoned in bodies, which are the sources of sin and evil. The soul desires to rise and return to God, but it can do so only if, with the help of God, it keeps itself free from the things of sense. The truly wise and virtuous man can temporarily, in ecstasy, be lifted above his sensible existence in a vision of God, while his own consciousness disappears in a vision of light. If one has kept oneself free from the sensible world, at death he will escape the transmigration of his soul into another body. Philo distinguished between "the heavenly man," who is in the image of God, and "the earthly man."[22]

Philo clearly adopted some Platonic and Neopythagorean ideas. His dualism of body and soul, transcendence of God, and transmigration of souls are also akin to Gnosticism. Nevertheless, he has not gone all the way. He has not made knowledge of the Father and of the soul's origin and destiny the basis of salvation. Though God used an intermediary, his Word, he is still the good Creator. Philo was not hostile to the Old Testament or Judaism; he even claims that the doctrines of the Greek philosophers were taught by Moses. Philo's philosophical religion is not Gnosticism, but Hellenistic mysticism.

For two decades after the Dead Sea scrolls were published, some biblical scholars thought that they are evidence of pre-Christian Jewish Gnosticism. The evidence is that they emphasize the importance of the knowledge which God reveals to the sect. That view of the scrolls is generally rejected today because their type of knowledge is not at all Gnostic, but rather consists of sectarian interpretation of the Hebrew Scriptures.

Some Christian Gnostics were familiar with the Old Testament, and that fact suggested that the books were written by Jewish Christians who were adherents of a Jewish Gnosticism before they became Christians. Two facts discredit that theory: gentile Christians knew and interpreted the Old Testament too,[23] and usually the Gnostic authors were intensely hostile to Jews and Judaism, including the Old Testament. A few biblical scholars have conjectured that Gnosticism began with a renegade Jewish sect that hated everything Jewish, but that theory is implausible compared to the theory that the Christian Gnostics were gentiles who were acquainted with the Old Testament and hated everything Jewish.

The Gospel of John was also thought to be evidence of Jewish Gnosticism, for it contains both Jewish-Christian ideas and terms and some Gnostic ideas and terms. But two facts expose the fallacy of that theory. (1) The gospel displays such bitter hostility to Jews and their Law that the author could not possibly have thought of himself and his beliefs as within the folds of Judaism. (2) With the exception of the Prologue, the Gnostic passages are distinct from the Jewish passages. That phenomenon does not fit a Jewish-Gnostic background of the gospel; instead, it fits the recent discovery that the book contains matter from a Jewish-Christian non-Gnostic source and gentile-Christian proto-Gnostic sources (see fuller discussion below). *Against.* Now we turn to the case against the existence of a pre-Christian Jewish Gnosticism. Here is the evidence:

1. No pre-Christian, Jewish-Gnostic document has ever been found. No ancient writer, either Jewish or Christian, mentions the existence of such a document.

2. No ancient writer mentions the existence of a pre-Christian Jewish-Gnostic sect.

3. The church fathers did not trace Gnostic origins to Judaism. Irenaeus[24] traces it (erroneously) to the Samaritan, Simon Magus. Hippolytus states that the heresy of the Gnostic Valentinus is of Pythagorean and Platonic origin.[25]

4. As we have seen, the case for a Jewish origin of Gnosticism is very weak.

5. Many Christian-Gnostic sects were not really monotheistic, which would be remarkable if their background was Jewish. Irenaeus (1. 25. 6) said that some Carpocratian Gnostics' "veneration of images is like that of the gentiles."

6. When Gnostic writers interpret the Old Testament, they display no Jewish understanding of it. They really "mess it up."

7. If a Jewish Gnosticism was the source of Christian Gnosticism, why do the writers not display evidence of knowledge of any Jewish literature other than the Old Testament, and usually only Genesis at that?

8. When Christian Gnostics discussed the Old Testament, Judaism, or the Jews, they were hostile to them. Significantly, Gnostics were hostile to the most basic beliefs in Judaism, namely, that only one God, the Creator, exists; that he is a good God; that the Jewish Law is good and should be observed. It strains our credulity to believe that any sect of Jews would be so hostile to *Judaism as a whole.* It is true that the Essenes at Qumran regarded the Jews outside their sect, as well as the gentiles, as "sons of darkness," but they were zealously loyal to the Jewish Law and the Jewish God, the Creator.

9. As we observed, the basic beliefs in Christian Gnosticism come from paganism, not Judaism. This fact, we believe, is decisive evidence.

Syncretism
   In the Hellenistic and early Roman periods a tremendous

amount of syncretism occurred in the Mediterranean world. Hellenistic Judaism combined Greek and Near Eastern elements with Judaism; Christianity combined elements from Judaism with features from pagan religions and pagan philosophy. Pagan philosophies borrowed from each other; mystery cults borrowed from each other. Many religions borrowed from philosophies. Plutarch did not merely add features to a certain philosophy; he was so eclectic that he created his own philosophy with parts from many sources.

Significant for the investigation of the origin of Christian Gnosticism is the fact that some of its features were already involved in the syncretistic process. That occurred particularly in Philo's voluminous writings and in the Hermetica. We cannot say with certainty that Gnosticism as a system existed before Christianity. We can say with certainty, however, that the process of syncretism out of which Christian Gnosticism was born was already in progress. Christian Gnosticism was syncretistic and became increasingly so as it expanded. Philosophy was the main source, but mystery religions were probably factors too.

CHRISTIAN GNOSTICISM

To determine what Christian Gnostics believed, scholars, prior to this century, had to rely heavily on the descriptions church fathers wrote when they were attacking those heretics. Scholars recognized the danger that the church fathers may have misrepresented the Gnostics because they were hostile to them. The discovery of Gnostic documents at Nag Hammadi has shown that the churchmen's descriptions are rather accurate after all. We will rely primarily on Gnostic documents, but we will not exclude additional information from patristic sources. In addition to the Nag Hammadi documents, some Gnostic writings were already known and were published in English translation in 1924.[26]

Christian Mysticism

Some early Christian writings are moving in the direction of Gnosticism, but are still essentially only Hellenistic mysticism. In Colossians, for example, God is "the Father" and Jesus is the Son in whom "all the fullness ["of God" is not in the Greek text] was pleased to dwell" (1:12, 19). A Platonic feature is that the Son "is the image of the invisible God" (1:15) and the new nature of Christians is being renewed in knowledge "according to the image of its Creator" (3:10). A Christian goal is to do good works and increase one's "knowledge of God," but this is Jewish, not Gnostic, in tone; the Greek word for knowledge here is *epignosis*, not *gnosis*. The author of Ephesians prays that God, "the Father of glory, may give you a spirit of wisdom and of revelation in the knowledge of him" (1:17). The church is "the fullness of him who fills all in all" (Eph. 1:23).

Ignatius, bishop of Antioch, wrote his letters about the same time that the Gospel of John was written. Although he too was not a Gnostic, he approached the borderline. He greeted the church at Ephesus by stating that it "is blessed with greatness in the fullness of God the Father." In his letters he writes that Jesus Christ is the "knowledge" (*gnosis*) of God (*Eph.* 17:2), and he is "our God" (*Eph.* 18:2)—but he is not consistent, for "there is [only] one God, who manifested himself through Jesus Christ, his Son" (*Mag.* 8:2). Evil comes from the Archon, "Ruler," of this age (*Mag.* 1). Ignatius comes close to Gnosticism when he states that the Son is God's "Logos proceeding from Silence" (Greek: *Sige*; *Mag.* 8:2). In some Gnostic mythology the Logos emanated from *Sige* and *Theos* (God). One feature in Ignatius is like John 5:19, 30— "the Lord was united to the Father and did nothing without him" (*Mag.* 7:1).

Early Christian Gnosticism

Contrary to Justin and Irenaeus, the Samaritans Simon Magus and Menander were not Gnostics; instead, their teachings were examples of Hellenistic syncretism. They were not Christians, for each claimed that he himself was the Messiah and Savior.

The earliest Christian passage that is Gnostic in thought is in a Q pericope[27] where the reading in Matthew is: "All things have been delivered to me by my Father; no one knows the Son except the Father, and no one knows the Father except the Son and anyone to whom the Son chooses to reveal him." Thus the Son is the Revealer who makes the Father known—a Gnostic idea. In Luke's version what is made known is who the Father is. Which reading is the original? The form in Matthew reminds us of "the Father knows me and I know the Father" in John

10:15. The pericope in Q is very unlike the rest the synoptic material and must have come from a different Christian community than the rest of Q.

In sources in the Gospel of John. The next earliest Christian-Gnostic writing is the hymn incorporated in the Prologue of the Gospel of John. We have noted that the hymn contains a non-Gnostic Jewish poem. The Christian Gnostic who composed the hymn reinterpreted the Word as Jesus himself. Thus, for the first time in Christianity, Jesus is viewed as the Logos through whom God made the cosmos. In this Gnostic hymn we have the birth of an explicit doctrine of Incarnation: "the Word became flesh." Translating directly from the Greek text, we find that the Gnostic hymn contributes other new features to Christian faith. The Word had "glory as the only-begotten from the Father, full of grace and truth." "We have all received from his fullness, grace upon grace." "No one has ever seen God" (thus God is invisible, as in Platonism). "The only-begotten God [changed to "Son" in later manuscripts to preserve monotheism] who is in the bosom of the Father, that one has declared" (him).

Since the Gospel of John probably was written in Alexandria around the year 100, the hymn probably was written there A.D. 80-100. Its features of special interest for Gnostic origins are the Incarnation and Jesus as the only-begotten God who has declared the Father (and thus made him known). Also significant is the fact that the Jewish features occur only in the Jewish poem—none in the Gnostic hymnist's own composition. That fact indicates that the hymnist had contact with Jews or at least Jewish literature but was not a Jew himself. He was attracted to the poem because in it the Logos was with God in the heavens from the beginning.

The author of John used also some other sources from early Gnosticism. In them we see Christian Gnosticism in the process of being born. Rudolph Bultmann called these sources in John "Revelation Speeches." He erred greatly in thinking that they were originally written in Aramaic by John the Baptist's sect, but he rightly recognized the existence of sources consisting of several documents of a Gnostic nature. That source material is difficult to separate from the composition of the author of John because his views are similar to it. Close examination of the syntax, literary style, and ideas, however, enables us to distinguish at least some of that source material.

After locating in John the passages that are clearly from early Gnostic sources, we arranged into categories those with ideas that are significant for the study of the beginnings of Gnosticism.[28] The dualism and antipathy between the spiritual realm and the material cosmos is understood in 3:31: "He who comes from above is above all; he who is from the earth is from the earth and from the earth he speaks." Christians are not from the world (Greek: *kosmos*), the Son chose them out of the world, and therefore the world hates them (15:18-19). The world hates Jesus because he testifies that its works are evil (7:7). The Son has conquered the world (16:33). In order to obtain life eternal a person must be born again: "It is necessary (that) you be born from above" (3:7; cf. 3:3).

And how is one reborn? What must one do to be saved? The basic method, apparently, is to hear the Son's word (Greek: *logos*) and believe in the One (the Father) who sent him (5:24; 10:26-28). They who are not from God do not listen to God's word (8:47). The Son is the exemplar in that he knows the Father and keeps the Father's word (8:55).

The Son's word is really the Father's word. "The word which you hear is not mine, but the Father's who sent me" (14:24). "What things I speak, even as the Father told me, thus I speak" (12:50; cf. 7:16). What is the content of the Son's word? The basic theme is the necessity of believing in the Son,[29] which is the equivalent of believing in the Father, for he who has seen the Son has seen the One who sent him (12:44-45). The Son is the Light of the world (8:12), and his disciples should believe in the Light (12:36). "Believing" is essentially the same as "knowing." Presumably it is the "word" that enables the disciples to know their Shepherd (10:14), to know the Son and whence he is (7:28). Apparently it is important for Christians to know that the Son "came forth from God; I have not come of myself, but he sent me" (8:42; cf. 16:28).[30]

A close relationship exists between the Father and the Son. "He who receives me receives the One who sent me" (13:20). He who hates the Son hates the Father also (15:23); the Father loves the disciples because they loved the Son (16:27). The Son is the Way to the Father: "I am the Way and the Truth and the Life. No one comes to the Father except through me" (14:6).

The term "work" has an important role in this source material. In 17:4 Jesus says to the Father, "I glorified you on earth, having completed the work which you gave to me to do" (cf. 4:34). What is the work which the Son completed? Apparently it is teaching the word that he has received from the Father. The plural, "works," has a different connotation. Jesus has shown many good works from the Father (10:32). The world hates Jesus because he testifies that its works are evil (7:7).

When we analyze these sources, we see that they do contain some Gnostic features: metaphysical dualism, rebirth, the Son and the Father with emphasis on their close relationship, and the necessity of knowing whence and whither and knowing the Son and the Father in order to attain life eternal. We did not find the belief that one must know the Father directly; instead one must know the Son, who is the Way to knowing the Father and hence is the Way to salvation.

Only a few Jewish terms appear: "walk," "works," and "Sons of Light." None are used in a Jewish sense, and we get the impression that the writers are outsiders with only a cursory knowledge of Judaism.

A striking characteristic of the sources is the tremendous elevation of Jesus' stature far above that in the synoptic gospels or the Gospel of Signs. He has become a god, a personal Redeemer, the only Way to the Father. Man no longer is saved directly by God.

The author of John displays a broad knowledge of the situation in his community. He knows and largely agrees with the Gnostics, but he also knows Jewish-Christian tradition (synoptic gospels, Gospel of Signs), the Christian controversy with Jews, and the wide range of Christian doctrinal and polemic problems. He has mixed his variety of materials together instead of synthesizing them into a unity.

Jesus is "the Son of Man" in six passages in John[31] and four of them refer to his ascension. In one (3:13-15) his prior descent from heaven is also mentioned. We have observed that in the synoptic gospels the descent to earth of the Son of Man is in the future, as in the Jewish background. In the Son-of-Man source in John the descent is in the past. Belief in the Son of Man's preexistence in heaven required his descent to earth *before* his ascension. We suspect that this logical and non-Gnostic adjustment in christology was the theme of the Son-of-Man source used in John. The author of John used that source as support for the doctrine of the Gnostic incarnated Son, who also was preexistent.

Other examples. Ignatius' letters reveal that contemporary with the writing of the Gospel of John the Docetic type of Gnosticism was invading the churches in Asia Minor. The Docetics' doctrines logically followed from their philosophical dualism in which flesh is evil. The Incarnation doctrine opened the way for separating "Jesus Christ" into two persons: Christ and Jesus. The spiritual Christ was united to the physical Jesus in the Incarnation, but did not die—Christ left him when Jesus was crucified. Thus Christ only "seemed to suffer" death.[32] Therefore the Docetics did not believe in the resurrection of Jesus. Because flesh is evil, the Docetics denied that Jesus was born from a virgin and was descended from David.[33] Similarly, "they abstain from the Eucharist and prayer because they do not confess that the Eucharist is the flesh of our Savior Jesus Christ" [*Smyr.* 7:1]. Ignatius explains the Docetics' disbelief by saying that God hid the *gnosis* of Jesus Christ's birth and death from the Archon of this aeon ("Ruler of this age," *Eph.* 19). Ignatius opposes Judaizers also. Some scholars have erred by concluding that they were also the Docetics; the error was the result of the assumption that Gnosticism came out of Judaism.

1 John too opposes Docetics; it denounces their teachers, who have appeared in some churches and been expelled, as "antichrists" and "false prophets." The author or authors—1 John may be composite—regard "Jesus Christ" as one person, but the false teachers separate Jesus and Christ by denying that "Jesus is the Christ," the Son of God (2:22; 5:5). They do not confess that "Jesus Christ has come in the flesh" (4:2-3).

Numerous Gnostic teachers arose in the second century. According to Irenaeus,[35] Saturninus in Antioch taught that the Father, who is unknown, made the angels, who in turn, made the world and mankind. The Father also made the celestial "powers and authorities." At the Creation a power sent "a spark of life" into man, which made him alive; "after death this spark of life returns to what is of the same nature as itself." The Savior is "unbegotten, incorporeal, and without form"; he is "Christ," who came to destroy wicked men and demons and to save good men. Christ appeared on earth in the form of man. Saturninus asserted that marriage and begetting children are from Satan [because sex is evil], and like the Pythagoreans, his disciples refused to eat meat. Christ came to destroy the God of the Jews, who is an angel.

The Gnostic Basilides taught in Alexandria in the second quarter of the second century. Irenaeus describes him also as a Docetist.[35] Basilides said that the Father sent *Nous,* "Mind," who appeared in the form of the man Jesus and was his first-begotten, into the world to free those who believe in him from the power of the angels who made the world. The chief of those angels is the God of the Jews; because he wanted to subjugate all the nations to his people, the Jews, the other nations resisted his nation. Simon of Cyrene was the person who was crucified, while the real Jesus became invisible and stood by and laughed before he ascended.

Basilides conceived of a celestial genealogy, a speculative device that became popular in Gnosticism. In his system the unbegotten Father begot *Nous* (Mind), which begot *Logos* (Reason), which begot Understanding, which begot *Sophia* (Wisdom) and Power, and they (*Sophia* is feminine gender) begot the powers, principalities, and first angels by whom the first heaven was made.

Cosmic genealogies originated in paganism. Hesiod (ca. 700 B.C.), a Greek, wrote in his *Theogony* that Chaos, Earth, and Love came into existence independently, unbegotten. Out of Chaos came Darkness and Night, Night begot Sleep and Death, and Earth begot Sky, to name a few. Gods were not the creators of the cosmos, but instead Earth and Sky begot the gods. The Orphics believed in a genealogy in which Earth and Sky sprang from Night. In *Poimandres* and Numenius we have cosmic genealogies in pagan Gnosticism in the second century A.D. Philo produced a brief Jewish genealogy in which the Father, the Creator, and the Mother, Knowledge or Wisdom, generated the Son, the world.[36]

In sharp contrast to ascetic Gnosticism is libertine Gnosticism; Carpocrates (2nd c.) provides an example. He probably lived in Alexandria. He taught that Jesus was human, the son of Joseph, but because his soul despised Jewish customs and the world-creating archons, or angels, the unbegotten Father gave Jesus' soul powers which enabled it to annihilate physical passions. The souls of Gnostics can achieve the same goal, and when they do, they are free to indulge in physical passions because they now have power over the world. The Carpocratians even went to the extreme of claiming that souls will not escape the endless reincarnation caused by the world-creating angels until the souls have committed all kinds of sins.

BR 162.3
W SS

Freeing the supreme God, the Father, from responsibility for creating the evil material world became a major concern of some Gnostics. Saturninus blamed the deed on an angel or angels. Cerinthus, a Docetist, called the supreme God "the First God," "the Power above all"; a lower power, who does not know the First God, made the world. Cerdo came to Rome and taught that the Father, who is the father of Jesus Christ, is unknown, but the God of the Old Testament is known. Marcion came to Rome too and expanded to the extreme Cerdo's doctrine of two Gods. Marcion vigorously attacked the Old Testament God, the Demiurge, the Maker of this awful world. Dualism and antipathy to Judaism were not the only reasons that Marcion espoused the doctrine; as a serious student of Scripture he added the bad traits of the Old Testament God: fondness for war, inconsistency of purpose, and reliance on law instead of love as a guide in human relations. Therefore Marcion rejected the entire Old Testament. Of the New Testament, he accepted only Paul's letters and Luke after he had removed their passages that do not fit his views.

Marcion claimed that Jesus came to destroy the works of the Demiurge, so the Demiurge caused his death. Marcion was an ascetic. Whereas Valentinus and Basilides each founded a school with disciples, Marcion founded a rival church, with local churches throughout the Roman Empire, which is one reason why the church fathers in alarm denounced him so bitterly.

Valentinus, a Christian Gnostic contemporary with Marcion, established a school in Alexandria in which he taught his own theological system. He was not a Docetic, did not teach the transmigration of souls, and did not separate the Father and the Creator into two Gods. Nevertheless, he was clearly a Gnostic, and his teaching enlightens our understanding of the Gospel of John. He had a very large following, and some of his disciples founded schools of their own. The following description of the doctrines is drawn from the Valentinian meditation, *The Gospel of Truth.*

Valentinians have received the gift of the true gospel [message, not book] from the Father through the power of the Word. The Son is the preexistent Logos, or Word, who came from the Fullness and is in the Mind and Thought of the Father. He is called the Savior and is Jesus Christ. He illumined those who were in the darkness caused by Forgetting; he gave them a

Way (18). The Son has revealed the Father's name (38). Jesus took the Father's Book of Life as his own and died for it (20) [a new explanation of Jesus' death!].

The Father is perfect, good, and the Father of Truth. He made the All, or Totality, which includes humanity. The All is not perfect, or complete, because it lacks knowledge of the Father and has forgotten whence it came. Souls originally were in the Father without knowing him; they received Error when they left him, which was Forgetfulness of where they came from. When the body dies, souls will perish unless they acquire Gnosis, which is knowledge of the Father and of whence they came and whither they should go. "Therefore if one is a Gnostic, he is from above" (22).

How does one acquire Gnosis? Not everyone will acquire it, because predestination has already determined who will be saved. The name of each saved person is written in the Book of Life; the Father utters this special name, and the Son or Gnostics teach it to the individual. "For he whose name has not been spoken is an agnostic" (21), i.e., he does not know and will perish. And how do Gnostics know whose name has not been uttered? He or she is the one who will not listen to Gnostic teaching. But he who has received his name knows whence and whither (22). To be saved the Gnostic must also know the Father; without that knowledge he is incomplete. "When the Father is known, then the Lack [Incompleteness] will not exist" (24). When the Father calls, the Gnostic ascends to him mystically (22).

They who know the Father have a very intimate relationship with him. "The Father is in them, and they are in the Father, because they are complete, inseparable from him who is the truly Good (One)" (42). The Father's love flows upon "the true brothers" (Valentinians; 43). When the body dies, the soul of the agnostic perishes, but the soul of the Gnostic ascends to the "place" from which it came and there it will have "rest."

The Gospel of Truth alludes to some New Testament material, but drastically reinterprets it. It has no interest in following the canonical gospels' portrait of Jesus. According to Irenaeus, Valentinus' followers made copious use of the Gospel of John (3.11.7).

The Gospel of Thomas, discovered in Coptic translation at Nag Hammadi, originally was written in Greek in the second century, probably in Alexandria. It lends credibility to the theory that a "Q Document" of sayings ascribed to Jesus could have existed, for it too is a string of such unconnected sayings—in fact, many of its sayings are in Q. Some of its sayings, however, are not in the Q material in Matthew and Luke, and this fact caused some scholars to leap to the conclusion that it contains previously unknown authentic sayings of Jesus. That conjecture is now discredited because (1) its previously unknown sayings are often Gnostic in nature and Jesus, as we know, was not a Gnostic, and (2) the Q material itself is of questionable authenticity too. The setting assumed in Thomas is a revelation of the ascended Jesus to the disciples on earth, recorded by the disciple Thomas.

Was the author's source(s) of the Q material the same that the authors of Matthew and Luke drew from, or were Matthew and Luke his sources? We have substantial evidence of the latter.[37]

Clear evidence of the lateness of Thomas is its Gnostic reinterpretation of synoptic sayings. Sometimes it calls the kingdom of God the "Kingdom of the Father" (76). A greater change is in sayings 49 and 50 where the kingdom is not a future one on earth, but the celestial Place of Light: "you come from it and to it you will return." To "Blessed are the persecuted" is added the interpretation that "it is they who have truly come to know the Father" (69).

The Gnostic ideas and terminology in *Thomas* are similar to those in the *Gospel of Truth*, a fact that suggests that *Thomas* too may be a product of the Valentinian school. For example:

Dualism. In commenting on the flesh (*sarx*) and spirit (*pneuma*) Jesus says, "I marvel at how this great wealth [spirit] has made its home in this poverty" [flesh] (29). The world is bad (27).

Know the Father. This is an essential goal, for which some Gnostics have been persecuted (69).

Know the Truth. "Your kings and your great men . . . are not able to know the Truth" (78).

Light. "Jesus said, 'It is I who am the Light which is above them all'" (77). The disciples "have come from the Light" (50).

Place. "The disciples said, 'Show us the Place where you are, for it is necessary for us to seek it'" (24). It is "the

Place of Life" (4).

Rest. "Seek a Place for yourselves within Rest" (60).

Sex. "Jesus said to them, '. . . when you make the male and the female into one and the same, so that the male not be male nor the female be female, . . . then you shall enter (the Kingdom)'" (22). Jesus will reveal himself to the disciples "when you take off your clothing without being ashamed" (37). (This extreme sexual asceticism was a characteristic of some later Christian sects known as Encratites.)

Whence and whither of souls. When the disciples asked "how our end will be," Jesus said, "Where the beginning is, there shall be the end. Blessed is he who shall stand at the beginning, and he shall know the end and shall not taste death" (18).

Women are inferior. "Simon Peter said to them [the disciples], 'Let Mary depart from us, because women are not worthy of the Life.' Jesus said: 'I shall lead her, so that I will make her male, that she too may become a living spirit, resembling you males. For every woman who makes herself male will enter the Kingdom of Heaven.'"(114). [What is the logic behind this? Is it that physical bodies are evil, and women produce them (i.e., babies), but if women abstain from sex, they will be like males and not bear children, and thus they will qualify to enter the Kingdom?]

Numerous other Gnostic sects arose, especially in the second half of the second century. Many were founded by disciples of earlier Gnostics. Dualism and anti-Judaism continued to be characteristic. The following Gnostics regarded "the God of the Jews" as inferior to a higher God: Cerdo, Saturninus, Marcion, Barbelo-Gnostics, Sethian-Ophites, Cainites, and Ptolemaeus.

The inferior nature of the physical world conflicted with the role of the physical in Christian doctrines. The most serious problem here was the question, How could a physical man, Jesus, possibly be a divine spirit, the Son of the Father? The doctrine of Incarnation in the Johannine Prologue was the earliest attempt at solution, but the Gospel of John as a whole still has the problem, for in it Jesus still has a physical resurrection. The Docetic solution was to separate a spiritual Christ from the physical Jesus and have him depart from Jesus at the crucifixion and ascend to heaven. Marcion had a less unorthodox solution: Jesus was raised with a spiritual body which ascended to heaven. Therefore Marcion revised Luke to make it agree; he changed the narrative of Jesus' post-resurrection appearance to the disciples. In Luke, when the disciples thought that Jesus was only a spiritual apparition, he invited them to handle him, "for a spirit has not flesh and bones as you see me have" (24:39). Marcion rewrote the line to read, "a spirit, such as you see me have, has not bones."[38]

A doctrine that was a problem for Gnostics was the belief in Jesus' parousia. If immortality is in heaven and there will be no kingdom of God on earth, what need is there for Jesus to return? One Gnostic solution to the problem was to claim that his Coming had already occurred.

The belief that there will be a general resurrection of the bodies of the dead conflicted with the Gnostic tenet that the real self is the spirit within the body. Even if the raised body is thought to be an incorruptible, spiritual body, as in Romans 15, its destination is immortality on earth, whereas the destination of the Gnostic soul is the Place of Rest in the heavens. Whereas Paul believed that the dead would be raised with a spiritual body that will remain on earth, the Naassene Gnostics believed that they would be raised with a spiritual body that will ascend and enter through the gate of heaven.[39] Also, logically the kingdom of God became the kingdom of heaven in Gnostic faith, encouraged by the pious substitution of "heaven" for "God" in the Gospel of Matthew.

To eliminate offensive Christian beliefs, Gnostics resorted to outright denial or to reinterpretation of them. Allegorization was one method; another was the quotation of scriptural passages out of context and the misinterpretation of them. Valentinus and others used the text, "Seek, and you will find," in Q as justification for the latter practice.[40]

The Gnostics antagonized the catholic Christians by disregarding ethics as well as by rejecting doctrines. This was especially true of the libertine Gnostics with their immorality. Ethics in general are not fostered much in Gnostic literature, a contrast to the synoptic gospels and Paul's letters. Irenaeus praises the righteous conduct of Old Testament patriarchs and prophets in contrast to the current heretics "who have despised the Lord's coming and become slaves of their own lusts."[41]

Catholic Christians attacked the Gnostics in many ways, including persecution. Eusebius reports from an unidentified writer that "those called Marcionites from the heresy of Marcion say that they have immense numbers of martyrs of Christ."[42] The Apostles' Creed proclaims as essential many Christian beliefs that Marcion and some other Gnostics rejected, including God is the Maker of heaven and earth, Jesus Christ is his only Son, the virgin birth, Jesus' resurrection, ascension, and future coming to earth to judge the living and the dead.

Gnosticism completely separated Christianity from its historical origins. The historical Jesus was utterly lost. Gnosticism freed Christianity from its Jewish roots: the Law, the Old Testament, Jewish nationalism, Jewish eschatology, Jewish ethics. (Paul had freed it from the Torah, and gentile Christians had already rejected Jewish nationalism.) That freedom appealed to gentiles accustomed to the mutual dislike between Jews and gentiles, reinforced by the recent Jewish revolts against Rome and the controversy between Jews and Christians. Gnosticism appealed also to the numerous Christians disillusioned with the failure of Jesus to usher in the new kingdom of God. No wonder that Gnosticism spread like wildfire in the second century!

OBSERVATIONS

A comprehensive examination of the ancient sources—
Jewish, Christian, and pagan—gives us new insights into the
old question, How did Christianity begin?

Most overwhelming is the recognition of the enormous
discrepancy between tradition and history, between traditional
beliefs about Christian origins and modern historical knowledge of what actually happened. Recognition of this basic fact
is not new, for it has been developing since the Renaissance,
especially in the last three centuries. What is new now is the
discovery of more details of the formation of the Christian
faith, details learned from archaeology, ancient literature, and
modern methods of historical research. The new understanding of the problems of the early Christians provides new
insight into the origin of the traditional doctrines and revises
historians' earlier reconstructions of Jesus' life. Prominent
among the methods is the detection by linguistic means of
source material and later insertions in ancient composite
writings, biblical and non-biblical.

We are surprised at the tremendous variety of thought
in the ancient world. We should all beware of hastily generalizing by saying, "Jews believed such and such," "Christians
believed such and such," "Greeks believed such and such," or
"Romans believed such and such." There were indeed some
ideas that each group generally held, but many other ideas
were accepted by only a portion of a group. Amazing variety
of ideas and practices existed not only among the groups, but
also within them, often resulting in internal tensions.

JESUS

Jesus Lived

Many myths arose about Jesus, but he himself was not
a myth. He was a historical person, even though a multitude

of unhistorical acts and sayings were assigned to him after his death. Soon after his crucifixion the disciples were preaching two major themes: the kingdom of God and the judgment day are coming soon, and Jesus was and still is (because he now is living in heaven) the Christ, the Jewish Messiah foretold in the Scriptures. If a small band of Jews had invented the whole story, they would have made Jesus fit Jewish expectations far better than he did. As we read carefully the early Christian writings, we can see the authors struggling to make Jesus fit prophecy. But his life did not fit it, and Christians had to misinterpret Scripture in a vain effort to harmonize Jesus and prophecy. The fact that Christian explanations were often inconsistent with each other also suggests that an original myth was not a guide to Christian faith.

The most severe discrepancy between prophecy and the historical Jesus was his crucifixion. The dominant theme in Jewish messianic expectation was that the Christ would, with the Lord's help, overthrow foreign rule over the world and establish the Lord's kingdom on earth. But instead, just the opposite occurred: a foreign ruler killed Jesus. If Jesus were created as a myth, his creators surely would have explained his disappearance from earth simply with an ascension story without the unnecessary and embarrassing feature of his death at the hands of a Roman governor. Many early Christian ideas are clearly the product of efforts to explain Jesus' death.

Certain other events in Jesus' life would not be in a narrative of a fictional Jesus. His baptism by John the Baptist implied that Jesus was repenting for his sins, which was contrary to the messianic expectation that the Christ would be sinless. The synoptic gospels supply improbable explanations of Jesus' baptism, while the Gospel of John conveniently slides around it (in it the Baptist says that he saw the Spirit descend on Jesus, but he does not say that he baptized Jesus). If the story of Jesus had been invented to present him as the Messiah of prophecy, he would be born in Bethlehem in the earliest gospel, Mark, and Matthew and Luke would not contain implausible stories to put his parents in Bethlehem for his birth and then move them to Nazareth. And he would have grown up in Bethlehem, not Nazareth; merely being born in Bethlehem is an inadequate fulfillment of the prophecy that the Messiah would come from Bethlehem (Micah 5:2; cited in

Matt. 2:6). Also, the dominant concept of the Christ in Palestine was that he would be a descendant of David. If Jesus were only a myth, Mark surely would have portrayed him as a "son of David."

What is mythological is the depiction of Jesus as having a virgin birth, receiving the Holy Spirit in visible form at his baptism, performing miracles, rising from the dead, ascending into heaven, and promising to return to earth in the future. The portrayal of him as the Son of Man and later as a god are, of course, mythological. These mythological features caused a few scholars to leap to the conclusion that the whole story is a myth.

Jesus Was Human

There are several major reasons for concluding that Jesus was completely human. First, Jesus and the earliest Christians thought so. We have observed ample evidence of that in the synoptic gospels and in Romans 1. Second, in Judaism and in primitive Christianity "Son of God" was a title for the human Messiah, or Christ. The title was first interpreted literally in the birth stories in Matthew and Luke where God's Spirit impregnates Mary, contrary to other passages in those gospels. The cause of the contradiction is the composite nature of the gospels. Third, the belief that Jesus was divine during his life on earth was introduced later by gentile Christians. Fourth, in the ancient superstitious world the belief in someone's divinity was readily accepted by the masses; in today's world, scientific knowledge disproves the claim that anyone died and arose from the grave, either as a human or as a deity. Fifth, Jesus believed that, in the lifetime of his audiences, a general resurrection of the dead and a judgment day would occur, and a supernatural kingdom of God would replace the current world order. Those events did not occur and never will, for the beliefs were founded on a superstitious view of the world. Anyone who is that mistaken is not divine.

Authentic or Unauthentic?

Our understanding of the historical Jesus is changing. Historians and biblical scholars have long recognized that a distinction must be made between the Jesus of history and the Christ of faith. What Jesus actually said and did was very different from the beliefs about him as the Christ and Savior that Christian communities created. Much of what the canonical gospels attribute to Jesus actually originated after his death in the churches' energetic efforts to persuade people that he was either the Messiah of Jewish expectations or a Savior of a pagan type. Throughout the twentieth century a major concern of scholars has been to find reliable criteria for determining which gospel traditions reflect Jesus' actual life. The number of canonical pericopes that scholars generally accept as authentic continues to decrease.

Unhistorical events were assigned to Jesus for various reasons, as we have seen. The miracle stories were intended in Jewish Christianity to represent Jesus as the Christ and in gentile churches to portray him as a god. Other incidents were created to bolster the claim that Jesus' life "fulfilled" the Scriptures; examples are details in the synoptic Passion story drawn from the Psalms.

Types of Unauthentic Sayings
Many of the sayings ascribed to Jesus in the Gospel of John are incompatible with the sayings in the synoptic gospels. This is especially the case with the Gnostic-type sayings, which disagree with the synoptics both in thought and in the kind of environment that produced them. The gospel sayings certainly cannot all be authentic!

Much of the teaching in the gospels, apart from the ethics in the synoptics, deals with problems in the churches, problems which did not arise until after Jesus' death, as we have observed. This type of teaching includes:

1. Sayings on persecution.

2. Sayings about Jesus' second coming: when and how he will return.

3. Sayings about John the Baptist: belittling his baptism; explaining his baptism of Jesus; interpreting him as Elijah redivivus.

4. The Son of Man sayings.

5. The disputes with the Pharisees and scribes over: Jesus' messiahship; the Law, both Written and Oral (Sabbath, divorce, fasting). The disputes over the Law began after Jesus' death; the Jerusalem church, founded by Jesus' disciples, observed the Law. Christian writings, except the gospels, never cite Jesus in support of their non-observance of

the Law—they surely would have if such support existed.

6. Kingdom of God sayings. Although Jesus' listeners probably raised questions about the coming of the kingdom of God, the apostles' audiences must have too, and they had many more years in which to ask them. The tone of the kingdom of God sayings is no different from that of sayings known with certainty to be unauthentic.

7. Ethical teaching. In chapter 6 we examined in detail the ethical teaching in the sayings of Jesus in the synoptic gospels. We found that virtually all the ethical standards were already in Judaism. If those sayings are authentic, Jesus' ethical teaching was not new. Although we would like to think that they are actual words of Jesus, their authenticity may well be questioned on the following grounds:

a. The sayings are based on the teachings of Pharisees, Essenes, and the Jewish sect that produced the *Testaments of the Twelve Patriarchs*. This is too wide a range of sources to emanate from one man, Jesus, especially since he was a carpenter (Mark 6:3[1]) who had never studied (John 7:15). This variety, however, would naturally be the result in a compilation of teachings from different churches with members drawn from several sects and backgrounds.

b. The inconsistency of some teachings in the synoptics indicates different sources, not just one man. "Blessed are the peacemakers" is not consistent with "I have not come to bring peace but a sword," or "division." If the universalism in the parable of the Good Samaritan was intended to extend to gentiles, then it is inconsistent with the exclusiveness in the story of Jesus and the Syrophoenician woman. Rarely is one individual as inconsistent as a group of individuals—or a group of churches!

c. Some of the teachings come from Jewish literature, a fact which indicates that learned men, not Jesus, brought them into Christianity from Jewish literature.

d. Since most of the other sayings that are presented as direct quotations of Jesus are unauthentic, it would be surprising if the gospel authors did not ascribe ethical teaching to him also.

e. Jesus surely was too busy with his urgent mission to call Jews to repent before it was too late for him to take time to give miscellaneous ethical teaching. The churches, on the other hand, needed such teaching for the training of their members, a practice in the synagogues.

Even though the ethical sayings probably were never uttered by Jesus, however as a Jew he must have agreed with some of them.

The kerygma, the proclamation of the early apostles, gives no indication that Jesus was a teacher. The usual explanation is that the apostles were mainly interested in proclaiming that Jesus is the Messiah and that the kingdom of God is coming soon. That indeed was their concern. But this poses another problem, usually ignored: If the apostles were not interested in Jesus' teaching, how could it have been well known in the churches decades later when the gospels were written? The kerygma certainly does not support the popular theory that an oral tradition of Jesus' teaching circulated among the early churches. Biblical scholars have long recognized that the miracle stories are not historical, but they preferred to think that the teaching of Jesus in the synoptic gospels must be authentic. One of the most significant insights into the gospels, however, is the realization that teaching, as well as miracles, could be assigned to Jesus after his death.

The late appearance of some sayings was explained as the result of the disciples' "remembering" them after Jesus' death. In Luke 24:6-8 two angels at Jesus' tomb tell women followers of Jesus, "Remember how he told you, while he was still in Galilee, that the Son of Man must . . . be crucified, and on the third day rise." In Acts 11:16 Peter, in his explanation of the conversion of gentiles, says he "remembered the word of the Lord, how he said, 'John baptized with water, but you shall be baptized with the Holy Spirit.'" (But in the gospels the Baptist, not Jesus, is the one who says this.) In Acts 20:35 Paul is portrayed as "remembering the words of the Lord Jesus, how he said, 'It is more blessed to give than to receive.'" (But Paul never knew Jesus.)

The author of the Gospel of John used this device too. In 2:17 he writes, "His disciples remembered that it has been written, 'Zeal for your house will consume me'" (Ps. 69:9). Thus the author portrays Jesus as quoting prooftexts. In 2:19 he ascribes to Jesus the saying, "Destroy this temple, and in three days I will raise it up." As in the saying in Luke 24, the reference to the resurrection faith arose after Jesus' death. In 2:22 the author in effect admits this when he states, "Then when he was raised from the dead, his disciples remembered that he said this." In John 16:2-4 Jesus predicts the Jewish persecution of Christians and adds, "But I have spoken these things to you so that when the hour [the persecution] has come, you will remember them, because I told you." Thus Jesus is represented as forecasting the persecution, a forecast "remembered" when (and not until) it happened.

For a summary of the evidence against the authenticity of the Jesus sayings, see Appendix, "The Case Against Authenticity."

Authentic Tradition

Contrary to efforts, past and current, to dejudaize Jesus and modernize him, three kinds of evidence demonstrate that Jesus' basic message was that his listeners should repent because the kingdom of God would soon appear.

1. The three earliest gospels, the synoptics, treat that message as his main theme.

2. The fact that they present the message in indirect speech as a summary of Jesus' preaching, rather than in direct speech, indicates its probable authenticity. A frequent practice of ancient writers was to put words into the mouths of historical characters as well as fictional ones. This clearly is the case with Stephen's speech in Acts 7 and the Gnostic speeches of Jesus in John. On the other hand, in any age people tend to remember the main theme of a person's speech better than they remember the actual words. Also, Jesus' basic message was more likely to be remembered because he must have repeated it many times to different groups of listeners.

3. The preaching and actions of the disciples after Jesus' death are incomprehensible if Jesus did not proclaim that the kingdom of God was coming soon.

A few miscellaneous sayings of Jesus in the synoptic gospels may be authentic. The saying in Mark 1:38, "Let us go on to the next towns, that I may preach there also, for that is why I came out," fits Jesus' situation and may be authentic. The author of Mark must not have composed it, for it does not mention the casting out of demons, which is a major concern in the author's own writing in the next verse and elsewhere. Mark names only one of the persons to whom Jesus said this, namely, "Simon" (Peter). Did Peter transmit this incident to the Christian community (Antioch?) from which Mark drew it? In Mark 3:35 Jesus says, "Whoever does the will of God is my brother, and sister, and mother." This subordination of family ties to the will of God could fit in either Jesus' situation or that of the apostles after his death. The former seems more probable, considering that it is doubtful that early Christians would create without reason a story of tension between Jesus and his mother. Similarly, we doubt that the apostles would create the pericope that Jesus' friends said, "He is beside himself" (Mark 3:21), that is, out of his mind.

Two probable historical facts are in John which are not in the synoptic gospels. These are the traditions that Jesus baptized (4:1) and that the crowds wanted to make him king (6:15).

The Historical Jesus

In summary, what do we really know about the historical Jesus? We know that he was a Jew, born and raised in Nazareth in Galilee, and either he or his father was a carpenter. Having heard about John the Baptist and his mission, he went to the Jordan River to repent and be baptized by him. He believed John's message that the judgment day and the kingdom of God on earth were imminent and therefore Jews should repent of their sins. When John was later imprisoned and killed by Herod Antipas, Jesus felt compelled to carry on the mission, as did John's (other?) disciples too. Women as well as men followed him (Mark 15:40-41).

We doubt that Jesus performed healings, but two factors could have caused him to try to do so: Popular demand for them, and the expectation that miracles would occur when the new kingdom came. On the other hand, his career may have been too short to perform many healings, and if Mark 1:38 is authentic, he preferred preaching anyway. In our chapter on miracles we saw ample cause for apostles to ascribe healings to Jesus later.

Whether Jesus taught more than his basic message we do not know. If he did, we cannot be sure that it was recorded. Authentic or not, the synoptic ethical teaching was not unique—it came straight out of Judaism.

Jesus' basic theme did not require that he be the Christ; the kingdom of God was coming whether he was the Messiah or not. But many Jews believed that the Messiah would usher in the new kingdom, so we should not be surprised if the crowds pressured him to become the messianic king, as John

6:15 and possibly Mark 11:8-10 indicate. That Jesus was regarded as the Christ before his death is shown by the Roman sign on his cross and the disciples' later faith in him.

The growing popular belief that Jesus was the Christ probably caused him to accept the role. He and/or some of his followers may have started a revolt; at least we know an insurrection occurred (Mark 15:7). That Jesus probably was involved with that revolt is suggested by his going into hiding and his title "King of the Jews." The early Christians suppressed knowledge of the revolt because they were forced to convince the Romans that they were loyal. The Temple authorities cooperated with the Romans by arresting Jesus and turning him over to Pilate, who ordered him to be crucified. Peter's denial that he knew Jesus is probably historical, for such an unflattering picture of the hero Peter would hardly be created by the churches which produced the synoptic gospels. Joseph of Arimathea may have buried his body. Crucifixion, a painful death, was a favorite Roman method of punishing rebels.

Was Jesus a Christian? The answer to this debatable question hinges on (1) the definition of "Christian" and (2) what Jesus believed and taught. The basic definition of a Christian in the first century was a person who believes that Jesus is the Christ. We have concluded that at first Jesus did not think of himself in those terms, but later the pressure of the crowds led him to do so. Thus at the end he was a Christian. But if we add to the definition the necessity of believing that Jesus was resurrected, ascended to heaven, and will return to earth, he was not a Christian, for those beliefs originated after his death. The same is true of the belief in his divinity. If we add also the belief that being a Christian requires acceptance of a religion that is separate from Judaism, Jesus does not fit that definition either. The assumption that Jesus was not a Christian underlies the classic distinction between "the Jesus of history" and "the Christ of faith."

JEWISH CHRISTIANS

Gentile Christianity as a separate movement first appeared with Paul's churches, but Jewish Christianity—in a limited form—goes back to Jesus himself, assuming that he reached the conclusion that he was the Christ. After his death,

Jewish Christians developed several forms of the new
religious movement, which was not a new religion, but a new
Jewish sect. From a Jewish point of view, Jerusalem was the
most conservative church. Hellenist Jewish Christians in
Palestine and Syria were much less traditional in their attitude
toward the Law and their interpretation of the messiahship.
Their Bible was the Septuagint, and they reinterpreted
numerous passages in it to support their new christology and
theology. As their numbers grew, the Jewish Christians
became increasingly concerned with internal and external
problems and issues, which they tried to solve in their
preaching and in their writings. As Jewish Christianity
expanded to Rome, Alexandria, and Asia Minor, it must have
added yet more variety in thought and practice.

A new recognition of the influence of the Jewish-
Christian churches is emerging. The synoptic gospels contain
Jewish ethics that were taught in those churches, and because
most gentile churches later adopted those gospels as scripture,
the ethics have been preserved in Christianity for two
millennia. If Jesus did not actually teach them, as we have
concluded, then the role of Jewish Christians was even greater
than scholars have thought; namely, Jewish Christians, not
Jesus, introduced those ethics into Christianity. They
contributed more emphasis on ethics and more specific rules
than either Paul or early gentile Christians. Jewish Christians
originated many major Christian doctrines, including belief in
Jesus' resurrection, ascension, and return to earth. They
created the doctrine of atonement and belief that Christianity is
the new Judaism.

The Jewish-Christian communities which produced the
synoptic gospels' traditions were located in Palestine (especially the coastal cities) and/or Syria (especially Antioch). The
evidence for this conclusion is considerable. Those are the
regions where Christianity first spread; the bulk of the
pericopes in Mark and the Q source are Jewish Christian in
thought and style, as are the passages composed by the
synoptic authors. Luke-Acts' interest in Samaria and the
Samaritans may indicate that it was written in Palestine. Some
of the synoptic sayings have their closest parallels in the
Testaments of the Twelve Patriarchs, which Howard Kee
believes emanated from sectarian Judaism in Syria.[2] The
synoptic gospels display no knowledge of Asia Minor, Rome,

or Alexandria and their churches.

Several types of evidence point to Antioch as the probable place of origin of the Gospel of Mark. The church there was founded by Greek-speaking Jewish Christians. In writing the story of the baptism of Jesus, the author of Mark definitely used the *Testament of Levi*, one of the books in the *Testaments of the Twelve Patriarchs*. Also, Antioch was a major base of the Roman army, and Mark displays knowledge of Latinisms, the Roman form of divorce, and the Roman army. The Syrian churches, like Mark, favored the adoptionist christology, that is, the belief that Jesus became the Christ at his baptism.

A puzzle is the presence of the Lord's Supper story, with its pagan concepts of body and blood, in Mark, which is Jewish Christian as a whole.[3] How could Mark include a gentile ritual in which blood was drunk, even symbolically, an idea repugnant to Jews? The usual explanation has been that the author was a gentile, but that does not explain the practice of the Lord's Supper in a Jewish-Christian church. The present writer is convinced that the explanation is that Mark was produced in a mixed church, with both Jewish and gentile members, and the gentiles brought in some gentile-Christian practices. And what Jewish-Christian church was the first to have gentile converts? Antioch (Acts 11:20). Influence of the cultic meal of Mithraism is the most probable source of the Lord's Supper. Mithraism was especially popular with the Roman soldiers, who were numerous at Antioch. The author of Mark depicts a Roman centurion as recognizing that Jesus is "the Son of God." Mark was a source for the Lord's Supper tradition in Matthew and Luke, and the practice in the local church probably was also a source in the case of Luke. Considering Matthew's loyalty to the Law, we may wonder if the Lord's Supper was actually celebrated in Matthew's church. Perhaps it was and the author felt constrained to accept it, yet he personally longed for strict observance of the Law.

RELATIONS BETWEEN CHRISTIANS AND JEWS

We have tried to give a full and unbiased report on the controversy between Christians and Jews up to the time of Justin. Many Christian scholars, desiring to foster good relations between Jews and Christians, have pointed out the

393

Christian faults and overlooked the Jewish responsibility.

Who was to blame, Jews or Christians? Both. Both were partly right and partly wrong. The Sadducees and Sanhedrin can be excused for turning Jesus over to Pilate to prevent or end—whichever was the case—a disastrous armed rebellion. (The destruction of Jerusalem in A.D. 70 as a result of a Jewish rebellion demonstrates that fear of the consequences of a revolt was warranted.) Jews were right in recognizing that Jesus was not the Messiah, not the Son of Man, and not a god. But Jews were wrong in their intolerance of Jewish sects and of gentiles and in their obsession with the Law. Both Jews and Christians were mistaken in believing that the Jewish Scriptures were inspired by the Holy Spirit; Jews were right in rejecting the Christian claim that Jesus is prophesied in their Scriptures. Both were wrong in believing in eschatology—though not all accepted it. Both Jews and Christians were mistaken in believing that God would send a Messiah. Christians were mistaken in believing that Jesus was the Messiah, or Christ, had risen and would return, and (in gentile Christianity) was divine.

The Sadducees and Pharisees were wrong to persecute Christians. In order to understand the intensity of Jewish emotions, we must realize that monotheism and observance of the Law were two of the most elemental features of Judaism, features that eventually were discarded by most Christians. Christians were wrong in placing all the blame for Jesus' death upon Jews. Both Jewish Christians and gentile Christians were wrong in their intolerance of non-Christian Jews, and the last group was just as intolerant of the other two. Christians apparently did not engage in physical persecution of Jews, even though Jews persecuted them. Scholars rightly regard as a gross injustice the Christian efforts to shift all responsibility for Jesus' death away from Pilate and on to Jews, but some treat the Jewish persecution of Jewish Christians as only "a family affair," a case of Jews against Jews. But that is a double standard! If Jewish Christians were Christians in one situation, they were Christians in the other also.

Paul and gentile Christians were definitely right in freeing religion from its bondage to the Law and Jewish nationalism. They made Christianity an international religion.

394

GENTILE CHRISTIANS

Gentile Christians retained some aspects of Jewish Christianity and rejected others. They kept the Jewish Bible, and eventually added both Jewish-Christian and gentile-Christian writings to their canon. They continued the practice of using passages in the Septuagint to support their own beliefs and many that they received from the Jewish Christians. Some gentile Christians continued to accept Jewish-Christian eschatological beliefs, but others spiritualized them or rejected them outright. Gentile Christians contributed the full deification of Jesus, using ideas in their own background to reinterpret the Jewish-Christian faith in his resurrection and ascension. Numerous gentile Christians developed a Gnostic interpretation of Christianity. Whereas mutual hostility prevailed between Jewish Christians and the scribes and Pharisees, mutual hostility existed also between gentile Christians and Jews in general. All Christians, both Jewish and gentile, rejected the idea that Christians should rebel against Rome, partly because they desired peaceful relations with them and partly because they believed that God would deal with the Romans when he established his kingdom.

INTERNAL CONTROVERSY

We have seen a huge variety of beliefs in early Christianity, and often one belief was at variance with another. Considering how vigorously many of the beliefs were held and promoted, we are not surprised to find evidence of internal strife. Tension existed over issues such as attitude toward the Romans, attitude toward the Law, what kind of Christ was Jesus, his humanity or divinity, the role of miracles in the Christian mission, and the mission to gentiles. Tension existed between Jewish Christians and gentile Christians, and between those who were loyal under persecution and those who committed apostasy in such times and wanted to rejoin when the danger was past. Above all, perhaps, was controversy between Gnostic Christians and non-Gnostic, or catholic (not Roman Catholic), Christians. The internal dissension led some Christian writers to try to promote internal harmony. That was a major motive of the author of Luke–Acts and the author of Ephesians. Consequently we find ascribed to Jesus in Mark 9:50, "Have salt in yourselves, and be at peace with one another." "A new commandment I give you, that you love one another" is in John 13:34 (cf. 15:12-17). In 1 John 3:23 the commandment that "we should believe in the name of his Son Jesus Christ and love one another" comes from God, not Jesus.

The growth of Christianity caused division within families as well as among churches. Some members of a family became converts while other members refused to join. That evidently is the situation in Mark 10:29-30 where Jesus promises reward for those who have left home and family "for my sake." Controversy and hatred within families is explicitly the consequence of becoming a disciple of Jesus, for he did not come to bring peace but division.[4]

CONSEQUENCES OF HISTORICAL INVESTIGATION

What are the effects of the new understanding of Christian beginnings? At first glance, they appear to be destructive. The Bible is not the Word of God after all. Many words and deeds attributed to Jesus are not authentic. He was not divine. Traditional doctrines and rituals do not have a solid foundation. Those conclusions come as a shock to conservative Christians. (Judaism and other world religions are in a similar predicament—much that their adherents have believed for centuries is not valid.)

But, we should ask, are the traditional beliefs and rituals really essential? Are they even desirable? Does the Bible, for example, have to be divinely inspired? Does it *all* have to be true? Is it really qualified to be the authoritative guide in religion? In fact, does Christianity have to have a Bible? The earliest Christians did not have a New Testament, and in the Sermon on the Mount some elements in the Old Testament are rejected. Moreover, the Bible has done a lot of harm through the years. Many heated arguments and many animosities have been engendered by conflicting interpretations of it; many antagonistic sects and many wars have resulted. Bestowing too much authority on the Bible has impeded the intellectual growth of civilization many, many times. Recognizing the real nature of the Bible and removing it from its pedestal is constructive in the long run.

The validity of a teaching, either doctrinal or ethical, does not depend on Jesus' having taught it; it stands or falls on its own merits. Neither is the validity of Christianity dependent upon the divinity of Jesus; he did not believe that he was divine. If Jesus had taught the necessity of believing that he is the divine Son, as portrayed in the Gospel of John, would that not make him egotistical? The authors of the synoptic gospels did not believe that Jesus was a deity who must be worshiped.

Traditional doctrines and rituals also are not essential. Is it reasonable that baptism in the name of someone will get us into heaven? Is it reasonable to believe that eating consecrated bread and drinking blood transformed into wine (or vice versa) will make us immortal? Even within the Christian tradition there are more sensible means of "salvation," particularly repentance and ethics. Few Christians realize how many routes to salvation are in the Bible.

In some respects a historical understanding of Jesus leads to a more positive view of him. We now realize that Jesus was not a vain individual who boasted, "No one comes to the Father except through me." We now know that it was the gospel writers, not Jesus, who were inconsistent. We now see that the wild misinterpretations of the Old Testament came not from him, but from the apostles and evangelists.

But after we have stripped away so many unauthentic gospel pericopes, is there anything left of Jesus to inspire us today? Indeed there is! Jesus believed that humanity was confronted with the threat of eternal damnation in the imminent Judgment, and he risked his life to save as many Jews as possible. And if he was involved in a revolt against the Romans, that fatal effort sprang from a desire to bring freedom to his people. He was mistaken on both counts, but his motivation was idealistic. Jesus cared!

Although the new historical knowledge greatly reduces the extent of our knowledge of Jesus, it greatly increases our understanding of Christian beginnings by allowing the gospels to supply more evidence about what was happening in the churches. By failing to place the gospel pericopes in their actual situation in the Christian communities, Christians through the centuries have not listened to what the gospels can tell us. Critics of historical scholarship in this field generally overlook this positive result.

Above all, a historical understanding of Christian beginnings reveals a tremendous variety of thought and practice in the early churches. Christian faith was not "cast in concrete," and if it could change so drastically in its first century, surely it can change today. The same could be said of Judaism from 150 B.C. to A.D. 100. Also, the situations and environments that produced Christianity are not ours. The ancient world was not the modern world. This fact too suggests that we are free to change.

Historical investigation can find and support elements in tradition that deserve to be preserved, such as the Judeo-Christian and Greek ideals of truth, righteousness, and justice. It can also open the way for the discovery and development of the new that is better than the old. Eliminating the false and erroneous opens the way for the discovery and acceptance of the true. As long as we cling to error and superstition, we will not let go and advance to truth and reason. The situation can be expressed in a parable:

> Intellectual progress in religion is like a plot of land that was covered with brush and weeds. When a farmer cleared away the brush and weeds, the land was barren; but when he sowed seed on it, valuable crops grew and fed livestock and humans. Verily, the second process was impossible without the first.

APPENDIX 1

CASE AGAINST AUTHENTICITY

In the course of this book we have often remarked that various sayings ascribed to Jesus are not authentic words of his. Readers may think that we prejudged them, but that is not the case. Before the book was written, the sayings were examined one by one, searching for evidence both for and against authenticity. We concluded that, with the exception of Jesus' basic message, all are questionable and many are definitely unauthentic. Because that conclusion is controversial, the types of evidence are collected here with a few examples so that readers may see the case as a whole. This admittedly results in some duplication of matter in the body of the book, but the importance of the question justifies a consolidated presentation of the evidence.

1. Inconsistency among the sayings is a type of evidence observed centuries ago, particularly the difference in ideas and attitudes between John and the synoptic gospels. In modern times biblical scholars have observed inconsistencies among the synoptics and even within the same gospel. In the synoptics for example, three different opinions concerning signs of the end are assigned to Jesus. In Mark 8:12 "no sign will be given to this generation"; Matthew 16:4 modifies this by adding that "only the sign of Jonah" will be given; in Matthew 16:1-3 Jesus criticizes the Sadducees and Pharisees for not discerning "the signs of the times" (thus signs are being given). It seems improbable that Jesus would be so inconsistent. Jesus' saying that he came not to sow peace but a sword (Matt. 10:34) can hardly be reconciled with his "Blessed are the peacemakers" in Matthew 5:9.

2. The Old Testament quotations in the canonical gospels are from the Greek Septuagint that the early Christian authors used, and not from an Aramaic or Hebrew text that Jesus would have used if he had quoted Scripture.

3. The Jesus sayings never refer to his baptism by John

nor do they mention his basic message. They never explain why he thought the kingdom of God was imminent. If the sayings are authentic, it is strange that they are not more closely related to his basic message.

4. In the sayings many Old Testament passages are used and interpreted in a new way, a Christian way. Many hours of searching must have been required to find the passages. A traveling prophet would not have time for such searching. Further, the way in which the quotations are combined and reinterpreted is like that of Jewish scribes, whose occupation was to interpret Scripture; this use of Scripture required much training that an unlearned man would not have.

5. We have observed that the ethics in the synoptic gospels display the teaching of a variety of Jewish sects. An unlearned man would not have such a wide range of knowledge, nor would an itinerant prophet have a library with him.

6. Sayings which conflict with Jesus' basic message are certainly suspect. A saying from Q^1 makes seeing miracles the basis for repentance, but miracles are not even mentioned in Jesus' call to repentance. The gospel sayings emphasize faith and belief, not repentance.

7. A type of evidence that is characteristic of many sayings is that they do not fit in Jesus' life, but they do fit the life of the early Christian communities.

a. One type consists of references to *beliefs* that originated after Jesus' death, including belief in his resurrection (Mark 8:31), ascension (John 3:13-14), and parousia, or return to earth (Matt. 24; 10:23). The traditional explanation is that Jesus was divine and therefore had foreknowledge (cf. John 2:25); when we recognize that Jesus was human, however, we realize that others must have originated the allusions after the beliefs had originated.

b. Some Jesus sayings refer to *events* which occurred after Jesus' death. The events include the general Jewish rejection of Christian preaching, the Jewish war against the Romans in A.D. 66-70, and the Christian mission to the gentiles. Often the events are "forecast" by Jesus. In Mark 14:27-28 Jesus predicts the disciples' desertion when he was arrested and Peter's vision of Jesus in Galilee later. Jesus forecasts the martyrdom of James and John, the sons of Zebedee, in Mark 10:39. The description of the war and the destruction of the Temple in Mark 13 is too detailed a prediction to be authentic.

Appendix 1

According to Luke 13:28-30 Jesus knew that most Jews would be thrust out of the kingdom of God (because they did not accept the Christian message) and that gentiles "will come from the east and west, and from the north and south, and sit at table in the kingdom of God." Trials of Jewish Christians by synagogue authorities are predicted by Jesus in Luke 12:11, and Christian martyrdom is "foreseen" in Mark 8:34-35.

"Forecasting" events that had already occurred was popular in the Greco-Roman world. Robert Grant gives this example: "In 212 B.C. the [Roman] praetor made public an oracle which (he said) he had received; it correctly predicted the battle of Cannae, which had occurred five years earlier, . . ."[2] A characteristic of the alleged predictions in the gospels is that the specific ones never predict any events that occurred after the author wrote; that fact alone should make us suspicious. "From the days of John the Baptist until now the kingdom of heaven suffers violence, and men of violence take it by force," is ascribed to Jesus in Matthew 11:12. "Until now" does not fit Jesus' time, for it indicates that many years have passed since John's death.

c. Some of Jesus' sayings do not fit in the *environment* in which he lived. The Gnostic type sayings in the Gospel of John are clear examples. Another example is the teaching on divorce in Mark 10:12, for Jewish women could not divorce their husbands in Palestine.

8. The controversies with the Pharisees are surely examples of setting back into Jesus' life the experiences of the churches. If Jesus had had the heated arguments with the Pharisees depicted in the gospels, they surely would have made similar accusations against him at his trial before the high priest and council. Instead we find that the Pharisees are not even mentioned there nor are the issues involved in the arguments.

Observance of the Sabbath and of fasting were issues between the churches and the Pharisees because the churches were breaking away from Judaism. Jesus and his disciples, however, were faithful to the Law, and there was no reason for them to adopt a policy of disobeying it. The fact that Jesus' disciples were not among the Jerusalem Christians who were persecuted by the Jewish authorities is strong evidence that Jesus did not preach contrary to Pharisaic teaching about the Law, for the disciples presumably would have the same attitude as their master.

401

9. Jesus' exclusion of John the Baptist from the kingdom of God (Luke 7:28 par) is very dubious, for Jesus preached the same message as his predecessor, who had lost his life as a result. The early Christians, however, had a strong reason for excluding him: his disciples had formed a rival sect.

10. Jesus' conversation with the Samaritan woman in John 4 must be fiction, for according to Acts 8, the apostles in the Jerusalem church were surprised that the Samaritans "had received the word of God" when Philip preached to them. The conversion of the Samaritans would not have been a surprising new development if Jesus had gone to them and caused "many to believe in him." However, Jesus' charge to the Twelve not to go among the gentiles or enter any town of the Samaritans (Matt. 10:5) is not authentic either, for it is only a statement of the author's prejudice.

11. In Acts the Old Testament, not Jesus, is the authority for Christian faith and teaching. Acts often cites the Jewish Scriptures, but it cites Jesus only once (20:35). If Jesus had actually taught the things attributed to him in the gospels, would not those sayings have had more impact on both apostolic preaching and the account in Acts? We suspect that the author of Luke-Acts knew that the Jesus sayings really originated in the churches.

12. A few gospel sayings of Jesus occur elsewhere in the New Testament, where they are not attributed to Jesus. "You shall love your neighbor as yourself" (Mark 12:31) is quoted in James 2:8, but it is cited as "according to Scripture" (Lev. 19:18), not as words of Jesus. The commandment to "love one another" in John 15:17 occurs also in Romans 12:10 and 1 John 4:7, and it is not credited to Jesus in either of the latter two. Paul in Romans urges Christians to "Bless those who persecute you" and "Repay no one evil for evil" (12:14, 17); the latter command is also in 1 Peter 3:9. These are similar to passages in the Sermon on the Mount, but Paul and the author of 1 Peter did not connect the sayings with Jesus. If Jesus uttered these commandments, why did the New Testament writers not acknowledge him as an authority?

13. The sophisticated reasoning based on Corban in Mark 7:9-13, placed on the lips of Jesus, is scribal reasoning, not that of an unlearned prophet.

14. In Mark 14:62 the Son of Man type of Christ (derived from *1 Enoch*) is combined with a feature from Psalm 110:1

(sitting at the right hand of God) and a feature from Daniel 7:13 (coming with the clouds of Heaven). Combining passages from different sources in this manner demonstrates literary knowledge and sophistication that Jesus did not have.

15. None of the Son of Man sayings can be authentic because the idea that Jesus was that supernatural Messiah originated among some churches to provide apocalyptic support for a Christ who would come down from heaven. As some scholars have noted, Jesus would have to be out of his mind to think that he was a supernatural being who had existed in heaven from the beginning of time and had descended to earth.

16. Jesus is portrayed as quoting Old Testament passages, but when those passages are used in other early Christian books, including those in the New Testament, the writers seem to be unaware that Jesus used them. In Mark 10:45 Jesus is depicted as applying to himself the idea of sacrificial death in Isaiah 53. When the same passage from Isaiah is applied in Hebrews 9:28 and *1 Clement* 16:14, the authors do not claim that Jesus used it. In Mark 12:10 Jesus applies to himself the passage in Psalm 118:22, "The stone which the builders rejected has become the head of the corner." The same verse is cited in Acts 4:11 and 1 Peter 2:7, but the writers are unaware that Jesus quoted it for the same purpose. The truth is that these verses were first applied thus in Jewish-Christian churches, and then gospel writers portrayed Jesus as doing the same.

17. A controversial issue within Christianity in the first century was the question of whether gentiles should be admitted. Some sayings of Jesus are for the conversion of gentiles and some are against it. This contradiction tells us that at least some of the sayings are unauthentic, and we observe that outside the gospels, no one cites Jesus as either for or against the mission.

18. Early Christian writers made statements on numerous problems confronting the apostles and their churches, and in the gospel sayings Jesus also makes statements concerning them, often with the same point of view. Yet before the gospels circulated generally and were used as sources (mid-2d c.), the writers did not refer to Jesus when they discussed the same problems. These sayings are a special category of those mentioned under type 7 above; namely, they do not fit into Jesus' life. Sayings about non-observance of the Law are in this category. In Mark and Q Jesus gives explanations of the delay

of the coming of the kingdom of God and the return of Jesus, but the Epistle of James, 2 Peter, and *1 Clement* display no knowledge of that when they address the problem.[3] In the gospels Jesus often speaks of his death, but that is unknown to non-gospel authors when they discuss it.

In the gospel sayings Jesus encourages Christians who are being persecuted, but he is not cited by the non-gospel writers when they encourage the persecuted.[4] Considering that persecution was a tremendous problem for the early Christians, it would be amazing indeed if Jesus had uttered such encouraging words and the writers did not mention them. Another example is the warning against false prophets, ascribed to Jesus, but not mentioned by the authors of 1 John, 2 Peter, and *Didache* when they deal with the problem.[5]

The "sayings of Jesus" in the gospels are similar in literary form to the chreiai in contemporary Greek literature. The ability to compose chreiai was taught in Greek schools of rhetoric. Although Chreiai could occur in oral speech too, the polished forms in the New Testament certainly suggest that their origin was in written composition. It is far more probable that the gospel authors, who wrote in Greek, had had some training in rhetoric than that Jesus had studied it.[6]

The above is not a complete list of the evidence, but that evidence is enough to demonstrate that the bulk of the "sayings of Jesus" was not uttered by Jesus, but originated among the early churches. The fact that those sayings were not generally regarded as words of Jesus until after the gospels were widely circulated among the churches is weighty evidence against the existence of an oral tradition of Jesus' teaching. The authors of the Gospels of Luke and John recognized the problem of explaining to readers why such sayings of Jesus were unknown until long after the crucifixion. They offered the explanations that the disciples did not understand the sayings or else remembered them later. To Jesus' prediction of the Passion of the Son of Man in Mark 10, Luke adds: "But they [the disciples] understood none of these things; this saying was hid from them, and they did not grasp what was said" (18:34). E, the author of John, expands this literary device by adding that the disciples "remembered" after Jesus' death. After a forecast of the Jewish persecution of Christians, Jesus says: "But I have said these things to you, that when their hour comes, you may remember that I told you of them" (16:4). After claiming that Jesus' entry into Jerusalem fulfilled Scripture, the author wrote: "The disciples did not understand this at first; but when Jesus was glorified, then they remembered that this had been written of him and had been done to him" (12:16). In 14:26 Jesus says that the Holy Spirit "will teach you all things, and bring to your remembrance all that I have said to you." Finally, in 14:29 E wrote, "I have told you before it happens, so that when it does happen, you may believe."

NOTES

Chapter 1, **Christian Beginnings**
1. Kirsopp Lake, in his Introduction to his translation, *Eusebius: The Ecclesiastical History*, I, xxxiv, in the Loeb Classical Library series.
2. Luke 24:27, 45-47. Early studies of the use of the Old Testament in the New Testament: Crawford H. Toy, *Quotations in the New Testament* (New York, 1884); James Rendel Harris, *Testimonies* (London, 1917, 1920); C. H. Dodd, *According to the Scriptures* (London, 1952).
3. For surveys of the history of biblical interpretation, see the following: Ronald E. Clements, *One Hundred Years of Old Testament Interpretation* (Philadelphia, 1976); Robert M. Grant (David Tracey's section not recommended), *A Short History of the Interpretation of the Bible*, rev. ed., (Philadelphia, 1984); Herbert F. Hahn, *The Old Testament in Modern Research*, 2nd ed. (Philadelphia, 1966); Edgar Krentz, *The Historical-Critical Method*, rev. ed. (Philadelphia, 1992); H. M. Teeple, *The Historical Approach to the Bible* (Evanston, IL, 1982).
4. Romans, 1 and 2 Corinthians, Galatians, Philemon, Philippians, Colossians, and 1 and 2 Thessalonians. Some scholars have doubts about Philippians and Colossians. A. Q. Morton and James McLeman concluded that only the first five are Pauline (in their *Christianity in the Computer Age* (New York and Evanston, 1964).
5. See Eric L. Titus, "Did Paul Write 1 Corinthians 13?," *Journal of Bible and Religion* 27 (1959):299-302.
6. See H. M. Teeple, "The Oral Tradition that Never Existed," *JBL* 89 (1970): 56-68.
7. Ernest C. Colwell, *The Greek of the Fourth Gospel* (Chicago, 1931).

Chapter 2, **Sources Outside the Bible**
1. See Millar Burrows, *What Mean These Stones?* (New Haven, 1941). Beware of Werner Keller's *The Bible as*

History, which seeks to defend the Bible.

2. Josephus, *Ant.* 18.1; *Wars* 2.8.

3. Edmund Wilson, "The Scrolls from the Dead Sea," *The New Yorker,* May 14, 1955; Millar Burrows, *The Dead Sea Scrolls* (New York, 1955), and *More Light on the Dead Sea Scrolls* (New York, 1958).

4. John Dominic Crossan, *Sayings Parallels* (Philadelphia, 1986); Robert W. Funk, *New Gospel Parallels* (Philadelphia, 1985).

5. Frederick C. Grant, *Roman Hellenism and the New Testament* (New York, 1962), 116.

6. Including Rudolf Bultmann, *Primitive Christianity in Its Contemporary Setting* (New York, 1956); Shirley Jackson Case, *The Origins of Christian Supernaturalism* (Chicago, 1946); Wilfred L. Knox, *Some Hellenistic Elements in Primitive Christianity* (London, 1944); Eduard Lohse, *The New Testament Environment,* rev. ed. (Nashville, 1974); Arthur Darby Nock, *Early Gentile Christianity and Its Hellenistic Background* (New York, 1964); John Herman Randall, Jr., *Hellenistic Ways of Deliverance and the Making of the Christian Synthesis* (New York/London, 1970).

7. See "conscience" in theological dictionaries.

8. Ugo Bianchi, *The Greek Mysteries* (Leiden, 1976); Walter Burkert, *Ancient Mystery Cults* (Cambridge, MA, 1987); George E. Mylonas, *Eleusis and the Eleusinian Mysteries* (Princeton, 1961); Maarten J. Vermaseren, *Cybele and Attis : The Myth and the Cult* (London, 1977); Harold R. Willoughby, *Pagan Regeneration* (Chicago, 1929); R. E. Witt, *Isis in the Graeco-Roman World* (Ithaca, NY, 1971). Willoughby's book is adapted from the first section of his 600-page doctoral dissertation at The University of Chicago. For superior studies of Mithraism and other cults, see the series, "Etudes Preliminaire aux Religions Orientales dans l'Empire Romain," published by E. J. Brill in Leiden, Netherlands.

9. Isaac Casaubon, *De rebus sacris et ecclesiasticis exercitationes XVI* ("Sixteen Exercises concerning Sacred and Ecclesiastical Matters"; London, 1614).

10. See Moses Hadas and Morton Smith, *Heroes and Gods* (New York, 1965).

11. Suetonius, *Domitian* 13.

Chapter 3, **The Jewish Background**

1. Whether there actually was an Exodus is debated. Although the accounts of the Exodus are mostly legendary, a migration of Israelites from Egypt to the Land of Canaan seems very, very probable. The belief that an Exodus occured made such a strong, widespread impression on the Israelites that it must have happened. Where there was so much smoke, there must have been a fire!

2. The practice of substituting "the Lord" for "Yahweh" in English versions of the Bible springs from the fact that the Septuagint does essentially the same thing by replacing *"Yahweh"* in the Hebrew text with *"Kurios,"* the Greek word for "Lord." It is still the practice in traditional Judaism to say *Adonai,* the Hebrew word for "Lord," when reading the Hebrew text. The Jewish substitutions (metonyms) are motivated by piety—the name Yahweh is too sacred to pronounce.

3. For a survey, see Richard A. Horsley and J. S. Hanson, *Bandits, Prophets, and Messiahs: Popular Movements at the Time of Jesus* (San Francisco, 1988).

4. See George F. Moore, *Judaism in the First Centuries of the Christian Era.* 2 vols. (Cambridge, MA, 1946), II, 376.

5. Norman Golb has advanced the theory that the Jews at Qumran were not Essenes, but Jewish leaders who fled Jerusalem during the First Jewish War against Rome. Many of us find the evidence against his theory to be decisive. Josephus' description of the Essenes (*Wars* 2.8) is quite similar to the evidence in the Dead Sea scrolls. Also, Golb assumes that all the Essenes were celibate, and then he stresses the fact that some women and children were buried at Qumran. But the scrolls uphold the sanctity of marriage, and Josephus says of the Essenes, "they do not absolutely deny the fitness of marriage" (ibid.). The large majority of the skeletons excavated at Qumran are those of men; this fits the theory that the majority of the men at Qumran were celibate Essenes, but some Essene families were allowed to live there too. Josephus states that another order of Essenes do marry (*Wars* 2.8.13). The presence of some non-Essene documents in the Qumran library does not indicate that non-Essenes lived at Qumran, for a large library like that of the Essenes would naturally contain the writings of more than their own sect.

6. See W. D. Davies, *Torah in the Messianic Age*

and/or the Age to Come (Philadelphia, 1952); H. M. Teeple, *The Mosaic Eschatological Prophet* (Philadelphia, 1957).

    7. Quoted by Eusebius, *H. E.* 4.22.7.

    8. Harry Elmer Barnes, *An Intellectual and Cultural History of the Western World* (New York, 1937), 82.

    9. Cited from Julius A. Bewer, *The Literature of the Old Testament*, 3rd ed. (New York, 1962), 323, n. 2.

Chapter 4, **John the Baptist**

    1. In Eusebius, *H. E.* 4.22.7.

    2. *Sib. Or.* 4:165-170.

    3. Ibid., 3:591-593.

    4. Isa. 29:18-19; 35:5-6; 61:1.

    5. The same passage from Malachi is attributed to Isaiah in Mark 1:2. This error probably is the result of a later insertion into Mark's citation of Isaiah. Note that the Malachi passage is not in Matthew and Luke; the reason may be it was not in Mark when the other two gospels incorporated it in Mark.

    6. Trypho's statement that "all of us Jews" expect that Elijah will come and anoint the Christ (*Dial.* 49) may be significant if Jews believed that a century earlier. In the synoptic gospels John's baptism of Jesus is clearly viewed as the occasion when God anointed Jesus with the Holy Spirit. Did the authors believe that John's role then was that of Elijah? We admit that there is no evidence for this interesting theory.

    7. Mark 9:13; Matt. 11:13-14; 17:12-13.

    8. Tertullian, *On the Soul* 35; Hippolytus, *Treatise on Christ and Antichrist* 46.

Chapter 5, **Jesus of Nazareth**

    1. *Time*, August 15, 1988, pp. 37-42.

    2. For a discussion of criteria, see M. Eugene Boring, "Criteria of Authenticity: The Lucan Beatitudes as a Test Case," *Forum* 1:4 (Dec. 1985).

    3. The most thorough study of the canonical birth stories is Raymond E. Brown's book, *The Birth of the Messiah* (Garden City, 1977). He rightly rejects the theory of a source derived from the sect of John the Baptist (pp. 246-247). For Jesus or his father as a carpenter, see chap. 25, n. 1, below.

    4. Ibid., pp. 161, 523.

    5. Philo, *Cher.* 12-15.

    6. Plutarch, *Numa* 4; *Symposiacs* 7.1.3.

7. Diogenes Laertius, *Vitae* 3.2; cited from Cartlidge and Dungan, *Sourcebook of Texts*, 2nd ed., p. 6.

8. Ignatius, *Eph.* 18.2; Justin, *Dial.* 43.1; 45.4.

9. Ignatius, *Eph.* 7.2.

10. There is no significance to whether "Spirit" is capitalized or not in English translation when it refers to God's Spirit. No words are capitalized in Hebrew and ancient Greek, so it is a matter of preference whether a modern translator capitalizes words.

11. "Chosen" and "elect" are two different English translations of the same Hebrew or Greek word in the text.

12. Cited by Jerome, *adv. Pelag.* 3.2.

13. The usual translation, "having received from the Father the promise of the Holy Spirit," errs in not recognizing that "of the Holy Spirit" here is an epexegetical, or explanatory, genitive, as Arndt and Gingrich recognized (*Gk.-Eng. Lexicon N. T.* 2nd ed., 280). The thought in the passage is not that Jesus received the promise, but that he received what was promised, namely, the Holy Spirit. Because Jesus had received the Spirit at his resurrection/ascension, he was able to give it to the disciples on Pentecost (Acts 2:4, 33).

14. Luke 8:1-3; Mark 15:40-41.

Chapter 6, **Ethical Teaching**

1. Although often translated as "Master," the word in the Greek text is *rabbi*, the usual term for "rabbi."

2. Many English translations place "with authority" in the next clause, so that it is Jesus' commanding unclean spirits that is with authority. The Nestle-Aland Greek text, however, connects the phrase with the teaching, which is consistent with verse 22. The author of Mark inserted the exorcism story in the midst of the teaching pericope, making the latter obscure.

3. Works which relied heavily on rabbinic parallels include: H. L. Strack and P. Billerbeck, *Kommentar z. Neuen Testament aus Talmud u. Midrash* (1922); I. Abrahams, *Studies in Pharisaism and the Gospels* (1917-1924); C. G. Montefiore, *Rabbinic Literature and Gospel Teachings* (1930).

4. H. Maldwyn Hughes, *The Ethics of Jewish Apocryphal Literature* (London, 1909).

5. For early rabbinic statements, see *Abot* 2.10; 4.11, 17.

6. The correct translation in Matt. 6:12 is not "debts,"

but "sins," as Arndt and Gingrich's Lexicon recognizes, for it is a metaphorical use of the Greek noun *opheilema*, "debt."
  7. Cited from Strack and Billerbeck, *Kommentar*, I, 146. Cf. *Pss. Sol.* 4.
  8. *Universal Jewish Encyclopedia*, VIII, 392.
  9. For references, see *OTP*, I, 863, n. 45b.
  10. Peacemakers are lauded also in the Jewish-Christian Epistle of James in the New Testament: "And the harvest of righteousness is sown in peace by those who make peace" (3:18).

Chapter 7, Jesus' Death

  1. Careful historical studies: G. F. Brandon, *Jesus and the Zealots* (New York, 1967); Gerard Sloyan, *Jesus on Trial* (Philadelphia, 1973); Paul Winter, *On the Trial of Jesus* (Berlin, 1961). Pierre van Paassen's *Why Jesus Died* (New York, 1949) is a popular account. Martin Hengel's *Was Jesus a Revolutionist?* (Philadelphia, 1971) is Christian apologetics.
  2. Josephus, *Ant*. 18.3.1-2.
  3. Josephus, *War* 2.4.1-3.
  4. Ibid., 2.8.1; see Acts 5:36-37. Acts errs in placing Theudas earlier than Judas the Galilean.
  5. *War* 2.8.1.
  6. *Ant*. 20.5.1; 20.8.6; *War* 2.13.5.
  7. *War* 2.13.4.
  8. E.P. Sanders (*Jesus and Judaism*, 314-15) cites several examples from Josephus of the Romans holding the Sanhedrin responsible for arresting insurrectionists.
  9. *Vita* 4.
  10. *War* 2.1.3.
  11. Mark 14:50; a "forecast" of this event is ascribed to Jesus in Mark 14:27.
  12. In R. H. Charles, *Apocrypha and Pseudepiqrapha*, II, 776; *OTP*, II, 498.

Chapter 8, Resurrection and Ascention

  1. For a detailed discussion, see H. M. Teeple, "The Historical Beginnings of the Resurrection Faith," in *Studies in the New Testament and Early Christian Literature*, edited by David E. Aune (Leiden, 1972), 107-120.
  2. In the *Apocalypse of Zephania* 4.7 angels come for wicked souls, fly them around in the air for three days, and then

cast them into eternal punishment. Apparently there is no resurrection of the body. Eduard Lohse (*The New Testament Environment*, 232) states that a popular view in the ancient world was that "the soul of the deceased remained for three days in the vicinity of the tomb before departing to the heights."

3. Julian Morgenstern, "The 'Son of Man' of Daniel 7:13f.: A New Interpretation," *JBL*, March 1961, p. 68.

4. In Acts 2:34-35; Heb. 1:13; Mark 12:36 par.

Chapter 9, The Primitive Church

1. Josephus, *Ant.* 15.10.4.

2. See Robert M. Grant, *Early Christianity and Society* (San Francisco, 1977), 100-101.

3. Josephus, *War* 2.8.4.

4. Ibid., 5.4.2.

5. See James H. Charlesworth, *Jesus Within Judaism* (New York, 1988), 116-117. For details see the map entitled "Archaeoloqy of Jerusalem," published by Pictorial Archive (Near Eastern History) in Jerusalem.

6. Joseph A. Fitzmeyer, S.J., "Jewish Christianity in Acts in the Light of the Dead Sea Scrolls," in J. A. Fitzmeyer, *Essays on the Semitic Backqround of the New Testament* (Missoula, MT, 1974), 300. "The many" (Greek: *ho plethos*) occurs in Acts 4:32; 6:2, 5; 15:12, 30 as a term for the Jerusalem Christian community, or church. Unfortunately, the RSV translates it differently in each occurrence, thus preventing the reader from recognizing the full signifance of the passage.

7. Josephus, *Ant.* 20.9.1.

8. Eusebius, *H. E.* 3.5.3.

9. "The Hebrews" and "the Hellenists" here differed from each other in both language and religious beliefs. The Hebrews probably spoke Aramaic, although the Hebrew language was still known to some Palestinian Jews, for the liturgy in the Temple and synagogues was in Hebrew, and most of the Dead Sea scrolls were written in Hebrew.

10. Marcel Simon, *St Stephen and the Hellenists in the Primitive Church* (London, 1958). The six parallels are: "false witness" (Mark 14:56; Acts 6:13); "will destroy this" Temple or place (Mark 14:58; Acts 6:14); see the Son of Man at the right hand of God (Mark 14:62; Acts 7:56); each prays for the forgiveness of his persecutors (Luke 23:34; Acts 7:60); each commits his spirit to God or to the Lord Jesus (Luke 23:46; Acts

7:59); they are buried by a "righteous man" (Luke 23:50) or "devout men" (Acts 8:2). These close similarities are too numerous to be accidental.

11. Acts 8:1; 11:19.

12. For Paul's own accounts of his life, see Gal. 1:11-2:21; 1 Cor. 1:14, 17; 2:1-5; 2 Cor. 2:12-13; 11:21-33.

13. Gal. 1:13-14.

14. Acts 8:1-3; 9:1-2; Gal. 1:13,23.

15. In Acts 9, 22, and 26.

16. See Charles H. Dodd, *The Bible and the Greeks* (London, 1935); Jewish literature as well as synagogue services influenced gentiles.

17. J. Louis Martyn, *History and Theology in the Fourth Gospel,* rev. ed. (Nashville, 1979); R. Alan Culpepper, *Anatomy of the Fourth Gospel: A Study in Literary Design* (Philadelphia, 1983).

18. Origen said that Peter was the second bishop of Antioch, and Eusebius said that he was the third bishop of Rome. Such statements are merely efforts to exalt Christian heroes, and are unreliable as history.

Chapter 10, **Baptism and Spirit**

1. *The Mithras Liturgy,* tr. and ed. by Marvin W. Meyer, 509-510 (on p. 5). It is also in H. D. Betz, ed., *The Greek Magical Papyri in Translation* and M. W. Meyer, ed., *The Ancient Mysteries.* Formerly some scholars thought erroneously that this document originated in the Hermetic cult. Non-Mithraic words and formulas were inserted later.

2. Origen, *Homily on Numbers* 3:1.

3. G. E. Mylonas, *Eleusis and the Eleusinian Mysteries* (Princeton, 1961), 241-249.

4. R. E. Witt, *Isis in the Graeco-Roman World* (Ithaca, NY, 1971, 160, 308, n. 63. Observe the large circular tub in the Palestrina mosaic, Plates 8 and 11.

5. Meyer, *Ancient Mysteries,* 207.

6. M. J. Vermaseren, *Corpus Inscriptionum et Monumentorum religionis Mithriacae* (The Hague, 1960), II, 498.

7. See M. J. Vermaseren, *Mithriaca I: The Mithraeum at Santa Maria Capua Vetere* (Leiden, 1971).

8. Justin, *Dial.* 14:1.

9. Ibid., *1 Apol.* 61.

10. *Hermas*, Mand. 4.3.6.
11. *Corpus Hermeticum*, Tractate 4.4.
12. Alan Richardson, ed., *A Theological Word Book of the Bible* (London, 1957), 157.
13. Ibid.
14. Justin, *1 Apol.* 61.
15. Alan H. M'Neile, *The Gospel According to Matthew* (London, 1955), 435.
16. D.-E. von Dobschutz, *Christian Life in the Primitive Church* (London, 1904), 20. For an example of Jewish sin-offering and prayer to atone for the sins of the dead, see 2 Maccabees 12:39-45 in the Apocrypha.
17. Cf. the Roman Catholic practice of intercessory prayers for the souls of Christian dead in purgatory.
18. See John Bright, *A History of Israel,* 3rd ed. (Philadelphia, 1981), 248-249, for a concise description.
19. God's Spirit: 1 Cor. 2:11; 6:11,19; 12:3; 2 Cor. 1:22; 1 Thess. 4:8. Jesus' Spirit: Gal. 4:6; Phil. 1:19.
20. Philo, *Decal.* 9, 11.
21. Talmud, Midrash *Tanhuma* 26c.
22. Talmud, *Pesach* 68b. The tradition that the Law was given on Pentecost begins in pre-Christian *Jubilees*: The harvest festival (Weeks, or Pentecost) was instituted with Abraham in the middle of the third month of the year (15:1), and that was the time of the year that the Lord gave the Ten Commandments to Moses (1:1).

Chapter 11, **Explaining Jesus' Death**
1. Ascribed to the risen Jesus in Luke 24:26, 46; ascribed to Paul, Acts 26:23.
2. Mark 8:31; 9:31; 10:33-34.
3. Several different words are used in English translations of the New Testament to designate the general idea of atonement. "Expiation" and "propitiation" have their origin in animal sacrifices. Technically expiation is directed against sins—it removes them. Propitiation is directed toward God—it turns away God's anger at the sinner. "Justification" is God's act of declaring a person to be just, or righteous. "Redemption" is a transaction in which a person gains something in exchange for payment. E.g., a slave could be redeemed and gain freedom when someone paid his master; in the redemption doctrine, Jesus' death was a payment which gave Christians release from

bondage to sin. All of these terms were applied to groups or classes of people as well as to individuals.

4. Observe the difference in outlook. In Acts 5:31 we have the Jewish-Christian view that salvation is for Jews; in *1 Clement* it is the gentile-Christian view that salvation is for the whole world.

5. The redactor of the Gospel of John makes it explicit that Jesus shed blood at his death. He inserts the detail that when a soldier pierced Jesus' side with a spear "immediately came out blood and water" (19:34).

6. Luke 22:37; Acts 8:32; 1 Pet. 2:21-25; *1 Clem.* 16:3-14; *Barn.* 5:2.

6a. Also 4 Macc. 17:22 and 2 Macc. 7:38.

7. This translation is made directly from the Septuagint (LXX), the Bible of the early Christians outside of Jerusalem. In the Psalms the chapter and verse divisions in the LXX differ from those in the Hebrew text.

8. Barnabas Lindars, *New Testament Apologetic: The Doctrinal Significance of the Old Testament Quotations* (London, 1961), 90.

9. A. D. Nock, *Early Gentile Christianity*, 10.

10. John Knox, *The Death of Christ* (New York, 1958), 154.

11. Basilides' system as described in Irenaeus 1.24.3-6.

12. *Gospel of Truth* 18-20.

Chapter 12, **The Problem of tbe Christ—A**

1. Acts 5:42; 8:5; 9:22.

2. Adolf Deissmann, *Licht vom Osten* ("Light from the Ancient East"), 4th ed. (Tuebingen, 1923), 231.

3. Eusebius, *H. E.*, 3.11-12.

4. E.g., Mark 1:1; 3:11; 5:7; 15:39.

5. *HBD*, 979.

6. In *BAR*, Mar/Apr 1990, 24.

7. Euripides, *Madness of Hercules* 796ff.

8. See S. J. Case, *Experience with the Supernatural*, (New York, 1929) 133-9; Joseph Klausner, *From Jesus to Paul* (New York, 1943), 108-112.

9. Rudolf Bultmann, *Theology of the New Testament* (New York, 1951), I, 128-9.

10. S=1:49; 11:27; E=1:34; 3:18; 20:31.

11. *Hermas*, Sim. 9.14.5.

12. Joseph A. Fitzmeyer, "The Contribution of Qumran Aramaic to the Study of the New Testament," *NTS* 20 (1974):382-407.
    13. For discussions of the Primal, or Primordial, Man, see Carl H. Kraeling, *Anthropos and Son of Man* (New York, 1927); Frederick H. Borsch, *The Son of Man in Myth and History* (London/Philadelphia, 1967), chap. 2; Richard Reitzenstein, *Poimandres* (Leipzig, 1904).
    14. See Arvid S. Kapelrud, *The Ras Shamra Discoveries and the Old Testament* (Norman, OK, 1963), 39-44; James B. Pritchard, ed., *The Ancient Near East* (Princeton, 1958), I, 92-118.
    15. *Larousse Encyclopedia of Mythology* (New York, 1959), 75, col. 1.
    16. Matt. 24:27=Luke 17:24; Matt. 24:37-39=Luke 17:26-27; Matt. 24:40-41=Luke 17:34-35; Matt. 24:44=Luke 12:40. For an excellent discussion of the Son of Man in Judaism, see James H. Charlesworth, "The Concept of the Messiah in the Pseudepigrapha," in *ANRW*, II.19.1, p. 207.
    17. Mark 8:38; 13:26; 14:62; "coming in [or with] the clouds of heaven" [from Dan. 7] is in the last two.
    18. John 1:51; 3:13, 14; 6:62; 8:28; 12:34.
    19. Matt. 12:32=Luke 12:10.
    20. Mark 8:31; 9:12, 31; 10:33; 14:21, 41.
    21. Mark 1:34; 3:12; 5:43; 7:36; 8:26.
    22. Hans Conzelmann in *RGG*, 3rd ed. (1959)1, III; Philip Vielhauer, "Gottesreich und Menschensohn in der Verkündigung Jesu," in *Festschrift für Guenther Dehn* (1957)1; Ferdinand Hahn, *Christologische Hoheitstitel; Ihre Geschichte im fruehen Christentum*, 2d Aufl. (Gottingen, 1964). See also H. M. Teeple, "The Origin of the Son of Man Christology," *JBL* 84 (1965):213-250.
    23. *1 Enoch* 48:4.

Chapter 13, **Problem of the Christ—B**
    1. Matt. 15:24; Mark 9:37; Luke 10:16; John 3:34; 13:20.
    2. Philo, *Mos.* 1. 158.
    3. Josephus, *Ant.* 18.4.1.
    4. Origen, *Contra Celsum* 1.57.
    5. H. M. Teeple, *Mosaic Eschatological Prophet,* (Philadelphia, 1957), 63-64.

6. Clementine *Homilies* 3.53; Clementine *Recognitians* 1.36.; Origen, *Com. on John* 6.4; 6.8; Novatian, *On the Trinity* 9; Cyprian, *Treatise* 12.
7. *Hermas*, Sim. 9.12.2; 9.14.5.
8. Ignatius, *Mag.* 6:1; 8:2. Yet Jesus is descended from David in *Eph.* 20:2.
9. *Eph.* 20:2 and *Mag.* 13:1, resp.
10. Philo, *Cher.* 125-27; *Immut.* 31; *Som.* 1.228-29; *Spec.* 1.81.
11. Philo, *Opif.* 9.
12. Émile Bréhier, *Les Idées philosophique et religieuses de Philon d'Alexandrie*, 3rd ed. *(Paris, 1950), 107-111.*
13. see. H. M. Teeple, *The Literary Origin of the Gospel of John* (Evanston, Ill., 1974), chap. 10.
14. Justin, *1 Apol.* 63.
15. Clement of Alexandria, *Instructor* 1.7.
16. Origen, *Celsum* 3.41.
17. Servant Songs: Isa. 42:1-4; 49:1-6; 50:4-9; 52:13-53:12. In them the servant is a prophet. The insertion of 49:3 reinterprets the servant as the nation Israel. Outside of the Songs, the Servant in Deutero-Isaiah is always Israel. This is strong evidence that the Songs are a source which Deutero Isaiah has incorporated. In Isa. 42:4 the Servant will establish justice in the earth "and the coastlands wait for his law." In this verse the Servant appears to be a king, probably the Persian king Cyrus, who freed Israel from Babylonian rule.
18. For a broad investigation of the subject see Wayne A. Meeks. *The Prophet-King: Moses Traditions and the Johannine Christology* (Leiden, 1967).
19. In *ANF*, X, 265.
20. In Hennecke, *New Testament Apocrypha*, I, 199.
21. Irenaeus 3.18.1; cited from *ANF*, I, 446.
22. Philo, *Mos.* 1.21.

Chapter 14, **Miracles**
1. See also Acts 8:7; 28:9.
2. 1 Cor. 12:10, 28; Heb. 2:4; Acts 2:43; 5:12; 8:7; 14:3; 15:12.
3. Mark 6:7; Matt. 10.1, Luke 9:1; 10:19-20.
4. Philostratus, *Apollonius of Tyana* 8.30.
5. Ibid., 3.39.

6. Ibid., 4.20.

7. Lucian, *The Lover of Lies* 16; cited from Cartlidge and Dungan, *Sourcebook of Texts for Comp. Study*, 2nd ed., 50.

8. Mark 7:32-37; 8:22-26.

9. Tacitus, *Histories* 4.81; also in Dio Cassius, *Roman History* 65.8 and Suetonius, *Vespasian* 7.

10. Pliny, *Natural History* 7.124; Philostratus, *Apollonius of Tyana* 3.38-39.

11. See Rom. 11:20 and Heb. 3:19 for examples.

12. Morton Smith, *Jesus the Magician*, 92.

13. S. J. Case, *Origins of Christian Supernaturalism*. 220, 221.

14. Matt. 11:20-21=Luke 10:13.

15. Matt. 12:28=Luke 11:20. "Finger of God" in Luke 11:20 instead of "Spirit of God"; cf. Exod. 8:19.

16. "Poor," not "afflicted," is the proper translation, as the LXX and Luke 4:18 show.

17. Matt. 4:1-11=Luke 4:1-13.

Chapter 15, **Lord's Supper**

1. Martin Dibelius, *From Tradition to Gospel* (London, 1934), 121.

2. George H. C. Macgregor, *Eucharistic Origins* (London, 1929), 48.

3. Matt. 26:26-29; Mark 14:22-25; Luke 22:17-20; John 6:53-57; 1 Cor. 10:16-21; 11:20-30. Luke has the cup—i.e., the wine—tradition twice; this is the result of combining in Luke two separate traditions. Codex D, Old Latin, and Syriac mss. omit the second cup in order to remove the duplication.

4. L. R. Farnell, *The Cults of the Greek States* (Oxford, 1896-1907), III, 195; see also p. 240 and Plate xvb. See REI slide lecture, *The Eleusinian Mysteries*, by David E. Aune.

5. H. R. Willoughby, *Pagan Regeneration*, 135. For a concise presentation of this cult, see REI slide lecture, *Cybele and Attis*, by Paul F. Gehl.

6. Justin, *1 Apol.* 66.

7. See Farnell, op. cit., V, chaps. 4-6.

8. F. Griffith and H. Thompson, *Demotic Magical Papyri of London and Leiden*. (London, 1904), I, 15, lff.

9. A. H. Sayce, "The Hittite Communion Table at Mar'ash," in *Proceedings of the Society of Biblical Archeology*,

Nov. 9, 1910, pp. 253-54.
    10. J. G. Frazer, *The Golden Bough*, VII, 161, n. 4.
    11. *Oxyrhynchus Papyri*, I, 110; III, 523.
    12. *Proceedings of the Society of Biblical Archeology*, Dec. 14, 1910, pp. 208-209.
    13. Robert Hawkins, *The Recovery of the Historic Paul* (Nashville, 1943), 189. This controversial book was a pioneering effort to distinguish between the authentic words written by Paul and the editorial material inserted later. When John Knight was a professor of religion at Willamette University, he told me that he had studied under Hawkins, and that though at first he was skeptical, he became convinced that Hawkins "had something."
    14. Walter Lowrie, *Art in the Early Church* (New York, 1947), 72. Some scholars have thought that the Lord's Supper originated as a memorial meal, but that idea was probably an afterthought.
    15. The four features in common are: Jesus gives thanks instead of a blessing before breaking the bread; he commands, "Do this in remembrance of me"; the covenant is "new," which is not the case in Matthew and Mark until scribes inserted the word in them in some manuscripts in the fifth century; in the Greek text the words, "and likewise the cup after supper," are identical in both passages, with a minor change in word order. (The last feature demonstrates the necessity of studying the N.T. in its original language, Greek, for the Greek word *hosautos* is translated as "likewise" in Luke and as "in the same way" in 1 Corinthians, which hides the fact that the same word is used in both passages.) Manuscripts of Luke were the source of the later insertion of "new" into the text of Matthew and Mark. Luke 22:19b-20 is not in Codex D, Old Latin, and Sinaitic and Curetonian Syriac manuscripts.
    16. Even this passage may be composite.
    17. Irenaeus, *Adv. Haer.* 5.2.3.
    18. See Arndt and Gingrich, *A Greek-English Lexicon of the New Testament*, 1st ed., (Cambridge/Chicago, 1957), 328.
    19. See H. M. Teeple, "How Mithra Won the West," in Society of Biblical Literature, *Seminar Papers* (Atlanta, 1988), 312-17. See also REI slide lectures: Lewis M. Hopfe, "The Cult of Mithras," and H. M. Teeple, "The Cult of Mithras: A Supplement." (In the Persian stage the god's name was Mitra,

or Mithra; in the Roman stage it was Mithras.)
    20. Ignatius, *Eph.* 20:2.
    21. Ibid., *Smyr.* 7:1.
    22. Cited from Finegan, *Light From the Ancient Past,* 1st ed. (Princeton, 1946), 385.
    23. The two frescoes mentioned here are reproduced in Josef Wilpert, *Die Malereien der Katakomben Roma* (Rome, 1903), which, in turn, are reproduced in the REI slide lecture, *Christian Catacomb Frescoes,* by H. M. Teeple, slides 20, 22, and 21, resp.
    24. Tertullian, *On Baptism* 1.
    25. Finegan, op. cit., 383.
    26. In Pierpont Morgan Library, New York. Photograph in *Biblical Archaeologist,* March 1978, p. 21.

Chapter 16, **Future—A**
    1. Papias in Irenaeus, *Adv. Haer.* 5.33.3.
    2. Rev. 20:14.
    3. The town was Pepuza; Epiphanius, *Heresies* 49.1.
    4. William H. Brownlee, *The Dead Sea Manual of DIscipline* (*BASOR,* Sup. Studies, nos. 10-12), p. 55.
    5. Acts 2:43; 5:12, 16; 14:3; 15:12.
    6. Matt. 13:44-45; 18:23; 20:1; 25:1. In Matt. 22:2 the author has added it to the Q parable in Luke 14:16.
    7. *Hermas,* Sim. 9.12.8.
    8. Kapelrud, *Ras Shamra Discoveries,* 51, 59.
    9. Cited from Case, *Experience with the Supernatural,* 252.
    10. See Moore, *Judaism,* II, 375-76.
    11. Papias as reported in Eusebius, *H. E.* 3.39.12.
    12. Justin, *Dial.* 80:5.
    13. Ibid., 32:1.
    14. We observe also that in *1 Enoch,* although the Son of Man is immortal, he is subservient to God, "the Lord of Spirits"; the Son of Man is the Lord's "Anointed One," or Messiah. God is superior to him because God has anointed him.
    15. Papias as reported in Eusebius, *H. E.* 3.39.12.
    16. Mark 8:38-9:1; 13:24-30.
    17. Justin, *Dial.* 28:2.
    18. Philo, *Legat.* 200-203.

Chapter 17, **Future — B**
1. See "Paradise" in Charlesworth, *OTP*, II, Index.
2. *1 Enoch* 91:16; 103:3-4.
3. Mark 12:23 par; John 5:29 and 11:24 (in John's sources).
4. Justin, *1 Apol.* 18; *2 Clem.* 19:3.
5. This is in the Son of Man source.
6. Rev. 20:4, 11-13. Christians, like Jews, gave special honor to their martyrs.
7. Irenaeus, *Adv. Haer.* 1.27.3.
8. *Tosephta Sanhedrin* 13, 5; *Rosh ha-Shanah* 17a.
9. See REI slide lecture, *Orphism*, by Larry J. Alderink.
10. *1 Enoch* 38:5-6.
11. 2 Thess. 1:5-8; Rom. 2:2-6; 14:10.
12. Polycarp, *Philip.* 2:1; 6:2.
13. Luke 17:35=Matt. 24:41; in adjoining verses the same is said of two men in a bed and two men in a field.

Chapter 18, **New Judaism**
1. Mark 14:12-16; Matt. 26:17-19; Luke 22:15.
2. See W. D. Davies, *Torah in the Messianic Age and/or the Age to Come* (Philadelphia, 1952); ibid., *The Setting of the Sermon on the Mount* (Cambridge, 1964); H. M. Teeple, *The Mosaic Eschatological Prophet.*
3. *Sib. Or.* 3.373-4, 757-9.
4. Gal. 3:24-26; 5:18.
5. In Matthew Jesus is like Moses in subtle ways: Pharaoh orders all male infants to be killed (Exod. 1:15-22), and Herod gives a similar order in Matt. 2:16; Jesus' parents flee to Egypt so that Jesus, like Moses, "comes out of Egypt"; Moses receives the Law on a mountain, and Jesus delivers the Sermon on the Mount on a mountain.
6. Mark 9:5; 10:51; 11:21; 14:45.
7. John 1:38, 49; 3:2, 26; 4:31; 6:25; 9:2; 11:8.
8. In Hebrews 4-6, *1 Clem.* 61; and *Martyr. of Poly.* 14.
9. *T. Moses* 6:1.
10. E.g., "our father Abraham" (*1 Clem.* 31); attack on Judaism per se, Ignatius, *Mag.* 8:1; 10:3.

Chapter 19, **Great Controversy—A**

1. Mark 12:35; 14:49.
2. Mark 14:58; 15:29. Although the words are presented as spoken by persons hostile to Jesus, the author of Mark agrees with the idea, as his remark about the tearing of the Temple curtain indicates.
3. Ignatius, *Mag.* 11.
4. In Acts 28:26-27; Matt. 13:14-15; John 12:40. It is used in Mark 8:17-18, where portions of it are placed on Jesus' lips and applied to his disciples.
5. In Mark 4:10; 7:17-23; 9:28; 10:10; 13:3-4. To understand what is meant by "the disciples" in the gospels, we must realize that the term often represents the apostles after Jesus' death, a fact discovered by Hermann Reimarus, professor of Hebrew and oriental [Near Eastern] languages at Hamburg, before his death in 1768.
6. Matt. adds 13:36-43 and 17:25-27; Luke adds "privately" to a Q saying (10:23).
7. Exod. 20:13 and Deut. 5:17; Exod. 20:14 and Deut. 5:18; Lev. 19:12; Lev. 19:18, resp.
8. Deut. 24:1; Exod. 21:24, Deut. 19:21, and Lev. 24:20.
9. Roman law, unlike Jewish law, permitted women to divorce their husbands.
10. Matt. 5:21-48 is a block from a written source, for in all six of its "But I say to you," the pronoun *ego* is included for emphasis; when the author of Matthew (19:9) adds the clause to a pericope he copies from Mark 10:11, he does not use *ego*.
11. Davies, *Torah in the Messianic Age*, chaps. 3 and 4.
12. Jer. 17:24; cf. Amos 8:5.

Chapter 20, **Great Controversy—B**

1. Cf. fasting in connection with initiation into some mystery cults.
2. Mark 2:19-20 is a different pericope with a different theme, added to verse 18 because both contain the catchword "fast."
3. See 1 Macc. 1:47-48, 62-63; 2 Macc. 6:18-20; 7:1.
4. The custom of giving firstborn "clean" animals to a priest to sacrifice is derived from the attitude expressed in Exod. 13:2, "Consecrate to me all the firstborn, . . . both of man and beast, it is mine."

5. Justin, *Dial.* 10:3.

6. Matt. 8:21-22=Luke 9:59-60.

7. R. V. G. Tasker, *The Old Testament in the New Testament* (London, 1954), 50-51.

8. Matt. 23:13=Luke 11:52. "Lawyers" here in Luke is another term for the scribes, who were lawyers in the sense that they interpreted the Law.

9. Josephus, *Ant.* 20.9.1.

10. In Eusebius, *H. E.* 2.23.4-18.

11. Donald W. Riddle, *Jesus and the Pharisees: A Study in Christian Tradition* (Chicago, 1928), 177, 179.

12. A. N. Sherwin-White, *Racial Prejudice in Imperial Rome* (Cambridge, 1967), 86. See this book for an accurate description of the situation.

13. Josephus, *Ant.* 19.5.2.

14. Ibid., *Apion* 2:11.

15. Diodorus Siculus 40, fr. 3-4.

16. Strabo 16.2.35-38 (760-762); Cicero, *pro Flacco* 53-69.

17. Justin, *1 Apol.* 35.

18. John Dominic Crossan, in his *The Cross that Spoke: The Origins of the Passion Narrative* (San Francisco, 1988), presents his proposition that the *Gospel of Peter* contains as a source the earliest Passion Narrative, which he calls the "Cross Gospel." His alleged "source," however, contains late features in Christian tradition rather than early ones, especially the shifting onto Jews the blame for Jesus' death. E.g., in it the Jewish people do to Jesus what the Roman soldiers do in the canonical gospels, and "the Jews" replace the chief priests and scribes of the synoptics.

19. Acts 9:23-24; 23:12-21; 25:7, 24; 26:2; 28:19.

20. Justin, *Dial.* 8:4.

21. See *IDB*, art. "Angels."

22. Josephus, *War* 2.8.7.

23. This does not apply to those Jews who believed that angels were wicked and had fallen from grace long ago, as in *1 Enoch* 6-36.

24. Clement Alex., *Stromata* ("Miscellanies") 6.5. This *Preaching of Peter* was written by a gentile Christian; the other *Preaching of Peter,* extracted in the *Clementine Homilies,* is Jewish Christian, ca. 200.

25. Justin, *Dial.* 10:1; Origen, *Celsum* 6.27.

Chapter 21, **Persecution**
  1. 2 Cor. 1:8; 4:8-10; 7:5; 12:10.
  2. Acts 13.50; 14:5, 19; 17:5-8; 18:12-13; 20:3, 19;
21:27-36; 23:12-13; 24:27-25:3.
  3. 2 Cor. 1:8; Acts 16:6; 21:27.
  4. Josephus, *Ant.* 20.9.1. Hegesippus' account in
Eusebius is legendary.
  5. Suetonius, *Life of Claudius* 25.4.
  6. This translation is an adaptation of those in Martyn,
History and Theology, rev. ed., 58, and Williams, ed., *Justin
Martyr: Dialogue with Trypho*, 33, n. 3. The text is preserved
in a copy of the Jewish Prayer Book discovered in 1896;
medieval Christians censored it in other copies.
  7. Martyn, op. cit., and Alan Culpepper, *Anatomy of the
Fourth Gospel* .
  8. John 9:22; 12:42; 16:2.
  9. Martyn, op. cit., 66.
  10. Ibid., 59-60.
  11. Justin, *1 Apol.* 31.
  12. Hermann L. Strack, *Introduction to the Talmud and
Midrash* (Philadelphia, 1931), 111.
  13. Justin, *Dial.* 16:4; 17:1; 117:3, resp.
  14. Israel Abrahams, *Studies in Pharisaism and the
Gospels*, 2nd Series (Cambridge, 1924), 67-69.
  15. Donald W. Riddle, *The Martyrs: A Study in Social
Control* (Chicago, 1931), 215.
  16. Quoted by Eusebius, *H. E.* 5.16.12.
  17. Cited from *A New Eusebius*, James Stevenson, ed.
(London, 1957), 2-3.
  18. Dio Cassius, *Epitome*, 67.14.
  19. Pliny, *Epistles* 10.96.
  20. Ibid., 10.97.
  21. Quoted by Eusebius, *H.E.* 4.9.
  22. Justin, *Dial.* 110.4.
  23. *Sib. Or.* 5:28-34; 8:70-71.
  24. *Martyr. Poly.* 2:1.
  25. Ibid., 14:2.
  26. Ignatius, *Eph.* 1:2.
  27. *Martyr. Poly.* 17:3.
  28. Ibid., 6:2.
  29. Ignatius, *Rom.* 4:1.
  30. Philo, *Mos.* 1.69.

31. *Hermas*, Sim. 8.6.4; cf. 9.19.1.

32. The verses that follow Mark 9:42 also discuss causes of stumbling, or sin, but they do not belong with verse 42 because the causes are in a completely different category. Mark joins them together on the basis of the catchwords "causes to sin"; observe the shift from "causes little ones" in one source to "causes you" in the other. The chapter ends with another example of the use of catchwords in joining source material: "salted" and "salt."

33. *The Martyrdom of Isaiah* consists of 1:1-3:12 and 5:1-16 of the *Ascension of Isaiah*.

34. Sometimes "cup" is a metaphor for martyrdom in Mark. In 10:39 James and John will drink the same cup that Jesus drinks ("baptism" here is also a metaphor for martyrdom), and in 14:36 Jesus prays to the Father as he is about to die, "Remove this cup from me." In Isaiah 51:17, 22 "the cup of his [God's] wrath" is the persecution which Jerusalem has suffered. Polycarp prayed to God that he "be numbered among the martyrs and share in the cup of your Christ" (*Martyr. Poly.* 14:2).

35. Tertullian, *Apology* 50.

Chapter 22, **Mission to Gentiles**

1. Talmud, *Shabbat* 31a.

2. Luke 9:51-55 is an exception. In this pericope one Samaritan town refuses to receive Jesus because he was going to Jerusalem. This probably indicates that some Samaritan towns were unfriendly to the apostles because they, the apostles, were Jews.

3. Talmud, *Shabbat* 88b.

4. Matt. 22:1-10=Luke 14:16-24.

5. Matt. 11:21-23=Luke 10:13-15.

6. Mark 7:24-30, Syrophoenician woman; Matt. 8:5-13=Luke 7:1-10, centurion's son.

7. The incident in Mark 5:1-20 is in gentile territory.

8. Acts 15:16-18; Amos 9:11 and Isa. 45:21.

9. Hosea 2:23; 1:10.

10. Justin, *1 Apol.* 53.

11. Ibid., *Dial.* 121.

12. *Hermas*, Mand. 1.1.

13. Justin, *1 Apol.* 67; see Ps. 119:12.

14. Ibid., 21.

15. E.g., Rom. 9:1; 2 Cor. 4:2; Heb. 9:9.
16. Cited by A. D. Nock in A. L. J. Rawlinson, ed., *Essays on the Trinity and Incarnation* (London, 1928); see also Adolf Deissmann, *Licht vom Osten*, 447. Cf. Mark 1:1.
17. Justin uses it: *1 Apol.* 65.
18. Acts 9:30; 10:1; 21:8.
19. Justin, *1 Apol.* 61, 65.
20. Ignatius, *Mag.* 9:1.
21. Samuele Bacchiocchi, *From Sabbath to Sunday* (Rome, 1977), 241.
22. Tertullian, *On Baptism* 5.

Chapter 23, **Deification of Jesus**

1. Described in Joseph Fitzmeyer, *A Wandering Aramean* (Missoula, MT, 1979), 90-94.
2. Rom. 1:7; 1 Cor. 1:3; 2 Cor. 1:2; Phil. 1:2.
3. W. W. Tarn, *The Greeks in Bactria and India* (Cambridge, 1938), 39.
4. *Papyri Oxyrhynchus* 110.
5. See Liddell & Scott, *A Greek-English Lexicon*, 7th ed. (New York, 1889), entry: *kurios*.
6. *Doctrina* 6:2; *Did.* 15:4; 16:1.
7. Rom. 9:28-29; 11:33-34; 14:10-11; 15:11. Jesus: Rom. 10:13.
8. In the Septuagint "the Lord raised up a Savior" (Greek: *soter*) for the people of Israel, namely Othniel and Ehud (Judg. 3:9, 15).
9. See Pauly-Wissowa, *Realencyklopaedie*, V, col. 1211ff.
10. Luke 2:11; Acts 13:23; in Acts 5:31 Savior is virtually a title.
11. *Hermas*, Sim. 9.14.5.
12. John 3:18; 1 John 4:9.
13. See Arndt & Gingrich, *Greek-English Lexicon*, 808.
14. Titus 2:13; 2 Pet. 1:1.
15. Bob Brier, *Ancient Egyptian Magic* (New York, 1981), 139.
16. Matt. 6:9=Luke 11:2.
17. Justin, *2 Apol.* 6.
18. *Hermas*, Vis. 3.7.3; Sim. 9.16.7; 9.12.5, resp.
19. Ignatius, *Mag.* 6:1.

20. Justin, *1 Apol.* 21, 23.
21. See Henri Frankfort, *Kingship and the Gods* (Chicago, 1948), chap. 2.
22. Plato, *Phaedo* 110.
23. Philo, *Opif.* 9.
24. See chapter 13, note 10, above.
25. John 8:24, 58; 18:5.
26. Cited from F. C. Grant, ed., *Hellenistic Religions*, 132-33.
27. In his letters to the Romans, Ephesians, and Smyrnians he refers to Jesus as "Jesus Christ my God."
28. Justin, *Dial.* 68:9.
29. Acts 2:24; Polycarp, *Philip.* 2:1.
30. Ignatius, *Mag.* 13:2.
31. 1 Cor. 12:4-6; 2 Cor. 13:14; 1 Pet. 1:2; *1 Clem.* 46:6; Ignatius, *Eph.* 9:1.
32. *Hermas*, Mand. 3.1.
33. *Hermas*, Sim. 9.1
34. Tertullian, *Against Praxeas* 29.
35. Irenaeus, *Adv. Haer.* 3.18.6; 3.22.1; Origen, *Com. John* 10.4.

Chapter 24. **Gnosticism**
1. Cited from W. K. C. Guthrie, *Orpheus and Greek Religion*, 2nd ed. (London, 1952), 173.
2. Philostratus, *Apollonius of Tyana* 1. 25.
3. Ibid., 3. 19.
4. Ibid., 1. 8.
5. Ibid., 1. 13.
6. Plato, *Cratylus* 400C.
7. Plato, *Phaedo* 65-66.
8. Ibid., 77.
9. Ibid., 80B.
10. Ibid., 80-82.
11. Ibid., 107.
12. Plato, *Timaeus* 28C.
13. As cited by Plutarch, *On the Generation of the Soul in the Timaeus* 1014B; see Plato, *Timaeus* 29-36.
14. Plato, *Politicus* 273B6-C2, as cited in Plutarch, ibid., 1015C.
15. Plutarch, ibid., 1015E.
16. Plutarch, *Platonic Questions* 1001C.

17. R. M. Grant, *Gods and the One God* (Philadelphia, 1986), 81.

18. *Poimandres* 31.

19. Plato, *Phaedo* 76E.

20. Plutarch, *On the E at Delphi* 10.

21. See Birger A. Pearson, "Friedlander Revisited. Alexandrian Judaism and Gnostic Origins," in *studia philonica* 2 (1973):23-39.

22. Philo, *Allegories of the Sacred Laws* 1. 31.

23. Some non-Christian gentiles also knew the Old Testament, as the Hermetica witnesses. See C. H. Dodd, *The Bible and the Greeks*, chap 12.

24. Irenaeus, *Adv. Haer.* 1. 23. 2.

25. Hippolytus, *Refutation of All Heresies* 6.16, 32.

26. Montague R. James, tr., *The Apocryphal New Testament* (Oxford, 1924; rev. ed. 1953).

27. Matt. 11:27=Luke 10:22.

28. Some similar passages are omitted because they are judged to have been composed by the author of John.

29. The classic Johannine statement of this is John 3:16-18, which agrees with the view in the proto-Gnostic source, but which on syntactical grounds we conclude is the evangelist's own composition. For Jesus as the Son in John, see pp. 259-60 above.

30. The idea that God sent men to preach to the people was a belief in both the Jewish and pagan environments. For example, the Lord sent Jeremiah to Topheth to prophesy (Jer. 19:14). Epictetus (*Diss.* 3.22.23-25; Loeb 2:139) said that the Cynic preacher was an envoy of God, sent "partly as a messenger, in order to show [mortals] that in questions of good and evil they have gone astray."

31. John 1:51; 3:13-15; 5:26-29; 6:53; 8:28; 12:23.

32. *Smyr.* 2. In opposition Ignatius pointed to the Johannine tradition that Jesus Christ appeared in the flesh after his resurrection.

33. *Mag.* 11; *Eph.* 18:2; 20:2;.

34. Irenaeus, *Adv. Haer.* 1. 24. 1-2.

35. Ibid., 1. 24. 3-7.

36. Philo, *On Drunkedness* 30.

37. The parable of the Mustard Seed is in all three synoptic gospels, but only in Matthew is the reading "kingdom of heaven." The parable is also in *Gospel of Thomas* 20, and

like Matt. 13:31, it reads "kingdom of heaven." Examination of the synoptic gospels discloses the "kingdom of heaven" is not a literary trait of Mark, Luke, or Q, but it is of Matthew. *Thomas* normally uses only "kingdom": (k. of heaven in 114), which suggests that in saying 20 the author of Thomas was using Matthew. In saying *Thomas* 39 the reading "keys of knowledge" is not in Matthew's form of the Q saying, but is in Luke's (Matt. 23:13=Luke 11:52). Possibly *Thomas* draws directly from Q, but the above evidence and the lateness of *Thomas* point to Matthew and Luke as the probable sources. Wolfhart Schrage and others have clearly demonstrated that *Thomas* is dependent upon the synoptic gospels.

38. Tertullian, *Against Marcion* 4:43.
39. Hippolytus, *Refutation of All Heresies* 5. 8. 24.
40. Tertullian, *Prescription Against Heretics* 9,10; Matt. 7:7=Luke 11:9. To counteract the tactic, Tertullian admonished his readers "not to seek anything beyond what they have believed," 10.
41. Irenaeus, *Adv. Haer.* 4. 27. 2.
42. Eusebius, *H. E.* 5.16.21.

Chapter 25. **Observations**
1. According to the parallel pericope in Matt. 13:55, however, it was Jesus' father who was the carpenter. Which preserves the original tradition, Matthew or Mark? Mark was written earlier, but the text could have been changed before our earliest manuscripts of Mark were written, several centuries later. Perhaps Matthew preserves the original tradition, and sometime the text in Mark was altered to eliminate the reference to Joseph as Jesus' father because it conflicts with the virgin birth. A reason is not apparent for Matthew to change the tradition from Jesus as carpenter to his father as the carpenter.
2. See H. C. Kee's introduction to the *Testaments of the Twelve Patriarchs* in *OTP*, I, 778.
3. The author of Mark, however, was not very familiar with Jewish customs, for in 14:12 he writes: "on the first day of Unleavened Bread, when they sacrificed the Passover lamb." But the lamb was sacrificed on the 14th of the month of Nissan, and the first day of Unleavened Bread was the 15th.
4. In Q. Luke 12:51-53; 14:26; similar in Matt. 10:34-39.

Appendix 1, **Case Against Authenticity**
1. Matt. 11:20-23=Luke 10:13-15.
2. R. M. Grant, *The Sword and the Cross* (New York, 1955), 18.
3. Mark 4:26-32; Q in Matt. 13:33=Luke 13:20-21; Jas. 5:7-8; 2 Peter 3:3-4, 8; *1 Clem.* 23:5.
4. Mark 8:34-38; Matt. 19:27-29; John 15:18-20; Heb. 10; 1 Pet. 4:13; 5:4.
5. Mark 13:22; Matt. 7:15; 2 Pet. 2:1; 1 John 4:1; *Didache* 16.
6. See Vernon K. Robins and Burton L. Mack, *Rhetoric in the Gospels: Argumentation in Narrative Elaboration* (Philadelphia, 1987).

BIBLIOGRAPHY OF SOURCES

BIBLE
Bible. English. R.S.V. *The New Oxford Annotated Bible*. H. G. May and B. M. Metzger, eds. New York: Oxford University Press, 1977. (Includes the Apocrypha).
— —. O.T. Hebrew. *Biblia Hebraica*. Rudolf Kittel, et al., eds. 7th ed. Stuttgart/New York: Württembergische Bibelanstalt/American Bible Society, 1951. (Hebrew text of the Hebrew Scriptures).
— —, —, Greek. *Septuaginta*. Alfred Rahlfs, ed. 4th ed. 2 vols. Stuttgart/New York: Württ. Bibelanstalt/Am. Bible Society, 1950. (Greek text of the Septuagint).
— —, N.T. Greek, *Novum Testamentum Graece*. E. Nestle, K. Aland, et al., eds. 26th ed. Stuttgart: Deutsche Bibelstiftung, 1979.
— —, —. Gospels. English. *Gospel Parallels: A Synopsis of the First Three Gospels*. Burton H. Throckmorton, ed. 4th ed. New York: Thomas Nelson & Sons, 1979.
— —. —. — —. — —;. *New Gospel Parallels*. Robert W. Funk, ed. 2 vols. Philadelphia: Fortress Press, 1985.
— —. —. — —. Greek. *Synopse der Drei Ersten Evangelien mit Beigabe der Johanneischen Parallelstellen*. Albert Huck, ed. 13th ed., rev. by Heinrich Greeven. Tübingen: Mohr (Paul Siebeck), 1981.
— —. —. — —. — —. *Synopsis Quattuor Evangeliorum*. Kurt Aland, ed. Stuttgart: Württ. Bibelanstalt/Am. Bible Society, 1964.

NEAR EASTERN SOURCES
The Book of the Dead. Trans. by E. A. Wallis Budge. Rev. ed. New York: University Books, 1960.
Budge, E. A. Wallis. *Amulets and Superstitions*. London: Oxford University Press, 1930.
Driver, Godfrey Rolles, ed. *Canaanite Myths and Legends*. 2d ed. Edinburgh: Clark, 1978.
Gaster. Theodor H., ed. *Thespis: Ritual, Myth, and Drama in the Ancient Near East*. Rev. ed. New York: Doubleday, 1961.
Glueck, Nelson. *Deities and Dolphins*. New York: Farrar,

Straus and Giroux, 1965. (The Nabataeans).

Hittite Myths. Ed. by Gary M. Beckman; trans. by Harry A. Hoffner, Jr. Atlanta: Scholars Press, 1991.

Kapelrud, Arvid S. *The Ras Shamra DIscoveries and the Old Testament*. Norman, OK: University of Oklahoma Press, 1963. (The Canaanites).

Mendelsohn, Isaac, ed. *Religions of the Ancient Near East: Sumero-Akkadian Religious Tests and Ugaritic Epics*. New York: Liberal Arts Press, 1955.

Mullen, E. Theodore, Jr. *The Divine Council in Canaanite and Early Hebrew Literature*. Harvard Semitic Monographs, 24. Chico, CA: Scholars Press, 1980. (Also entitled *The Assembly of the Gods*).

Pritchard, James B., ed. *The Ancient Near East in Pictures Relating to the Old Testament*. 2d ed. Princeton: Princeton University Press, 1969.

— —. *Ancient Near Eastern Texts Relating to the Old Testament*. 3d ed. Princeton: Princeton University Press, 1969.

Simpson, William Kelly, ed. *The Literature of Ancient Egypt: An Anthology of Stories, Instructions, and Poetry*. New ed. New Haven/ London: Yale University Press, 1973.

Zabkar, Louis V., ed. *Hymns to Isis in Her Temple at Philae*. Hanover, NH: University Press of New England, 1988.

JEWISH SOURCES

The Babylonian Talmud. Ed. by I. Epstein. 34 vols. London: Soncino Press, 1948-52.

Charles, Robert H., ed. *The Apocrypha and Pseudepigrapha of the Old Testament*. 2 vols. Oxford: Clarendon Press, 1913.

Charlesworth, James H., ed. *The Old Testament Pseudepigrapha*. 2 vols. Garden City, NY: Doubleday, 1983, 1985.

Gaster, Theodor H., trans. *The Dead Sea Scriptures*. 3d ed. Garden City, NY: Doubleday, 1976.

Josephus. *The Works of Flavius Josephus*. William Whiston, trans. Philadelphia: Henry T. Coates, n.d.

— —. *The Jewish War*. Trans. by G. A. Williamson; rev. by E. Mary Smallwood. New York: Dorset Press, 1985.

Josephus. (See Loeb Classical Library for Greek and English texts).

Bibliography

The Mishnah. Trans. by Herbert Danby. London: Oxford University Press, 1933.

The Mishnah: A New Translation. Trans. by Jacob Neusner. New Haven: Yale University Press, 1988.

Philo. (See Loeb Classical Library).

The Talmud Bavl: The Steinsaltz Edition. New York: Random House, 1989-. (Hebrew and Aramaic text with English trans.).

CHRISTIAN SOURCES

Ante-Nicene Fathers. Ed by A. Cleveland Coxe and (vol. 9) E. C. Richardson. 9 vols. Buffalo, NY: Christian Literature Publishing Co., 1885-1887. Sup., vol. 10, ed. by Allan Menzies. Grand Rapids: Eerdmans, 1951.

The Apostolic Fathers. Trans. by Robert M. Grant, et al. 4 vols. New York: Nelson, 1964-66.

The Apostolic Fathers. Ed. & trans. by Edgar J. Goodspeed. New York: Harper, 1950.

The Apostolic Fathers. Ed. & trans. by Kirsopp Lake. Loeb Classical Library. 2 vols. London/New York: Heinemann/Putnam's, 1912-1913.

Ayer, Joseph Cullen, Jr., ed. *A Source Book for Ancient Church History.* New York: Scribner's, 1949.

Eusebius. *Eusebius: The Ecclesiastical History.* Ed. & trans. by J. E. L. Oulton and H. J. Lawlor. Loeb Classical Library. 2 vols. London/Cambridge, MA: Heinemann/Harvard University Press, 1926, 1932.

The Fathers of the Church: A New Translation. 93 vols. New York/Washington, DC: Fathers of the Church/Catholic University of America, 1948-.

Grant, Robert M., ed. & trans. *Gnosticism.* New York: Harper, 1961.

— —, ed. & trans. *Second-Century Christianity: A Collection of Fragments.* London: Society for the Promotion of Christian Knowledge (S.P.C.K.), 1946.

Hennecke, Edgar, ed. *New Testament Apocrypha.* Ed. by Wilhelm Schneemelcher. Eng. trans. ed. by R. McL. Wilson. 2 vols. Philadelphia: Westminster Press, 1963, 1965.

James, Montague Rhodes, ed. & trans. *The Apocryphal New Testament.* Rev. ed. Oxford: Clarendon Press, 1953.

Justin. *Justin Martyr: The Dialogue with Trypho.* Ed. & trans.

Bibliography

by A. Lukyn Williams. London: S.P.C.K., 1930.

Robinson, James M., ed. *The Nag Hammadi Library*. 3d ed. Leiden: E.J. Brill, 1988. (1st ed.: Harper & Row, 1977).

Stevenson, James, ed. *A New Eusebius*. London: S.P.C.K., 1957.

GREEK AND ROMAN SOURCES

Apuleius. *The Golden Ass, being the Metamorphoses of Lucius Apuleius*. Trans. by W. Adlington; rev. by S. Gaselee. Loeb Classical Library. Cambridge, MA/London: Harvard University Press/William Heinemann, 1915.

Athanassakis, Apostolos N., ed. *The Orphic Hymns*. Missoula, MT: Scholars Press, 1977.

Barrett, Charles K., ed. *The New Testament Background: Selected Documents*. London: S.P.C.K., 1957.

Betz, Hans Dieter, ed. *The Greek Magical Papyri in Translation, Including the Demotic Spells*. 2d ed., vol. 1. Chicago: University of Chicago Press, 1986.

Bianchi, Ugo. *The Greek Mysteries*. Leiden: E.J. Brill, 1976. (photographs).

Corpus Cultus Cybelae Attidisque (CCCA). Ed. by M. J. Vermaseren. 7 vols. Leiden: E. J. Brill, 1977-89. (Mystery cult of Cybele and Attis).

Corpus Cultus Deae Syria (CCDS). Ed. by P.-L. van Berg. Leiden: E. J. Brill, 1972.

Corpus Cultus Iovis Sabazii (CCIS). Ed. by E. N. Lane, 3 vols. Leiden: E. J. Brill, 1983-89. (Mystery cult of Sabazios).

Corpus Hermeticum. Ed. by A. D. Nock and A.-J. Festugiere. 4 vols. Paris: Société d'Édition, 1945-54. (Greek text and French trans. of the Hermetica).

Danker, Frederick W., ed. & trans. *Benefactor: Epigraphic Study of Graeco-Roman and New Testament Semantic Field*. St. Louis: Clayton Publishing House, 1982.

Dungan, David L., and David R. Cartlidge, eds. *Sourcebook of Texts for the Comparative Study of the Gospels*. 3d ed. Missoula, MT: Scholars Press, 1973.

Grant, Frederick C., ed. *Hellenistic Religions*. New York: Liberal Arts Press, 1953.

Grant, Robert M., ed. & trans. *Gnosticism*. (See above). (Contains Eng. trans. of four Hermetica tractates, including *Poimandres* and *Concerning Rebirth*).

Bibliography

Guthrie, Kenneth Sylvan, ed. & trans. *The Pythagorean Sourcebook and Library: An Anthology of Ancient Writings which Relate to Pythagoras and Pythagorean Philosophy.* Grand Rapids, MI: Phanes Press, 1987.

Horsley, G. H. R., ed. *New Documents Illustrating Early Christianity.* No. 1-. North Ryde, Australia: Macquarie University, 1981-.

Iamblichus. *On the Pythagorean Way of Life.* Trans. & ed. by John Dillon & Jackson Hershbell. Atlanta: Scholars Press, 1991.

Lucian. *De Dea Syria.* Ed. by Harold W. Attridge and Robert A. Oden. Missoula, MT: Scholars Press, 1987.

Myer, Marvin W., ed. *The Ancient Mysteries: A Sourcebook.* San Francisco: Harper & Row, 1987.

Posidonius. Ed. by L. Edelstein and I. G. Kidd. 2 vols. Cambridge: Cambridge University Press, 1988-89.

Robbins, Vernon K., ed. *Ancient Quotes and Anecdotes.* Sonoma, CA: Polebridge Press, 1989.

Robinson, James M., ed. *The Nag Hammadi Library.* (See above)

SOURCES IN PUBLISHER'S SERIES

Etudes Preliminare aux Religions Orientales dans l'Empire Romain, published by E. J. Brill, Leiden.

Loeb Classical Library, published by Harvard University Press.

REI Slide Lectures Series: A Series, Archaeology. J Series, Early Judaism. MR Series, Mystery Religions. NT Series, New Testament Manuscripts. OT Series, Old Testament and Its Near Eastern Background. Published by Religion and Ethics Institute.

Texts and Translations: Graeco-Roman Religion Series, published by Scholars Press.

INDEX